MAKING SENSE
OF
THE Social
World

RELATED TITLES IN RESEARCH METHODS AND STATISTICS FROM PINE FORGE PRESS

Investigating the Social World: The Process and Practice of Research, Fifth Edition by Russell K. Schutt

Investigating the Social World: The Process and Practice of Research, Fifth Edition With SPSS Student Version 14.0 by Russell K. Schutt

The Practice of Research in Social Work by Rafael J. Engel and Russell K. Schutt

The Practice of Research in Criminology and Criminal Justice, Second Edition by Ronet K. Bachman and Russell K. Schutt

Designing Surveys: A Guide to Decisions and Procedures, Second Edition by Ronald F. Czaja and Johnny Blair

A Guide to Field Research, Second Edition by Carol A. Bailey

Adventures in Social Research, Fifth Edition by Earl Babbie, Fred Halley, and Jeanne Zaino

Adventures in Social Research With SPSS Student Version 11.0, Fifth Edition by Earl Babbie, Fred Halley, and Jeanne Zaino

Adventures in Criminal Justice Research, Third Edition by George Dowdall, Kim Logio, Earl Babbie, and Fred Halley

Social Statistics for a Diverse Society, Fourth Edition by Chava Frankfort-Nachmias and Anna Leon-Guerrero

Social Statistics for a Diverse Society, Fourth Edition With SPSS Student Version 13.0 by Chava Frankfort-Nachmias and Anna Leon-Guerrero

Multiple Regression: A Primer by Paul Allison

Experimental Design and the Analysis of Variance by Robert K. Leik

How Sampling Works by Richard Maisel and Caroline Hodges Persell

OTHER PINE FORGE PRESS TITLES OF INTEREST

Social Problems by Anna Leon-Guerrero

Sociology: Exploring the Architecture of Everyday Life, Sixth Edition by David Newman

The McDonaldization of Society, Revised New Century Edition, by George Ritzer

This Book Is Not Required, Third Edition by Inge Bell, Bernard McGrane, and John Gunderson

Explorations in Classical Sociological Theory by Kenneth Allan

Sociology in the Classical Era by Laura Edles and Scott Appelrouth

Illuminating Social Life, Third Edition by Peter Kivisto

Race, Ethnicity, Gender, and Class, Fifth Edition by Joseph Healey

Diversity and Society by Joseph Healey

Production of Reality, Fourth Edition by Jodi O'Brien

Second Thoughts, Third Edition by Janet Ruane and Karen Cerulo

MAKING SENSE OF THE Social World

Methods of Investigation

SECOND EDITION

DANIEL F. CHAMBLISS
Hamilton College

RUSSELL K. SCHUTT
University of Massachusetts, Boston

PINE FORGE PRESS
An Imprint of Sage Publications, Inc.
Thousand Oaks • London • New Delhi

For information:

Pine Forge Press
An imprint of Sage Publications, Inc.
2455 Teller Road
Thousand Oaks, California 91320
E-mail: order@sagepub.com

Sage Publications Ltd.
1 Oliver's Yard
55 City Road
London EC1Y 1SP
United Kingdom

Sage Publications India Pvt. Ltd.
B-42, Panchsheel Enclave
Post Box 4109
New Delhi 110 017 India

Printed in the United States of America

Library of Congress Cataloging-in-Publication Data

Chambliss, Daniel F.
Making sense of the social world : methods of investigation / Daniel F. Chambliss, Russell K. Schutt.— 2nd ed.
    p. cm.
Includes bibliographical references and index.
ISBN 1-4129-2717-X (paper w/cd)

    1. Social problems—Research. 2. Social sciences—Research. I. Schutt, Russell K. II. Title.
HN29.C468 2006
361.1072—dc22

                                    2005027858

This book is printed on acid-free paper.

06   07   08   10   9   8   7   6   5   4   3   2

Acquiring Editor:	Jerry Westby
Editorial Assistant:	Kim Suarez
Production Editor:	Kristen Gibson
Copy Editor:	Marjorie Cappellari
Typesetter:	C&M Digitals (P) Ltd.
Indexer:	Mary Mortensen
Cover Designer:	Candice Harman

Brief Contents

Detailed Contents

About the Authors

Daniel F. Chambliss, Ph.D., is the Eugene M. Tobin Distinguished Professor of Sociology at Hamilton College in Clinton, New York, where he has taught since 1981. He received his Ph.D. from Yale University in 1982; later that year, his thesis research received the American Sociological Association's Medical Sociology Dissertation Prize. In 1988, he published the book *Champions: The Making of Olympic Swimmers,* which received the Book of the Year Prize from the United States Olympic Committee. In 1989, he received the American Sociology Association's Theory Prize for work on organizational excellence based on his swimming research. Recipient of both Fulbright and Rockefeller Foundation fellowships, Professor Chambliss published his second book, *Beyond Caring: Hospitals, Nurses and the Social Organization of Ethics,* in 1996; for that work, he was awarded the ASA's Elliot Freidson Prize in Medical Sociology. His research and teaching interests include organizational analysis, higher education, social theory, and comparative research methods. He is currently Director of the Project for Assessment of Liberal Arts Education at Hamilton College, funded by the Andrew W. Mellon Foundation, and is a member of the Middle States Commission on Higher Education.

Russell K. Schutt, Ph.D., is Professor of Sociology and Director of the Graduate Program in Applied Sociology at the University of Massachusetts, Boston, and Lecturer on Sociology in the Department of Psychiatry (Beth Israel-Deaconess Medical Center) at the Harvard Medical School. He completed his B.A., M.A., and Ph.D. degrees at the University of Illinois at Chicago and was a Postdoctoral Fellow in the Sociology of Social Control Training Program at Yale University. In addition to five editions of *Investigating the Social World: The Process and Practice of Research,* two editions of a coauthored brief edition of this text (with Dan Chambliss) and two coauthored versions—for the fields of social work (with Ray Engel) and criminal justice (with Ronet Bachman)—he is the author of *Organization in a Changing Environment,* coeditor (with Stephanie Hartwell) of *The Organizational Response to Social Problems,* and coauthor (with Gerald Garrett) of *Responding to the Homeless: Policy and Practice.* He has authored and coauthored numerous journal articles, book chapters, and research reports on homelessness, mental health, organizations, law, and teaching research methods. He recently directed a large translational research project at the Harvard Medical School for the Women's Health Network program of the Massachusetts Department of Public Health, and he is now co-investigator on a project funded by the National Cancer Institute, "University of Massachusetts Boston/Dana-Farber Harvard Cancer Center Comprehensive Cancer Partnership Program: Educating Underserved Communities about Cancer Clinical Trials." His primary research focuses on social factors that shape the impact of housing, employment, and services for severely mentally ill persons and on the service preferences of homeless persons and service personnel. He has also studied influences on well-being, satisfaction, and cognitive functioning; processes of organizational change and the delivery of case management; decision making in juvenile justice and in union admissions; political participation; media representations of mental illness; and HIV/AIDS prevention.

Preface

If you have been eager to begin your first course in social science research methods, we are happy to affirm that you've come to the right place. We have written this book in order to give you just what you were hoping for—an introduction to research that is interesting, thoughtful, and thorough.

But what if you've been looking toward this course with dread, putting it off for longer than you should, wondering why all this "scientific" stuff is required of students who were really seeking something quite different in their major? Well, even if you had just some of these thoughts, we want you to know that we've had your concerns in mind, too. In *Making Sense of the Social World* we introduce social research with a book that combines professional sophistication with unparalleled accessibility: Any college student will be able to read and understand it—even enjoy it—while experienced social science researchers, we hope, can learn from our integrated approach to the fundamentals. And whatever your predisposition to research methods, we think you'll soon realize that understanding them is critical to being an informed citizen in our complex, fast-paced, social world.

TEACHING AND LEARNING GOALS

Our book will introduce you to social science research methods that can be used to study diverse social processes and to improve our understanding of social issues. Each chapter illustrates important principles and techniques in research methods with interesting examples drawn from formal social science investigations and everyday experiences.

Even if you never conduct a formal social science investigation after you complete this course, you will find that improved understanding of research methods will sharpen your critical faculties. You will become a more informed consumer, and thus a better user, of the results of the many social science studies that shape social policy and popular beliefs. Throughout this book, you will learn what questions to ask when critiquing a research study and how to evaluate the answers. You can begin to sharpen your critical teeth on the illustrative studies throughout the book. Exercises at the end of each chapter will allow you to find, discuss, critique, and actually do similar research.

If you are already charting a course toward a social science career, or if you decide to do so after completing this course, we aim to give you enough "how to" instruction so that you can design your own research projects. We also offer "doing" exercises at the end of each chapter that will help you try out particular steps in the research process.

But our goal is not just to turn you into a more effective research critic or a good research technician. We do not believe that research methods can be learned by rote or applied mechanically. Thus you will learn the benefits and liabilities of each major research approach as well as the rationale for using a combination of methods in some situations. You will also come to appreciate why the results of particular research studies must be interpreted within the context of prior research and through the lens of social theory.

ORGANIZATION OF THE BOOK

The first two chapters introduce the why and how of research in general. Chapter 1 shows how research has helped us understand how social relations have changed in recent years and what the impact of these changes has been. Chapter 2 illustrates the basic stages of research with studies of domestic violence, Olympic swimmers, and environmental disasters. The next three chapters discuss how to evaluate the way researchers design their measures, draw their samples, and justify their statements about causal connections.

We discuss experiments in Chapter 5 and thus introduce the first of three primary methods of data collection. In Chapters 6 and 7 we cover the other two most common methods of data collection: surveys and qualitative methods (including participant observation, intensive interviews, and focus groups).

Chapters 8 and 9 shift the focus from collecting data to analyzing it. Since qualitative research strategies often blend the processes of collecting and analyzing data, you may want to read Chapter 8, on methods of analyzing qualitative data, as a companion to Chapter 7, on methods of collecting qualitative data. Chapter 9 presents the basic statistical methods that are used to analyze the results of quantitative studies. We will examine the results of the 2004 General Social Survey to see how these statistics are used. Chapter 10 covers the review of prior research, the development of research proposals, and the writing and reporting of research results.

DISTINCTIVE FEATURES OF THIS EDITION

In making changes for this edition, we feel we have advanced even further in pursuit of our goal of making research methods one of your most enjoyable and engaging courses. We have incorporated valuable suggestions from many faculty reviewers and students who have used the book over the several years since it was first released.

A new chapter on qualitative data analysis—This new chapter draws attention to the distinctive features of qualitative data analysis and illustrates several different approaches. Although some of this material was included in the first edition's qualitative methods chapter, this new chapter allows us to go into much greater detail. There is a new section in this chapter on visual sociology and more on computer-assisted qualitative data analysis.

An expanded appendix on secondary data resources—The appendix on sources of secondary data has been greatly expanded and now includes instructions for using the resources available at the Inter-university Consortium on Political and Social Research (ICPSR).

New sections on writing techniques and on preparing a literature review—Our last chapter now includes tips for writing clearly and a new section on writing a composite literature review.

Changes to improve clarity of presentation about traditionally difficult topics—We have added a fuller discussion of conceptualization; significantly modified the section on units and levels of analysis, including a better explanation of the ecological fallacy; and reworked our explanation of the varieties of longitudinal research designs. Occasionally, we have added mnemonics—memory tricks—to help students remember important distinctions. Many of the exhibits have been slightly modified for increased clarity (better titling, better design, etc.), and throughout the book we continue to edit and rewrite paragraphs to maximize the transparency of the arguments. Sometimes difficult ideas are presented in here, but understanding our sentences, we hope, should never be difficult.

More use of research from around the globe—Reflecting the increasingly global scope of social science research, we have included more examples from researchers in other countries or about persons from countries outside the United States. Chapters 1 and 8 illustrate this change.

Updated and expanded treatment of human subjects issues—We have added more details about how to consider ethical issues involving the treatment of human subjects in research and we have recognized the increasing role of university IRBs in student research.

As in the first edition, our text also offers other distinctive features:

Brief examples of social research that illustrate particular points in each chapter and show how research techniques are used to answer important social questions— Whatever your particular substantive interests in social science, you'll find some interesting studies that will arouse your curiosity.

Integrated treatment of causality and experimental design—We have combined the discussions on causation and experimental design so we could focus on the issues that are most often encountered in research in sociology, criminal justice, education, social work, communications, and political science.

Realistic coverage of ethical concerns and ethical decision making—Like the parent volume, *Investigating the Social World*, this text presents ethical issues that arise in the course of using each method of data collection, rather than as a discrete topic that can be isolated from the rest of the research process.

Engaging end-of-chapter exercises—We organize the exercises under the headings of "discussing," "finding," "critiquing," and "doing." New exercises have been added and some of the old ones have been omitted. The result is a set of learning opportunities that should greatly facilitate the learning process.

Software-based learning opportunities—The CD-ROM that accompanies the textbook includes review exercises to help you master the concepts of social research, a portion of the 2004 General Social Survey so you can try out quantitative data analysis (if your school provides access to the SPSS statistical package), and a qualitative data analysis program, HyperRESEARCH™, with which you can practice qualitative data analysis. Appendix B in this volume provides a guide to using HyperRESEARCH software and Appendix D is an introduction to SPSS.

Aids to effective study—Lists of main points and key terms provide quick summaries at the end of each chapter. In addition, key terms are highlighted in boldface type when first introduced and defined in the text. Definitions of key terms can also be found in the glossary/index at the end of the book. The Pine Forge Press Web site (www.pineforge.com/isw/index.htm) includes other review questions. An instructor's manual includes more exercises that have been specially designed for collaborative group work in and outside of class. Appendix A, "Finding Information," provides up-to-date information about using the Internet, and Appendix C lists secondary data sources.

Acknowledgments

First, we would like to thank Jerry Westby, Senior Editor at Pine Forge Press, our main managerial contact and source of encouragement as we developed our text. Other members of the Pine Forge Press and Sage team helped in multiple ways: Denise Simon provided expert assistance with the review of the reviews, and Marjorie Cappellari did a superb job of copyediting.

The reviewers for this edition helped us to realize the potential for this revision. We are very grateful for the wisdom and critical acumen of the following:

Manfred Kuechler, Hunter College

Kristen Zgoba, Rutgers University

Ann Marie Kinnell, The University of Southern Mississippi

Julio Borquez, University of Michigan–Dearborn

Ed Nelson, California State University, Fresno

Colin Olson, University of New Mexico

Vera Lopez, Arizona State University

Sandy D. Alvarez, Indiana State University

Matthew W. Brosi, Oklahoma State University

Juanita M. Firestone, University of Texas at San Antonio

Laura Hecht, California State University, Bakersfield

Keith F. Durkin, Ohio Northern University

Dena Hanley, University of Akron

Reviewers of the first edition proposal were:

Diane C. Bates, Sam Houston State University

Mark Edwards, Oregon State University

David Folz, University of Tennessee, Knoxville

Ann Marie Kinnell, University of Southern Mississippi

Ronald Perry, Arizona State University

Chenyang Xiao, Washington State University

David Zehr, Plymouth State College

Sharlene Hesse-Biber and Ann Dupuis contributed a version of Hyper-RESEARCH for the accompanying CD-ROM, as well as some text in Chapter 8 and an appendix about the program. Elizabeth Schneider again contributed to the appendix on "Finding Information" that draws on her comparable work with Russ (her husband) for the 5th edition of *Investigating the Social World.* We thank Megan Reynolds for reviewing the interactive exercises, many of which had been written for the last edition by Kathryn Stoeckert, and we thank Matt Philbin and Colin Godfrey for programming the exercises.

We also have some personal "thank you's." Dan wishes gratefully to acknowledge the assistance, in many areas, of Marcia Wilkinson, who as typist, transcriber, organizer and administrative aide, and daily conscience is simply irreplaceable. My students at Hamilton College have been a blessing throughout: Chris Takacs helped to design and create several of the new exhibits, solving intellectual problems through graphic displays. Shauna Sweet told me where the book was good and where it wasn't, clarified the regression effect, and showed me how people actually should read contingency tables. Katey Healy-Wurzburg, in one of many moments of intellectual brilliance, explained the underlying rhetorical problem of the ecological fallacy; and Erin Voyik, as a teaching assistant in my Methods class, laid out for me time and again what students do and don't actually understand, and enjoy, about social research methods. There are many others, students and colleagues alike, who have contributed without recognition; let's just say that all of intellectual life is communal, and we fully appreciate that fact. And finally, Dan hopes that his wife Susan Morgan enjoyed, at least vicariously, the thrills he felt in working on this book as much as he enjoyed sharing them with her.

Russ is grateful to the many reviewers of the first four editions of *Investigating the Social World,* as well as to the many staff and consultants at Pine Forge Press and Sage Publications who helped to make that text a success. He is also grateful for the superb assistance of Megan Reynolds with preparing this edition, as well as for the speedy assistance of Tracey Newman on the first edition. He also expresses his appreciation to his many research collaborators with whom he has shared so many fascinating and educational experiences and from whom he has learned so much, and for the many fine students at the University of Massachusetts, Boston, who continue to renew his enthusiasm for quality teaching. Most importantly, he thanks his wife, Beth, for her ongoing support and love, and his daughter, Julia, for being such a marvelous young woman.

Finally, Dan wants to say that Russ Schutt is a wonderful coauthor, with whom he is honored to work: totally responsible and respectful, hard-working, serious in his scholarship but without a trace of arrogance; his generous personality has allowed this collaboration to sail along beautifully. Russ adds that Dan is the perfect model of the gentleman and scholar, whose research savvy and keen intelligence are matched to a warm and caring persona. We both like to think that our talents are almost entirely complementary. We are immensely grateful for the chance to work together.

Chapter 1

Science, Society, and Social Research

Are social ties weakening in modern society? It's a key question for social scientists. It was a central issue in Emile Durkheim's (1906) studies of European societies around the turn of the last century. It was the focus of David Riesman's *The Lonely Crowd,* a study of "organization men," at mid-century. And it's the key question for Robert Putnam's (2000) national bestseller, *Bowling Alone.* As you might surmise from the title, Putnam's answer to that question is rather pessimistic; moreover, he identifies so many adverse consequences to "the collapse of American community" that we must hasten to point out that he does suggest that the "collapse" can, with effort, be reversed.

The evidence of weakening social ties in the last decades of the twentieth century is substantial. During roughly the last four decades, Putnam (2000:31–32) reports that the rate of voting in U.S. presidential elections declined by 14 percentage points (to 49%), the percentage of voters who had actually done some work for a political party had dropped by almost half (to 2.5%), church attendance slid by about 10 percentage points (to 37%), and union membership plunged to half of its earlier level (to 15%). Even the frequency of having a social evening with neighbors has declined by more than 10 percentage points (to about 50% of single people).

It's the social science research presented in *Bowling Alone* that makes the book's argument so compelling. It is not just Robert Putnam's opinion, nor is it a collection of anecdotes obtained from quick "man-on-the-street" media interviews, or what "everyone knows" or what "we've always believed." Instead, Putnam examines a great deal of evidence about social ties and reviews much of the research done by others. In the rest of this chapter, you will learn how Putnam's study and other social science investigations are helping to answer questions about social ties. By the chapter's end, you should know what is "scientific" in social science and appreciate how the methods of science can help us understand the workings of society. And you may also find yourself developing new respect for the challenges that the social world presents to even careful social scientists, as you might already realize if you know that the voting rate in presidential elections, which Putnam reported as 48% in 1996, edged up to 50% in 2000 and to 53% in 2004 (Bureau of the Census, 2004–2005:12, 239; Gray, 2004:1).

WHAT IS THE PROBLEM?

You may have your own interests in studying social ties; for instance, to:

Improve your own social connections. Perhaps you're transferring to a new school or planning to buy a home in a new community. Maybe you want to help your child develop a more supportive network of friends. Maybe you want to understand what factors create strong marriages so you can have one. Such personal motivations often stimulate social research.

Reverse the decline of social ties in your own community. Community leaders may need information for planning "get out the vote" campaigns; others may want to increase volunteering for community improvement activities—and may hire you to do research on the current state of social ties. Law enforcement agencies may need to understand the bases of social cohesion in gangs or other criminal groups. Policy motivations like these could lead to much social research about social ties.

Understand the consequences of weakening social ties. People with fewer social ties seem to have poorer health, both mental and physical. Communities with weaker social networks seem to have more crime. Organizations with poorer interpersonal relations seem to have less satisfied employees. The desire to identify and understand such consequences is an important academic motivation for research.

How to proceed? What methods should you use, and how much can you trust the conclusions of other studies? Should we turn our sociological backs to the Putnam research because the rate of voting in presidential elections has increased in the 2000 and 2004 elections, reversing the decline that Putnam (2000:35) termed "merely the most visible symptom of a broader disengagement from community life"? It is questions like these that this book will help you to answer.

Consider the topic of social trust—the belief that people can be trusted (an attitude that strengthens social ties). Responses to several surveys indicate that the fraction of the American population that believes that "most people can be trusted" has dropped from about 55% to about 35%—and plunged to 25% among high school students (Exhibit 1.1). But it turns out that this change is not due to shifts in individual attitudes; instead, the decline in social trust among the population as a whole is due to the lower levels of trust among younger age cohorts. For example, only 50% of people born after 1960 agree that "most people are honest," compared to 75% of those born before 1930 (Putnam, 2000:140–141).

Could you have predicted the results of this survey research? Opinions about the state of social ties can be based on direct experience or on what other people have said or written. Do you see how different people, with different experiences, can come to different conclusions about social issues?

People come to different conclusions about the social world for another reason: It's easy to make errors in logic, particularly when we are analyzing the social world, in which we ourselves are conscious participants. We can call some of these errors "everyday errors" because they occur so frequently in the nonscientific, unreflective conversations that we hear on a daily basis.

Our favorite example of such errors in reasoning comes from a letter to Ann Landers, the newspaper advice columnist (sadly, now deceased). See if you can spot the problems here: The letter was written by a woman who had just moved, with her two pet cats, from an apartment in the city to a house out in the country. In the city, she had not let the cats go outside, but she felt guilty about keeping them locked up. When they arrived at the country house, she let the cats out—but they tiptoed cautiously to the door, looked outside, then went right back into the living room and lay down!

Exhibit 1.1 Four Decades of Dwindling Trust: U.S. Adults and Teenagers, 1960–1999

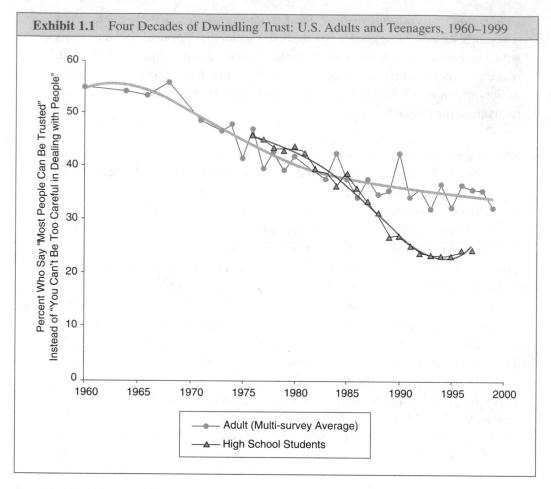

Source: Reprinted with permission of Touchstone Books, a division of Simon & Schuster, Inc., from *Bowling Alone: The Collapse and Revival of American Community* by Robert D. Putnam. Copyright 2000.

The woman concluded that people shouldn't feel guilty about keeping their cats indoors, since even when they have the chance, cats don't really want to play outside.

Did you spot this person's errors in reasoning?

- *Overgeneralization.* She observed only two cats, both of which were previously confined indoors. Maybe they aren't like most cats.
- *Selective or inaccurate observation.* She observed the cats at the outside door only once. But maybe if she let them out several times, they would become more comfortable with going out.

- *Illogical reasoning.* She assumed that other people feel guilty about keeping their cats indoors. But maybe they don't.
- *Resistance to change.* She was quick to conclude that she had no need to change her approach to the cats. But maybe she just didn't want to change her own routines and was eager to believe that she was managing her cats just fine already.

You don't have to be a scientist or use sophisticated research techniques to avoid these four errors in reasoning. If you recognize them and make a conscious effort to avoid them, you can improve your own reasoning. In the process, you also will be taking the advice of your parents (or minister, teacher, or other adviser) not to stereotype people, to avoid jumping to conclusions, and to look at the big picture. These are the same kinds of mistakes that the methods of social science are designed to help us avoid.

Let's look at each kind of error in turn.

Overgeneralization

Overgeneralization occurs when we unjustifiably conclude that what is true for *some* cases is true for *all* cases. We are always drawing conclusions about people and social processes from our own interactions with them, but sometimes we forget that our experiences are limited. The social (and natural) world is, after all, a complex place. Maybe someone made a wisecrack about the ugly shoes you're wearing today, but that doesn't mean that "everyone is talking about you." Or there may have been two drunk-driving accidents following fraternity parties this year, but by itself this doesn't mean that all fraternity brothers are drunk drivers. Or maybe you had a boring teacher in your high school chemistry class, but that doesn't mean all chemistry teachers are boring. We can interact with only a small fraction of the individuals who inhabit the social world, especially in a limited span of time; rarely are they completely typical people. One heavy Internet user found that his online friendships were "much deeper and have better quality" than his other friendships (Parks & Floyd, 1996). Would his experiences generalize to yours? To those of others?

Selective or Inaccurate Observation

We also have to avoid **selective** or **inaccurate observation**—choosing to look only at things that are in line with our preferences or beliefs. When we dislike individuals or institutions, it is all too easy to notice their every failing. For example, if we are convinced that heavy Internet users are antisocial, we can find many confirming instances. But what about elderly people who serve as Internet pen pals for grade school children, or therapists who deliver online counseling? If we acknowledge only the instances that confirm our predispositions, we are victims of our own selective observation. Exhibit 1.2 depicts the difference between selective observation and overgeneralization.

Our observations can also simply be inaccurate. When you were in high school, maybe your mother complained that you were "always staying out late with your friends." Perhaps that was inaccurate; you only stayed out late occasionally. And when you complained that she "yelled" at you, even though her voice never actually increased in volume, that too was an inaccurate observation. In social science, we try to be more precise than that.

Such errors often occur in casual conversation and in everyday observation of the world around us. What we think we have seen is not necessarily what we really have seen (or heard, smelled, felt, or tasted). Even when our senses are functioning fully, our minds have to interpret what we have sensed (Humphrey, 1992). The optical illusion in Exhibit 1.3, which can be viewed as either two faces or a vase, should help you realize that even simple visual perception requires interpretation.

Exhibit 1.2   The Difference Between Overgeneralization and Selective Observation

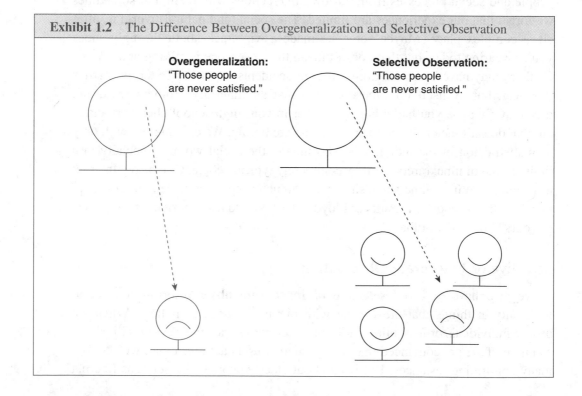

Exhibit 1.3   An Optical Illusion

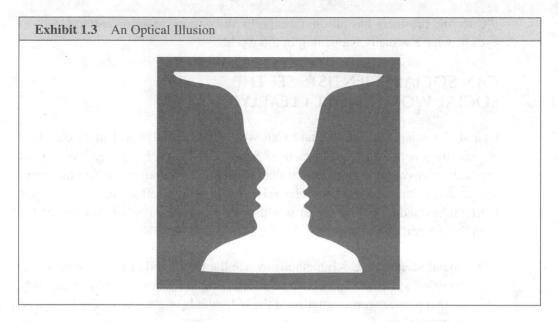

Illogical Reasoning

When we prematurely jump to conclusions or argue on the basis of invalid assumptions, we are using **illogical reasoning.** For example, we might think that people who don't have many social ties just aren't friendly, even if we know they have just moved into a community and started a new job. Obviously, that's not logical. On the other hand, an unquestioned assumption that everyone seeks social ties or benefits from them overlooks some important considerations, such as the impact of childhood difficulties on social trust and the exclusionary character of many tightly knit social groups. Logic that seems impeccable to one person can seem twisted to another—but the problem usually is caused by people having different assumptions rather than just failing to "think straight."

Resistance to Change

Resistance to change, the reluctance to change our ideas in light of new information, is a common problem. After all, we know how tempting it is to make statements that conform to our own needs rather than to the observable facts ("I can't live on that salary!"). It can also be difficult to admit that we were wrong once we have staked out a position on an issue ("I don't want to discuss this anymore."). Excessive devotion to tradition can stifle adaptation to changing circumstances ("This is how we've always done it, that's why."). People often accept the recommendations of those in positions of authority without question

("Only the president has all the facts."). In all of these ways, we often close our eyes to what's actually happening in the world.

CAN SOCIAL SCIENTISTS SEE THE SOCIAL WORLD MORE CLEARLY?

Can social science do any better? Can we see the social world more clearly if we use the methods of social science? **Science** relies on logical and systematic methods to answer questions, and it does so in a way that allows others to inspect and evaluate its methods. So **social scientists** develop, refine, apply, and report their understanding of the social world more systematically, or "scientifically," than the general public does:

- Social science research methods reduce the likelihood of overgeneralization by using systematic procedures for selecting individuals or groups to study, so that they are representative of the individuals or groups to which we wish to generalize.
- To avoid illogical reasoning, social researchers use explicit criteria for identifying causes and for determining whether these criteria are met in a particular instance.
- Social science methods can reduce the risk of selective or inaccurate observation by requiring that we measure and sample phenomena systematically.
- Scientific methods lessen the tendency to answer questions about the social world from ego-based commitments, excessive devotion to tradition, and/or unquestioning respect for authority. Social scientists insist: Show us the evidence!

Science: A set of logical, systematic, documented methods for investigating nature and natural processes; the knowledge produced by these investigations.

Social science: The use of scientific methods to investigate individuals, societies, and social processes; the knowledge produced by these investigations.

Social Research in Practice

Although all social science research seeks to minimize errors in reasoning, different projects may have different goals. The four most important goals of social research are description, exploration, explanation, and evaluation. Let's look at examples of each.

Description: How Often Do Americans "Neighbor?"

During the last quarter of the twentieth century, the annual (biennial since 1996) General Social Survey (GSS) has investigated a wide range of characteristics, attitudes, and behaviors. Each year, more than 1,000 adults in the United States complete GSS phone interviews; many questions are repeated from year to year so that trends can be identified. Robert Putnam often used GSS data in his investigation of social ties in America.

Survey responses indicate that "neighboring" has been declining throughout this period. As indicated in Exhibit 1.4 (Putnam, 2000:106), the percentage of GSS respondents who reported spending "a social evening with someone who lives in your neighborhood . . . about once a month or more often" was 60% for married people in 1975 and about 65% for singles. By 1998, the comparable percentages were 45% for married people and 50% for singles. This is **descriptive research** because the findings simply *describe* differences or variations in social phenomena.

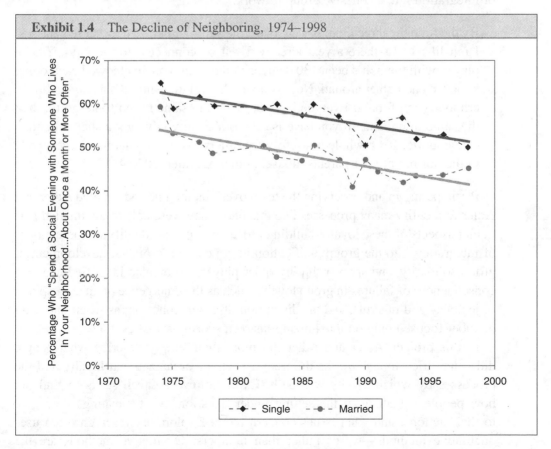

Exhibit 1.4   The Decline of Neighboring, 1974–1998

Source: Reprinted with permission of Touchstone Books, a division of Simon & Schuster, Inc., from *Bowling Alone: The Collapse and Revival of American Community* by Robert D. Putnam. Copyright 2000.

Exploration: How Do Athletic Teams Build Player Loyalty?

Organizations like combat units, surgical teams, and athletic teams must develop intense organizational loyalty among participants if they are to maximize their performance. How do they do it? It was this question that motivated Patricia and Peter Adler (2000) to study college athletics. To investigate this question, Peter Adler joined his college basketball team as a "team sociologist," while Patti participated in some team activities as his wife and as a professor in the school. They recorded observations and comments at the end of each day for a period of five years. They also interviewed at length the coaches and all 38 basketball team members during that period.

Careful and systematic review of their notes led Adler and Adler to conclude that intense organizational loyalty emerged from five processes: domination, identification, commitment, integration, and goal alignment. We won't review each of these processes here, but the following quote indicates how they found the process of integration into a cohesive group to work.

By the time the three months were over [the summer before they started classes] I felt like I was there a year already, I felt so connected to the guys. You've played with them, it's been 130 degrees in the gym, you've elbowed each other, knocked each other around. Now you've felt a relationship, it's a team, a brotherhood type of thing. Everybody's got to eat the same rotten food, go through the same thing, and all you have is each other. So you've got a shared bond, a camaraderie. It's a whole houseful of brothers. And that's home to everybody in the dorm, not your parents' house. (Adler & Adler, 2000:43)

Participating in and observing the team over this long period enabled Adler and Adler to identify many processes like this one. They were able to distinguish particular aspects of these loyalty-building processes, such as identifying three modes of integration into the group: unification in opposition to others, development of group solidarity, and sponsorship by older players. They also identified negative consequences of failures in group loyalty, such as the emergence of an atmosphere of jealousy and mistrust, and the disruption of group cohesion, as when one team member focused only on maximizing his own scoring statistics.

In this project, Adler and Adler did more than simply describe what people did—they tried to *explore* the different aspects of organizational loyalty and the processes by which loyalty was built. **Exploratory research** seeks to find out how people get along in the setting under question, what meanings they give to their actions, and what issues concern them. Exploratory research often uses qualitative methods—words rather than numbers. Qualitative methods are the focus of Chapter 7.

Explanation: Does Social Context Influence Adolescent Outcomes?

Often, social scientists want to *explain* social phenomena, usually by identifying causes and effects. Bruce Rankin at Koc University in Turkey and James Quane at Harvard (Rankin & Quane, 2002) analyzed data collected in a large survey of African American mothers and their adolescent children in order to test the effect of social context on adolescent outcomes. Their source of data was a study funded by the MacArthur Foundation, *Youth Achievement and the Structure of Inner City Communities,* in which face-to-face interviews were conducted with more than 636 youth living in 62 poor and mixed-income urban Chicago neighborhoods.

Explanatory research like this seeks to identify causes and effects of social phenomena and to predict how one phenomenon will change or vary in response to some variation in some other phenomenon. Rankin and Quane (2002) were most concerned with determining the relative importance of three different aspects of social context—neighborhoods, families, and peers—on adolescent outcomes (both positive and negative). In order to make this determination, they had to conduct their analysis in a way that allowed them to separate the effects of neighborhood characteristics like residential stability and economic disadvantage from parental involvement in child-rearing and other family features, and from peer influence. They found that neighborhood characteristics affect youth outcomes primarily by influencing the extent of parental monitoring and the quality of peer groups.

Evaluation: Does More Social Capital Result in More Community Participation?

The "It's Our Neighbourhood's Turn" project (Onze Burrt aan Zet, or OBAZ) in the city of Enschede, the Netherlands, was one of a series of projects initiated by the Dutch Interior and Kingdom Relations ministry to increase the quality of life and safety of individuals in the most deprived neighborhoods in the Netherlands. In the fall of 2001, residents in three of the city's poorest neighborhoods were informed that their communities had received funds to use for community improvement and that residents had to be actively involved in formulating and implementing the improvement plans (Lelieveldt 2003:1). Political scientist Herman Lelieveldt (2004:537) at the University of Twente, the Netherlands, and others then surveyed community residents to learn about their social relations and their level of local political participation; a second survey was conducted one year after the project began.

Lelieveldt wanted to *evaluate* the impact of the OBAZ project—to see whether the "livability and safety of the neighborhood" could be improved by taking steps like those Putnam (2000:408) recommended to increase "social capital," meaning that citizens would spend more time connecting with our neighbors than we do today . . . more casual socializing with friends and neighbors.

It turned out that residents who had higher levels of social capital participated more in community political processes. However, not every form of social capital made much of a difference. Neighborliness—the extent to which citizens are engaged in networks with their neighbors—was an important predictor of political participation, as was a feeling of obligation to participate. By contrast, a sense of trust in others (something which Putnam emphasizes) was not consistently important (Lelieveldt 2004:535, 547–548): Those who got more involved in the OBAZ political process tended to *distrust* their neighbors. When researchers focus their attention on social programs like the OBAZ project, they are conducting **evaluation research**—research that describes or identifies the impact of social policies and programs.

Certainly many research studies have more than one such goal—all studies include some description, for instance. But clarifying your primary goal can often help when deciding how to do your research.

HOW WELL HAVE WE DONE OUR RESEARCH?

Social scientists want **validity** in their research findings—they want to find the truth. The goal of social science is not to reach conclusions that other people will like or that suit our personal preferences. We shouldn't start our research determined to "prove" that our college's writing program is successful, or that women are portrayed unfairly in advertisements, or that the last presidential election was rigged, or that homeless people are badly treated. We may learn that all of these are true, or aren't; but our goal as social scientists should be to learn the truth, even if it's sometimes unpleasant. The goal is to figure out how and why some part of the social world operates as it does and to reach valid conclusions. We reach the goal of validity when our statements or conclusions about empirical reality are correct. In *Making Sense of the Social World: Methods of Investigation,* we will be concerned with three kinds of validity: measurement validity, **generalizability**, and causal validity (also known as internal validity). We will learn that invalid measures, invalid generalizations, or invalid causal inferences result in invalid conclusions.

Measurement validity: Exists when an indicator measures what we think it measures.

Generalizability: Exists when a conclusion holds true for the population, group, setting, or event that we say it does, given the conditions that we specify.

Causal validity (internal validity): Exists when a conclusion that A leads to, or results in, B is correct.

Measurement Validity

Measurement validity is our first concern, because without having measured what we *think* we've measured, we don't even know what we're talking about. So when Putnam (2000:291) introduces a measure of "social capital" that has such components as number of club meetings attended and number of times worked on a community project, we have to stop and consider the validity of this measure. Measurement validity is the focus of Chapter 3.

Problems with measurement validity can occur for many reasons. In studies of Internet forums, for instance, researchers have found that some participants use fictitious identities, even pretending to be a different gender (men posing as women, for instance) (Donath, 1999). Therefore, researchers could not rely on gender as disclosed in the forums when identifying differences in usage patterns between men and women; it's difficult to measure gender in these forums. Similarly, if you ask people, "Are you an alcoholic?" they probably won't say yes, even if they are; the question elicits less valid information than would be forth-coming by asking them how many drinks they consume, on average, each day. Some college men may be hesitant to admit to watching reruns of *The Simpsons* on television six hours a day, so researchers use electronic monitoring devices on TV sets to measure what programs people watch and how often.

Generalizability

The **generalizability** of a study is the extent to which it can inform us about persons, places, or events that were *not* directly studied. For instance, if we ask our favorite students how much they enjoyed our Research Methods course, can we assume that other students (perhaps not as favored) would give the same answers? Maybe they would—but probably not. Generalizability is the focus of Chapter 4.

Generalizability is always an important consideration when you review social science research. Even the huge, international National Geographic (2000) survey of Internet users had some limitations in generalizability. Only certain people were included in the sample: people who were connected to the Internet, who had heard about the survey, and who actually chose to participate. This meant that many more respondents came from wealthier countries, which had higher rates of computer and Internet use, than from poorer countries. However, the inclusion of individuals from 178 countries and territories does allow some interesting comparisons among countries.

There are two kinds of generalizability: sample and cross-population.

Sample generalizability: Exists when a conclusion based on a sample, or subset, of a larger population holds true for that population.

> ***Cross-population generalizability:*** Exists when findings about one group, population, or setting hold true for other groups, populations, or settings (see Exhibit 1.5). Also called ***external validity.***

Sample generalizability is a key concern in survey research. Political polls such as the Gallup Poll or Zogby International may study a sample of 1,400 likely voters, for example, and then generalize their findings to the entire American

Exhibit 1.5 Sample and Cross-Population Generalizability

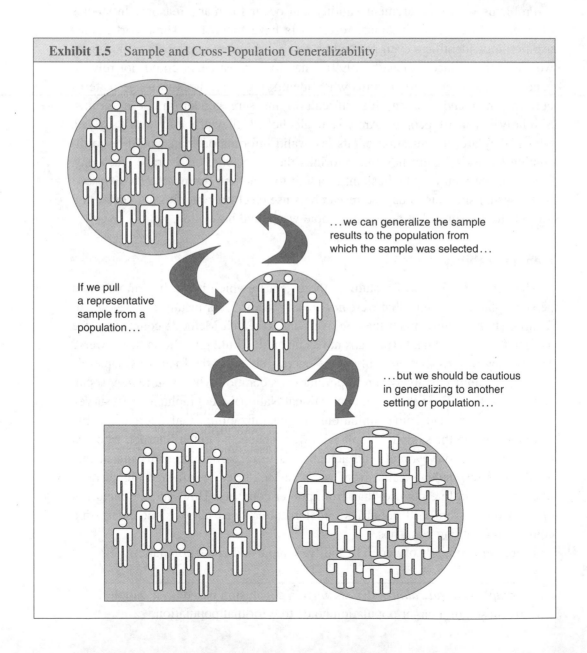

If we pull a representative sample from a population . . .

. . . we can generalize the sample results to the population from which the sample was selected . . .

. . . but we should be cautious in generalizing to another setting or population . . .

population of 80,000,000 likely voters. No one would be interested in the results of political polls if they represented only the tiny sample that actually was surveyed rather than the entire population.

Cross-population generalizability occurs to the extent that the results of a study hold true for multiple populations; these populations may not all have been sampled, or they may be represented as subgroups within the sample studied. We can only wonder about the cross-population generalizability of Putnam's findings about social ties in the United States. Has the same decline occurred in Mexico, Argentina, Britain, or Thailand?

Causal Validity

Causal validity, also known as **internal validity,** refers to the truthfulness of an assertion that A causes B. It is the focus of Chapter 5.

Most research seeks to determine what causes what, so social scientists frequently must be concerned with causal validity. For example, Gary Cohen and Barbara Kerr (1998) asked whether computer-mediated counseling could be as effective as face-to-face counseling for mental health problems—that is, whether one type of counseling leads to better results than the other. They could have compared people who had voluntarily experienced one of these types of treatment, but it's quite likely that individuals who sought out a live person for counseling would differ, in important ways, from those who sought computer-mediated counseling. Younger people tend to use computers more; so do more educated people. Or maybe less sociable people would be more drawn to computer-mediated counseling. So normally it would be hard to tell if different results from the two therapies were caused by the therapies themselves or by different kinds of people going to each.

So Cohen and Kerr designed an experiment in which students seeking counseling were assigned randomly (by a procedure somewhat like flipping a coin) to either computer-mediated or face-to-face counseling. In effect, people going to one kind of counseling were just like people going to another. The result? There was no difference in the outcomes; students in both groups benefited the same amount (see Exhibit 1.6). By using the random assignment procedure, Cohen and Kerr strengthened the causal validity of this conclusion.

On the other hand, even in properly randomized experiments, causal findings can be mistaken because of some factor that was not recognized during planning for the study. If the computer-mediated counseling sessions were conducted in a modern building with all the latest amenities, while face-to-face counseling was delivered in a rundown building, this might have led to different outcomes for reasons quite apart from the type of counseling. And Cohen and Kerr didn't have a group that received no counseling. Maybe just a little quiet time or getting older would provide the same benefits as therapy.

Exhibit 1.6 Partial Evidence of Causality

Pre-counseling Anxiety Score	Type of Counseling	Post-counseling Anxiety Score
35	Computer-mediated	28
35	Face-to-face	29

Pre-counseling anxiety score: 35	Computer-mediated counseling	→	Post-counseling anxiety score: 28

Pre-counseling anxiety score: 35	Face-to-face counseling	→	Post-counseling anxiety score: 29

So establishing causal validity can be quite difficult. In subsequent chapters, you will learn in more detail how experimental designs and statistics can help us evaluate causal propositions, but the solutions are neither easy nor perfect. We always have to consider critically the validity of causal statements that we hear or read.

CONCLUSION

This first chapter should have given you an idea of what to expect in the rest of the book. Social science provides us with a variety of methods for avoiding everyday errors in reasoning and for coming to valid conclusions about the social world. We will explore different kinds of research, using different techniques, in the chapters to come, always asking, "Is this answer likely to be correct?" The techniques are fairly simple but powerful nonetheless if properly executed. You will also learn some interesting facts about social life. We have already seen, for instance, some evidence that

- Social ties of many sorts have declined in the United States in the last 25 years, *but*
- Social ties can be strengthened by organizational processes that build loyalty, as happens on athletic teams, *and*
- Neighborhoods in which social ties are weaker may result in less effective forms of parenting, but both parenting and peer group quality have stronger effects on adolescent outcomes, *and*
- Government programs to increase social capital in neighborhoods can increase local political participation, *and*
- Students may benefit as much from computer-mediated counseling as from face-to-face counseling.

Remember, you must ask a direct question of each research project you examine: How valid are its conclusions? The theme of *validity* ties the chapters in this book together. Each technique will be evaluated in terms of its ability to help us with measurement validity, generalizability, and causal validity.

To illustrate the process of doing research, in Chapter 2 we describe studies of domestic violence, community disaster, student experience of college, and other topics. We will review the types of problems that social scientists study, the role of theory, the major steps in the research process, and other sources of information that may be used in social research. We stress the importance of considering scientific standards in social research and review generally accepted ethical guidelines.

Then, in Chapters 3, 4, and 5 we return to the subject of validity—the three kinds of validity and the specific techniques used to maximize the validity of our measures, our generalizations, and our causal assertions.

Four methods of data collection are introduced in Chapters 5, 6, 7, and 8. Experimental studies are presented in Chapter 5 as the best method for establishing causal connections. Survey research is the most common method of data collection in sociology, and in Chapter 6 we devote a lot of attention to the different types of surveys. Chapter 7 shows how qualitative methods like participant observation, intensive interviewing, and focus groups can uncover aspects of the social world that we are likely to miss in experiments and surveys, while Chapter 8, on qualitative data analysis, illustrates several approaches that researchers can take to the analysis of the data they collect in qualitative projects.

Some people say "you can prove anything with statistics." It isn't true, if you understand a few basic ideas. Chapter 9 is not a substitute for an entire course in statistics, but it gives you a good idea of how to honestly use statistics in reporting the results of your own studies using quantitative methods and in critically interpreting the results of research reported by others. Finally, Chapter 10 focuses on how to review prior research, how to propose new research, and how to report original research. We give special attention to how to formulate research proposals and how to critique, or evaluate, reports of research that you encounter.

Throughout these chapters, we will try to make the ideas interesting and useful to you, both as a consumer of research (as reported in newspapers, for instance) and as a potential producer (if, say, you do a survey in your college or neighborhood). Each chapter ends with several helpful learning tools. Lists of key terms and chapter highlights will help you to review, and exercises will help you to apply your knowledge. Social research isn't rocket science, but it does take some clear thinking, and these exercises should give you a chance to practice.

A closing thought: Vince Lombardi, legendary coach of the Green Bay Packers of the National Football League during the 1960s, used to say that championship football was basically a matter of "four yards and a cloud of dust." Nothing too fancy, no razzle-dazzle plays, no phenomenally talented players doing it all alone—just solid, hard-working, straight-ahead fundamentals. This may sound strange, but excellent social research can be done—can "win games"—in the same way. We'll show you how to do surveys that get the right answers, interviews that discover people's true feelings, and experiments that pinpoint what causes what. And we'll show you how to avoid getting bamboozled by every "Studies Show . . . We're Committing More Crimes!" article you see in the newspaper. It takes a little effort initially, but we think you will find it worthwhile, and even enjoyable.

KEY TERMS

Causal validity (internal validity)
Cross-population generalizability (external
  validity)
Descriptive research
Evaluation research
Explanatory research
Exploratory research
Generalizability
Illogical reasoning

Inaccurate observation
Measurement validity
Overgeneralization
Resistance to change
Sample generalizability
Science
Selective (inaccurate) observation
Social science
Validity

HIGHLIGHTS

• Four common errors in everyday reasoning are overgeneralization, selective or inaccurate observation, illogical reasoning, and resistance to change. These errors result from the complexity of the social world, subjective processes that affect the reasoning of researchers and those they study, researchers' self-interestedness, and unquestioning acceptance of tradition or of those in positions of authority.

- Social science is the use of logical, systematic, documented methods to investigate individuals, societies, and social processes, as well as the knowledge produced by these investigations.

- Social research can be motivated by personal interest, policy guidance and program management needs, or academic concerns.

- Social research can be descriptive, exploratory, explanatory, or evaluative—or some combination of these.

- Valid knowledge is the central concern of scientific research. The three components of validity are measurement validity, generalizability (both from the sample to the population from which it was selected and from the sample to other populations), and causal (internal) validity.

> To assist you in completing the Web Exercises, please access the Study Site at http://www.pineforge.com/mssw2 where you'll find the Web Exercises with accompanying links. You'll find other useful study materials like self-quizzes and e-flashcards for each chapter, along with a group of carefully selected articles from research journals that illustrate the major concepts and techniques presented in the book.

EXERCISES

Discussing Research

1. Select a social issue that interests you, like Internet use or crime. List at least four of your beliefs about this phenomenon. Try to identify the sources of each of these beliefs. Write down your answers, pass them in to a discussion leader, and compare.

2. Review letters to the editor and opinion pieces in your local newspaper about some particular current event that you and other students select in advance. Identify any of the errors in reasoning in this material: overgeneralization, selective or inaccurate observation, illogical reasoning, or resistance to change. Rate each letter or opinion piece as more or less credible, on a scale from 1 to 5 (where 5 means that you think the author's statements are unquestionably true). Compare your statements and ratings with the others in your small group. Present a summary of your group's conclusions to the class. Lead a discussion of the strengths and weaknesses illustrated by each example and then conduct a class-wide vote to choose the most glaring example of each error.

3. Find a report of social science research in an article in a daily newspaper. What were the major findings? How much evidence is given about measurement validity, generalizability, and causal validity of the findings? What additional design features might have helped to improve the study's validity? Compare answers submitted by different students and vote, as a class, for the articles that do the "best" and "worst" jobs of describing study methodology.

Finding Research

1. Read the abstracts (initial summaries) of each article in a recent issue of a major social science journal. (Ask your instructor for some good journal titles.) On the basis of the abstract only, classify each research project represented in the articles as primarily descriptive, exploratory, explanatory, or evaluative. Note any indications that the research focused on other types of research questions.

2. From the news, record statements of politicians or other leaders about some social phenomenon. Which statements do you think are likely to be in error? What evidence could the speakers provide to demonstrate the validity of these statements?

3. Check out Robert Putnam's Web site (http://www.bettertogether.org) and review survey findings about social ties in several cities. Prepare a 5- to 10-minute class presentation on what you have found about social ties and the ongoing research-based efforts to understand them.

Critiquing Research

1. The National Geographic Society studied the use of the Internet and social ties in countries around the world. Review the design of their survey and some of the results at their Web site (http://survey2000.nationalgeographic.com).

2. Compare the methods used in the OBAZ project (http://www.essex.ac.uk/ecpr/events/jointsessions/paperarchive/edinburgh/ws22/Lelieveldt.pdf) with those used in a Canadian study by Barry Wellman concerning the impact of Internet use on community social relations (http://www.chass.utoronto.ca/~wellman/publications/neighboring/neighboring_netville.pdf). Did these studies investigate the same issues? How did the design of these research projects differ? Did they ask similar questions of the same types of people? Which approach do you think is more likely to result in valid causal conclusions?

Doing Research

1. What topic would you focus on if you could design a social research project without any concern for costs? What are your motives for studying this topic?

2. Develop four questions that you might investigate about the topic you just selected. Each question should reflect a different research motive: description, exploration, explanation, or evaluation. Be specific. Which question most interests you? Why?

Chapter 2

The Process and Problems of Social Research

In Chapter 1, we introduced the reasons *why* we do social research: to describe, explore, explain, and evaluate. Each type of social research can have tremendous impact. Alfred Kinsey's descriptive studies of the sex lives of Americans, conducted in the 1940s and 1950s, were at the time a shocking exposure of the wide variety of sexual practices that apparently staid, "normal" people engaged in behind closed doors—and the studies helped introduce the unprecedented sexual openness we see 50 years later. At around the same time, Gunnar Myrdal's exploratory book, *An American Dilemma* (1944/1964), forced our grandparents and great-grandparents to confront the tragedy of institutional racism; Myrdal's research was an important factor in the 1954 Supreme Court decision *Brown v. Topeka Board of Education* that ended school segregation in America. The explanatory "broken windows" theory of crime, which was developed during the 1980s, dramatically changed police practices in our cities. And evaluative social research today actively influences advertising campaigns, federal housing programs, the organization of military units (from Army fire teams to Navy submarine crews), drug treatment programs, and corporate employee benefit plans.

We now introduce the *how* of social research. In this chapter, you will learn about the process of specifying a research question, developing an appropriate research strategy and design with which to investigate that question, choosing appropriate units of analysis, and conforming to scientific and ethical guidelines during the investigation. By the chapter's end, you should be ready to formulate a question, to design a strategy for answering this question, and to begin to critique previous studies that addressed this question.

WHAT IS THE QUESTION?

A **social research question** is a question about the social world that you seek to answer through the collection and analysis of firsthand, verifiable, empirical data. Questions like this may emerge from your own experience, from research by other investigators, from social theory, or from a "request for research" issued by a government agency that needs a study of a particular problem.

Some researchers of the health care system, for example, have had personal experiences as patients with serious diseases, or as nurses or aides working in hospitals, or as family members touched directly and importantly by doctors and hospitals. They may want to learn why our health care system failed or helped them. Feminist scholars study violence against women in hopes of finding solutions to this problem, as part of a broader concern with improving women's lives. One colleague of ours, Veronica Tichenor, was fascinated by a prominent theory of family relations that argues that men do less housework than women because they earn more money; so Professor Tichenor did research on couples in which the woman made far more money than the man, to test the theory. (She found, by the way, that the women still did more of the housework.) Some researchers working for large corporations or major polling firms conduct marketing studies simply to make money. So a wide variety of motives can push a researcher to ask research questions.

A good research question doesn't just spring effortlessly from a researcher's mind. You have to refine and evaluate possible research questions in order to find one that is worthwhile. It's a good idea to develop a list of possible research questions as you are thinking about a research area. At the appropriate time, you can narrow your list to the most interesting and feasible candidate questions.

What makes a research question "good"? Many social scientists evaluate their research questions in terms of three criteria: *feasibility* given the time and resources available, *social importance*, and *scientific relevance* (King, Keohane, & Verba, 1994):

- Can you start and finish an investigation of your research question with available resources and in the time allotted? If so, your research question is feasible.
- Will an answer to your research question make a difference in the social world, even if it only helps people understand a problem they consider important? If so, your research question is socially important.
- Does your research question help to resolve some contradictory research findings or a puzzling issue in social theory? If so, your research question is scientifically relevant.

Here's a good example of a question that is feasible, socially important, and scientifically relevant: Does arresting accused spouse abusers on the spot prevent repeat incidents? Beginning in 1981, The Police Foundation and the Minneapolis Police Department began an experiment to find the answer. The Minneapolis experiment was first and foremost scientifically relevant: It built on a substantial body of contradictory theory regarding the impact of punishment on criminality (Sherman & Berk, 1984). Deterrence theory predicted that arrest would deter individuals from repeat offenses, but labeling theory predicted that arrest would make repeat offenses more likely. The researchers found one prior experimental study of this issue, but it had been conducted with juveniles. Studies among adults had not yielded consistent findings. Clearly, the Minneapolis researchers had good reason for conducting a study.

As you consider research questions, you should begin the process of consulting and then reviewing the published literature. Your goal here and in subsequent stages of research should be to develop a research question and specific expectations that build on prior research and that use the experiences of prior researchers to chart the most productive directions and design the most appropriate methods. Appendix A describes how to search the literature, and Chapter 10 includes detailed advice for writing up the results of your search in a formal review of the relevant literature that you find.

WHAT IS THE THEORY?

Theories have a special place in social research because they help us make connections to general social processes and large bodies of research. Building and evaluating theory is, therefore, one of the most important objectives of social science. A social theory is a logically interrelated set of propositions about empirical reality (i.e., the social world as it actually exists). You may know, for instance, about conflict theory, which proposes that (1) people are basically self-interested; (2) power differences between people and groups reflect the different resources available to groups; (3) ideas (religion, political ideologies, etc.) reflect the power arrangements in a society; (4) violence is always a potential resource and the one that matters most; and so on (Collins, 1975). These statements are related to each other, and the sum of conflict theory (entire books are devoted to it) is a sizable collection of such statements. Dissonance theory in psychology, deterrence theory in criminology, and labeling theory in sociology are other examples of social theories.

Theory: A logically interrelated set of propositions about empirical reality.

Social theories suggest the areas on which we should focus and the propositions that we should consider testing. For example, Sherman and Berk's (1984) domestic violence research in the Minneapolis spouse abuse experiment was actually a test of predictions that they derived from two varying theories on the impact of punishment on crime (Exhibit 2.1):

Deterrence theory expects punishment to deter crime in two ways. General deterrence occurs when people see that crime results in undesirable punishments, that "crime doesn't pay." The persons who are punished serve as examples of what awaits those who engage in proscribed acts. Specific deterrence occurs when persons who are punished decide not to commit another offense so they can avoid further punishment (Lempert & Sanders, 1986:86–87). Deterrence theory leads to the prediction that arresting spouse abusers will lessen their likelihood of reoffending.

Labeling theory distinguishes between primary deviance, the acts of individuals that lead to public sanction, and secondary deviance, the deviance that occurs in response to public sanction (Hagan, 1994:33). Arrest or some other public sanction for misdeeds labels the offender as deviant in the eyes of others. Once the offender is labeled, others will treat the offender as a deviant, and he or she is then more likely to act in a way that is consistent with the deviant label. Ironically, the act of punishment stimulates more of the very behavior that it was intended to eliminate. This theory suggests that persons arrested for domestic assault are more likely to reoffend than those who are not punished, which is the reverse of the deterrence theory prediction.

How do we find relevant social theory and prior research? You may already have encountered some of the relevant material in courses pertaining to research questions that interest you, but that won't be enough. The social science research community is large and active, and new research results appear continually in scholarly journals and books. The World Wide Web contains reports on some research even before it is published in journals (like some of the research reviewed in Chapter1). Conducting a thorough literature review in library sources and checking for recent results on the Web are essential steps for evaluating scientific relevance. (See Appendix A for instructions on how to search the literature and the Web.)

Exhibit 2.1   Two Social Theories and Their Predictions About the Effect of Arrest on Domestic Assault

	Rational choice theory	**Symbolic interactionism**
Theoretical assumption	People's behavior is shaped by calculations of the costs and benefits of their actions.	People give symbolic meanings to objects, behaviors, and other people.
Criminological component	Deterrence theory: People break the law if the benefits of doing so outweigh the costs.	Labeling theory: People label offenders as deviant, promoting further deviance.
Prediction (effect of arrest for domestic assault)	Abusing spouse, having seen the costs of abuse (namely, arrest), decides not to abuse again.	Abusing spouse, having been labeled as "an abuser," abuses more often.

Source: Data from Sherman & Berk, 1984:267.

WHAT IS THE STRATEGY?

When conducting social research, we try to connect theory with empirical data—the evidence we obtain from the real world. Researchers may make this connection in one of two ways:

- By starting with a social theory and then testing some of its implications with data. This is called **deductive research**; it is most often the strategy used in quantitative methods.
- By collecting the data and then developing a theory that explains it. This **inductive research** process is typically used with qualitative methods.

A research project can use both deductive and inductive strategies.

Let's examine the two different strategies in more detail. We can represent both within what is called the **research circle.**

Deductive Research

In deductive research, we start with a theory, and then try to find data that will confirm or deny it. Exhibit 2.2 shows how deductive research starts with a

Exhibit 2.2   The Research Circle

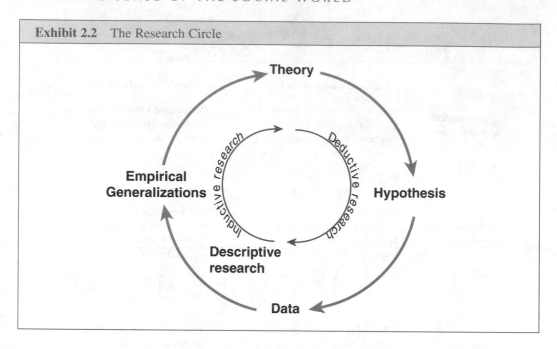

theoretical premise and logically *deduces* a specific expectation. Let's begin with an example of a theoretical idea: When people have emotional and personal connections with coworkers, they will be more committed to their work. We could extend this idea to college life by deducing that if students know their professors well, they will be more engaged in their work. And from this we can deduce a more specific expectation—or **hypothesis**—that smaller classes, which allow more student-faculty contact, will lead to higher levels of engagement. Now that we have a hypothesis, we can collect data on levels of engagement in small and large classes and compare them. We can't always directly test the general theory, but we can test specific hypotheses that are deduced from it.

A hypothesis states a relationship between two or more **variables**—characteristics or properties that can vary, or change. Classes can be large, like a 400-student introductory psychology course, or they can be small, like an upper-level seminar. Class size is thus a *variable*. And hours of homework done per week can also vary (obviously); you can do 2 hours, or 20. So, too, can "engagement" vary, as measured in any number of different ways. (Nominal designations like religion are variables, too, because they can vary between Protestant, Catholic, Jew, and so on.)

But a hypothesis doesn't just state that there is a connection between variables; it suggests that one variable actually influences another—that a change in the first one somehow propels (or predicts, influences, or causes) a change in the second. It says that *if* one thing happens, *then* another thing is likely: *If* you stay up too late, *then* you will be tired the next day. *If* you smoke cigarettes for many years, *then* you may develop heart disease or cancer. *If* a nation loses a major war, *then* its government is more likely to collapse. And so on.

So in a hypothesis, we suggest that one variable influences another—or that the second in some ways "depends" on the first. We may believe, again, that students' reported enthusiasm for a class "depends" on the size of the class. Hence we call enthusiasm the **dependent variable**—the variable that *depends* on another, at least partially, for its level. If cigarettes damage your health, then health is the dependent variable; if lost wars destabilize governments, then government stability is the dependent variable; if enthusiasm for a course depends (in some degree) on class size, then enthusiasm is the dependent variable.

The predicted result in a hypothesis, then, is called the dependent variable. And the hypothesized cause is called the **independent variable**, because in the stated hypothesis it doesn't depend on any other variable.

These terms—hypothesis, variable, independent variable, and dependent variable—are used repeatedly in this book and are widely used in all fields of natural and social science, so they are worth knowing well!

Hypothesis: A tentative statement about empirical reality, involving a relationship between two or more variables. Example: The higher the poverty rate in a community, the higher the percentage of community residents who are homeless.

Variable: A characteristic or property that can vary (take on different values or attributes). Examples: poverty rate, percentage of community residents who are homeless.

Independent variable: A variable that is hypothesized to cause, or lead to, variation in another variable. Example: poverty rate.

Dependent variable: A variable that is hypothesized to vary depending on or under the influence of another variable. Example: percentage of community residents who are homeless.

You may have noticed that sometimes an increase in the independent variable leads to a corresponding increase in the dependent variable; in other cases it leads to a decrease. An increase in your consumption of fatty foods will often lead to a corresponding increase in the cholesterol levels in your blood. But an increase in cigarette consumption leads to a decrease in health. In the first case, we say that the **direction of association** is positive; in the second, we say it is negative. Either way, you can clearly see that a change in one variable leads to a predictable change in the other.

In both explanatory and evaluative research you should say clearly what you expect to find (your hypothesis), and design your research accordingly to test that hypothesis. Doing this strengthens the confidence we can place in the results. So the deductive researcher (to use a poker analogy) states her expectations in advance, shows her hand, and lets the chips fall where they may. The data are accepted as a fair picture of reality.

Domestic Violence and the Research Circle

The Sherman and Berk (1984) study of domestic violence is a good example of how the research circle works. Sherman and Berk's study was designed to test a hypothesis based on deterrence theory: "Arrest for spouse abuse reduces the risk of repeat offenses." In this hypothesis, arrest or release is the independent variable, and variation in the risk of repeat offenses is the dependent variable (it is hypothesized to depend on arrest).

Sherman and Berk tested their hypothesis by setting up an experiment in which the police responded to complaints of spouse abuse in one of three ways, one of which was to arrest the offender. When the researchers examined their data (police records for the persons in their experiment), they found that of those arrested for assaulting their spouse, only 13% repeated the offense, compared to a 26% recidivism rate for those who were separated from their spouse by the police but were not arrested. This pattern in the data, or **empirical generalization**, was consistent with the hypothesis that the researchers deduced from deterrence theory. The theory thus received support from the experiment (see Exhibit 2.3).

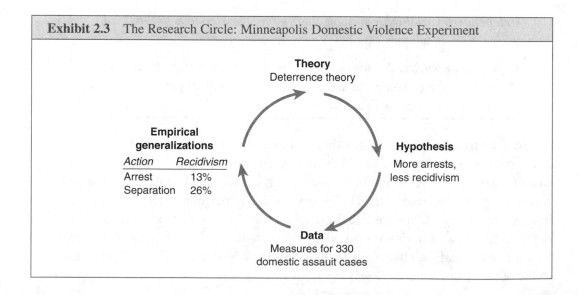

Exhibit 2.3   The Research Circle: Minneapolis Domestic Violence Experiment

Theory
Deterrence theory

Empirical generalizations

Action	Recidivism
Arrest	13%
Separation	26%

Hypothesis
More arrests, less recidivism

Data
Measures for 330 domestic assault cases

Inductive Research

In contrast to deductive research, **inductive research** begins with specific data, which are then used to develop ("induce") a theory to account for the data. (Hint: when you start *in* the data, you are doing *in*ductive research.)

One way to think of this process is in terms of the research circle. Rather than starting at the top of the circle with a theory, the inductive researcher starts at the bottom of the circle with data and then moves up to a theory. Some researchers committed to an inductive approach even resist formulating a research question before they begin to collect data. Their technique is to let the question emerge from the social situation itself (Brewer & Hunter, 1989:54–58). In the research for his book *Champions: The Making of Olympic Swimmers,* Dan Chambliss (1988) spent several years living and working with world-class competitive swimmers who were training for the Olympics. Chambliss entered the research with no definite hypotheses and certainly no developed theory about how athletes became successful, or what their lives were like, or how they related to their coaches and teams. He simply wanted to understand who these people were, and he decided to report on whatever struck him as most interesting in his research.

As it turned out, what Chambliss learned was not how special these athletes were, but actually how ordinary they were. Becoming an Olympic athlete was less about innate talent, special techniques, or inspired coaching than it was about actually paying attention to all the little things that make one perform better in one's sport. His theory was "induced" from what he learned in his studies (Chambliss, 1988), from being immersed "in" the data.

Research designed using an inductive approach, as in Chambliss's study, can result in new insights and provocative questions. **Inductive reasoning** also enters into deductive research when we find unexpected patterns in data collected for testing a hypothesis. Sometimes such patterns are **anomalous** in that they don't seem to fit the theory being proposed, and they can be **serendipitous** in that we may learn exciting, surprising new things from them. Even if we do learn inductively from such research, the adequacy of an explanation formulated after the fact is necessarily less certain than an explanation presented prior to the collection data. Every phenomenon can always be explained in some way. Inductive explanations are more trustworthy if they are tested subsequently with deductive research. Great insights and ideas can come from inductive studies, but verifiable proof comes from deductive research.

An Inductive Study of Response to a Disaster

Qualitative research is often inductive: The researcher begins by observing social interaction or interviewing social actors in depth and then developing an explanation for what has been found. The researchers often ask questions like, "What is going on here?" "How do people interpret these experiences?" or "Why do people do what they do?" Rather than testing a hypothesis, the researchers are trying to make sense of some social phenomenon.

In 1972, for example, towns along the 17-mile Buffalo Creek hollow in West Virginia were wiped out when a dam at the top of a hollow broke, sending 132 million gallons of water, mud, and garbage crashing down through the towns that bordered the creek. After the disaster, sociologist Kai Erikson went to the Buffalo Creek area and interviewed survivors. In the resulting book, *Everything in Its Path,* Erikson (1976) described the trauma suffered by those who survived the disaster. His explanation of their psychological destruction—an explanation that grew out of his interviews with the residents—was that people were traumatized not only by the violence of what had occurred, but also by the "destruction of community" that ensued during the recovery efforts. Families were transplanted all over the area with no regard for placing them next to their former neighbors. Extended families were broken up in much the same way, as federal emergency housing authorities relocated people with little concern for whether they knew the people with whom they would be housed. Church congregations were scattered, lifelong friends were resettled miles apart, and entire neighborhoods simply vanished, both physically—that is, their houses were destroyed—and socially. Erikson's explanation grew out of his in-depth immersion in his data—the conversations he had with the people themselves.

Inductive explanations such as Erikson's feel authentic because we hear what people have to say "in their own words," and we see the social world "as they see it." These explanations are richer and more finely textured than they often are in deductive research; on the other hand, they are probably based on fewer cases and drawn from a more limited area.

Descriptive Research: A Necessary Step

Both deductive and inductive research move halfway around the research circle, connecting theory with data. Descriptive research does not go that far, but it is still part of the research circle shown earlier in Exhibit 2.2. Descriptive research starts with data and proceeds only to the stage of making **empirical generalizations**; it does not generate entire theories.

Valid description is actually critical in all research. The Minneapolis Domestic Violence Experiment was motivated in part by a growing body of descriptive research indicating that spouse abuse is very common: 572,000 cases of women victimized by a violent partner each year; 1.5 million women (and 500,000 men) requiring medical attention each year due to a domestic assault (Buzawa & Buzawa, 1996:1–3).

Much important research for the government and private organizations is primarily descriptive: How many poor people live in this community? Is the health of the elderly improving? How frequently do convicted criminals return to crime? Description of social phenomena can stimulate more ambitious deductive and inductive research. Simply put, good description of data is the cornerstone for the scientific research process and an essential component of understanding the social world.

WHAT IS THE DESIGN?

Researchers usually start with a question, although some begin with a theory or a strategy. If you're very systematic, the *question* is related to a *theory,* and an appropriate *strategy* is chosen for the research. All of these, you will notice, are critical defining issues for the researcher. If your research question is trivial (how many shoes are in my closet?), or your theory sloppy (more shoes reflect better fashion sense), or your strategy inappropriate (I'll look at lots of shoes and see what I learn), the project is doomed from the start.

But let's say you've settled these first three elements of a sound research study. Now we must begin a more technical phase of the research: the design of a study. From this point on, we will be introducing a number of terms and definitions that may seem arcane or difficult. In every case, though, these terms will help to clarify your thinking. Like exact formulae in an algebra problem or precisely the right word in an essay, these technical terms help, or even require, scientists to be absolutely clear about what they are thinking—and to be precise in describing their work to other people.

An overall research strategy can be implemented through several different types of research design. One important distinction between research designs is whether data are collected at one point in time—a **cross-sectional research design**—or at two or more points in time—a **longitudinal research design**. Another important distinction is between research designs that focus on individuals—the **individual unit of analysis**—and those that focus on groups, or aggregates of individuals—the **group unit of analysis**.

Cross-Sectional Designs

In a cross-sectional design, all of the data are collected at one point in time. In effect, you take a "cross-section"—a slice that cuts across an entire population—and use that to see all the different parts, or sections, of that population. Imagine cutting out a slice of a tree trunk, from bark to core. In looking at this cross-section, one can see all the different parts, including the rings of the tree. In social research, you might do a cross-sectional study of a college's student body, with a sample that includes freshmen through seniors. This "slice" of the population, taken at a single point in time, would allow one to compare the different groups.

But cross-sectional studies, because they use data collected at only one time, suffer from a serious weakness: They don't directly measure the impact of time. For instance, you may see that seniors at your college write more clearly than do freshmen. You might conclude, then, that it's because of what transpired over time, that is, what they learned in college. But in fact it may be because this year's seniors were recruited under a policy that favored better writers. In other words, the cross-sectional study doesn't distinguish if the seniors have learned a lot in college, or if they were just better than this year's freshmen when they first enrolled.

Or let's say that in 2006 you conduct a study of the American workforce and you find that older workers make more money than younger workers. You may conclude (erroneously) that "as one gets older, one makes more money." But you didn't actually observe that happening because you didn't track actual people over time. It *may* be that the older generation (say, people born in 1945) have just enjoyed higher wages all along than have people born in 1975.

With a cross-sectional study, we can't be sure which explanation is correct, and that's a big weakness. Of course, we could ask workers what they made when they first started working, or we could ask college seniors what test scores they received when they were freshmen, but we are then injecting a "longitudinal" element into our cross-sectional research design. Because of the fallibility of memory and the incentives for distorting the past, it's not a good way to study change over time.

Longitudinal Designs

In longitudinal research, data are collected over time. By measuring independent and dependent variables at each of several different times, the researcher can determine whether change in the independent variable does in fact precede change in the dependent variable—that is, whether the hypothesized cause comes before the effect, as a true cause must. In a cross-sectional study, when the data are all collected at one time, you can't really show if the cause occurs first; in longitudinal studies, though, you can see if a cause occurs and then, later in time, an effect occurs. So if possible to do, longitudinal research is always preferable.

But collecting data more than once takes time and work. Often researchers simply cannot, or are unwilling to, delay completion of a study for even one year in order to collect follow-up data. Still, many research questions really should have a long follow-up period: What is the impact of job training on subsequent employment? How effective is a school-based program in improving parenting skills? Under what conditions do traumatic experiences in childhood result in later mental illness? The value of longitudinal data is great, so every effort should be made to develop longitudinal research designs whenever they are appropriate.

There are basically two longitudinal research designs, with variations possible on each one. In the first, you conduct a simple *cross-sectional* study, but then *repeat* that study several times; therefore this approach is referred to as a *repeated cross-sectional,* or *trend,* design. The frequency of follow-up measurement can vary, ranging from a simple before-and-after design with just one follow-up, to studies in which various indicators are measured every month for many years. In such trend studies, the population from which the sample is selected may be defined broadly or narrowly, but members of the sample are rotated or completely replaced each time a measurement is done. In effect, you look at the population over time, drawing a new sample at each of a number of different points in time. You are looking for trends in the population.

The second major longitudinal design is called a *panel* study. A panel study uses a single group of people who are questioned or studied at multiple points across time; the same people are asked questions on multiple occasions, so how they change and develop as individuals can be studied.

Let's consider these two longitudinal designs and one variation—cohort studies—to see how they are done and what are their strengths and weaknesses.

Exhibit 2.4　Three Types of Research Design

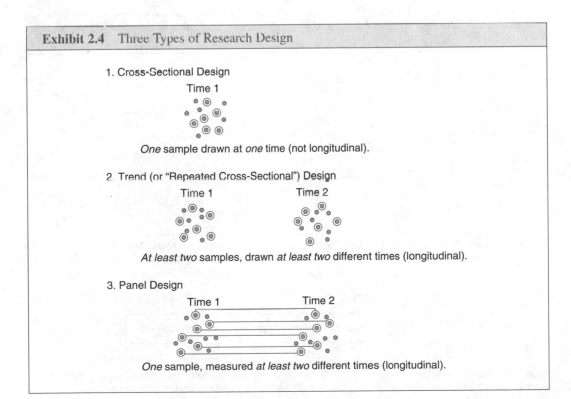

1. Cross-Sectional Design

Time 1

One sample drawn at *one* time (not longitudinal).

2. Trend (or "Repeated Cross-Sectional") Design

Time 1　　　　　Time 2

At least two samples, drawn *at least two* different times (longitudinal).

3. Panel Design

Time 1　　　　　Time 2

One sample, measured *at least two* different times (longitudinal).

Trend Designs

Trend designs, also known as repeated cross-sectional studies, are conducted as follows:

1. A sample is drawn from a population at Time 1, and data are collected from the sample.

2. As time passes, some people leave the population and others enter it.

3. At Time 2, a different sample is drawn from this population.

The Gallup polls, begun in the 1930s, are a well-known example of trend studies. One Gallup poll, for instance, asks people how well they believe the American president is doing his job (Exhibit 2.5). Every so often, the Gallup organization takes a sample of the American population (usually about 1,400 people) and asks them this question. Each time, they ask a different, though roughly equivalent, group of people the question; they aren't talking to the same people every time. Then they use the results of a series of these questions to analyze trends in support for presidents. That is, they can see when support for presidents is high, and when it is low, in general. This is a *trend study*.

Exhibit 2.5 George W. Bush Approval Ratings, Before and After Sept. 11, 2001: A Trend Study by the Gallup Organization

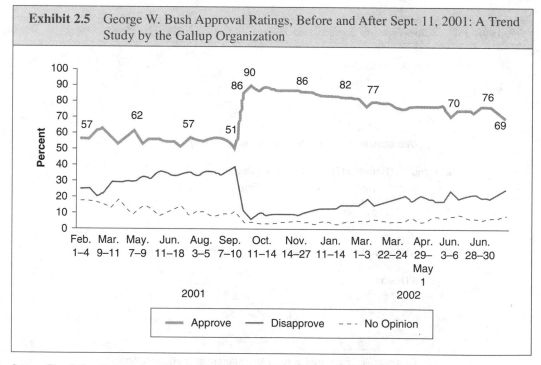

Source: The Gallup Organization. August 20, 2002. Poll Analyses, July 29, 2002. Bush Job Approval Update. http://www.gallup.com/poll/releases/pr020729.asp. © 2002 by the Gallup Organization; used by permission.

When the goal is to determine whether a population has changed over time, trend (or repeated cross-sectional) designs are appropriate. Has racial tolerance increased among Americans in the past 20 years? Are employers more likely to pay maternity benefits today than they were in the 1950s? Are college students today more involved in their communities than college students were 10 years ago? These questions concern changes in populations as a whole, not changes in individuals.

Panel Designs

When we need to know whether individuals in the population changed, we must turn to a **panel design.** In the Mellon Foundation Assessment Project at Hamilton College, underway as this book is being written, a panel of 100 students just entering college was selected from the first-year class to be interviewed once a year for each of their four years at Hamilton. The goal is to determine which experiences in their college career are valuable, and which are a hindrance to their education. By following the same people over a long period of time, we can see how changes happen in the lives of individual students.

Panel designs allow clear identification of changes in the units (individuals, groups, or whatever) we are studying. Here is the process for conducting fixed-sample panel studies:

1. A sample (called a *panel*) is drawn from a population at Time 1, and data are collected from the sample (for instance, 100 freshmen are selected and interviewed).

2. As time passes, some panel members become unavailable for follow-up, and the population changes (some students transfer to other colleges, or decline to continue participating).

3. At Time 2, data are collected from the same people (the panel) as at Time 1, except for those people who cannot be located (the remaining students are re-interviewed).

A panel design allows us to determine how individuals change as well as how the population as a whole has changed; this is a great advantage. However, panel designs are difficult to implement successfully and often are not even attempted, for two reasons:

1. *Expense and attrition*—It can be difficult and expensive to keep track of individuals over a long period, and inevitably the proportion of panel members who can be located for follow-up will decline over time. Panel studies often lose more than one-quarter of their members through attrition (Miller, 1991:170).

2. *Subject fatigue*—Panel members may grow weary of repeated interviews and drop out of the study, or they may become so used to answering the standard questions in the survey that they start giving stock answers rather than actually thinking about their current feelings or actions (Campbell, 1992). This is called the problem of *subject fatigue.*

Because panel studies are so useful, social researchers have developed increasingly effective techniques for keeping track of individuals and overcoming subject fatigue. But if your resources do not permit use of these techniques to maintain an adequate panel and you plan to do a cross-section study instead, remember that it is preferable to use a repeated cross-sectional design rather than a one-time-only cross-sectional study.

Cohort Studies

Trend and panel studies can both track the results of an event (such as World War II) or the progress of a specific historical generation (for instance, people born in 1985). In this case, the historically specific group of people being studied is known as a *cohort,* and this cohort makes up the basic population for your trend or panel study. If you were doing a trend study, the cohort would be the population from which you draw your different samples. If you were doing a panel study, the cohort provides the population from which the panel itself is drawn. Examples of cohorts include:

- *Birth cohorts*—Those who share a common period of birth (those born in the 1940s, 1950s, 1960s, and so on)
- *Seniority cohorts*—Those who have worked at the same place for about 5 years, about 10 years, and so on
- *School cohorts*—Freshmen, sophomores, juniors, seniors

Trend or repeated cross-sectional design: A longitudinal study in which data are collected at two or more points in time from different samples of the same population.

Panel design: A longitudinal study in which data are collected from the same individuals—the panel—at two or more points in time.

Cohort: Individuals or groups with a common starting point. Examples include the college class of 1997, people who graduated from high school in the 1980s, General Motors employees who started work between 1990 and the year 2000, and people who were born in the late 1940s or the 1950s (the "baby boom generation"). Cohorts can form the initial population for either trend or panel studies.

We can see the value of longitudinal research in comparing two studies that estimated the impact of public and private schooling on high school students' achievement test scores. In an initial cross-sectional (not longitudinal) study, James Coleman, Thomas Hoffer, and Sally Kilgore (1982) compared standardized achievement test scores of high school sophomores and seniors in public, Catholic, and other private schools. They found that test scores were higher in the private (including Catholic) high schools than in the public high schools.

But was this difference a causal effect of private schooling? Perhaps the parents of higher performing children were choosing to send them to private schools rather than to public ones. So James Coleman and Thomas Hoffer (1987) went back to the high schools and studied the test scores of the former sophomores two years later, when they were seniors; in other words, the researchers used a panel (longitudinal) design. This time they found that the verbal and math achievement test scores of the Catholic school students had increased more over the two years than the scores of the public school students had. Irrespective of students' initial achievement test scores, the Catholic schools seemed to "do more" for their students than did the public schools. The researchers' causal conclusion rested on much stronger ground because they used a longitudinal panel design.

Units and Levels of Analysis

Finally, as a social science student you probably understand by now that groups don't act or think like individuals do. They are different units of analysis. "Units of analysis" are the things you are studying, whose behavior you want to understand. Often these are people, but they can also be, for instance, families, groups, colleges, governments, or nations. All of these could be units of analysis for your research. The unit of analysis is the entity you are studying and trying to learn about.

As these examples suggest, units exist at different *levels* of analysis, from the most micro (small) to the most macro (large). Individual people are easily seen and talked to, and you can learn about them quite directly. A university, however, although you can certainly visit it and walk around it, is harder to visualize, and data regarding it may take longer to gather. Finally, a nation is not really a "thing" at all and can never be seen by human eyes; understanding such a unit may require many years of study. People, universities, and nations exist at different *levels* of social reality.

Sometimes researchers confuse levels of analysis, mistakenly using data from one level to draw conclusions about a different level. Even the best social scientists fall into this trap. In Emile Durkheim's classic (1951) study of suicide, for example, nationwide suicide rates were compared for Catholic and Protestant countries (in an early stage of his research). Obviously, the data on suicide were collected for individual people, and religion was tallied for individuals as well. Then Durkheim used aggregated numbers to characterize entire countries as being high or low suicide countries and as Protestant (England, Germany, Norway) or Catholic (Italy, France, Spain) countries. He found that Catholic countries had lower rates of suicide than Protestant countries. His accurate finding was about countries, then, not about people; the unit of analysis was the country, and he ranked countries by their suicide rates. Yes, the data were collected from individuals and were about individuals, but it had been combined (aggregated) so as to describe entire nations. Thus, Durkheim's units of analysis were countries. So far, so good.

But Durkheim then made his big mistake. He used his findings from one level of analysis to make statements about units at a different level. He used country data to draw conclusions about individuals, claiming that Catholic individuals were less likely than Protestant individuals to commit suicide. Much of his later discussion in *Suicide* was about why Catholic individuals would be less likely to kill themselves.

Confusions about levels of analysis can take several forms (Lieberson, 1985). Durkheim's mistake was to use findings from a "higher" level (countries) to draw conclusions about a "lower" level (individuals). This is called the *ecological fallacy,* because the "ecology"—the broader surrounding setting, in this case a country—is mistakenly believed to determine what happens for individuals. The ecological fallacy occurs when group-level data are used to draw conclusions about individual-level processes. It's a mistake, and a common one.

Try to spot the ecological fallacy in each of the following deductions. The first half of each sentence is true, but the second half doesn't logically follow from the first:

- Richer countries have higher rates of heart disease; therefore, richer people have higher rates of heart disease.
- Florida counties with the largest number of black residents have the highest rates of Ku Klux Klan membership; therefore, blacks join the Klan more than whites.
- In fall 2000, the presidential election was very close; therefore, Americans wanted a divided government.

In each case, a group-level finding from data is used to draw (erroneous) conclusions about individuals. In rich countries, yes, there is more heart disease, but actually it's among the poor individuals within those countries. Florida counties with more black people attract more white individuals to the Klan. And although America (as a whole) was certainly divided in the 2000 election, just as certainly many individual Americans, both Republican and Democratic, had no ambivalence whatsoever about who was their favorite candidate. *America* as a whole may want a divided government, but relatively few *Americans* do. A researcher who draws such hasty conclusions about individual-level processes from group-level data is committing an **ecological fallacy**.

So conclusions about processes at the individual level must be based on individual-level data; conclusions about group-level processes must be based on data collected about groups. (See Exhibit 2.6.)

Exhibit 2.6 Levels of Analysis: Data from one level of analysis should lead to conclusion only about that level of analysis.

INCORRECT

Level of Analysis	Data Findings	::Therefore::	(Incorrect) Conclusion	Levels of analysis
NATION	Protestant counties have high suicide rates		New York State Votes Republican	STATE
	Rich countries have high rates of heart disease			
GROUP	Most counties in New York State vote Republican		Platoons with high promotion rates have high morale	GROUP
INDIVIDUAL	Individual soldiers who get promoted have high morale		Individual Protestants are more likely to commit suicide	INDIVIDUAL
			Rich people are more likely to have heart disease	

Down slope line (\) indicates Ecological Fallacy; Up slope line (/) indicates Reductionism.

CORRECT

Level of Analysis	Data Findings	::Therefore::	Conclusion	Levels of analysis
NATIONS	(Data about nations)		(Conclusion about nations)	NATIONS
STATES	(Data about states)		(Conclusion about states)	STATES
COUNTIES	(Data about counties)		(Conclusion about counties)	COUNTIES
ORGANIZATIONS	(Data about organizations)		(Conclusion about organizations)	ORGANIZATIONS
GROUPS	(Data about groups)		(Conclusion about groups)	GROUPS
INDIVIDUALS	(Data about individuals)		(Conclusion about individuals)	INDIVIDUALS

Remember that conclusions about individual processes based on group-level data are not necessarily wrong. We just don't know for sure. Suppose, for example, that we find that communities with higher average incomes have lower crime rates. Perhaps there is something about affluence that improves community life such that crime is reduced; that's possible. Or it may be that the only thing special about these communities is that they have more individuals with higher incomes, who tend to commit fewer crimes. Even though we collected data at the group level and analyzed them at the group level, they may reflect a causal process at the individual level (Sampson & Lauritsen, 1994:80–83). The ecological fallacy just reminds us that we can't *know* about individuals without having individual-level information.

Confusion between levels of analysis also occurs in the other direction, when data from the individual level are used to draw conclusions about group behavior. For instance, you may know the personal preferences of everyone on a hiring committee, and so you try to predict whom the committee will decide to hire; but you could easily be wrong. Or you may know two good individuals who are getting married, and so you think that the marriage (the higher-level unit) will be good too. But often, such predictions are wrong, because groups as units don't work like individuals. Nations often go to war even when most of their people (individually) don't want to. Adam Smith, in the 1700s, famously pointed out that millions of people (individuals) acting selfishly could in fact produce an economy (a group) that acted selflessly, helping everyone. You can't predict higher-level processes or outcomes from lower-level ones. You can't, in short, reduce group behavior to individual behavior added up; doing so is called **reductionism** (since it "reduces" group behaviors to that of individuals), and it's basically the reverse of the ecological fallacy.

Both involve confusion of levels of analysis.

Unit of analysis: The level of social life on which a research question is focused, such as individuals, groups, towns, or nations.

BUT IS IT ETHICAL?

Thus far, we've only described how one conducts research, not whether the research project is morally justifiable. But every scientific investigation, whether in the natural or social sciences, has an ethical dimension to it. First and foremost, the scientific concern with validity requires that scientists be honest and reveal their methods. Otherwise, how can we determine if the requirement of validity has been met? Scientists also have to consider the uses to which their findings will be put. Most important, because social science is concerned with society and the human beings in that society, social researchers have some unique ethical concerns.

Honesty and Openness

Research distorted by political or personal pressures to find particular outcomes or to achieve the most marketable results is unlikely to be carried out in an honest and open fashion. And what about the ethics of concealing from your subjects that you're even doing research? Carolyn Ellis (1986) spent several years living in and studying two small fishing communities on Chesapeake Bay in Massachusetts. Living with these "fisher folk," as she called them, she learned quite a few fairly intimate details about their lives, including their less-than-perfect hygiene habits (many simply smelled bad from not bathing). When the book was published, many townspeople were enraged that Ellis had lived among them and then, in effect, betrayed their innermost secrets without having told them that she was planning to write a book. There was enough detail in the book, in fact, that some of the fisher folk could be identified, and Ellis had never fully disclosed to the fisher folk that she was doing research. The episode stirred quite a debate among professional sociologists as well.

Here's another example of hiding one's motives from one's subjects. In the early 1980s, Professor Erich Goode spent three and a half years doing research on the National Association to Aid Fat Americans. Professor Goode was interested primarily in how overweight people managed their identity and enhanced their own self-esteem by forming support groups. Twenty years after the research, in 2002, Goode published an article in which he revealed that in doing the research he met and engaged in romantic and sexual relationships with more than a dozen women in that organization. There was a heated discussion among the editors and board members of the journal in which the article was published, not only about the ethics of the researcher doing such a thing but also about the ethics of the journal then publishing an article that also seemed to take inappropriate advantage of the unusual subject matter (Goode, 2002).

Openness about research procedures and results goes hand in hand with honesty in research design. Openness is also essential if researchers are to learn from the work of others. In the 1980s, there was a long legal battle between a U.S. researcher, Robert Gallo, and a French researcher, Luc Montagnier, about which of them first discovered the virus that causes AIDS. (Scientists are like other people in their desire to be first.) Enforcing standards of honesty and encouraging openness about research is the best solution for these problems.

The Uses of Science

Scientists must also consider the uses to which their research is put. For example, during the 1980s Murray Straus, a prominent researcher of family violence (wife battering, child abuse, corporal punishment, and the like) found in his research that in physical altercations between husband and wife, the wife was, in fact, just as likely as the husband to throw the first punch. This is a startling finding when taken by itself. But Straus also learned that regardless of who actually hit first, the wife nearly always wound up being physically injured far more severely than the man. Whoever started the fight, she lost it (Straus & Gelles, 1988). In this respect (as well as in certain others), Straus's finding that "women hit first as often as men" is quite misleading when taken by itself. When Straus published his findings, a host of social scientists and feminists protested loudly on the grounds that his research was likely to be misused by those who believe that wife battering is not, in fact, a serious problem. It seemed to suggest that, really, men are no worse in their use of violence than are women. Do researchers have an obligation to try to correct what seem to be misinterpretations of their findings?

Social scientists who conduct research on behalf of organizations and agencies may face additional difficulties when the organization, not the researcher, controls the final report and the publicity it receives. If organizational leaders decide that particular research results are unwelcome, the researcher's desire to have findings used appropriately and reported fully can conflict with contractual obligations. This possibility cannot be avoided entirely, but because of it, researchers should acknowledge their funding source in reports.

Research on People

Formal procedures for the protection of human subjects in research grew out of some widely publicized abuses of human subjects. A defining event occurred in 1946 when the Nuremberg war crimes trials exposed horrific medical experiments conducted by Nazi doctors and others in the name of "science." Many Americans were also shocked to learn in the 1970s that researchers funded by the U.S. Public Health Service had infected 600 low-income African-American men with syphilis in the 1930s without their knowledge and had then studied the "natural" course of the illness. Many participants were not informed of their illness and were denied treatment until 1972, even though a cure (penicillin) was developed in the 1950s.

Egregious violations of human rights like these resulted, in the United States, in the creation of a National Commission for the Protection of Human Subjects of Biomedical and Behavioral Research; its 1979 "Belmont Report" (Department of Health, Education, and Welfare, 1979) established basic ethical principles that were translated into specific regulations in 1991 as the "Federal Policy for the Protection of Human Subjects."

The federal government, professional associations, special university review boards, and ethics committees in other organizations all set standards for the treatment of human subjects. Federal regulations require that every institution that seeks federal funding for biomedical or behavioral research on human subjects have an **Institutional Review Board (IRB)** that reviews research proposals. IRBs at universities and other agencies apply ethics standards that are set by federal regulations, but these standards can be expanded or specified by the IRB itself

(Sieber, 1992:5, 10). In order to promote adequate review of ethical issues, the regulations require that IRBs include members with diverse backgrounds. The Office for Protection from Research Risks in the National Institutes of Health monitors IRBs, with the exception of research involving drugs, which is the responsibility of the Federal Drug Administration.

The American Sociological Association (ASA) and other professional social science organizations have adopted ethics guidelines for practicing sociologists that are more specific than the federal regulations. Professional organizations also review complaints of unethical practices when asked.

The code of ethics of the American Sociological Association (1997) is available in print and is posted on the ASA Web site at http://www.asanet.org/members/ecoderev.html. Its standards concerning the treatment of human subjects cover those emphasized by most organizations of social scientists:

- Research should cause no harm to subjects.
- Participation in research should be voluntary, and therefore subjects must give their informed consent to participate in the research.
- Researchers should fully disclose their identity.
- Anonymity or confidentiality must be maintained for individual research participants unless it is voluntarily and explicitly waived.
- The benefits of a research project should outweigh any foreseeable risks.

The difficulties involved in applying these guidelines are illustrated well by a well-known prison simulation study (Haney, Banks, & Zimbardo, 1973). The study was designed to investigate the impact of social position on behavior—specifically, the impact of being either a guard or a prisoner in a prison, a "total institution." The researchers selected apparently stable and mature young male volunteers and asked them to sign a contract to work for two weeks as a guard or a prisoner in a simulated prison. Within the first two days after the "prisoners" were incarcerated by the guards in a makeshift basement prison, the prisoners became passive and disorganized, while the guards became verbally and physically aggressive. Five "prisoners" were soon released for depression, uncontrollable crying, fits of rage, and in one case a psychosomatic rash; on the sixth day the researchers terminated the experiment. Through discussions in special postexperiment encounter sessions, feelings of stress among the participants who played the role of prisoner seemed to be relieved; follow-up during the next year indicated no lasting negative effects on the participants and some benefits in the form of greater insight.

This study has long been the focus of vigorous debate over the meaning of "harm to subjects." Would you ban such experiments because of the potential for harm to subjects? Does the fact that the experiment yielded significant insights—insights that could be used to improve prisons—make any difference (Reynolds, 1979:133–139)? Do you believe that this benefit outweighed the foreseeable risks?

The requirement of informed consent is more difficult to define than may first appear. To be informed, consent must be given by persons who are competent to consent, have consented voluntarily, are fully informed about the research, and have comprehended what they have been told (Reynolds, 1979). The researcher's actions and body language must help to convey his or her verbal assurance that consent is voluntary. Children cannot legally give consent to participate in research, but they must have the opportunity to give or withhold their *assent* to participate in research to which their legal guardians have consented (Sieber, 1992). Can prisoners give informed consent? Can students who are asked to participate in research by their professor? Can participants in covert experiments? These situations require extra care. Fully informed consent is difficult in studies like the prison simulation study because signing consent forms prior to participation may change participants' responses, as well as participation in the research (Larson, 1993:114). Experimental researchers whose research design requires some type of subject deception try to get around this problem by withholding some information before the experiment begins but then debriefing subjects at the end. In the **debriefing**, the researcher explains to the subject what happened in the experiment and why and responds to questions (Sieber, 1992:39–41).

In the prison simulation, all of the participants signed consent forms, but how could they have been fully informed in advance? The researchers themselves did not realize that the study participants would experience so much stress so quickly, that some "prisoners" would have to be released for severe negative reactions within the first few days, or that even those who were not severely stressed would soon be begging to be released from the mock prison. If this risk was not foreseeable, was it acceptable for the researchers to presume in advance that the benefits would outweigh the risks?

For his study of homosexual behavior in public bathrooms, *Tearoom Trade,* Laud Humphreys (1970) decided that truly informed consent would be impossible to obtain. Instead, he first served as a lookout—a "watch queen"—for men who were entering a public bathroom in a city park with the intention of having sex. In a number of cases, he then left the bathroom and copied the license plate numbers of the cars driven by the men. One year later, he visited the homes of the men and interviewed them as part of a larger study of social issues. Humphreys changed his appearance so that the men did not recognize him. His conclusions, seemingly, were benign—the men who engaged in what were viewed as deviant acts were for the most part married, suburban men whose families were unaware of their sexual practices. But debate has continued ever since the publication of this research about Humphreys' failure to tell the men what he was really doing in the bathroom or why he had come to their homes for the interview. If you were to serve on your university's IRB, would you allow this research to be conducted?

Sometimes subjects are tested without their knowledge in ways that are directly and knowingly harmful to them. We mentioned earlier one such case—the Tuskegee Syphilis Study. Beginning in 1932, the U.S. Public Health Service conducted a panel study of about 600 poor black men diagnosed with syphilis in Macon County, Alabama. The men, told that they had "bad blood," were deliberately not treated, even after penicillin became widely available during World War II. Treating the men with penicillin might have cured them. The details finally were exposed 40 years later, in 1972—while the study was still being carried out (Jones, 1993). A scandal ensued, and in 1997 President Clinton officially apologized, on behalf of the government, to the survivors. Those who were left untreated suffered from a terrible disease, which could have been cured rather easily—all in the name of science.

Maintaining confidentiality is another key ethical obligation; it should be reflected in a statement in the informed consent agreement about how each subject's privacy will be protected (Sieber, 1992). Procedures, such as locking records and creating special identifying codes, must be created to minimize the risk of access by unauthorized persons. However, statements about confidentiality should be realistic. In 1993, sociologist Rik Scarce was jailed for five months for contempt of court, after refusing to testify to a grand jury about so-called "eco-terrorists." Scarce, a Ph.D. candidate at Washington State University at the time, was researching radical environmentalists and may have had information about a 1991 "liberation" raid on an animal research lab at Washington State. Scarce was eventually released from jail, but he never did violate the confidentiality he claimed to have promised his informants. Laws allow research records to be subpoenaed and may require reporting child abuse. A researcher also may feel compelled to release information if a health- or life-threatening situation arises and participants need to be alerted.

The potential of withholding a beneficial treatment from some subjects is also cause for ethical concern. Sometimes, in an ethically debatable practice, researchers will actually withhold treatments from some subjects, knowing that those treatments would probably help the people, in order to accurately measure *how much* they helped. For example, in some recent studies of AIDS drugs conducted in Africa, researchers provided different levels of AIDS-combating drugs to different groups of patients with the disease. Some patients received no drug therapy at all, despite the fact that all indications were that the drug treatments would help them. From the point of view of pure science, this makes sense: You can't really know how effective the drugs are unless you try different treatments on different people who start from the same situation (i.e., having AIDS). But the research has provoked a tremendous outcry across the world because many people find the practice of deliberately not treating people—in particular, impoverished black people living in Third World countries—to be morally repugnant.

The extent to which ethical issues are a problem for researchers and their subjects varies dramatically with research design. Most survey research, in particular, creates few ethical problems (Reynolds, 1979:56–57). On the other hand, some experimental studies in the social sciences that have put people in uncomfortable or embarrassing situations have generated vociferous complaints and years of debate about ethics (Reynolds, 1979; Sjoberg, 1967). Moreover, adherence to ethical guidelines must take into account each aspect of the research procedures. For example, full disclosure of "what is really going on" in an experimental study is unnecessary if subjects are unlikely to be harmed.

What it comes down to is that the researcher must think through in advance the potential for ethical problems, must make every effort to foresee all possible risks and to weigh the possible benefits of the research against these risks, must establish clear procedures that minimize the risks and maximize the benefits, and must inform research subjects in advance about the potential risks.

Ultimately, these decisions about ethical procedures are not just up to you, as a researcher, to make. Your university's IRB sets the human subjects protection standards for your institution and may even require that you submit your research proposal to them for review. Before submitting a project for review, you should also consult with individuals with different perspectives to develop a realistic risk/benefit assessment (Sieber, 1992:75–108).

CONCLUSION

Social researchers can find many questions to study, but not all questions are equally worthy. The ones that warrant the expense and effort of social research are feasible, socially important, and scientifically relevant.

Selecting a worthy research question does not guarantee a worthwhile research project. The simplicity of the research circle presented in this chapter belies the complexity of the social research process. In the following chapters, we will focus on particular aspects of that process. Chapter 3 examines the interrelated processes of conceptualization and measurement, arguably the most important parts of research. Measurement validity is the foundation for the other two aspects of validity, which are discussed in Chapters 4 and 5. Chapter 4 reviews the meaning of generalizability and the sampling strategies that help us to achieve this goal. Chapter 5 introduces the third aspect of validity—causal validity—and illustrates different methods for achieving causal validity and explains basic experimental data collection. The next two chapters introduce approaches to data collection—surveys and qualitative research—that help us, in different ways, to achieve validity.

Ethical issues also should be considered in the evaluation of research proposals and completed research studies. As the preceding examples show, ethical issues in social research are no less complex than the other issues that researchers confront. And it is inexcusable to jump into research on people without any attention to ethical considerations.

You are now forewarned about the difficulties that all scientists, but social scientists in particular, face in their work. We hope that you will return often to this chapter as you read the subsequent chapters, when you criticize the research literature, and when you design your own research projects. To be conscientious, thoughtful, and responsible—this is the mandate of every social scientist. If you formulate a feasible research problem, ask the right questions in advance, try to adhere to the research guidelines, and steer clear of the most common difficulties, you will be well along the road to fulfilling this mandate.

KEY TERMS

Anomalous
Cohort
Cross-sectional research design
Deductive research
Dependent variable
Direction of association
Ecological fallacy
Empirical generalization
Group unit of analysis
Hypothesis
Independent variable
Individual unit of analysis
Inductive reasoning

Inductive research
Institutional Review Board (IRB)
Longitudinal research design
Panel design
Research circle
Serendipitous or anomalous
   findings
Social research question
Theory
Trend Study (repeated cross-sectional
   design)
Units of analysis
Variable

HIGHLIGHTS

• Research questions should be feasible (within the time and resources available), socially important, and scientifically relevant.

• Building social theory is a major objective of social science research. Investigate relevant theories before starting social research projects, and draw out the theoretical implications of research findings.

• The type of reasoning in most research can be described as primarily deductive or inductive. Research based on deductive reasoning proceeds from general ideas, deduces specific expectations from these ideas, and then tests the ideas with empirical data. Research based on inductive reasoning begins with ("in!") specific data and then develops (induces) general ideas or theories to explain patterns in the data.

• It may be possible to explain unanticipated research findings after the fact, but such explanations have less credibility than those that have been tested with data collected for the purpose of the study.

- The scientific process can be represented as circular, with connections from theory, to hypotheses, to data, and to empirical generalizations. Research investigations may begin at different points along the research circle and traverse different portions of it. Deductive research begins at the point of theory; inductive research begins with data but ends with theory. Descriptive research begins with data and ends with empirical generalizations.

- Scientific research should be conducted and reported in an honest and open fashion. Contemporary ethical standards also require that social research cause no harm to subjects, that participation be voluntary as expressed in informed consent, that researchers fully disclose their identity, that benefits to subjects outweigh any foreseeable risks, and that anonymity or confidentiality be maintained for participants unless it is voluntarily and explicitly waived.

> To assist you in completing the Web Exercises, please access the Study Site at http://www.pineforge.com/mssw2 where you'll find the Web Exercises with accompanying links. You'll find other useful study materials like self-quizzes and e-flashcards for each chapter, along with a group of carefully selected articles from research journals that illustrate the major concepts and techniques presented in the book.

EXERCISES

Discussing Research

1. Classify two research projects you have read about, perhaps in other courses, as primarily inductive or deductive. Did you notice any inductive components in the primarily deductive projects? How much descriptive research was involved? Did the findings have any implications that you think should be investigated in a new study? What new hypotheses are implied by the findings?

2. Using one of the research projects on which you focused in Exercise 1, identify the stages of the project corresponding to the points on the research circle. Did the research cover all four stages? Identify the theories and hypotheses underlying the study. What data were collected? What were the findings (empirical generalizations)?

3. Research problems posed for explanatory studies must specify hypotheses and variables, which need to be stated properly and need to correctly imply any hypothesized causal relationship. Some lessons on the practice CD-ROM accompanying your textbook will help you to learn the language of variables and hypotheses.

To use these lessons, choose one of the four "Variables and Hypotheses" exercises from the opening menu. About 10 hypotheses are presented in the lesson. After reading each hypothesis, name the dependent and independent variables and state the direction (positive or negative) of the relationship between them. The program will evaluate your answers. If an answer is correct, the program will repeat it and go on to the next question. If you have made an error, the program will explain the error to you and give you another chance to respond. If your answer is unrecognizable, the program will instruct you to check your spelling and try again.

4. Earlier in the chapter we mentioned Erich Goode's research on "fat Americans" that prompted a vigorous debate in the journal in which it was published. Should researchers avoid any personal relationships with their subject? What might people find unethical in Goode's research? What, exactly, do you find unethical or troubling in it? Discuss this in your class.

5. In this chapter we discussed a number of cases of questionable research ethics. List what you think are the three "most unethical" cases, as you see them. For each one, say why you think it was worse than the other cases.

6. The ecological fallacy consists of drawing conclusions about individuals from group-level data. Think of two examples that you know, or can imagine, of an ecological fallacy. State for each case how this is different from making an unjustified generalization about individuals. (This is a difficult exercise!)

Finding Research

1. State a problem for research—some feature of social life that interests you. If you have not already identified a problem for study, or if you need to evaluate whether your research problem is doable, a few suggestions should help to get the ball rolling and keep you on course.

   a. Jot down several questions that have puzzled you about people and social relations, perhaps questions that have come to mind while reading textbooks or research articles, talking with friends, or hearing news stories.
   b. Now take stock of your interests, your opportunities, and the work of others. Which of your research questions no longer seem feasible or interesting? What additional research questions come to mind? Pick out one question that is of interest and seems feasible and that has probably been studied before.
   c. Do you think your motives for doing the research affect how the research is done? How? Imagine several different motives for doing the research. Might any of them affect the quality of your research? How?
   d. Write out your research question in one sentence; then elaborate on it in one paragraph. List at least three reasons why it is a good research question for you to investigate. Then present your question to your classmates and instructor for discussion and feedback.

2. Review Appendix A, Finding Information, and then search the literature (and the Internet) on the research question you identified. Copy down at least five citations to articles (with abstracts from Sociological Abstracts) and two Web sites reporting research that seems highly relevant to your research question. Look up at least two of these articles and one of the Web sites. Inspect the article bibliographies and the links in the Web site and identify at least one more relevant article and Web site from each source.

Write a brief description of each article and Web site you consulted and evaluate its relevance to your research question. What additions or changes to your thoughts about the research question are suggested by the sources?

3. You can read descriptions of major social theories at this Web site: http://ryoung001 .homestead.com/AssessingTheory.html. Which description do you find most appealing? Can you state several of the predictions from this theory as "if-then" hypotheses? What are the independent variables? The dependent variables?

4. You've been assigned to write a paper on domestic violence and the law. To start, you would like to find out what the American Bar Association's stance is on the issue. Go to the American Bar Association Commission on Domestic Violence's Web site (http://www.abanet.org/domviol/mrdv/identify.html).

What is the American Bar Association's definition of domestic violence? How do they suggest one can identify a person as a victim of domestic violence? What do they identify as "basic warning signs"?

Critiquing Research

1. Using recent newspapers or magazines, find three articles that report on large interview or survey research studies. Describe each study briefly, then say (a) whether the study design was longitudinal or cross-sectional, and (b) if that mattered, that is, if the study's findings would possibly have been different using the alternative design.

2. Search the journal literature for three studies concerning some social program or organizational policy, after you review the procedures in Appendix A. Several possibilities are research on Project Head Start, on the effects of welfare payments, on boot camps for offenders, and on standardized statewide testing in the public schools. Would you characterize the findings as largely consistent or inconsistent? How would you explain discrepant findings?

3. Criticize one of the studies described in this chapter in terms of its adherence to each of the ethics guidelines for social research. List each guideline and indicate what problem or problems might have occurred as a result of deviation from it. How would you weigh the study's contribution to knowledge and social policy against its potential risks to human subjects?

Doing Research

1. Formulate four research questions about support for capital punishment. Provide one question for each research purpose: descriptive, exploratory, explanatory, and evaluative.

2. State four hypotheses in which support for capital punishment is the dependent variable and some other variable is the independent variable.

    a. Justify each hypothesis in a sentence or two.
    b. Propose a design to test each hypothesis. Design the studies to use different longitudinal designs and different units of analysis. What difficulties can you anticipate with each design?

3. Write a statement for one of your proposed research designs that states how you will ensure adherence to each ethical guideline for the protection of human subjects. Which standards for the protection of human subjects might pose the most difficulty for researchers on your proposed topic? Explain your answers and suggest appropriate protection procedures for human subjects.

Chapter 3

Conceptualization and Measurement

Every time you begin to review or design a research study, you will have to answer two questions: (1) What do the main concepts mean in this research? (2) How are the main concepts measured? Both questions must be answered to evaluate the validity of any research. For instance, to study a hypothesized link between religious fundamentalism and terrorism, you may conceptualize terrorism as "nongovernmental political violence," and measure incidents of terrorism by counting for a 5-year period the number of violent attacks that have explicit political aims. You will also need to define and measure "religious fundamentalism," no easy task. What counts? And how should you decide what counts? We cannot make sense of a researcher's study until we know how the concepts were *defined* and *measured*. Nor can we begin our own research until we have defined our concepts clearly and constructed valid measures of them.

In this chapter, we briefly address the issue of conceptualization, or defining your main terms. We then describe measurement sources such as available archive data, questions, observations, and less direct, or unobtrusive, measures. We then discuss the level of measurement reflected in different measures. The final topic is to assess the validity and reliability of these measures. By the chapter's end, you should have a good understanding of measurement, the first of the three legs (measurement, generalizability, and causality) on which a research project's validity rests.

WHAT DO WE HAVE IN MIND?

A May 2000 *New York Times* article (Stille, 2000) announced that the "social health" of the United States had risen a bit, after a precipitous decline in the 1970s and 1980s. Should we be relieved? Concerned? What, after all, does "social health" mean? To social scientist Marc Miringoff, it has to do with social and economic inequalities. To political pundit William J. Bennett, it is more a matter of moral values. In fact, the **concept** of social health means different things to different people. Most agree that it has to do with "things that are not measured in the gross national product" and is supposed to be "a more subtle and more meaningful way of measuring what's important to [people]" (Stille, 2000:A19). But until we agree on a definition of social health, we can't decide whether it has to do with child poverty, trust in government, out-of-wedlock births, alcohol-related traffic deaths, or some combination of these or other phenomena.

Conceptualization

A continuing challenge for social scientists, then, rests on the fact that many of our important topics of study (social health, for instance) are not clearly defined things or objects (like trees or rocks), but are abstract concepts or ideas. A concept is an image or idea, not a simple object. Some concepts are relatively simple, such as a person's age or sex: almost everyone would agree what it means to be 14 years old or female. But other concepts are more ambiguous. For instance, if you want to count the number of families in Chicago, what counts as a family? A husband and wife with two biological children living in one house—yes, that's a family.

Do cousins living next door count? Cousins living in California? Or maybe the parents are divorced; or the children adopted; or maybe the children are grown. Maybe two women live together with one adopted child and one biological child fathered by a now-absent man. So perhaps "living together" is what defines a family—or is it biology? Or is it a crossing of generations—that is, the presence of adults and children? The particular definition you develop will affect your research findings, and some people probably won't like it whatever you do, but how you define "family" obviously affects your results.

Often social concepts can be used sloppily or even misleadingly. Nowadays you may hear that "the economy" is doing well, but it may seem to you that many people are worse off. Typically, in news reports "the economy" refers to the Gross Domestic Product—the total amount of economic activity (value of goods and services, precisely) in the country in a given year. When the GDP goes up, reporters say "the economy is improving." But that's very different from saying that the average working person makes more money than he or she would have 20 years ago—in fact, he or she makes less. We could use the concept of "the economy" to refer to the economic well-being of actual people, but that's not typically in fact how it's used.

Defining concepts clearly can be quite difficult because many concepts have several meanings and can be measured in many ways. What is meant, for instance, by the idea of "power?" The classic definition, provided by German sociologist Max Weber, is that power is the ability to meet your goals over the objections of other people. That definition implies that unknown people can be quite powerful, whereas certain presidents of the United States have been relatively powerless. A different definition might equate power to one's official position; in that case, the president of the United States would be powerful. Or perhaps power is equated with prestige, so famous intellectuals like Albert Einstein would be considered powerful. Or maybe power is defined as having wealth, so that rich people are seen as powerful.

And even if we can settle on a definition, how then do we actually measure power? Should we ask a variety of people if a certain person is powerful? Should we review their acts over the last 10 years and see when they exerted their will over others? Should we try to uncover the true extent of their wealth and use that? How about power at a lower level, say, as a member of student government? The most visible and vocal people in your student assembly may be, in fact, quite unpopular and perhaps not very powerful at all—just loud. At the same time, there may be students who are members of no official body whatsoever, but somehow they always get what they want. Isn't that power? From these varied cases, you can see that power can be quite difficult to conceptualize.

Or describing what causes "crime," or even what causes "theft," is inherently problematic, since the very definition of these terms is spectacularly flexible and indeed forms part of their interest for us. What counts as theft varies dramatically, depending on the thief—a next-door neighbor, a sister, or a total stranger wandering through town—and what item is taken: a bottle of water, your watch, a lawn mower, a skirt, your reputation, or $5. Indeed, part of what makes social science interesting are the debates over, for instance, what is a theft, or what is crime.

So conceptualization—working out what your key terms will mean, in your research—is a crucial part of the research process. Definitions need to be explicit. Sometimes conceptualization is easy: "Older men are more likely to suffer myocardial infarction than younger men," or "Career military officers mostly vote for Republican candidates in national elections." Most of the concepts used in those statements are easily understood and easy to measure (sex, age, military status, voting). In other cases, conceptualization is quite difficult: "As people's moral standards deteriorate, the family unit starts to die," or "intelligence makes you more likely to succeed."

Conceptualization, then, is the process of matching up terms (family, sex, happiness, power) to clarified definitions for them—really, figuring out what are the social "things" you'll be talking about.

Concept: A mental image that summarizes a set of similar observations, feelings, or ideas.

Conceptualization: The process of specifying what we mean by a term. In deductive research, **conceptualization** helps to translate portions of an abstract theory into testable hypotheses involving specific variables. In inductive research, conceptualization is an important part of the process used to make sense of related observations.

It is especially important to define clearly concepts that are abstract or unfamiliar. When we refer to concepts like "social control," "anomie," or "social status," we cannot count on others knowing exactly what we mean. Even experts may disagree about the meaning of frequently used concepts if they base their conceptualizations on different theories. That's OK. The point is not that there can be only one definition of a concept, but that we have to specify clearly what we mean when we use a concept, and we should expect others to do the same.

Conceptualization also involves creating concepts, or thinking about how to conceive of the world: What things go together? How do we slice up reality? Cell phones, for instance, may be seen as communication devices, like telephones, radios, telegraphs, or two tin cans connected by a string. But they can also be conceived in another way: a college administrator we know, seeing students leaving class outside her building, said, "Cell phones have replaced cigarettes." She reconceptualized cell phones, seeing them not as communication tools but as something to fiddle with, like cigarettes, chewing gum wrappers, keys on a lanyard, or the split ends of long hair. In conceptualizing the world, we create the lenses through which we see it.

Our point is not that conceptualization problems are insurmountable, but that (1) you need to develop and clearly state what you *mean* by your key concepts, and (2) your measurements will need to be clear and consistent with the definitions you've settled on (more on that topic shortly).

Variables and Constants

After we define the concepts for a study, we must identify variables that correspond to those concepts. For example, we might be interested in what affects students' engagement in their academic work—when they are excited about their studies, when they become eager to learn more, and so on. Our main concept, then, would be "engagement." We could use any number of different variables to measure engagement: the student's reported interest in classes, a teacher's evaluation of student engagement, the number of hours spent on homework, or an index including a number of different questions. Any of these variables could show a high or low level of student engagement. If we are to study variation in engagement, we must identify variables to measure that are most pertinent to our theoretical concerns.

You should be aware that not every concept in a particular study is represented by a variable. In our student engagement study, all of the students *are* students—there is no variation in that. So "student," in this study, is called a **constant** (it's always the same), not a variable.

There are many variables that could measure student engagement. Which variables should we select? It's very tempting, and all too common, to simply try to "measure everything," by including in a study every variable we can think of. We could collect self-reports of engagement, teacher ratings, hours studied per week, pages of essays written for class, number of visits to the library per week, frequency of participation in discussion, times met with professors, and on and on. This haphazard approach will inevitably result in the collection of some useless data and the failure to collect some important data. Instead, we should take four steps:

1. Examine the theories that are relevant to our research question to identify those concepts that would be expected to have some bearing on the phenomena we are investigating.

2. Review the relevant research literature and assess the utility of variables used in prior research.

3. Consider the constraints and opportunities for measurement that are associated with the specific setting(s) we will study. Distinguish constants from variables in this setting.

4. Look ahead to our analysis of the data. What role will each variable play in our analyses?

Remember: A few well-chosen variables are better than a barrel full of useless ones.

HOW WILL WE KNOW WHEN WE'VE FOUND IT?

Once we have defined our concepts in the abstract—that is, after conceptualizing—and we have identified the variables that we want to measure, we must develop our measurement procedures. The goal is to devise **operations** that actually measure the concepts we intend to measure—in other words, to achieve measurement validity.

Exhibit 3.1 represents the **operationalization** process in three studies. The first researcher defines his or her concept, binge drinking, and chooses one variable—frequency of heavy episodic drinking—to represent it. This variable is then measured with responses to a single question, or *indicator:* "How often within the last 2 weeks did you drink five or more drinks containing alcohol in a row?" Because "heavy" drinking is defined differently for men and women (relative to their different metabolisms), the question is phrased in terms of "four or more drinks" for women. The second researcher defines her concept—poverty—as having two aspects or dimensions, subjective poverty and absolute poverty. Subjective poverty is measured with responses to a survey question: "Would you say that you are poor?" Absolute poverty is measured by comparing family income to the poverty threshold. The third researcher decides that her concept—social class—is defined by a position on three measured variables: income, education, and occupational prestige.

Operationalization: The process of specifying the operations that will indicate the value of cases on a variable.

Measures can be based on activities as diverse as asking people questions, reading judicial opinions, observing social interactions, coding words in books, checking census data tapes, enumerating the contents of trash receptacles, or drawing urine and blood samples. Experimental researchers may operationalize a concept by manipulating its value; for example, to operationalize the concept of exposure to anti-drinking messages, some subjects may listen to a talk about binge drinking while others do not. We will focus here on the operations of using

Exhibit 3.1   Concepts, Variables, and Indicators: Operationalizing Concepts

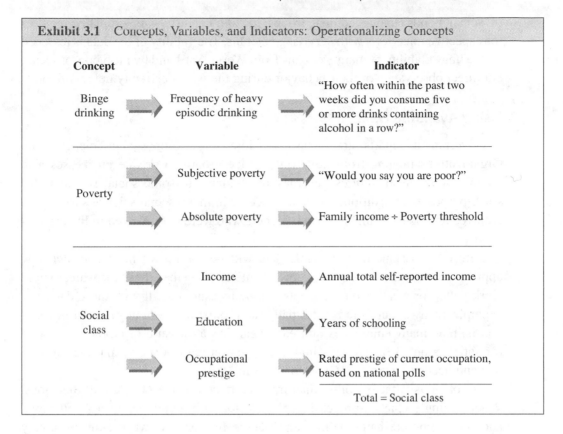

Concept	Variable	Indicator
Binge drinking	Frequency of heavy episodic drinking	"How often within the past two weeks did you consume five or more drinks containing alcohol in a row?"
Poverty	Subjective poverty	"Would you say you are poor?"
	Absolute poverty	Family income ÷ Poverty threshold
Social class	Income	Annual total self-reported income
	Education	Years of schooling
	Occupational prestige	Rated prestige of current occupation, based on national polls

Total = Social class

published data, asking questions, observing behavior, and using unobtrusive means of measuring people's behavior and attitudes.

The variables and measurement operations chosen for a study should be consistent with the purpose of the research question. Suppose we hypothesize that college students who go abroad for their junior year have a more valuable experience than those who remain at their college. If our purpose is *evaluation* of different junior-year options, we can operationalize "junior-year programs" by comparing (1) traditional coursework at home, (2) study in a foreign country, and (3) internships at home that are not traditional college courses. A simple question, asking students in each program, for example, "How valuable do you feel your experience was?" would help to provide the basis for determining the relative value of these programs. But if our purpose is *explanation,* we would probably want to interview students to learn what features of the different programs made them valuable, to find out the underlying dynamics of educational growth.

Time and resource limitations also must be taken into account when we select variables and devise measurement operations. For many sociohistorical questions (such as "How has the poverty rate varied since 1950?"), census data or other published counts must be used. On the other hand, a historical question about the types of social bonds among combat troops in 20th-century wars probably requires retrospective interviews with surviving veterans. The validity of the data is lessened by the unavailability of many veterans from World War I and by problems of recall, but direct observation of their behavior during the war is certainly not an option.

Using Available Data

Government reports are rich, accessible sources of social science data. Organizations ranging from nonprofit service groups to private businesses also compile a wealth of figures that may be available to some social scientists for some purposes. In addition, the data collected in many social science surveys are archived and made available for researchers who were not involved in the original survey project.

Before we assume that available data will be useful, we must consider how appropriate they are for our concepts of interest, whether other measures would work better, or whether our concepts can be measured at all with these data. For example, many organizations informally (and sometimes formally) use turnover— that is, how many employees quit each year—as a measure of employee morale (or satisfaction). If turnover is high (or retention rates are low), morale must be bad and needs to be raised. Or so the thinking goes.

But obviously, factors other than morale affect whether people quit their jobs. When a single chicken-processing plant is the only employer in a small town, and other jobs are hard to find, and people live on low wages, turnover may be very low even among miserable workers. In the "dot-com" companies of the late 1990s, turnover was high—despite amazingly good conditions, salary, and morale—because the industry was so hungry for good workers that companies competed ferociously to attract them. Maybe the concepts "morale" and "satisfaction," then, can't be measured adequately by the most easily available data, that is, turnover rates.

We also cannot assume that available data are accurate, even when they appear to measure the concept. "Official" counts of homeless persons have been notoriously unreliable because of the difficulty of locating homeless persons on the streets, and government agencies have at times resorted to "guesstimates" by service providers. Even available data for such seemingly straightforward measures as counts of organizations can contain a surprising amount of error. For example, a 1990 national church directory reported 128 churches in a Midwest county; an intensive search in that county in 1992 located 172 churches (Hadaway, Marler, & Chaves, 1993:744).

When legal standards, enforcement practices, and measurement procedures have been taken into account, comparisons among communities become more credible. However, such adjustments may be less necessary when the operationalization of a concept is relatively unambiguous, as with the homicide rate: Dead is dead. And when a central authority imposes a common data-collection standard, as with the FBI's Uniform Crime Reports, data become more comparable across communities. But careful review of measurement operations is still important, because procedures for classifying a death as a homicide can vary between jurisdictions and over time.

Another rich source of already-collected data is survey datasets archived and made available to university researchers by the Inter-University Consortium for Political and Social Research. One of its most popular survey datasets is the General Social Survey (GSS). The GSS is administered regularly by the National Opinion Research Center (NORC) at the University of Chicago to a sample of more than 1,500 Americans (annually until 1994; biennially since then). GSS questions vary from year to year, but an unchanging core of questions includes measures of political attitudes, occupation and income, social activities, substance abuse, and many other variables of interest to social scientists. This dataset can easily be used by college students to explore a wide range of interesting topics. However, when surveys are used in this way, after the fact, researchers must carefully evaluate the survey questions. Are the available measures sufficiently close to the measures needed that they can be used to answer the new research question?

Constructing Questions

Asking people questions is the most common, and probably most versatile, operation for measuring social variables. Do you play on a varsity team? What is your major? How often, in a week, do you go out with friends? How much time do you spend on schoolwork? Most concepts about individuals are measured with such questions. In this section, we'll introduce some options for writing single questions, explain why single questions can sometimes be inadequate measures, and then examine the use of multiple questions to measure a concept.

In principle, questions, asked perhaps as part of a survey, can be a straightforward and efficient means by which to measure individual characteristics, facts about events, level of knowledge, and opinions of any sort. In practice, though, survey questions can easily result in misleading or inappropriate answers. All questions proposed for a survey must be screened carefully for their adherence to basic guidelines and then tested and revised until the researcher feels some confidence that they will be clear to the intended respondents (Fowler, 1995). Some variables may prove to be inappropriate for measurement with any type of question. We have to recognize that memories and perceptions of the events about which we might like to ask can be limited.

Specific guidelines for reviewing questions are presented in Chapter 6; here, our focus is on the different types of survey questions.

Single Questions

Measuring variables with single questions is very popular. Public opinion polls based on answers to single questions are reported frequently in newspaper articles and TV newscasts: "Do you favor or oppose U.S. policy in Iraq?" "If you had to vote today, for which candidate would you vote?" Social science surveys also rely on single questions to measure many variables: "Overall, how satisfied are you with your job?" "How would you rate your current health?"

Single questions can be designed with or without explicit response choices. The question that follows is a **closed-ended**, or **fixed-choice, question**, because respondents are offered explicit responses from which to choose. It has been selected from the Core Alcohol and Drug Survey distributed by the Core Institute, Southern Illinois University, for the FIPSE Core Analysis Grantee Group (Presley, Meilman, & Lyerla, 1994).

Compared with other campuses with which you are familiar, this campus's use of alcohol is . . . (Mark one)

___ *Greater than other campuses*

___ *Less than other campuses*

___ *About the same as other campuses*

Most surveys of a large number of people contain primarily fixed-choice questions, which are easy to process with computers and analyze with statistics. However, fixed-response choices can obscure what people really think unless the choices are designed carefully to match the range of possible responses to the question.

Most important, response choices should be mutually exclusive and exhaustive, so that every respondent can find *one and only one* choice that applies to him or her (unless the question is of the "Check all that apply" variety). To make response choices exhaustive, researchers may need to offer at least one option with room for ambiguity. For example, a questionnaire asking college students to indicate their school status should not use freshman, sophomore, junior, senior, and graduate student as the only response choices. Most campuses also have students in a "special" category, so you might add "Other (please specify)" to the five fixed responses to this question. If respondents do not find a response option that corresponds to their answer to the question, they may skip the question entirely or choose a response option that does not indicate what they are really thinking.

Researchers who study small numbers of people often use **open-ended questions**, which don't have explicit response choices and allow respondents to write in their answers. The next question is an open-ended version of the earlier fixed-choice question:

How would you say alcohol use on this campus compares to that on other campuses?

An open-ended format is preferable when the full range of responses cannot be anticipated, especially when questions have not been used previously in surveys or when questions are asked of new groups. Open-ended questions also can allow clear answers when questions involve complex concepts. In the previous question, for instance, "alcohol use" may cover how many students drink, how heavily they drink, if the drinking is public or not, if it affects levels of violence on campus, and so on.

Just like fixed-choice questions, open-ended questions should be reviewed carefully for clarity before they are used. For example, if respondents are asked, "When did you move to Boston?" they might respond with a wide range of answers: "In 1944." "After I had my first child." "When I was 10." "20 years ago." Such answers would be very hard to compile. To avoid such ambiguity, rephrase the question to clarify the form of the answer, for instance, "In what year did you move to Boston?" Or provide explicit response choices (Center for Survey Research, 1987).

Indexes and Scales

When several questions are used to measure one concept, the responses may be combined by taking the sum or average of responses. A composite measure based on this type of sum or average is termed an **index.** The idea is that idiosyncratic variation in response to particular questions will average out, so that the main influence on the combined measure will be the concept that all the questions focus on. In addition, the index can be considered a more complete measure of the concept than can any one of the component questions.

Creating an index is not just a matter of writing a few questions that seem to focus on a concept. Questions that seem to you to measure a common concept might seem to respondents to concern several different issues. The only way to know that a given set of questions does, in fact, form an index is to administer the questions to people like those you plan to study. If a common concept is being measured, people's responses to the different questions should display some consistency.

Because of the popularity of survey research, indexes already have been developed to measure many concepts, and some of these indexes have proved to be reliable in a range of studies. Usually it is much better to use such an index than it is to try to form a new one. Use of a preexisting index both simplifies the work of designing a study and facilitates comparison of findings from other studies.

The questions in Exhibit 3.2 represent a short form of an index used to measure depression; it is called the Center for Epidemiologic Studies Depression Index

Exhibit 3.2   Example of an Index: Excerpt From the Center for Epidemiologic Studies Depression Index (CES-D)

At any time during the past week . . . *(Circle one response on each line)*	*Never*	*Some of the time*	*Most of the time*
a. Was your appetite so poor that you did not feel like eating?	1	2	3
b. Did you feel so tired and worn out that you could not enjoy anything?	1	2	3
c. Did you feel depressed?	1	2	3
d. Did you feel unhappy about the way your life is going?	1	2	3
e. Did you feel discouraged and worried about your future?	1	2	3
f. Did you feel lonely?	1	2	3

Source: Lenore Radloff, 1977. "The CES-D Scale: A Self-Report Depression Scale for Research in the General Population." *Applied Psychological Measurement, 1:* 385–401. Reprinted by permission of Sage Publications, Inc. Copyright 1977 West Publishing Company/Applied Psychological Measurement Inc. Reproduced by permission.

(CES-D). Many researchers in different studies have found that these questions form a reliable index. Note that each question concerns a symptom of depression. People may well have one particular symptom without being depressed; for example, persons who have been suffering from a physical ailment may say that they have a poor appetite. By combining the answers to questions about several symptoms, the index reduces the impact of this idiosyncratic variation. (This set of questions uses what is termed a "matrix" format, in which a series of questions that concern a common theme are presented together, with the same response choices.)

Usually an index is calculated by simply averaging responses to the questions, so that every question counts equally. But sometimes, either intentionally by the researcher or by happenstance, questions on an index arrange themselves in a kind of hierarchy in which an answer to one question effectively provides answers to others. For instance, a person who supports abortion on demand almost certainly supports it in cases of rape and incest as well. Such questions form a **scale**. In a scale, we give different weights to the responses to different questions before summing or averaging the responses. Responses to one question might be counted two or three times as much as responses to another. For example, based on Christopher Mooney and Mei Hsien Lee's (1995) research on abortion law reform, a scale to indicate support for abortion might give a "1" to agreement that abortion should be allowed "when the pregnancy resulted from rape or incest" and a

"4" to agreement with the statement that abortion should be allowed "whenever a woman decided she wanted one." A "4" rating is much stronger, in that anyone who gets a "4" would also probably agree to all "lower-number" questions as well.

Making Observations

Asking questions, then, is one way to operationalize, or measure, a variable. *Observations* can also be used to measure characteristics of individuals, events, and places. The observations may be the primary form of measurement in a study, or they may supplement measures obtained through questioning.

Direct observations can be used as indicators of some concepts. For example, Albert J. Reiss Jr. (1971) studied police interaction with the public by riding in police squad cars, observing police-citizen interactions, and recording the characteristics of the interactions on a form. Notations on the form indicated such variables as how many police-citizen contacts occurred, who initiated the contacts, how compliant citizens were with police directives, and whether or not police expressed hostility toward the citizens.

Often, observations can supplement what is initially learned from interviews or survey questions, putting flesh on the bones of what is otherwise just a verbal self-report. In Chambliss's (1996) book, *Beyond Caring,* a theory of the nature of moral problems in hospital nursing that was originally developed through interviews was expanded with lessons learned from observations. Chambliss found, for instance, that in interviews nurses described their daily work as exciting, challenging, dramatic, and often even heroic. But when Chambliss himself sat for many hours and watched nurses work, he found that their daily lives were rather humdrum and ordinary, even to them. Occasionally there were bursts of energetic activity and even heroism—but the reality of day-to-day nursing was far less exciting than interviews would lead one to believe. Indeed, Chambliss's original theory was modified to include a much broader role for routine in hospital life.

Direct observation is often the method of choice for measuring behavior in natural settings, as long as it is possible to make the requisite observations. Direct observation avoids the problems of poor recall and self-serving distortions that can occur with answers to survey questions. It also allows measurement in a context that is more natural than an interview. But observations can be distorted, too. Observers do not see or hear everything, and what they do see is filtered by their own senses and perspectives. Moreover, in some situations the presence of an observer may cause people to act differently from the way they would otherwise (Emerson, 1983). If you set up a video camera in an obvious spot on campus, in order to monitor traffic flows, you may well change the flow—just because people will see the camera and avoid it (or come over to make faces). We will discuss these issues in more depth in Chapter 8, but it is important to begin to consider them whenever you read about observational measures.

Content Analysis

Content analysis is a research method for systematically analyzing and making inferences from text (Weber, 1985:9). You can think of a content analysis as a "survey" of documents ranging from newspapers, books, or TV shows to persons referred to in other communications, themes expressed in government documents, or propositions made in tape-recorded debates. Words or other features of these units are then "coded" to measure the variables involved in the research question (Weber, 1985). As a simple example of content analysis, you might look at a variety of women's magazines over the past 25 years, and count the number of articles in each year devoted to various topics, such as makeup, weight loss, relationships, sex, and so on. You might count the number of articles on different subjects as a measure of the media's emphasis on women's anxiety about these issues and see how that emphasis (i.e., the number of articles) has increased or decreased over the past quarter-century. At the simplest level, you could code articles by whether key words ("fat," "weight," "pounds," etc.) appeared in the titles.

After coding procedures are developed, their reliability should be assessed by comparing different coders' results for the same variables. Computer programs for content analysis can be used to enhance reliability (Weitzman & Miles, 1994). The computer is programmed with certain rules for coding text so that these rules will be applied consistently.

Collecting Unobtrusive Measures

Unobtrusive measures allow us to collect data about individuals or groups without their direct knowledge or participation. In their recently revised classic book, Eugene Webb and his colleagues (2000) identified four types of unobtrusive measures: physical trace evidence, archives (available data), simple observation, and contrived observation (using hidden recording hardware or manipulation to elicit a response). These measures provide valuable supplements or alternatives to more standard survey-based measures, because they are not affected by an interviewer's appearance or how he or she asks questions. We have already considered some types of archival and observational data (Webb, Campbell, Schwartz, & Sechrest, 2000).

The physical traces of past behavior are one type of unobtrusive measure that provides creative opportunities. Patterns of grass wear on a campus quad show where most people walk. To measure the prevalence of drinking in college dorms or fraternity houses, we might count the number of empty bottles of alcoholic beverages in the surrounding dumpsters. Student interest in their college courses might be measured by counting the number of times that books on reserve as optional reading are checked out, or the number of class handouts left in recycling bins outside a lecture hall. The most popular stalls in restrooms can be determined by their high rate of toilet paper replacement.

Potential unobtrusive measures are everywhere. Webb and his colleagues (2000:37) suggested measuring the interest in museum exhibits by the frequency with which tiles in front of the exhibits needed to be replaced. If auto mechanics note the radio dial settings in cars brought in for repairs, they can target their advertising to those stations to which their customers listen most. A quick glance at the hands of men in a bar could help you see if the patrons do heavy manual work (calluses).

Unobtrusive measures can also be created from such diverse forms of media as newspaper archives, magazine articles, TV or radio talk shows, legal opinions, historical documents, personal letters, or e-mail messages. Researchers may read and evaluate the text of Internet listservs, as Fox and Roberts (1999) did in a study of British physicians. We could even learn about cities by comparing their telephone directory yellow pages! For example, we find that Sarasota, Florida, has many pages devoted to nursing homes and hospital appliances; Chattanooga, Tennessee, which has approximately the same number of people, rather than having pages devoted to medical care, has many pages listing churches. Admittedly, that's a rough way to compare cities, but it may alert us to key differences between them.

Combining Measurement Operations

The choice of a particular measurement method—questions, observations, archives, and the like—is often determined by available resources and opportunities, but measurement is improved if this choice also takes into account the particular concept or concepts to be measured. Responses to questions such as "How socially adept were you at the party?" or "How many days did you use sick leave last year?" are unlikely to provide valid information on shyness or illness. Direct observation or company records may work better. On the other hand, observations at cocktail parties may not fully answer our questions about why some people are shy; we may just have to ask people. Or if a company keeps no record of sick leave, we may have to ask direct questions and hope for accurate memories. Every choice of a measurement method entails some compromise between the perfect and the possible.

Triangulation—the use of two or more different measures of the same variable— can strengthen measurement considerably (Brewer & Hunter, 1989:17). When we achieve similar results with different measures of the same variable, particularly when they are based on such different methods as survey questions and field-based observations, we can be more confident of the validity of each measure. In surveys, for instance, people may say that they would return a lost wallet they found on the street. But field observation may prove that in practice many succumb to the temptation to keep the wallet. The two methods produced different results. In a contrasting example, post-combat interviews of American soldiers in World War II found that most GIs never fired their weapons in battle; and the written, archival records of ammunition resupply patterns confirmed this interview finding (Marshall, 1978). If results diverge when using different measures, it may indicate that we are sustaining more measurement error than we can tolerate.

Divergence between measures could also indicate that each measure actually operationalizes a different concept. An interesting example of this interpretation of divergent results comes from research on crime. Crime statistics are often inaccurate measures of actual crime; what gets reported to the police and shows up in official statistics is not at all the same thing as what happens according to victimization surveys (in which random people are asked if they have been a crime victim). Social scientists generally regard victim surveys as a more valid measure of crime than police-reported crime. We know, for instance, that rape is a dramatically underreported crime, with something like four to ten times the number of rapes occurring as are reported to police. But auto theft is an *overreported* crime: More auto thefts are reported to police than actually occur. This may strike you as odd, but remember that almost everyone who owns a car also owns car insurance; if their car is stolen, they will definitely report it to the police in order to claim the insurance. Some other people might report a car stolen when it hasn't been, because of the financial incentive. (By the way, insurance companies are quite good at discovering this scam, so it's a bad way to make money.)

Murder, however, is generally reported to police at roughly the same rate at which it actually occurs (i.e., official police reports generally match victim surveys). When someone is killed, it's very difficult to hide the fact. A body is missing, a human being doesn't show up for work, people find out. At the same time, it's very hard to pretend that someone was murdered when they weren't. There they are, still alive, in the flesh. Unlike rape or auto theft, there are no obvious incentives for either underreporting or overreporting murders. The official rate is generally valid.

So if you can, it's best to use multiple measures of the same variable; that way each measure helps to check the validity of the others.

HOW MUCH INFORMATION DO WE REALLY HAVE?

There are many ways of collecting information, or different *operations* for gathering data: asking questions, using previously gathered data, analyzing texts, and so on. Some of this data contains mathematically detailed information; it represents a higher level of measurement. There are four **levels of measurement:** nominal, ordinal, interval, and ratio. Exhibit 3.3 depicts the differences among these four levels.

Level of measurement: The mathematical precision with which the values of a variable can be expressed. The nominal level of measurement, which is qualitative, has no mathematical interpretation; the quantitative levels of measurement—ordinal, interval, and ratio—are progressively more precise *mathematically*.

Exhibit 3.3 Levels of Measurement

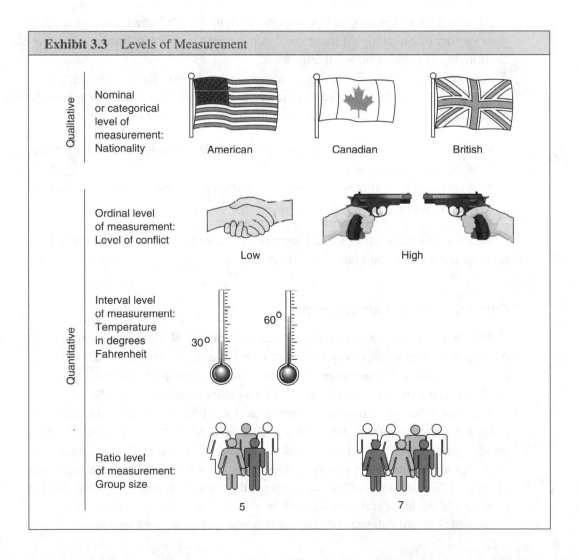

Nominal Level of Measurement

The **nominal level of measurement** identifies variables whose values have no mathematical interpretation; they vary in kind or quality, but not in amount. "State" (referring to the United States) is one example. The variable has 50 attributes (or categories or qualities), but none of them is more "state" than another. They're just different. Religious affiliation is another nominal variable, measured in categories: Christian, Moslem, Hindu, Jewish, and so on. Nationality, occupation, and region of the country are also measured at the nominal level. A person may be Spanish or Portuguese, but one nationality does not represent more nationality than another—just a different nationality (see Exhibit 3.3). A person may be a doctor or a truck driver, but one does not represent three units more occupation than the other. Of course, more people may identify themselves as being of one nationality than of another, or one occupation may have a higher average income than another occupation, but these are comparisons involving variables other than "nationality" or "occupation" themselves.

Although the attributes of nominal variables do not have a mathematical meaning, they must be assigned to cases with great care. The attributes we use to measure, or categorize, cases must be mutually exclusive and exhaustive:

- A variable's attributes or values are **mutually exclusive** if every case can have only one attribute.
- A variable's attributes or values are **exhaustive** when every case can be classified into one of the categories.

When a variable's attributes are mutually exclusive and exhaustive, every case corresponds to one—and only one—attribute.

Ordinal Level of Measurement

The first of the three quantitative levels is the **ordinal level of measurement**. At this level, you specify only the order of the cases, in "greater than" and "less than" distinctions. At the coffee shop, for example, you might choose between a small, medium, or large cup of decaf—that's ordinal measurement.

The properties of variables measured at the ordinal level are illustrated in Exhibit 3.3 by the contrast between the level of conflict in two groups. The first group, symbolized by two people shaking hands, has a low level of conflict. The second group, symbolized by two people pointing guns at each other, has a high level of conflict. To measure conflict, we could put the groups "in order" by assigning the number 1 to the low-conflict group and the number 2 to the high-conflict group, but the numbers would indicate only the relative position or order of the cases.

As with nominal variables, the different values of a variable measured at the ordinal level must be mutually exclusive and exhaustive. They must cover the range of observed values and allow each case to be assigned no more than one value.

Interval Level of Measurement

At the **interval level of measurement**, numbers represent fixed measurement units but have no absolute zero point. This level of measurement is represented in Exhibit 3.3 by the difference between two Fahrenheit temperatures. Note, for example, that 60 degrees is 30 degrees higher than 30 degrees; but 60 is not "twice as hot" as 30. Why not? Because heat does not "begin" at 0 degrees on the Fahrenheit scale. The numbers can therefore be added and subtracted, but ratios of them (2 to 1 or "twice as much") are not meaningful. There are thus few true interval-level measures in the social sciences; most are ratio-level, because they have zero points.

Sometimes, though, social scientists will create indexes by combining responses to a series of variables measured at the ordinal level and then treat these indexes as interval-level measures. An index of this sort could be created with responses to the Core Institute's questions about friends' disapproval of substance use (see Exhibit 3.4). The survey has 13 questions on the topic, each of

---

Exhibit 3.4   Ordinal Measures: Core Alcohol and Drug Survey. Responses could be combined to create an interval scale (see text).

26. How do you think your close friends feel (or would feel) about you...
(mark one for each line)

Columns: Don't disapprove / Disapprove / Strongly disapprove

	Don't disapprove	Disapprove	Strongly disapprove
a. Trying marijuana once or twice	○	○	○
b. Smoking marijuana occasionally	○	○	○
c. Smoking marijuana regularly	○	○	○
d. Trying cocaine once or twice	○	○	○
e. Taking cocaine regularly	○	○	○
f. Trying LSD once or twice	○	○	○
g. Taking LSD regularly	○	○	○
h. Trying amphetamines once or twice	○	○	○
i. Taking amphetamines regularly	○	○	○
j. Taking one or two drinks of an alcoholic beverage (beer, wine, liquor) nearly every day	○	○	○
k. Taking four or five drinks nearly every day	○	○	○
l. Having five or more drinks in one sitting	○	○	○
m. Taking steroids for body building or improved athletic performance	○	○	○

Source: Core Institute, Core Alcohol and Drug Survey, 1994. Carbondale, IL: Core Institute.

which has the same three response choices. If "Don't disapprove" is valued at 1, "Disapprove" is valued at 2, and "Strongly disapprove" is valued at 3, the summed index of disapproval would range from 13 to 39. A score of 20 could be treated as if it were four more units than a score of 16. Or the responses could be averaged to retain the original 1–3 range.

Ratio Level of Measurement

A **ratio level of measurement** represents fixed measuring units with an absolute zero point. Zero, in this situation, means absolutely no amount of whatever the variable indicates. On a ratio scale, 10 is two points higher than 8 and is also two times as great as 5. Ratio numbers can be added and subtracted, and because the numbers begin at an absolute zero point, they can also be multiplied and divided (so ratios can be formed between the numbers).

For example, people's ages can be represented by values ranging from 0 years (or some fraction of a year) to 120 or more. A person who is 30 years old is 15 years older than someone who is 15 years old ($30 - 15 = 15$) and is also twice as old as that person ($30/15 = 2$). Of course, the numbers also are mutually exclusive and exhaustive, so that every case can be assigned one and only one value. Age (in years) is clearly a ratio-level measure.

Exhibit 3.3 displays an example of a variable measured at the ratio level. The number of people in the first group is 5, and the number in the second group is 7. The ratio of the two groups' sizes is then 1.4, a number that mirrors the relationship between the sizes of the groups. Note that there does not actually have to be any "group" with a size of 0; what is important is that the numbering scheme begins at an absolute zero—in this case, the absence of any people.

Comparison of Levels of Measurement

Exhibit 3.5 summarizes the types of comparisons that can be made with different levels of measurement, as well as the mathematical operations that are legitimate with each. All four levels of measurement allow researchers to assign different values to different cases. All three quantitative measures allow researchers to rank cases in order.

Researchers choose levels of measurement in the process of operationalizing variables; the level of measurement is not inherent in the variable itself. Many variables can be measured at different levels, with different procedures. Age can be measured as young or old; 0–10, 11–20, 21–30, and so on; or as 1, 2, or 3 years old. We could gather the data by asking people their age, by having an observer guess ("Now *there's* an old guy!"), or by searching through hospital records for exact dates and times of birth. Any of these approaches could work, depending on our research goals.

Exhibit 3.5 Properties of Measurement Levels

Examples of comparison statements	Appropriate math operations	Relevant level of measurement			
		Nominal	Ordinal	Interval	Ratio
A is equal to (not equal to) B	= (≠)	✓	✓	✓	✓
A is greater than (less than) B	> (<)		✓	✓	✓
A is three more than (less than) B	+ (−)			✓	✓
A is twice (half) as large as B	× (/)				✓

Usually, though, it is a good idea to measure variables at the highest level of measurement possible. The more information available, the more ways we have to compare cases. We also have more possibilities for statistical analysis with quantitative than with qualitative variables. Even if your primary concern is only to compare teenagers to young adults, you should measure age in years rather than in categories; you can always combine the ages later into categories corresponding to "teenager" and "young adult."

Be aware, however, that other considerations may preclude measurement at a high level. For example, many people are very reluctant to report their exact incomes, even in anonymous questionnaires. So asking respondents to report their income in categories (such as less than $10,000, $10,000–$19,999, $20,000–$29,999, and so on) will elicit more responses, and thus more valid data, than asking respondents for their income in dollars.

DID WE MEASURE WHAT WE WANTED TO MEASURE?

Do the operations developed to measure our variables actually do so—are they valid? If we have weighed our measurement options, carefully constructed our questions and observational procedures, and selected sensibly from the available data indicators, we should be on the right track. But we cannot have much confidence in a measure until we have empirically evaluated its *validity*. We must also evaluate the *reliability* of our measures. The reliability of a measure is the degree to which it produces a consistent answer; such reliability (consistency) is a prerequisite for measurement validity.

Measurement Validity

In Chapter 1, you learned that measurement validity refers to how well your indicators measure what they are intended to measure. For instance, a good measure of a person's age is the current year minus the year given on their birth certificate. Very probably, the resulting number accurately represents the person's age. A less valid measure would be for the researcher to ask the person (who may lie, or forget), or for the researcher to simply guess. Measurement validity can be assessed with four different approaches: face validation, content validation, criterion validation, and construct validation.

Face Validity

Researchers apply the term **face validity** to the confidence gained from careful inspection of a concept to see if it is appropriate "on its face." More precisely, we can say that a measure has face validity if it obviously pertains to the meaning of the concept being measured more than to other concepts (Brewer & Hunter, 1989:131). For example, a count of the number of drinks people have consumed in the past week would be a face valid measure of their alcohol consumption.

Although every measure should be inspected in this way, face validation in itself does not provide convincing evidence of measurement validity. Face validity has some plausibility but often not much. For instance, let's say that Sara is having some worries about her boyfriend, Jeremy. She wants to know if he loves her. So she asks him, "Jeremy, do you really love me?" He replies, "Sure, baby, you know I do." And yet he routinely goes out with other women, only calls Sara once every three weeks, and isn't particularly nice to her when they do go out. His answer that he loves her has a certain "face validity," but Sara should probably look for other validating measures. (At the least, she might ask her friends if they think his claim has validity.)

Content Validity

Content validity establishes that the measure covers the full range of the concept's meaning. To determine that range of meaning, the researcher may solicit the opinions of experts and review literature that identifies the different aspects, or dimensions, of the concept. A measure of student engagement based on how much one talks in class won't count the quiet, but attentive and hardworking, person in the front row. Or if you measure power by listing only elected government officials, you may miss the most important people altogether.

Criterion Validity

Criterion validity is established when the results from one measure match those obtained with a more direct or an already validated measure of the same phenomenon (the "criterion"). A measure of blood-alcohol concentration, for instance, could be the criterion for validating a self-report measure of drinking. In other words, if Jason says he hasn't been drinking, we establish criterion validity by giving him a "breathalyzer" test. Observations of drinking by friends or relatives could also, in some limited circumstances, serve as a criterion for validating a self-report.

The criterion that researchers select can be measured either at the same time as the variable to be validated or after that time. **Concurrent validity** exists when a criterion conducted at the same time yields scores that are closely related to scores on a measure. A store might validate a test of sales ability by administering the test to its current salespeople and then comparing their test scores to their actual sales performance. Or a measure of walking speed based on mental counting might be validated concurrently with a stopwatch. With **predictive validity**, a measure is validated by predicting scores on a criterion measured in the future—for instance, SAT scores are validated when they predict a student's college grades.

Criterion validation greatly increases our confidence that a measure works, but for many concepts of interest to social scientists, it's difficult to find a criterion. Yes, if you and your roommate are together every evening, you can count the beers he drinks. You definitely know about his drinking. But if we are measuring feelings or beliefs or other subjective states, such as feelings of loneliness, what direct indicator could serve as a criterion? How do you know he's lonely? Even with variables for which a reasonable criterion exists, the researcher may not be able to gain access to the criterion—as would be the case with a tax return or employer document that we might wish we could use as a criterion for self-reported income.

Construct Validity

Measurement validity also can be established by relating a measure to other measures specified in a theory. This validation approach, known as **construct validity**, is commonly used in social research when no clear criterion exists for validation purposes.

A historically famous example of construct validity is provided by the work of Theodor W. Adorno, Nevitt Sanford, Else Frenkel-Brunswik, and Daniel Levinson (1950), in their book *The Authoritarian Personality*. Adorno and his colleagues, working in the United States and Germany immediately after World War II, were interested in a question that troubled much of the world during the 1930s and 1940s: Why were so many people attracted to Nazism and to its Italian and Japanese fascist allies? Hitler was not an unpopular leader in Germany. In fact, in January 1933 he came to power by being elected chancellor (something like president) of Germany, although some details of the election were a bit suspicious. Millions of people supported him enthusiastically. Why did so many Germans, during the 1930s, come to nearly worship Adolf Hitler and believe strongly in his program—which proved, of course, to be so disastrous for Europe and the rest of the world? The Adorno research group proposed the existence of what they called an "authoritarian personality," a type of person who would be drawn to a dictatorial leader of the Hitler type. Their key concept, then, was "authoritarianism."

But of course there's no such "thing" as authoritarianism; it's not like a tree, something you can look at. It's a *construct,* an idea that we use to help make sense of the world. To establish construct validity of this idea, the researchers created a number of different scales made up of interview questions. One scale was called the "anti-Semitism" scale, in which hatred of Jews was measured. Another measure was a "fascism" scale, measuring a tendency toward favoring a militaristic, nationalist government. Another was the "political and economic conservatism" scale, and so on. Adorno and his colleagues interviewed lots of Germans and found that high scores on these different scales tended to correlate; a person who scored high on one tended to score high on the others. Hence they determined that the "authoritarian personality" was a legitimate construct. The idea of authoritarianism, then, was validated through construct validity.

In short, a construct ("authoritarianism") was validated through the use of a number of other measures that all tended to be high or low at the same time. Simultaneous high scores on them validated the idea of authoritarianism.

Construct and criterion validation, then, compare scores on one measure to scores on other measures that are predicted to be related. Distinguishing the two forms (construct and criterion) matters less than thinking clearly about the comparison measures and whether they actually represent different views of the same phenomenon. For example, correspondence between scores on two different self-report measures of alcohol use is a weak indicator of measurement validity. A person just reports in two different ways how much she drinks; of course the two will be related. But the correspondence of a self-report measure with an observer-based measure of substance use is a much stronger demonstration of validity. The subject (a) reports how much she drinks, and then (b) an observer reports on the subject's drinking. If the results match up, it's strong evidence of validity.

Reliability

Reliability means that a measurement procedure yields consistent scores (or that the scores change only to reflect actual changes in the phenomenon). If a measure is *reliable,* it is affected less by random error, or chance variation, than if it is unreliable. Reliability is a prerequisite for measurement validity: We cannot really measure a phenomenon if the measure we are using gives inconsistent results. Let's say, for example, that you would like to know your weight and have decided on two different measures: the scales in the bathroom and your mother's estimate. Clearly, the scales are more reliable, in the sense that they will show pretty much the same thing from one day to the next, unless your weight actually changes. But your mother, bless her, may say "You're so skinny!" on Sunday; but on Monday, when she's not happy, she may say "You look terrible! Have you gained weight?" Her estimates may bounce around quite a bit. The bathroom scales are not so fickle; they are *reliable*.

This doesn't mean that the scales are *valid*—in fact, if they are spring-operated and old, they may be off by quite a few pounds. But they will be off by the same amount every day—hence not valid, but *reliable* nonetheless.

There are four possible indications of unreliability. For example, a test of your knowledge of research methods would be unreliable if every time you took it you received a different score even though your knowledge of research methods had not changed in the interim, not even as a result of taking the test more than once. This is test-retest reliability. Similarly, an index composed of questions to measure knowledge of research methods would be unreliable if respondents' answers to each question were totally independent of their answers to the others. The index has interitem reliability if the component items are closely related. A measure also would be unreliable if slightly different versions of it resulted in markedly different responses (it would not achieve alternate-forms reliability). Finally, an assessment of the level of conflict in social groups would be unreliable if ratings of the level of conflict by two observers were not related to each other (it would then lack interobserver reliability).

Test-Retest Reliability

When researchers measure an unchanging phenomenon at two different times, the degree to which the two measurements are related is the **test-retest reliability** of the measure. If you take a test of your math ability and then retake the test two months later, the test is reliable if you receive a similar score both times, presuming that your math ability stayed constant. Of course, if events between the test and the retest have changed the variable being measured, then the difference between the test and retest scores should reflect that change.

Interitem Reliability (Internal Consistency)

When researchers use multiple items to measure a single concept, they must be concerned with **interitem reliability** (or internal consistency). For example, if the questions in Exhibit 3.2 reliably measure depression, the answers to the different questions should be highly associated with one another. The stronger the association among the individual items, and the more items that are included, the higher the reliability of the index.

Alternate-Forms Reliability

When researchers compare subjects' answers to slightly different versions of survey questions, they are testing **alternate-forms reliability** (Litwin, 1995: 13–21). A researcher may reverse the order of the response choices in an index or may modify the question wording in minor ways, and then readminister the index to subjects. If the two sets of responses are not too different, alternate-forms reliability is established.

A related test of reliability is the **split-halves reliability** approach. A survey sample is divided in two by flipping a coin or using some other random assignment method. The two forms of the questions are then administered to the two halves of the sample. If the responses of the two halves of the sample are about the same, the reliability of the measure is established.

Interobserver Reliability

When researchers use more than one observer to rate the same people, events, or places, **interobserver reliability** is their goal. If observers are using the same instrument to rate the same thing, their ratings should be very similar. If they are similar, we can have much more confidence that the ratings reflect the phenomenon being assessed rather than the orientations of the observers.

Assessing interobserver reliability is most important when the rating task is complex. Consider a commonly used measure of mental health, the Global Assessment of Functioning Scale (GAFS), a bit of which is shown in Exhibit 3.6. The rating task seems straightforward, with clear descriptions of the subject characteristics that are supposed to lead to high or low GAFS scores. But in fact the judgments that the rater must make while using this scale are very complex. They are affected by a wide range of subject characteristics, attitudes, and behaviors as well as by the rater's reactions. As a result, interobserver agreement is often low on the GAFS, unless the raters are trained carefully.

Can We Achieve Both Reliability and Validity?

The reliability and validity of measures in any study must be tested after the fact to assess the quality of the information obtained. But then, if it turns out that a measure cannot be considered reliable and valid, little can be done to save the study. Hence it is supremely important to select in the first place measures that are likely to be both reliable and valid. The Dow Jones Industrials Index is a perfectly *reliable* measure of the state of the American economy—any two observers of it will see the same numbers—but its validity is shaky: There's more to the economy than the rise and fall of stock prices. In contrast, a good therapist's interview of a married couple may produce a *valid* understanding of their relationship, but such

Exhibit 3.6 The Challenge of Interobserver Reliability: Excerpt From the Global Assessment of Functioning Scale (GAFS)

Consider psychological, social, and occupational functioning on a hypothetical continuum of mental health-illness. Do not include impairment in functioning due to physical (or environmental) limitations.

Code (Note: Use intermediate codes when appropriate, e.g., 45, 68, 72.)

100 **Superior functioning in a wide range of activities, life's problems never seem to get out of hand, is sought by others because of his or her many positive qualities. No**
91 **symptoms.**

90 **Absent or minimal symptoms** (e.g., mild anxiety before an exam), **good functioning in all areas, interested and involved in a wide range of activities, socially effective, generally satisfied with life, no more than everyday problems or concerns** (e.g., an occasional
81 argument with family members).

80 **If symptoms are present, they are transient and expectable reactions to psychosocial stressors** (e.g., difficulty concentrating after family argument); **no more than slight impairment in social, occupational, or school functioning** (e.g., temporarily falling
71 behind in schoolwork).

70 **Some mild symptoms** (e.g., depressive mood and mild insomnia) **OR some difficulty in social, occupational, or school functioning** (e.g., occasional truancy or theft within the household), **but generally functioning pretty well, has some meaningful interpersonal**
61 **relationships.**

60 **Moderate symptoms** (e.g., flat affect and circumstantial speech, occasional panic attacks) **OR moderate difficulty in social, occupational, or school functioning** (e.g., few friends,
51 conflicts with peers or co-workers).

50 **Serious symptoms** (e.g., suicidal ideation, severe obsessional rituals, frequent shoplifting) **OR any serious impairment in social, occupational, or school functioning** (e.g., no
41 friends, unable to keep a job).

40 **Some impairment in reality testing or communication** (e.g., speech is at times illogical, obscure, or irrelevant) **OR major impairment in several areas, such as work or school, family relations, judgment, thinking, or mood** (e.g., depressed man avoids friends, neglects family, and is unable to work, child frequently beats up younger children, is
31 defiant at home, and is failing at school).

30 **Behavior is considerably influenced by delusions or hallucinations OR serious impairment in communication or judgment** (e.g., sometimes incoherent, acts grossly inappropriately, suicidal preoccupation) **OR inability to function in almost all areas** (e.g.,
21 stays in bed all day, no job, home, or friends).

20 **Some danger of hurting self or others** (e.g., suicide attempts without clear expectation of death, frequently violent, manic excitement) **OR occasionally fails to maintain minimal personal hygiene** (e.g., smears feces) **OR gross impairment in communication** (e.g.,
11 largely incoherent or mute).

10 **Persistent danger of severely hurting self or others** (e.g., recurrent violence) **OR persistent inability to maintain minimal personal hygiene OR serious suicidal act with**
1 **clear expectation of death.**

0 Inadequate information.

Source: Reprinted with permission from the *Diagnostic and Statistical Manual of Mental Disorders,* Fourth Edition. Copyright © 1994 American Psychiatric Association.

interviews are often not reliable, because another interviewer could easily reach different conclusions.

Finding measures that are both reliable and valid can be challenging. Don't just choose the first measure you find or can think of. Consider the different strengths of different measures and their appropriateness to your study. Conduct a pretest in which you use the measure with a small sample and check its reliability. Provide careful training to ensure a consistent approach if interviewers or observers will administer the measures. In most cases, however, the best strategy is to use measures that have been used before and whose reliability and validity have been established in other contexts. But even the selection of "tried and true" measures does not absolve researchers from the responsibility of testing the reliability and validity of the measure in their own studies.

Remember that a reliable measure is not necessarily a valid measure, as Exhibit 3.7 illustrates. This discrepancy is a common flaw of self-report measures

Exhibit 3.7   The Difference Between Reliability and Validity: Drinking Behavior

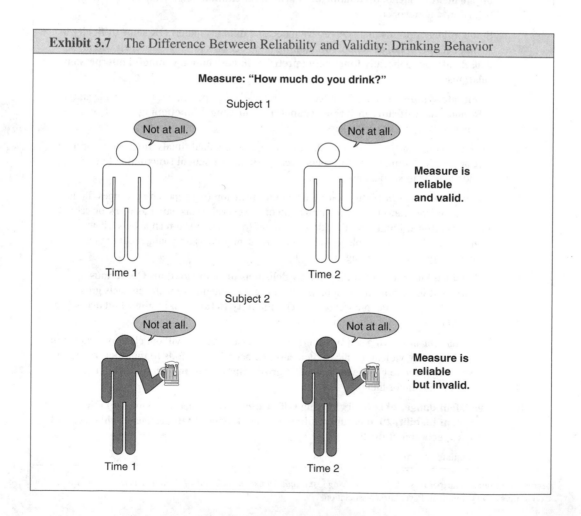

of substance abuse. People's answers to the questions are consistent, but they are consistently misleading: A number of respondents will not admit to drinking, even though they drink a lot. The multiple questions in self-report indexes of substance abuse are answered by most respondents in a consistent way, so the indexes are reliable. As a result, some indexes based on self-report are reliable but invalid. Such indexes are not useful and should be improved or discarded.

CONCLUSION

Remember always that measurement validity is a necessary foundation for social research. Gathering data without careful conceptualization or conscientious efforts to operationalize key concepts often is a wasted effort.

The difficulties of achieving valid measurement vary with the concept being operationalized and the circumstances of the particular study. The examples in this chapter of difficulties in achieving valid measures should sensitize you to the need for caution.

Planning ahead is the key to achieving valid measurement in your own research; careful evaluation is the key to sound decisions about the validity of measures in others' research. Statistical tests can help to determine whether a given measure is valid after data have been collected, but if it appears after the fact that a measure is invalid, little can be done to correct the situation. If you cannot tell how key concepts were operationalized when you read a research report, don't trust the findings. And if a researcher does not indicate the results of tests used to establish the reliability and validity of key measures, remain skeptical.

KEY TERMS

Alternate-forms reliability
Closed-ended (fixed-choice)
  question
Concept
Conceptualization
Concurrent validity
Constant
Construct validity
Content analysis
Content validity
Criterion validity
Exhaustive
Face validity
Index
Interitem reliability
Interobserver reliability
Interval level of measurement
Level of measurement
Mutually exclusive
Nominal level of measurement
Open-ended question
Operationalization
Operations
Ordinal level of measurement
Predictive validity
Ratio level of measurement
Reliability
Scale
Split-halves reliability
Test-retest reliability
Triangulation
Unobtrusive measure

HIGHLIGHTS

- Conceptualization plays a critical role in research. In deductive research, conceptualization guides the operationalization of specific variables; in inductive research, it guides efforts to make sense of related observations.

- Concepts may refer to either constant or variable phenomena. Concepts that refer to variable phenomena may be very similar to the actual variables used in a study, or they may be much more abstract.

- Concepts are operationalized in research by one or more indicators, or measures, which may derive from observation, self-report, available records or statistics, books and other written documents, clinical indicators, discarded materials, or some combination.

- Indexes and scales measure a concept by combining answers to several questions and so reducing idiosyncratic variation. Several issues should be explored with every intended index: Does each question actually measure the same concept? Does combining items in an index obscure important relationships between individual questions and other variables? Is the index multidimensional?

- If differential weighting, based on differential information captured by questions, is used in the calculation of index scores, then we say that the questions constitute a scale.

- Level of measurement indicates the type of information obtained about a variable and the type of statistics that can be used to describe its variation. The four levels of measurement can be ordered by complexity of the mathematical operations they permit: nominal (or qualitative), ordinal, interval, and ratio (most complex). The measurement level of a variable is determined by how the variable is operationalized.

- The validity of measures should always be tested. There are four basic approaches: face validation, content validation, criterion validation (either predictive or concurrent), and construct validation. Criterion validation provides the strongest evidence of measurement validity, but often there is no criterion to use in validating social science measures.

- Measurement reliability is a prerequisite for measurement validity, although reliable measures are not necessarily valid. Reliability can be assessed through a test-retest procedure, an interitem comparison of responses to alternate forms of the test, or the consistency of findings among observers.

To assist you in completing the Web Exercises, please access the Study Site at http://www.pineforge.com/mssw2 where you'll find the Web Exercises with accompanying links. You'll find other useful study materials like self-quizzes and e-flashcards for each chapter, along with a group of carefully selected articles from research journals that illustrate the major concepts and techniques presented in the book.

EXERCISES

Discussing Research

1. Pick one important, frequently used concept such as "power," "the economy," "fundamentalism," "poverty," "authoritarianism," "racism," or some other concept suggested by your instructor. Then find five uses of it in newspapers, magazines, or journals. Is the concept defined clearly in each article? How similar are the definitions? Write up what you have found in a short report.

2. Look at our definition of "terrorism" on the first page of this chapter. Do you agree with this definition? For each component of the definition (e.g., "political," "nongovernmental," etc.) give an example that might contradict the definition. Propose an alternative definition that might be better.

3. Do you and your classmates share the same beliefs about the meanings of important concepts? First, divide your class into several groups, each group having at least six students. Then, assign each group a concept from the following list: violence, stress, social support, mental illness, social norms. In each group, each student should independently write a brief definition of his or her concept and some different examples supporting it. Finally, all students who have worked on the same concept should meet together, compare their definitions and examples, and try to reach agreement on the meaning of the concept. Discuss what you learned from this effort.

4. Propose an open-ended question to measure one of the concepts you discussed in the preceding exercises. Compare your approach to those adopted by other students.

Finding Research

1. What are some of the research questions you could attempt to answer with available statistical data? Visit your library and ask for an introduction to the government documents collection. Inspect the U.S. Bureau of the Census Web site (www.census.gov) and find the population figures broken down by city and state. List five questions that you could explore with such data. Identify six variables implied by these research questions that you could operationalize with the available data. What are three factors that might influence variation in these measures, other than the phenomenon of interest? (Hint: Consider how the data are collected.)

2. How would you define "alcoholism?" Write a brief definition. Based on this conceptualization, describe a method of measurement that would be valid for a study of alcoholism (as you define it). Now go to the National Council on Alcohol and Drug Dependence (NCADD) Web site (www.ncadd.org/facts/defalc.html) and read their official "Definition of Alcoholism." What is the definition of alcoholism used by NCADD? How is alcoholism conceptualized? How does this compare to your definition?

Critiquing Research

1. Shortly before the year 2000 national census of the United States, a heated debate arose in Congress over whether instead of a census—a total headcount—a sample should

---

Exhibit 3.8 Selected Shelter Staff Survey Questions

1. What is your current job title? _____

2. What is your current employment status?
   Paid, full-time 1
   Paid, part-time (less than 30 hours per week) 2

3. When did you start your current position? _____ / _____ / _____
                                              Month   Day   Year

4. In the past month, how often did you help guests deal with each of the
   following types of problems? (*Circle one response on each line.*)

	Very often						Never
Job training/placement....................	1	2	3	4	5	6	7
Lack of food or bed........................	1	2	3	4	5	6	7
Drinking problems..........................	1	2	3	4	5	6	7

5. How likely is it that you will leave this shelter within the next year?
   Very likely... 1
   Moderately... 2
   Not very likely.. 3
   Not likely at all.. 4

6. What is the highest grade in school you have completed at this time?
   First through eighth grade... 1
   Some high school.. 2
   High school diploma.. 3
   Some college... 4
   College degree... 5
   Some graduate work.. 6
   Graduate degree.. 7

7. Are you a veteran?
   Yes... 1
   No.. 2

Source: Schutt & Fennell, 1992.

be used to estimate the number and composition of the U.S. population. As a practical matter, might a sample be more accurate in this case than a census? Why?

2. Develop a plan for evaluating the validity of a measure. Your instructor will give you a copy of a questionnaire actually used in a study. Pick out one question and define the concept that you believe it is intended to measure. Then develop a construct validation strategy involving other measures in the questionnaire that you think should be related to the question of interest—if it measures what you think it measures.

3. The questions in Exhibit 3.8 are selected from a survey of homeless shelter staff (Schutt & Fennell, 1992). First, identify the level of measurement for each question. Then

rewrite each question so that it measures the same variable but at a different level. For example, you might change a question that measures age at the ratio level, in years, to one that measures age at the ordinal level, in categories. Or you might change a variable measured at the ordinal level to one measured at the ratio level. For the categorical variables, those measured at the nominal level, try to identify at least two underlying quantitative dimensions of variation, and write questions to measure variation along these dimensions. For example, you might change a question asking which of several factors the respondent thinks is responsible for homelessness to a series of questions that ask how important each factor is in generating homelessness.

What are the advantages and disadvantages of phrasing each question at one level of measurement rather than another? Do you see any limitations on the types of questions for which levels of measurement can be changed?

4. A lengthy assessment of different measures of substance abuse is available at a site maintained by the National Institute on Alcoholism and Alcohol Abuse (http://www .niaaa.nih.gov/publications/Assesing%20Alcohol/selfreport.htm). Read through the summary of instruments (or review the instrument "fact sheets" at this NIAAA site). Pick two instruments. What concept of substance abuse is reflected in each measure? Is either measure multidimensional? What do you think the relative advantages of each measure might be? What evidence is provided about their reliability and validity? What other test of validity would you suggest?

Doing Research

1. Some people have said in discussions of international politics that "democratic governments don't start wars." How could you test this hypothesis? Clearly state how you would operationalize (1) "democratic," and (2) "start."

2. Now it's time to try your hand at operationalization with survey-based measures. Formulate a few fixed-choice questions to measure variables pertaining to the concepts you researched for Exercise 1 under "Discussing Research," such as poverty, power, or racism. Arrange to interview one or two other students with the questions you have developed. Ask one fixed-choice question at a time, record your interviewee's answer, and then probe for additional comments and clarifications. Your goal is to discover what respondents take to be the meaning of the concept you used in the question and what additional issues shape their response to it.

When you have finished the interviews, analyze your experience: Did the interviewees interpret the fixed-choice questions and response choices as you intended? Did you learn more about the concepts you were working on? Should your conceptual definition be refined? Should the questions be rewritten, or would more fixed-choice questions be necessary to capture adequately the variation among respondents?

3. Now try index construction. You might begin with some of the questions you wrote for Exercise 2. Write four or five fixed-choice questions that each measure the same concept. (For instance, you could ask questions to determine whether someone is alienated.) Write each question so it has the same response choices (a "matrix" design). Now conduct a literature search to identify an index that another researcher used to measure your concept

or a similar concept. Compare your index to the published index. Which seems preferable to you? Why?

4. List three attitudinal variables.

    a. Write a conceptual definition for each variable. Whenever possible, this definition should come from the existing literature—either a book you have read for a course or the research literature that you have been searching. Ask two class members for feedback on your definitions.

    b. Develop measurement procedures for each variable: Two measures should be single questions and one should be an index used in prior research (search the Internet and the journal literature in Soc Abstracts or Psych Abstracts). Ask classmates to answer these questions and give you feedback on their clarity.

    c. Propose tests of reliability and validity for the measures.

5. Exercise your cleverness on this question: For each of the following, suggest two unobtrusive measures that might help you discover (a) how much of the required reading for this course students actually complete; (b) where are the popular spots to sit in a local park, and (c) which major U.S. cities have the highest local taxes.

Chapter 4

Sampling

An old history professor was renowned for his ability, at semester's end, to finish grading large piles of student papers (many of them undistinguished) in a matter of a few short hours. When asked by a younger colleague how he accomplished this feat, the codger replied with a snort, "You don't have to eat the whole tub of butter to know if it's rancid." Harsh, but true.

That is the essence of sampling: A small portion, carefully chosen, can reveal the quality of a much larger whole. A survey of 1,400 Americans telephoned one Saturday afternoon can tell us very accurately how 40,000,000 will vote for president on the following Tuesday morning.

A quick check of reports from a few selected banks can tell the Federal Reserve how strong inflation is. And when you go to the doctor with a possible case of mononucleosis, and he orders a blood test, the phlebotomist needn't take all of your blood to see if you have too many atypical lymphocytes. Sampling techniques tell us how to select cases that can lead to valid generalizations about a

population, or the entire group you wish to learn about. In this chapter we define the key components of sampling strategy and then present the types of sampling one may use in a research study, along with the strengths and weaknesses of each.

HOW DO WE PREPARE TO SAMPLE?

Define Sample Components and the Population

To understand how sampling works, you'll first need a few useful definitions. A **sample** is a subset of the population that we want to learn about. The individual members of this sample are called **elements,** or elementary units. These are the cases that we actually study. In order to select these elements, we often rely on some list of all elements in the population—a **sampling frame.**

Population: The entire set of individuals or other entities to which study findings are to be generalized.

Sample: A subset of a population used to study the population as a whole.

Elements: The individual members of the population whose characteristics are to be measured.

Sampling frame: A list of all elements or other units containing the elements in a population.

Sampling units: Units listed at each stage of a multistage sampling design.

Sometimes our sources of information are not actually the elements in our study. For example, for a survey about educational practices a researcher might first sample schools, and then, within sampled schools, interview a sample of teachers. The schools and the teachers are both termed **sampling units,** because we sample from both (Levy & Lemeshow, 1999:22). The schools are selected in the first stage of the sample, so they are the *primary sampling units* (and in this case, the elements in the study). The teachers are *secondary sampling units* (but they are not elements, because they are used to provide information about the entire school) (see Exhibit 4.1).

It is important to know exactly what population a sample can represent when you select or evaluate sample components: The population for a study is the aggregation of elements that we actually focus on and sample from, not some larger

Exhibit 4.1   Sample Components in a Two-Stage Study

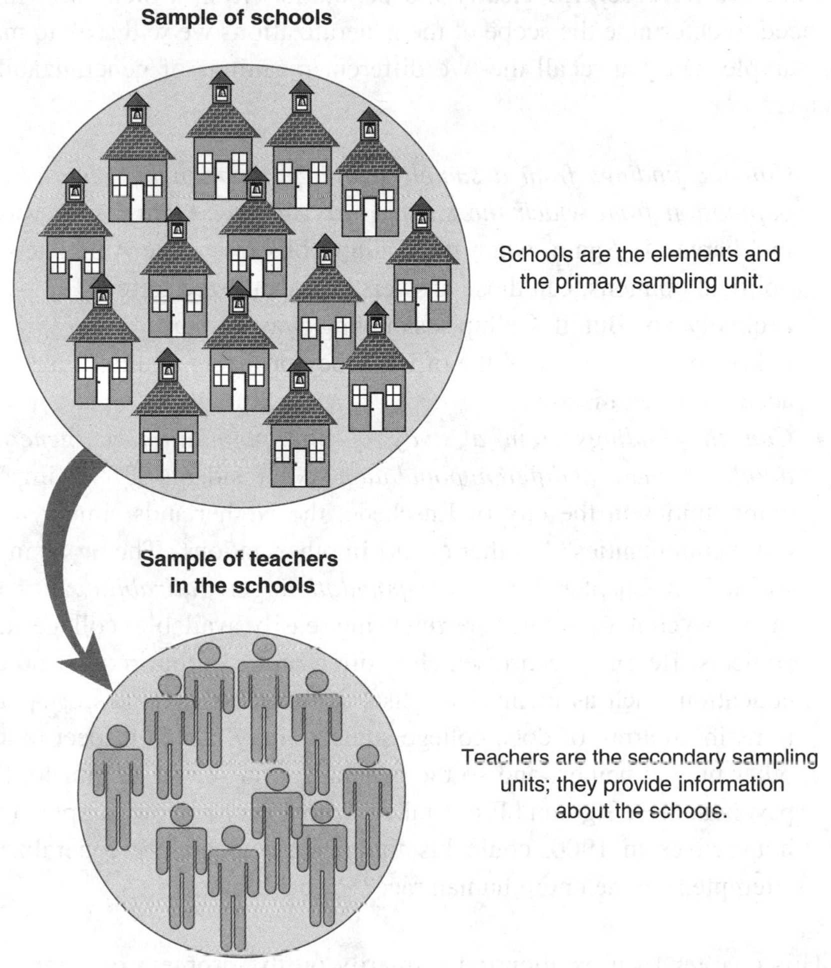

Sample of schools

Schools are the elements and
the primary sampling unit.

**Sample of teachers
in the schools**

Teachers are the secondary sampling
units; they provide information
about the schools.

aggregation that we really wish we could have studied. If we sample students in one high school, the population for our study is the student body of that school, not all high school students in the nation.

Some populations, such as frequent moviegoers, are not identified by a simple criterion such as a geographic boundary or an organizational membership. Clear definition of such a population is difficult but quite necessary. Anyone should be able to determine just what population was actually studied, so we would have to define clearly the concept of "frequent moviegoers" and specify how we determined their status.

Evaluate Generalizability

Once we have defined clearly the population from which we will sample, we need to determine the scope of the generalizations we will seek to make from our sample. Do you recall the two different meanings of generalizability from Chapter 1?

- *Can the findings from a sample of the population be generalized to the population from which the sample was selected?* This issue was defined in Chapter 1. Again, when the Gallup polls ask some Americans for their political opinions, can those answers be generalized to the U.S. population? Probably so. But if Gallup's sampling was haphazard—say, if they just talked to some people in the office—they probably couldn't make the same accurate generalizations.
- *Can the findings from a study of one population be generalized to another, somewhat different population?* Are residents of three impoverished communities in the city of Enschede, the Netherlands similar to those in other communities? In other cities? In other nations? The problem here was defined in Chapter 1 as *cross-population generalizability.* For example, many psychology studies are run using (easily available) college students as subjects. Because such research is often on tasks that require no advanced education, such as memorizing lists of nonsense syllables or spotting patterns in an array of dots, college students may in this respect be like most other human beings, and so the generalization seems legitimate. But when psychoanalyst Sigmund Freud talked with a very narrow sample of Viennese housewives in 1900, could his findings be accurately generalized (as he attempted) to the entire human race? Probably not.

This chapter focuses attention primarily on the problem of sample generalizability: Can findings from a sample be generalized to the population from which the sample was drawn? This is really the most basic question to ask about a sample, and social research methods provide many tools with which to address it.

But researchers often project their theories onto groups or populations much larger than, or simply different from, those they have actually studied. The population to which generalizations are made in this way can be termed the **target population**—a set of elements larger than or different from the population that was sampled and to which the researcher would like to generalize any study findings. Because the validity of cross-population generalizations cannot be tested empirically, except by conducting more research in other settings, we will not focus much attention on this problem here.

Assess the Diversity of the Population

Sampling is unnecessary if all the units in the population are identical. The blood in one person is constantly being mixed and stirred, so it's very homogeneous—any pint is the same as any other. Physicists don't need to select a representative sample of all atomic particles to learn about basic physical processes. They can study a single atomic particle, because it is identical to every other particle of its type.

What about people? Certainly all people are not identical, but if we are studying physical or psychological processes that are the same among all people, sampling is not needed to achieve generalizable findings. Psychologists and social psychologists often conduct experiments on college students to learn about processes that they think are identical across individuals. Field researchers who observe group processes in a small community sometimes make the same assumption. But we must always bear in mind that we don't really know how generalizable our findings are to populations that we haven't actually studied.

So we usually conclude that we must study the larger population in which we are interested, if we want to be able to make generalizations about it. For this purpose, we must obtain a **representative sample** of the population to which generalizations are sought (see Exhibit 4.2).

Representative sample: A sample that "looks like" the population from which it was selected in all respects that are potentially relevant to the study. The distribution of characteristics among the elements of a representative sample is the same as the distribution of those characteristics among the total population. In an unrepresentative sample, some characteristics are overrepresented or underrepresented.

Consider a Census

In some circumstances, it may be feasible to skirt the issue of generalizability by conducting a **census**—studying the entire population of interest—rather than drawing a sample. This is what the federal government tries to do every 10 years with the U.S. Census. Censuses also include studies of all the employees (or students) in small organizations, studies comparing all 50 states, and studies of the entire population of a particular type of organization in some area.

The reason that social scientists don't often attempt to collect data from all the members of some large population is simply that doing so would be too expensive and time-consuming—the 2000 U.S. Census cost more than $2.7 billion (Holmes, 1994)! But fortunately, a well-designed sampling strategy can result in a representative sample of the same population at far less cost.

Exhibit 4.2   Representative and Unrepresentative Samples

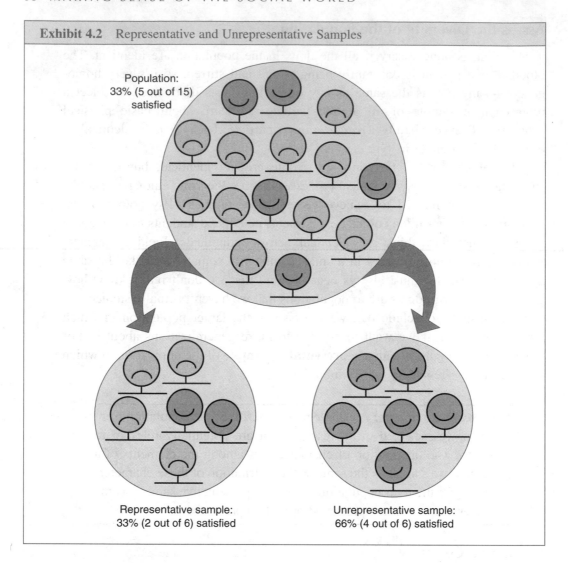

Population:
33% (5 out of 15)
satisfied

Representative sample:
33% (2 out of 6) satisfied

Unrepresentative sample:
66% (4 out of 6) satisfied

WHAT SAMPLING METHOD SHOULD WE USE?

Certain features of samples make them more or less likely to represent the population from which they are selected; the more representative the sample, the better. The crucial distinction about samples is whether they are based on a probability (more representative) or a nonprobability (less representative) sampling method. **Probability sampling methods** allow us to know in advance how likely it is that any element of a population will be selected. Sampling methods that do not let us know in advance the likelihood of selecting each element are termed **nonprobability sampling methods.**

Probability sampling methods rely on a random, or chance, selection procedure, which is in principle the same as flipping a coin to decide which of two people "wins" and which one "loses." Heads and tails are equally likely to turn up in a coin toss, so both persons have an equal chance to win. That chance, their **probability of selection,** is 1 out of 2, or .5.

Probability of selection: The likelihood that an element will be selected from the population for inclusion in the sample. In a census of all the elements of a population, the probability that any particular element will be selected is 1.0. If half the elements in the population are sampled on the basis of chance (say, by tossing a coin), the probability of selection for each element is one-half, or .5. As the size of the sample as a proportion of the population decreases, so does the probability of selection.

There is a natural tendency to confuse the concept of **random sampling,** in which cases are selected only on the basis of chance, with a haphazard method of sampling. On first impression, "leaving things up to chance" seems to imply not exerting any control over the sampling method. But to ensure that nothing but chance influences the selection of cases, the researcher must proceed very methodically. The researcher must follow carefully controlled procedures if a purely random process is to occur.

Two problems are often cause for concern when drawing random samples:

1. If the sampling frame is incomplete, a sample selected randomly from that list will not really be a random sample of the population. You should always consider the adequacy of the sampling frame. Even for a simple population like a university's student body, the registrar's list is likely to be at least somewhat out of date at any given time.

2. Nonresponse is a major hazard in survey research, because nonrespondents are likely to differ systematically from those who take the time to participate. If the response rate is low (say, below 65%), you should not assume that findings from even a random sample will be generalizable to the population.

Probability Sampling Methods

Probability sampling methods are those in which the probability of selection is known and is not zero (so there is some chance of selecting each element). These methods randomly select elements and therefore have no systematic **bias;** nothing but chance determines which elements are included in the sample. This feature of probability samples makes them much more desirable than nonprobability samples when the goal is to generalize to a larger population.

However, even a randomly selected sample will have some degree of sampling error—some deviation from the characteristics of the population. In general, both the size of the sample and the homogeneity (sameness) of the population affect the degree of error due to chance. In spite of what you might think, the *proportion* of the population that the sample represents does not affect sample representativeness, unless that proportion is very large—it is the number of cases in the sample that is important. To elaborate:

The larger the sample, the more confidence we can have in the sample's representativeness. If we randomly pick 5 people to represent the entire population of our city, our sample is unlikely to be very representative of the entire population in terms of age, gender, race, attitudes, and so on. But if we randomly pick 100 people, the odds of having a representative sample are much better; with a random sample of 1,000, the odds become very good indeed.

The more homogeneous the population, the more confidence we can have in the representativeness of a sample of any particular size. That's why blood testing works—blood is homogeneous in any specific individual's body. Or let's say we plan to draw samples of 50 people from each of two communities to estimate mean family income. One community is very diverse, with family incomes varying from $12,000 to $85,000. In the other, more homogeneous community, family incomes are concentrated in a narrow range, from $41,000 to $64,000. The estimated mean family income based on the sample from the homogeneous community is more likely to be representative than is the estimate based on the sample from the more heterogeneous community. With less variation to represent, fewer cases are needed to represent the homogeneous community.

The fraction of the total population that a sample contains does not affect the sample's representativeness, unless that fraction is large. This isn't obvious, but it is mathematically true. The raw number of cases matters more than the proportion of the population. Other things being equal, a sample of 1,000 from a population of 1 million (with a sampling fraction of 0.001, or 0.1%) is much better than a sample of 100 from a population of 10,000 (although the sampling fraction in this case is 0.01, or 1%, which is 10 times higher). The size of the samples is what makes representativeness more likely, not the proportion of the whole that the sample represents. We can regard any sampling fraction under 2% with about the same degree of confidence (Sudman, 1976:184). In fact, sample representativeness is not likely to increase much until the sampling fraction is quite a bit higher.

Polls to predict presidential election outcomes illustrate both the value of random sampling and the problems that it cannot overcome. In most presidential elections, pollsters have predicted accurately the outcomes of the actual votes by using random sampling and, these days, phone interviewing to learn whom likely voters intend to vote for. Exhibit 4.3 shows how close these sample-based predictions have been in the last 11 contests. The exceptions were the 1980 and 1992 elections, when third-party candidates had an unpredicted effect. Otherwise, the small discrepancies between the votes predicted through random sampling and the actual votes can be attributed to random error.

The Gallup poll did quite well in predicting the result of the remarkable 2000 presidential election. The final Gallup prediction was that George W. Bush would win with 48% (Al Gore was predicted to receive only 46%, and Green Party candidate Ralph Nader was predicted to secure 4%). Although the race turned out to be much closer, with Gore actually winning the popular vote (before losing in the Electoral College), Gallup accurately noted that there appeared to have been a late-breaking trend in favor of Gore (Newport, 2000).

But election polls have produced some major errors in prediction. In 1948, pollsters mistakenly predicted that Thomas E. Dewey would beat Harry S. Truman, based on the random sampling method that George Gallup had used successfully since 1934. The problem? Pollsters stopped collecting data several weeks before the election, and in those weeks many people changed their minds (Kenney, 1987). So the sample was systematically biased by underrepresenting shifts in voter sentiment just before the election.

Exhibit 4.3 Election Outcomes: Predicted[1] and Actual

Winner/Year	Polls	Result
Kennedy (1960)	51%	50%
Johnson (1964)	64%	61%
Nixon (1968)[2]	43%	43%
Nixon (1972)	62%	62%
Carter (1976)	48%	50%
Reagan (1980)[2]	47%	51%
Reagan (1984)	59%	59%
Bush (1988)	56%	54%
Clinton (1992)[2]	49%	43%
Clinton (1996)[2]	52%	50%
Bush, G. W. (2000)[2]	48%	48%
Bush, G. W. (2004)	49%	51%

Source: 1960–1992 poll data: The Gallup Poll (Loth, 1992). 1996 poll data: The Gallup Poll (www.gallup.com/poll/data/96prelec.html).

1. Polls one week prior to election.
2. There was also a third-party candidate.

Now that we have sung the praises of probability-based samples in general, we need to introduce the different types of random samples. The four most common types of random sample are simple random sampling, systematic random sampling, cluster sampling, and stratified random sampling.

Simple Random Sampling

Simple random sampling identifies cases strictly on the basis of chance. Both flipping a coin and rolling a die can be used to identify cases strictly on the basis of chance, but these procedures are not very efficient tools for drawing a sample. A **random number table** simplifies the process considerably. The researcher numbers all the elements in the sampling frame and then uses a systematic procedure for picking corresponding numbers from the random number table. (Exercise 1 under "Doing Research" at the end of this chapter explains the process step by step.) Alternatively, a researcher may use a lottery procedure. Each case number is written on a small card, and then the cards are mixed up and the sample selected from the cards. A computer program can also easily generate a random sample of any size.

Phone surveys often use a technique called **random digit dialing** in order to draw a random sample. A machine dials random numbers within the phone prefixes corresponding to the area in which the survey is to be conducted. Random digit dialing is particularly useful when a sampling frame (list of elements) is unavailable, because the dialing machine can just skip ahead if a phone number is not in service.

The probability of selection in a true simple random sample is equal for each element. If a sample of 500 is selected from a population of 17,000 (that is, a sampling frame of 17,000), then the probability of selection for each element is 500/17,000, or .03. Every element has an equal chance of being selected, just like the odds in a toss of a coin (1/2) or a roll of a die (1/6). Thus, simple random sampling is an *equal probability of selection method (EPSEM)*.

Systematic Random Sampling

Systematic random sampling is a variant of simple random sampling. The first element is selected randomly from a list or from sequential files, and then every *n*th element is selected. This is a convenient method for drawing a random sample when the population elements are arranged sequentially. It is particularly efficient when the elements are not actually printed (that is, there is no sampling frame) but instead are represented by folders in filing cabinets.

In almost all sampling situations, systematic random sampling yields what is essentially a simple random sample. The exception is a situation in which the

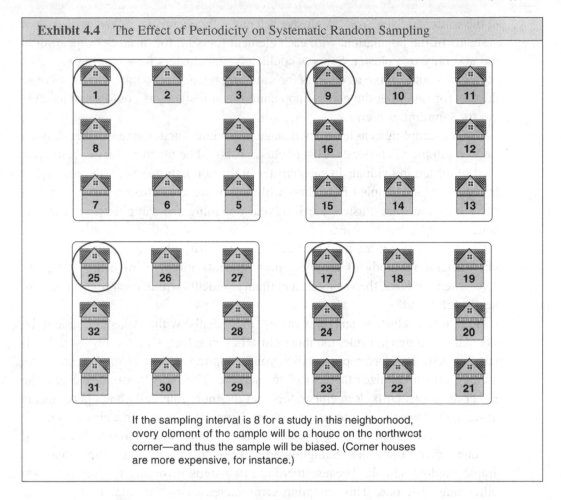

Exhibit 4.4 The Effect of Periodicity on Systematic Random Sampling

If the sampling interval is 8 for a study in this neighborhood, ovory olomont of tho oamplo will bo a houoo on tho northwcot corner—and thus the sample will be biased. (Corner houses are more expensive, for instance.)

sequence of elements is affected by **periodicity**—that is, the sequence varies in some regular, periodic pattern. For example, the houses in a new development with the same number of houses on each block (eight, for example) may be listed by block, starting with the house in the northwest corner of each block and continuing clockwise. If the **sampling interval** is 8, the same as the periodic pattern, all the cases selected will be in the same position (see Exhibit 4.4). But in reality, periodicity and the sampling interval are rarely the same, so this usually isn't a problem.

Cluster Sampling

Cluster sampling is useful when a sampling frame—a definite list—of elements is not available, as often is the case for large populations spread out across a wide geographic area or among many different organizations. We don't have a good list of all the Catholics in America, or all the businesspeople in Arizona, or all the waiters in New York. A **cluster** is a naturally occurring, mixed aggregate of elements of the population, with each element (person, for instance) appearing in one and only one cluster. Schools could serve as clusters for sampling students, city blocks could serve as clusters for sampling residents, counties could serve as clusters for sampling the general population, and restaurants could serve as clusters for sampling waiters.

Cluster sampling is at least a two-stage procedure. First, the researcher draws a random sample of clusters. (A list of clusters should be much easier to obtain than a list of all the individuals in each cluster in the population.) Next, the researcher draws a random sample of elements within each selected cluster. Because only a fraction of the total clusters are involved, obtaining the sampling frame at this stage should be much easier.

Cluster samples often involve multiple stages, with clusters within clusters, as when a national study of middle school students might involve first sampling states, then counties, then schools, and finally students within each selected school (see Exhibit 4.5).

How many clusters and how many individuals within clusters should be selected? As a general rule, the more clusters you select, with the fewest individuals in each, the more representative your sampling will be. Unfortunately, this strategy also maximizes the cost of the sample. The more clusters selected, the higher the travel costs. Remember, too, that the more internally homogeneous the clusters, the fewer cases needed per cluster. Homogeneity within a cluster is good.

Cluster sampling is a very popular method among survey researchers, but it has one general drawback: Sampling error is greater in a cluster sample than in a simple random sample, because there are two steps involving random selection rather than just one. This sampling error increases as the number of clusters decreases, and it decreases as the homogeneity of cases per cluster increases. This

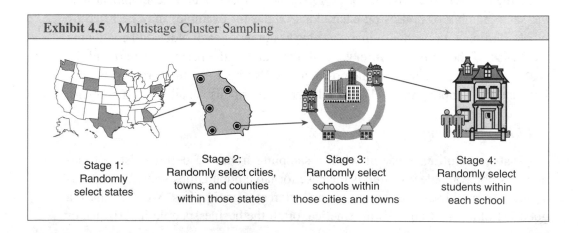

Exhibit 4.5   Multistage Cluster Sampling

Stage 1:
Randomly
select states

Stage 2:
Randomly select cities,
towns, and counties
within those states

Stage 3:
Randomly select
schools within
those cities and towns

Stage 4:
Randomly select
students within
each school

is another way of restating the points above: It's better to include as many clusters as possible in a sample and it's more likely that a cluster sample will be representative of the population if cases are relatively similar within clusters.

Stratified Random Sampling

Suppose you want to survey soldiers of an army to determine their morale. Simple random sampling would produce large numbers of enlisted personnel—that is, of lower ranks—but very few, if any, generals. But you want generals in your sample. **Stratified random sampling** ensures that various groups will be included.

First, all elements in the population (that is, in the sampling frame) are distinguished according to their value on some relevant characteristic (army rank, for instance: generals, captains, privates, etc.). That characteristic forms the sampling strata. Next, elements are sampled randomly from within these strata: so many generals, so many captains, and so on. Of course, in order to use this method more information is required prior to sampling than is the case with simple random sampling. Each element must belong to one and only one stratum.

For "proportionate to size" sampling, the size of each stratum in the population must be known. This method efficiently draws an appropriate representation of elements across strata. Imagine that you plan to draw a sample of 500 from an ethnically diverse neighborhood. The neighborhood population is 15% black, 10% Hispanic, 5% Asian, and 70% white. If you drew a simple random sample, you might end up with somewhat disproportionate numbers of each group. But if you created sampling strata based on race and ethnicity, you could randomly select cases from each stratum, in exactly the same proportions. This is termed **proportionate stratified sampling,** and it eliminates any possibility of sampling error in the sample's distribution of ethnicity. Each stratum would be represented exactly in proportion to its size in the population from which the sample was drawn (see Exhibit 4.6).

In **disproportionate stratified sampling,** the proportion of each stratum that is included in the sample is intentionally varied from what it is in the population. In the case of the sample stratified by ethnicity, you might select equal numbers of cases from each racial or ethnic group: 125 blacks (25% of the sample), 125 Hispanics (25%), 125 Asians (25%), and 125 whites (25%). In this type of sample, the probability of selection of every case is known but unequal between strata. You know what the proportions are in the population, and so you can easily adjust your combined sample statistics to reflect these true proportions. For instance, if you want to combine the ethnic groups and estimate the average income of the total population, you would have to "weight" each case in the sample to reflect its representation in the population.

Exhibit 4.6 Stratified Random Sampling

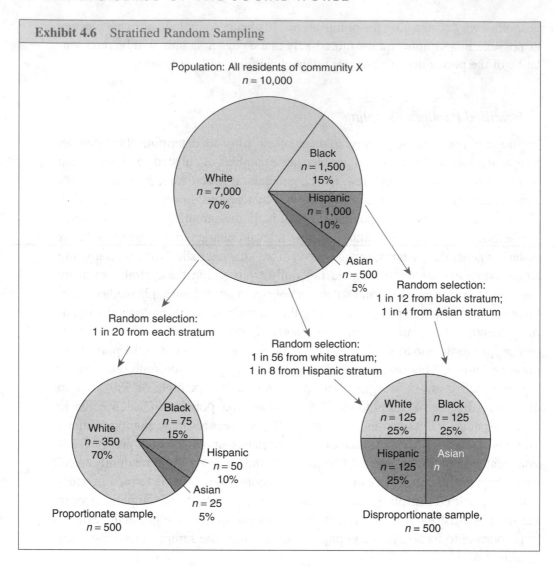

Why would anyone select a sample that is so unrepresentative in the first place? The most common reason is to ensure that cases from smaller strata are included in the sample in sufficient numbers to allow separate statistical estimates and to facilitate comparisons between strata. Remember that one of the determinants of sample quality is sample size. The same is true for subgroups within samples. If a key concern in a research project is to describe and compare the incomes of people from different racial and ethnic groups, then it is important that the researchers base the mean income of each group on enough cases to be a valid representation. If few members of a particular minority group are in the population, they need to be oversampled.

Nonprobability Sampling Methods

Nonprobability sampling methods are often used in qualitative research; they also are used in quantitative studies when researchers are unable to use probability selection methods. There are four common nonprobability sampling methods: availability sampling, quota sampling, purposive sampling, and snowball sampling. Because they do not use a random selection procedure, we cannot expect a sample selected with any of these methods to yield a representative sample. Nonetheless, these methods are useful when random sampling is not possible, with a research question that calls for an intensive investigation of a small population, or for a preliminary, exploratory study.

Availability Sampling

Elements are selected for **availability sampling** (sometimes called "convenience" sampling) because they're available or easy to find. For example, sometimes people stand outside stores in a shopping mall asking passersby to answer a few questions about their shopping habits. That may make sense; but asking the same people for their views on the economy doesn't. In certain respects, regular mall shoppers are not representative people.

An availability sample is often appropriate at key points in social research—for example, when a field researcher is exploring a new setting and trying to get some sense of prevailing attitudes, or when a survey researcher conducts a preliminary test of a new set of questions. Intensive qualitative research efforts also often rely on availability samples. Howard Becker's classic work on jazz musicians, for instance, was based on groups Becker himself played in (Becker, 1963).

Availability sampling often masquerades as a more rigorous form of research. Popular magazines periodically survey their readers by printing a questionnaire for readers to fill out and mail in. For many years *Playboy* magazine has conducted a sex survey among its readers using this technique. But usually only a small fraction of readers return the questionnaire, and these respondents might—how to say it?—have more interesting sex lives than other readers of *Playboy,* not to mention the rest of us (or so they claim).

Quota Sampling

Quota sampling is intended to overcome the most obvious flaw of availability sampling—that the sample will just consist of whoever or whatever is available, whether or not it represents the population. In this approach, quotas are set to ensure that the sample represents certain characteristics in proportion to their prevalence in the population.

Suppose that you want to sample 500 adult residents of a town. You know from the town's annual report what the proportions of town residents are in terms of gender, employment status, and age. In order to draw a quota sample of a certain size, you then specify that interviews must be conducted with 500 residents who will match the town population in terms of gender, employment status, and age.

The problem is that even when we know that a quota sample is representative of the particular characteristics for which quotas have been set, we have no way of knowing if the sample is representative in terms of any other characteristics. In Exhibit 4.7, for example, quotas have been set for gender only. Under the circumstances, it's no surprise that the sample is representative of the population only in terms of gender, not in terms of race.

Of course, you must know the relevant characteristics of the entire population to set the right quotas. In most cases researchers know what the population looks like in terms of no more than a few of the characteristics relevant to their concerns. And in some cases they have no such information on the entire population.

If you're now feeling skeptical of quota sampling, you've gotten the drift of our remarks. Nonetheless, in situations in which you can't draw a random sample, it may be better to establish quotas than to have no quotas at all.

Exhibit 4.7   Quota Sampling

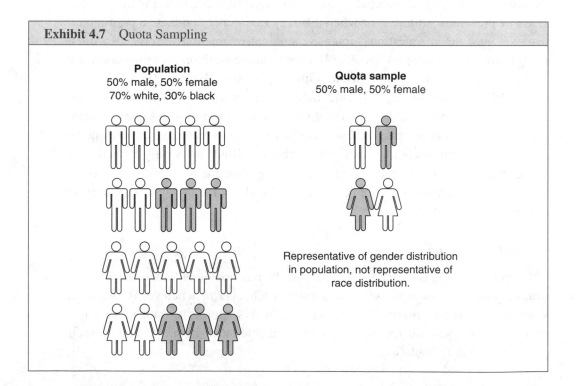

Population
50% male, 50% female
70% white, 30% black

Quota sample
50% male, 50% female

Representative of gender distribution
in population, not representative of
race distribution.

Purposive Sampling

In **purposive sampling,** each sample element is selected for a purpose, usually because of the unique position of the sample elements. Purposive sampling may involve studying the entire population of some limited group (directors of shelters for homeless adults) or a subset of a population (mid-level managers with a reputation for efficiency). Or a purposive sample may be a "key informant survey," which targets individuals who are particularly knowledgeable about the issues under investigation.

Herbert Rubin and Irene Rubin (1995:66) suggest three guidelines for selecting informants when designing any purposive sampling strategy. Informants should be:

1. "Knowledgeable about the cultural arena or situation or experience being studied." (p. 66)

2. "Willing to talk." (p. 66)

3. "Represent[ative of] the range of points of view." (p. 66)

In addition, Rubin and Rubin suggest continuing to select interviewees until you can pass two tests:

4. *Completeness.* "What you hear provides an overall sense of the meaning of a concept, theme, or process." (p. 72)

5. *Saturation.* "You gain confidence that you are learning little that is new from subsequent interview[s]." (p. 73)

Adhering to these guidelines will help to ensure that a purposive sample adequately represents the setting or issues studied.

Of course, purposive sampling does not produce a sample that represents some larger population, but it can be exactly what is needed in a case study of an organization, community, or some other clearly defined and relatively limited group.

Snowball Sampling

For **snowball sampling,** you identify one member of the population and speak to him or her, then ask that person to identify others in the population and speak to them, then ask them to identify others, and so on. The sample thus "snowballs" in size. This technique is useful for hard-to-reach or hard-to-identify, interconnected populations (at least some members of the population know each other). An example of a study using snowball sampling is Patricia Adler's (1993) study of southern California drug dealers. Wealthy philanthropists, top business executives, or Olympic athletes, all of whom may have reason to refuse a "cold call" from an unknown researcher, might be sampled effectively using the snowball technique. However, researchers using snowball sampling normally cannot be confident that their sample represents the total population of interest, so generalizations must be tentative.

CONCLUSION

Sampling is a powerful tool for social science research. Probability sampling methods allow a researcher to use the laws of chance, or probability, to draw samples from which population parameters can be estimated with a high degree of confidence. A sample of just 1,000 or 1,500 individuals can be used to estimate reliably the characteristics of the population of a nation comprising millions of individuals.

But researchers do not come by representative samples easily. Well-designed samples require careful planning, some advance knowledge about the population to be sampled, and adherence to systematic selection procedures—all so that the selection procedures are not biased. And even after the sample data are collected, the researcher's ability to generalize from the sample findings to the population is not completely certain.

The alternatives to random, or probability-based, sampling methods are almost always much less palatable for quantitative studies, even though they are typically much cheaper. Without a method of selecting cases likely to represent the population in which the researcher is interested, research findings will have to be carefully qualified. Qualitative researchers whose goal is to understand a small group or setting in depth may necessarily have to use unrepresentative samples, but they must keep in mind that the generalizability of their findings will not be known. Additional procedures for sampling in qualitative studies will be introduced in Chapter 7.

Social scientists often seek to generalize their conclusions from the population that they studied to some larger target population. Careful design of appropriate sampling strategies is what makes such generalizations possible.

KEY TERMS

Availability sampling	Element
Bias	Nonprobability sampling method
Census	Periodicity
Cluster	Population
Cluster sampling	Probability of selection
Disproportionate stratified sampling	Probability sampling method

Proportionate stratified sampling
Purposive sampling
Quota sampling
Random digit dialing
Random number table
Random sampling
Representative sample
Sample

Sampling frame
Sampling interval
Sampling unit
Simple random sampling
Snowball sampling
Stratified random sampling
Systematic random sampling
Target population

HIGHLIGHTS

• Sampling theory focuses on the generalizability of descriptive findings to the population from which the sample was drawn. It also considers whether statements can be generalized from one population to another.

• Sampling is unnecessary when the elements that would be sampled are identical, but the complexity of the social world often makes it difficult to argue that different elements are identical. Conducting a complete census of a population also eliminates the need for sampling, but the resources required for a complete census of a large population are usually prohibitive.

• Nonresponse undermines sample quality: It is the obtained sample, not the desired sample, that determines sample quality.

• Probability sampling methods rely on a random selection procedure to ensure no systematic bias in the selection of elements. In a probability sample, the odds of selecting elements are known, and the method of selection is carefully controlled.

• A sampling frame (a list of elements in the population) is required in most probability sampling methods. The adequacy of the sampling frame is an important determinant of sample quality.

• Simple random sampling and systematic random sampling are equivalent probability sampling methods in most situations. However, systematic random sampling is inappropriate for sampling from lists of elements that have a regular, periodic structure.

• Stratified random sampling uses prior information about a population to make sampling more efficient. Stratified sampling may be either proportionate or disproportionate. Disproportionate stratified sampling is useful when a research question focuses on a stratum or on strata that make up a small proportion of the population.

• Cluster sampling is less efficient than simple random sampling but is useful when a sampling frame is unavailable. It is also useful for large populations spread out across a wide area or among many organizations.

• Nonprobability sampling methods can be useful when random sampling is not possible, when a research question does not concern a larger population, and when a preliminary exploratory study is appropriate. However, the representativeness of nonprobability samples cannot be determined.

To assist you in completing the Web Exercises, please access the Study Site at http://www.pineforge.com/mssw2 where you'll find the Web Exercises with accompanying links. You'll find other useful study materials like self-quizzes and e-flashcards for each chapter, along with a group of carefully selected articles from research journals that illustrate the major concepts and techniques presented in the book.

EXERCISES

Discussing Research

1. Propose a sampling design that would be appropriate if you were to survey students on your campus only. Define the population, identify the sampling frame(s), and specify the elements and any other units at different stages. Indicate the exact procedure for selecting people to be included in the sample.

2. Propose a different sampling design for conducting your survey in a larger population, such as your city, state, or the entire nation.

Finding Research

1. Locate one or more newspaper articles reporting the results of an opinion poll. What information does the article provide on the sample that was selected? What additional information do you need to determine whether the sample was a representative one?

2. From professional journals, select five articles that describe research using a sample drawn from some population. Identify the type of sample used in each study, and note any strong and weak points in how the sample was actually drawn. Did the researchers have a problem due to nonresponse? Considering the sample, how confident are you in the validity of generalizations about the population based on the sample? Do you need any additional information to evaluate the sample? Do you think a different sampling strategy would have been preferable? What larger population were the findings generalized to? Do you think these generalizations were warranted? Why or why not?

3. Research on time use has been flourishing all over the world in recent years. Search the Web for sites that include the words "time use" and see what you find. Choose one site and write a paragraph about what you learned from it.

4. Check out the "people" section of the U.S. Bureau of the Census Web site (www .census.gov). Based on some of the data you find there, write a brief summary of some aspect of the current characteristics of the American population.

Critiquing Research

1. Shere Hite's popular book *Women and Love* (1987) is a good example of the claims that are often made based on an availability sample. In this case, however, the sample didn't necessarily appear to be an availability sample because it consisted of so many people. Hite distributed 100,000 questionnaires to church groups and many other organizations and received back 4.5%; 4,500 women took the time to answer some or all of her 127 essay questions regarding love and sex. Is Hite's sample likely to represent American

women in general? Why or why not? You might take a look at the book's empirical generalizations and consider whether they are justified.

2. In newspapers or magazines, find three examples of poor sampling, where someone's conclusions—either in formal research or in their everyday reasoning—are weakened by the selection of cases they've looked at. How is their sampling flawed, and how might that systematically distort their findings? Don't just say "their cases might not be typical"—try to guess, for instance, the direction of error. For example, did they pick unusually friendly or accessible people, or the most well-known examples? And how might that affect their findings?

Doing Research

1. Select a random sample using a table of random numbers (either one provided by your instructor or one from a Web site, such as http://www.bmra.com/extras/man-rand .htm). Compute a statistic based on your sample, and compare it to the corresponding figure for the entire population. Here's how to proceed:

   a. First select a very small population for which you have a reasonably complete sampling frame. One possibility would be the listing of some characteristic of states in a U.S. Census Bureau publication, such as average income or population size. Another possible population would be the list of asking prices for houses advertised in your local paper.

   b. Next, create a sampling frame, a numbered list of all the available elements in the population. If you are using a complete listing of all elements, as from a U.S. Census Bureau publication, the sampling frame is the same as the list. Just number the elements (states). If your population is composed of housing ads in the local paper, your sampling frame will be those ads that contain a housing price. Identify these ads, and then number them sequentially, starting with 1.

   c. Decide on a method of picking numbers out of the random number table, such as taking every number in each row, row by row, or moving down or diagonally across the columns. Use only the first (or last) digit in each number if you need to select 1 to 9 cases or only the first (or last) two digits if you want fewer than 100 cases.

   d. Pick a starting location in the random number table. It's important to pick a starting point in an unbiased way, perhaps by closing your eyes and then pointing to some part of the page.

   e. Record the numbers you encounter as you move from the starting location in the direction you decided on in advance, until you have recorded as many random numbers as the number of cases you need in the sample. If you are selecting states, 10 might be a good number. Ignore numbers that are too large (or small) for the range of numbers used to identify the elements in the population. Discard duplicate numbers.

   f. Calculate the average value in your sample for some variable that was measured (for example, population size in a sample of states, or housing price for the housing ads). Calculate the average by adding up the values of all the elements in the sample and dividing by the number of elements in the sample.

   g. Go back to the sampling frame and calculate this same average for all the elements in the list. How close is the sample average to the population average?

   h. Estimate the range of sample averages that would be likely to include 90% of the possible samples.

Causation and Experimental Design

Identifying causes—figuring out why things happen—is the goal of most social science research. Unfortunately, valid explanations of the causes of social phenomena do not come easily. Why did the homicide rate in the United States drop for 15 years and then start to rise in 1999 (Butterfield, 2000:12)? Was it because of changes in the style of policing (Radin, 1997:B7) or because of changing attitudes among young people (Butterfield, 1996a)? Was it due to variation in patterns of drug use (Krauss, 1996) or to tougher prison sentences (Butterfield, 1996a) or to more stringent handgun regulations (Butterfield, 1996b)? Did better emergency medical procedures result in higher survival rates for victims (Ramirez, 2002)? If we are to evaluate these alternative explanations we must design our research strategies carefully.

This chapter considers the meaning of causation, the criteria for achieving causally valid explanations, the ways in which experimental and quasi-experimental research designs seek to meet these criteria, and the difficulties that can sometimes result in invalid conclusions. By the end of the chapter, you should have a good grasp of the meaning of causation and the logic of experimental design. Most social research, both academic and applied, uses data collection methods other than experiments. But because experimental designs are the best way to evaluate causal hypotheses, a better understanding of them will help you to be aware of the strengths and weaknesses of other research designs that we will consider in subsequent chapters.

CAUSAL EXPLANATION

A cause is an explanation for some characteristic, attitude, or behavior of groups, individuals, or other entities (such as families, organizations, or cities) or for events. For example, Sherman and Berk (1984) conducted a study to determine whether adults who were accused of a domestic violence offense would be less likely to repeat the offense if police arrested them rather than just warned them. Their conclusion that this hypothesis was correct meant that they believed police response had a **causal effect** on the likelihood of committing another domestic violence offense.

> *Causal effect:* The finding that change in one variable leads to change in another variable, *ceteris paribus* (other things being equal). *Example:* Individuals arrested for domestic assault tend to commit fewer subsequent assaults than similar individuals who are accused in the same circumstances but are not arrested.

More specifically, a causal effect is said to occur if variation in the independent variable is followed by variation in the dependent variable, when all other things are equal (*ceteris paribus*). For instance, we know that for the most part men earn more income than women do. But is this because they are men—or could it be due to higher levels of education, or to longer tenure in their jobs (with no pregnancy breaks), or is it the kinds of jobs men go into as compared to those that women choose? We want to know if men earn more than women, *ceteris paribus*—other things (job, tenure, education, etc.) being equal.

We admit that you can legitimately argue that "all" other things can't literally be equal: We can't compare the same people at the same time in exactly the same circumstances except for the variation in the independent variable (King, Keohane, & Verba, 1994). However, you will see that we can design research to create conditions that are very comparable so that we can isolate the impact of the independent variable on the dependent variable.

WHAT CAUSES WHAT?

Five criteria should be considered in trying to establish a causal relationship. The first three criteria are generally considered as requirements for identifying a causal effect: (1) empirical association, (2) temporal priority of the independent variable, and (3) nonspuriousness. You must establish these three to claim a causal relationship. Evidence that meets the other two criteria—(4) identifying a causal mechanism, and (5) specifying the context in which the effect occurs—can considerably strengthen causal explanations.

Research designs that allow us to establish these criteria require careful planning, implementation, and analysis. Many times, researchers have to leave one or more of the criteria unmet and are left with some important doubts about the validity of their causal conclusions, or they may even avoid making any causal assertions.

Association

The first criterion for establishing a causal effect is an empirical (or observed) **association** (sometimes called a *correlation*) between the independent and dependent variables. They must vary together so when one goes up (or down), the other goes up (or down) at the same time. For example: When cigarette smoking goes up, so does lung cancer. The longer you stay in school, the more money you will make later in life. Single women are more likely to live in poverty than married women. When income goes up, so does overall health. In all of these cases, a change in an independent variable correlates, or is associated with, a change in a dependent variable. If there is no association, there cannot be a causal relationship. For instance, empirically there seems to be no correlation between the use of the death penalty and a reduction in the rate of serious crime. That may seem unlikely to you, but empirically it is the case: There is no correlation. So there cannot be a causal relationship.

Time Order

Association is necessary for establishing a causal effect, but it is not sufficient. We must also ensure that the variation in the independent variable came before variation in the dependent variable—the cause must come before its presumed effect. This is the criterion of **time order,** or the temporal priority of the independent variable. Motivational speakers sometimes say that to achieve success (the dependent variable in our terms), you need to really believe in yourself (the independent variable). And it is true that many very successful politicians, actors, and businesspeople seem remarkably confident—there is an association. But it may well be that their confidence is the result of their success, not its cause. Until you know which came first, you can't establish a causal connection.

Nonspuriousness

The third criterion for establishing a causal effect is **nonspuriousness.** *Spurious* means false or not genuine. We say that a relationship between two variables is **spurious** when it is actually due to changes in a third variable, so what appears to be a direct connection is in fact not one. Have you heard the old adage "Correlation does not prove causation"? It is meant to remind us that an association between two variables might be caused by something else. If we measure children's shoe sizes and their academic knowledge, for example, we will find a positive association. However, the association results from the fact that older children have larger feet as well as more academic knowledge; a third variable (age) is affecting both shoe size and knowledge, so that they correlate. But one doesn't cause the other. Shoe size does not cause knowledge, or vice versa. The association between the two is, we say, spurious.

If this point seems obvious, consider a social science example. Do schools with better resources produce better students? There is certainly a correlation, but consider the fact that parents with more education and higher income tend to live in neighborhoods that spend more on their schools. These parents are also more likely to have books in the home and to provide other advantages for their children (see Exhibit 5.1). Maybe parents' income causes variation in both school resources and student performance. If so, there would be an association between school resources and student performance, but it would be at least partially spurious. What we want, then, is *non*spuriousness.

Mechanism

A causal **mechanism** is the process that creates the connection between the variation in an independent variable and the variation in the dependent variable that it is hypothesized to cause (Cook & Campbell, 1979:35; Marini & Singer, 1988). Many social scientists (and scientists in other fields) argue that no causal explanation is adequate until a mechanism is identified.

For instance, there seems to be an empirical association at the individual level between poverty and delinquency: Children who live in impoverished homes seem

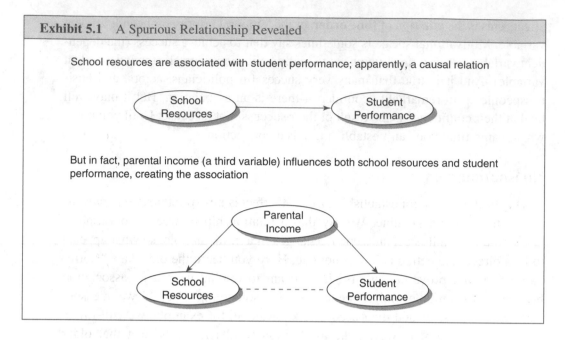

Exhibit 5.1   A Spurious Relationship Revealed

School resources are associated with student performance; apparently, a causal relation

School Resources → Student Performance

But in fact, parental income (a third variable) influences both school resources and student performance, creating the association

Parental Income

School Resources - - - - - Student Performance

more likely to be involved in petty crime. But why? Some researchers have argued for a *mechanism* of low parent/child attachment, inadequate supervision of children, and erratic discipline as the means by which poverty and delinquency are connected (Sampson & Laub, 1994). In this way, figuring out some aspects of the process by which the independent variable influenced the variation in the dependent variable can increase confidence in our conclusion that there was a causal effect (Costner, 1989).

Context

No cause has its effect apart from some larger **context** involving other variables. When, for whom, and in what conditions does this effect occur? A cause is really one among a set of interrelated factors required for the effect (Hage & Meeker, 1988; Papineau, 1978). Identification of the context in which a causal effect occurs is not itself a criterion for a valid causal conclusion, and it is not always attempted; but it does help us to understand the causal relationship.

You may hypothesize, for example, that if you offer employees higher wages to work harder, they will indeed work harder; and in the context of America, this seems to indeed be the case. Incentive pay causes harder work. But in noncapitalist societies, workers often want only enough money to meet their basic needs and would rather work less than drive themselves hard just to have more money.

In America, the correlation of incentive pay with greater effort seems to work; in medieval Europe, for instance, it did not (Weber, 1992).

As another example, in America in the 1960s, children of divorced parents ("from a broken home") were more likely to suffer from a variety of problems; they lived in a context of mostly intact families. In 2006, many parents are divorced, and the causal link between divorced parents and social pathology no longer seems to hold (Coontz, 1997).

WHY EXPERIMENT?

Experimental research provides the most powerful design for testing causal hypotheses because it allows us to confidently establish the first three criteria for causality—association, time order, and nonspuriousness. **True experiments** have at least three features that help us meet these criteria:

1. Two comparison groups (in the simplest case, an experimental group and a control group), to establish association

2. Variation in the independent variable before assessment of change in the dependent variable, to establish time order

3. Random assignment to the two (or more) comparison groups, to establish nonspuriousness

We can determine whether an association exists between the independent and dependent variables in a true experiment because two or more groups differ in terms of their value on the independent variable. One group receives some "treatment" that is a manipulation of the value of the independent variable. This group is termed the **experimental group.** In a simple experiment, there may be one other group that does not receive the treatment; it is termed the **control group.**

Experimental group: In an experiment, the group of subjects that receives the treatment or experimental manipulation.

Control group: A comparison group that receives no treatment.

Consider an example in detail (see the simple diagram in Exhibit 5.2). Does drinking coffee improve one's writing of an essay? Imagine a simple experiment. Suppose you believe that drinking two cups of strong coffee before class will help you in writing an in-class essay. But other people think that coffee makes them too nervous and "wired" and so doesn't help in writing the essay. To test your hypothesis ("coffee drinking causes improved performance"), you need to

Exhibit 5.2 A True Experiment

Experimental Group:	R O_1	X	O_2
Comparison Group:	R O_1		O_2

Key: R = Random assignment
O = Observation (pretest [O_1] or posttest [O_2])
X = Experimental treatment

	O_1	X	O_2
Experimental Group	Pretest Essay	Coffee	Posttest Essay
Comparison Group	Pretest Essay		Posttest Essay

compare two groups of subjects, a control group and an experimental group. First, the two groups will sit and write an in-class essay. Then, the control group will drink no coffee while the experimental group will drink two cups of strong coffee. Next, both groups will sit and write another in-class essay. At the end, all of the essays will be graded and you will see which group improved more. Thus, you may establish *association.*

You may find an association outside the experimental setting, of course, but it won't establish time order. Perhaps good writers hang out in cafés and coffee houses, and then start drinking lots of coffee. So there would be an association, but not the causal relation we're looking for. By controlling who gets the coffee, and when, we establish *time order.*

All true experiments have a **posttest**—that is, a measurement of the outcome in both groups after the experimental group has received the treatment. In our example, you grade the papers. Many true experiments also have **pretests** that measure the dependent variable before the experimental intervention. A pretest is exactly the same as a posttest, just administered at a different time. Strictly speaking, though, a true experiment does not require a pretest. When researchers use random assignment, the groups' initial scores on the dependent variable and on all other variables are very likely to be similar. Any difference in outcome between the experimental and comparison groups is therefore likely to be due to the intervention (or to other processes occurring during the experiment), and the likelihood of a difference just on the basis of chance can be calculated.

Finally, it is crucial that the two groups be more or less equal at the beginning of the study. If you let students choose which group to be in, the more ambitious students may pick the coffee group, hoping to stay awake and do better on the paper. Or people who simply don't like the taste of coffee may choose the non-coffee group. Either way, your two groups won't be equivalent at the beginning of the study, and so any difference in their writing may be the result of that initial difference (a source of spuriousness), not the drinking of coffee.

So you randomly sort the students into the two different groups. You can do this by flipping a coin for each one of them, or by pulling names out of a hat, or by using a random number table as described in the previous chapter. In any case, the subjects themselves should not be free to choose, nor should you (the experimenter) be free to put them into whatever group you want. (If you did that, you might unconsciously put the better students into the coffee group, hoping to get the results you're looking for.) Thus we hope to achieve nonspuriousness.

Note that the random assignment of subjects to experimental and comparison groups is not the same as random sampling of individuals from some larger population (see Exhibit 5.3). In fact, **random assignment (randomization)** does not help at all to ensure that the research subjects are representative of some larger population; instead, representativeness is the goal of random sampling. What random assignment does—create two (or more) equivalent groups—is useful for ensuring internal validity, not generalizability.

Matching is another procedure sometimes used to equate experimental and comparison groups, but by itself it is a poor substitute for randomization. Matching of individuals in a treatment group with those in a comparison group might involve pairing persons on the basis of similarity of gender, age, year in school, or some other characteristic. The basic problem is that, as a practical matter, individuals can be matched on only a few characteristics; unmatched differences between the experimental and comparison groups may still influence outcomes.

These defining features of true experimental designs give us a great deal of confidence that we can meet the three basic criteria for identifying causes: association, time order, and nonspuriousness. However, we can strengthen our understanding of causal connections, and increase the likelihood of drawing causally valid conclusions, by also investigating causal mechanism and causal context.

WHAT IF A TRUE EXPERIMENT ISN'T POSSIBLE?

Often, testing a hypothesis with a true experimental design is not feasible. A true experiment may be too costly or take too long to carry out; it may not be ethical to randomly assign subjects to the different conditions; or it may be too late to do

Exhibit 5.3   Random Sampling Versus Random Assignment

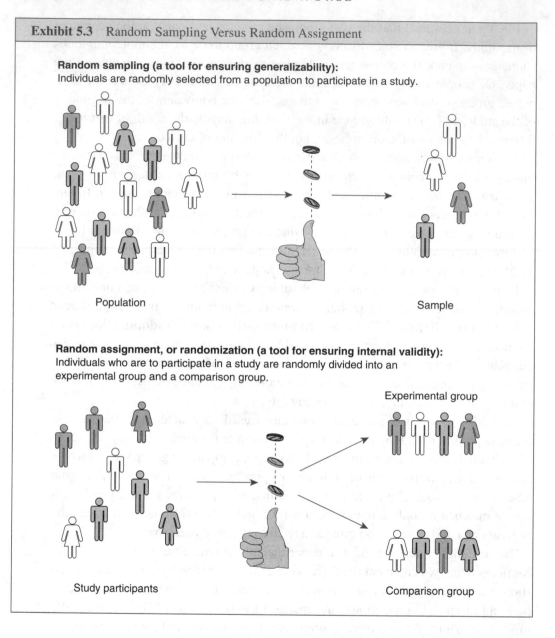

Random sampling (a tool for ensuring generalizability):
Individuals are randomly selected from a population to participate in a study.

Population   Sample

Random assignment, or randomization (a tool for ensuring internal validity):
Individuals who are to participate in a study are randomly divided into an
experimental group and a comparison group.

Experimental group

Study participants   Comparison group

so. Researchers may instead use "quasi-experimental" designs that retain several
components of experimental design but differ in important details.

In **quasi-experimental design**, a comparison group is predetermined to be
comparable to the treatment group in critical ways, such as being eligible for the
same services or being in the same school cohort (Rossi & Freeman, 1989:313).
These research designs are only "quasi"-experimental because subjects are not

randomly assigned to the comparison and experimental groups. As a result, we cannot be as confident in the comparability of the groups as in true experimental designs. Nonetheless, in order to term a research design quasi-experimental, we have to be sure that the comparison groups meet specific criteria.

We will discuss here the two major types of quasi-experimental designs, as well as one type—ex post facto (after the fact) control group design—that is often mistakenly termed quasi-experimental (other types can be found in Cook & Campbell, 1979, and Mohr, 1992):

- *Nonequivalent control group designs*—**Nonequivalent control group designs** have experimental and comparison groups that are designated before the treatment occurs but are not created by random assignment.
- *Before-and-after designs*—**Before-and-after designs** have a pretest and posttest but no comparison group. In other words, the subjects exposed to the treatment serve, at an earlier time, as their own control group.
- *Ex post facto control group designs*—These designs use nonrandomized control groups designated after the fact.

Exhibit 5.4 diagrams one study using the ex post facto control group design and another study using the multiple group before-and-after design, one type of before-and-after design. (The diagram for an ex post facto control group design is the same as for a nonequivalent control group design, but the two types of experiment differ in how people are able to join the groups.)

If quasi-experimental designs are longitudinal, they can establish time order. Where these designs are weaker than true experiments is in establishing the nonspuriousness of an observed association—that it does not result from the influence of some third, uncontrolled variable. On the other hand, because these quasi-experiments do not require the high degree of control necessary in order to achieve random assignment, quasi-experimental designs can be conducted using more natural procedures in more natural settings, so we may be able to achieve a more complete understanding of causal context. In identifying the mechanism of a causal effect, though, quasi-experiments are neither better nor worse than experiments.

Nonequivalent Control Group Designs

In this type of quasi-experimental design, a comparison group is selected so as to be as comparable as possible to the treatment group. Two selection methods can be used:

Individual matching—Individual cases in the treatment group are matched with similar individuals in the comparison group. This can sometimes create a comparison

Exhibit 5.4 Quasi-Experimental Designs

Nonequivalent control group design:

Experimental group:		O_1	X_a	O_2
Comparison group 1:		O_1	X_b	O_2
Comparison group 2:		O_1	X_c	O_2
		Pretest	*Treatment*	*Posttest*
Team Interdependence	Group	Team performance	Independent tasks	Team performance
	Hybrid	Team performance	Mixed tasks	Team performance
	Individual	Team performance	Individual tasks	Team performance

Before-and-after design:
Soap-opera suicide and actual suicide (Phillips, 1982)

Experimental group:	O_{11}	X_1	O_{21}
	O_{12}	X_2	O_{22}
	O_{13}	X_3	O_{23}
	O_{14}	X_4	O_{24}
	Pretest	*Treatment*	*Posttest*
	Suicide rate	Soap-opera suicides	Suicide rate

Key: O = Observation (pretest or posttest)
   X = Experimental treatment

Source: Ruth Wageman, 1995. "Interdependence and Group Effectiveness." *Administrative Science Quarterly,* *40:*145–180. Reprinted with permission.

group that is very similar to the experimental group, such as when Head Start participants were matched with their siblings to estimate the effect of participation in Head Start. However, in many studies it may not be possible to match on the most important variables.

Aggregate matching—In most situations when random assignment is not possible, the second method of matching makes more sense: identifying a comparison group that matches the treatment group in the aggregate rather than trying to match individual cases. This means finding a comparison group that has similar distributions on key variables: the same average age, the same percentage female, and so on. For this design to be considered quasi-experimental, however, it is important that individuals must themselves have chosen to be in the treatment group or the control group.

Nonequivalent control group designs allow you to determine whether an association exists between the presumed cause and effect.

Before-and-After Designs

The common feature of before-and-after designs is the absence of a comparison group: All cases are exposed to the experimental treatment. The basis for comparison is instead provided by the pretreatment measures in the experimental group. These designs are thus useful for studies of interventions that are experienced by virtually every case in some population, such as total coverage programs like Social Security or single-organization studies of the effect of a new management strategy.

The simplest type of before-and-after design is the fixed-sample panel design. As you may recall from Chapter 2, in a panel design the same individuals are studied over time, the research may entail one pretest and one posttest. However, this type of before-and-after design does not qualify as a quasi-experimental design because comparing subjects to themselves at just one earlier point in time does not provide an adequate comparison group. Many influences other than the experimental treatment may affect a subject following the pretest—for instance, basic life experiences for a young subject.

David P. Phillips's (1982) study of the effect of TV soap-opera suicides on the number of actual suicides in the United States illustrates a more powerful **multiple group before-and-after design.** In this design, before-and-after comparisons are made of the same variables between different groups. Phillips identified 13 soap-opera suicides in 1977 and then recorded the U.S. suicide rate in the weeks prior to and following each TV story. In effect, the researcher had 13 different before-and-after studies, one for each suicide story. In 12 of these 13 comparisons, deaths due to suicide increased from the week before each soap-opera suicide to the week after (see Exhibit 5.5). Phillips also found similar increases in motor-vehicle deaths and crashes during the same period, some portion of which reflects covert suicide attempts. (Despite his clever design, however, some prominent researchers have disputed his findings.)

Another type of before-and-after design involves multiple pretest and posttest observations of the same group. **Repeated measures panel designs** include several pretest and posttest observations, allowing the researcher to study the process by which an intervention or treatment has an impact over time; hence, they are better than a simple before-and-after study.

Time series designs include many (preferably 30 or more) such observations in both pretest and posttest periods. They are particularly useful for studying the impact of new laws or social programs that affect large numbers of people and that are readily assessed by some ongoing measurement. For example, we might use a time series design to study the impact of a new seat-belt law on the severity of injuries in

Exhibit 5.5   Real Suicides and Soap-Opera Suicides

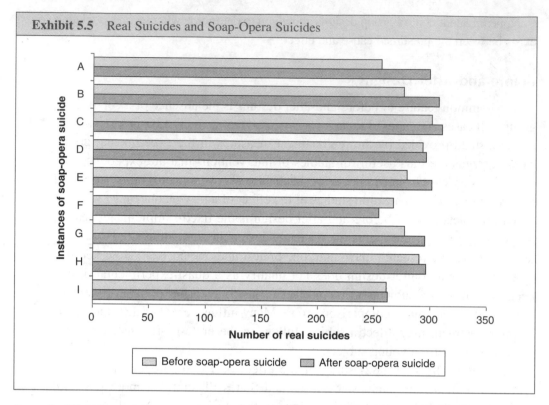

Source: David P. Phillips, 1982. "The Impact of Fictional Television Stories on U.S. Adult Fatalities: New Evidence on the Effect of the Mass Media on Violence." *American Journal of Sociology, 87* (May 1982):1340. Copyright © 1982 by the University of Chicago Press. Reprinted with permission.

automobile accidents, using a monthly state government report on insurance claims. Special statistics are required to analyze time series data, but the basic idea is simple: identify a trend in the dependent variable up to the date of the intervention, then project the trend into the postintervention period. This *projected* trend is then compared to the *actual* trend of the dependent variable after the intervention. A substantial disparity between the actual and projected trends is evidence that the intervention or event had an impact (Rossi & Freeman, 1989:260–261, 358–363).

How well do these before-and-after designs meet the five criteria for establishing causality? The before-after comparison enables us to determine whether an *association* exists between the intervention and the dependent variable (because we can determine whether there was a change after the intervention). They also clarify whether the change in the dependent variable occurred after the intervention, so *time order* is not a problem. However, there is no control group so we cannot rule out the influence of extraneous factors as the actual cause of the change we observe; *spuriousness* may be a problem. Some other event may have occurred during the study that resulted in a change in posttest scores. Overall, the longitudinal nature of before-and-after designs can help to identify causal mechanisms, while the loosening of randomization requirements makes it easier to conduct studies in natural settings, where we learn about the influence of contextual factors.

Ex Post Facto Control Group Designs

The **ex post facto control group design** appears to be very similar to the nonequivalent control group design and is often confused with it, but it does not meet as well the criteria for quasi-experimental designs. Like nonequivalent control group designs, this design has experimental and comparison groups that are not created by random assignment. But unlike the groups in nonequivalent control group designs, the groups in ex post facto designs are designated after the treatment has occurred. The problem with this is that if the treatment takes any time at all, people with particular characteristics may select themselves for the treatment or avoid it. Of course, this makes it difficult to determine whether an association between group membership and outcome is spurious. However, the particulars will vary from study to study; in some circumstances we may conclude that the treatment and control groups are so similar that causal effects can be tested (Rossi & Freeman, 1989:343–344).

Susan Cohen and Gerald Ledford's (1994) study of the effectiveness of self-managing teams used a well-constructed ex post facto design. They studied a telecommunications company with some work teams that were self-managing and some that were traditionally managed (meaning that a manager was responsible for the team's decisions). Cohen and Ledford found the self-reported quality of work life to be higher in the self-managing groups than in the traditionally managed groups.

WHAT ARE THE THREATS TO VALIDITY IN EXPERIMENTS?

Experimental designs, like any research design, must be evaluated for their ability to yield valid conclusions. Remember, there are three kinds of validity: internal (or causal), external (or generalizability), and measurement. True experiments are good at producing internal validity, but they fare less well in achieving external validity (generalizability). Quasi-experiments may provide more generalizable results than true experiments but are more prone to problems of internal invalidity. Measurement validity is also a central concern for both kinds of research, but even true experimental design offers no special advantages or disadvantages in measurement.

In general, nonexperimental designs such as those used in survey research and field research offer less certainty of internal validity, a greater likelihood of generalizability, and no particular advantage or disadvantage in terms of measurement

Exhibit 5.6   Threats to Internal Validity

Problem	Example	Type
Selection	Girls who choose to see a therapist are not representative of population.	Noncomparable Groups
Mortality	Students who most dislike college drop out, so aren't surveyed.	Noncomparable Groups
Instrument Decay	Interviewer tires losing interest in later interviews, so poor answers.	Noncomparable Groups
Testing	If someone has taken the SAT before, they are familiar with the format, so do better.	Endogenous Change
Maturation	Everyone gets older in high school; it's not the school's doing.	Endogenous Change
Regression	The lowest-ranking students on IQ must improve their rank; they can't do worse.	Endogenous Change
History	The O.J. Simpson trial affects members of diversity workshops.	History
Contamination	"John Henry" effect; people in study compete with one another.	Contamination
Experimenter Expectation	Researchers unconsciously help their subjects, distorting results.	Treatment Misidentification
Placebo Effect	Fake pills in medical studies produce improved health.	Treatment Misidentification
Hawthorne Effect	Workers enjoy being subjects and work harder.	Treatment Misidentification

validity. We will introduce survey and field research designs in the following chapters; in this section we focus on the ways in which experiments help (or don't help) to resolve potential problems of internal validity and generalizability.

Threats to Internal Causal Validity

The following sections discuss 10 threats to validity (also referred to as "sources of invalidity") that occur frequently in social science research (see Exhibit 5.7). These "threats" exemplify five major types of problems that arise in research design.

Noncomparable Groups

The problem of noncomparable groups occurs when the experimental group and the control group are not really comparable—that is, when something interferes with the two groups being essentially the same at the beginning (or end) of a study.

- *Selection bias*—Occurs when the subjects in your groups are initially different. If the ambitious students decide to be in the "coffee" group, you'll think their performance was helped by coffee—but it could have been their ambition.

Everyday examples of selection bias are everywhere. Harvard graduates are very successful people; but Harvard *admits* students who are likely to be successful anyway. Maybe Harvard itself had no effect on them. A few years ago, a psychotherapist named Mary Pipher wrote a bestseller called *Reviving Ophelia* (1994), in which she described the difficult lives of—as she saw it—typical adolescent girls. Pipher painted a stark picture of depression, rampant eating disorders, low self-esteem, academic failure, suicidal thoughts, and even suicide itself. Where did she get this picture? From her patients—that is, from adolescent girls who were in deep despair, or at least were unhappy enough to seek help. If Pipher had talked with a comparison sample of girls who hadn't sought help, perhaps the story would not have been so bleak.

In the Sherman and Berk (1984) domestic violence experiment in Minneapolis, some police officers sometimes violated the random assignment plan when they thought the circumstances warranted arresting a suspect who had been randomly assigned to receive just a warning; thus, they created a selection bias in the experimental group.

- *Mortality*—Even when random assignment works as planned, the groups can become different over time because of **mortality, or differential attrition;** this can also be called "deselection." That is, the groups become different because subjects are more likely to drop out of one of the groups for various reasons. At some colleges, satisfaction surveys show that seniors are more likely to rate their colleges positively than are freshmen. But remember that the freshmen who really hated the place may have transferred out, so *their* ratings aren't included with senior ratings. In effect, the lowest scores are removed; that's a mortality problem. This is not a likely problem in a laboratory experiment that occurs in one session, but some laboratory experiments occur over time, and so differential attrition can become a problem. Subjects who experience the experimental condition may become more motivated to continue in the experiment than comparison subjects.

Note that whenever subjects are not assigned randomly to treatment and comparison groups, the threat of selection bias or mortality is very great. Even if the comparison group matches the treatment group on important variables, there is no guarantee that the groups were similar initially in terms of either the dependent variable or some other characteristic. However, a pretest helps the researchers to determine and control for selection bias.

- *Instrument Decay*—Measurement instruments of all sorts wear out, producing different results for cases studied later in the research. An ordinary spring-operated bathroom scales, for instance, becomes "soggy" after some years, showing slightly heavier weights than would be correct. Or a college teacher—a kind of instrument for measuring student performance—gets tired after reading too many papers one weekend and starts giving everyone a B. Research interviewers can get tired or bored, too, leading perhaps to shorter or less thoughtful answers from subjects. In all these cases, the measurement instrument has "decayed," or worn out.

Endogenous Change

The next three problems, subsumed under the label **endogenous change,** occur when natural developments in the subjects, independent of the experimental treatment itself, account for some or all of the observed change between pretest and posttest.

- *Testing*—Taking the pretest can itself influence posttest scores. As the Kaplan SAT prep courses attest, there is some benefit to just getting used to the test format. Having taken the test beforehand can be an advantage. Subjects may learn something or may be sensitized to an issue by the pretest and, as a result, respond differently the next time they are asked the same questions, on the posttest.
- *Maturation*—Changes in outcome scores during experiments that involve a lengthy treatment period may be due to maturation. Subjects may age, gain experience, or grow in knowledge—all as part of a natural maturational experience—and thus respond differently on the posttest than on the pretest. In many high school yearbooks, seniors are quoted as saying, for instance, "I started at West Geneva High as a boy and leave as a man. WGHS made me grow up." Well, he probably would have grown up anyway, high school or not. WGHS wasn't the cause.
- *Regression*—Subjects who are chosen for a study because they received very low scores on a test may show improvement in the posttest, on average, simply because some of the low scorers were having a bad day. Whenever

subjects are selected for study because of extreme scores (either very high or very low), the next time you take their scores they will likely "regress," or move toward the average. For instance, suppose you give an IQ test to third graders and then pull the bottom 20% of the class out for special attention. The next time that group (the 20%) takes the test, they'll almost certainly do better—and not just because of testing practice. In effect, they *can't* do worse—they were at the bottom already. On average, they must do better. A football team that goes 0–12 one season almost has to improve. A first-time novelist writes a wonderful book, and gains worldwide acclaim and a host of prizes. The next book is not so good, and critics say "The praise went to her head." But it didn't; she *couldn't* have done better. Whenever you pick people for being on an extreme end of a scale, odds are that next time they'll be more average. This is called **regression.**

Regression effects: A source of causal validity that occurs when subjects who are chosen for a study because of their extreme scores on the dependent variable become less extreme on the posttest due to natural cyclical or episodic change in the variable.

Testing, maturation, and regression effects are generally not a problem in experiments that have a control group because they would affect the experimental group and the comparison group equally. However, these effects could explain any change over time in most before-and-after designs, because these designs do not have a comparison group. Repeated measures, panel studies, and time series designs are better in this regard because they allow the researcher to trace the pattern of change or stability in the dependent variable up to and after the treatment. Ongoing effects of maturation and regression can thus be identified and taken into account.

History

History, or **external events** during the experiment (things that happen outside the experiment), could change subjects' outcome scores. Examples are newsworthy events that have to do with the focus of an experiment and major disasters to which subjects are exposed. If you were running a series of diversity workshops for some insurance company employees while the O. J. Simpson trial was taking place, for instance, participants' thoughts on race relations at the end of the workshops may say less about you than about O. J. Simpson, or about their own relationship with the judicial system. This problem is often referred to as a **history effect**—history during the experiment, that is. It is a particular concern in before-and-after designs.

Causal conclusions can be invalid in some true experiments because of the influence of external events. For example, in an experiment in which subjects go to a special location for the treatment, something at that location unrelated to the treatment could influence these subjects. External events are a major concern in studies that compare the effects of programs in different cities or states (Hunt, 1985:276–277).

Contamination

Contamination occurs in an experiment when the comparison and treatment groups somehow affect each other. When comparison group members know they are being compared, they may increase their efforts just to be more competitive. This has been termed **compensatory rivalry,** or the **John Henry effect,** named after the "steel driving man" of the folk song, who raced against a steam drill in driving railroad spikes and killed himself in the process. Knowing that they are being denied some advantage, comparison group subjects may as a result increase their efforts to compensate. On the other hand, comparison group members may become demoralized if they feel that they have been left out of some valuable treatment and may perform worse than expected as a result. Both compensatory rivalry and demoralization thus distort the impact of the experimental treatment.

The danger of contamination can be minimized if the experiment is conducted in a laboratory, if members of the experimental group and the comparison group have no contact while the study is in progress, and if the treatment is relatively brief. Whenever these conditions are not met, the likelihood of contamination increases.

Treatment Misidentification

Sometimes the subjects experience a "treatment" that wasn't intended by the researcher. The following are three possible sources of **treatment misidentification:**

Expectancies of experiment staff—Change among experimental subjects may be due to the positive expectancies of the experiment staff who are delivering the treatment rather than to the treatment itself. Even well-trained staff may convey their enthusiasm for an experimental program to the subjects in subtle ways. This is a special concern in evaluation research when program staff and researchers may be biased in favor of the program for which they work and are eager to believe that their work is helping clients. Such positive staff expectations thus create a **self-fulfilling prophecy.** However, in experiments on the effects of treatments such as medical drugs, **double-blind procedures** can be used: Staff delivering the treatments do not know which subjects are getting the treatment and which are receiving a placebo—something that looks like the treatment but has no effect.

Placebo effect—In medicine, a *placebo* is a chemically inert substance (a sugar pill, for instance) that looks like a drug but actually has no direct physical effect. Research shows that such a pill can actually produce positive health effects in two-thirds of patients suffering from relatively mild medical problems (Goleman, 1993:C3). In other words, if you wish that a pill will help, it often actually does.

In social science research, such ***placebo effects*** occur when subjects think their behavior should improve through an experimental treatment and then it does—not from the treatment, but from their own belief. Researchers might then misidentify the treatment as having produced the effect.

Hawthorne effect—Members of the treatment group may change in terms of the dependent variable because their participation in the study makes them feel special. This problem could occur when treatment group members compare their situation to that of members of the control group who are not receiving the treatment, in which case it would be a type of contamination effect. But experimental group members could feel special simply because they are in the experiment. This is termed a **Hawthorne effect,** after a famous productivity experiment at the Hawthorne electric plant outside Chicago. No matter what conditions the researchers changed in order to improve or diminish productivity (for instance, increasing or decreasing the lighting in the plant), the workers seemed to work harder simply because they were part of a special experiment. Oddly enough, some more recent scholars suggest that in the original Hawthorne studies there was actually a selection bias, not a true Hawthorne effect—but the term has stuck (see Bramel & Friend, 1981). Hawthorne effects are also a concern in evaluation research, particularly when program clients know that the research findings may affect the chances for further program funding.

Process analysis is a technique for avoiding treatment misidentification (Hunt, 1985:272–274). Periodic measures are taken throughout an experiment to assess whether the treatment is being delivered as planned. For example, Drake et al. (1996) collected process data to monitor the implementation of two employment service models that they tested. One site did a poorer job of implementing the individual placement and support model than the other site, although the required differences between the experimental conditions were still achieved. Process analysis is often a special focus in evaluation research because of the possibility of improper implementation of the experimental program.

Generalizability

The need for generalizable findings can be thought of as the Achilles heel of true experimental design. The design components that are essential for a true experiment and that minimize the threats to causal validity make it more difficult to achieve sample generalizability—being able to apply the findings to some clearly defined larger population—and cross-population generalizability—generalizing across subgroups and to other populations and settings.

Sample Generalizability

Subjects who can be recruited for a laboratory experiment, randomly assigned to a group, and kept under carefully controlled conditions for the duration of the study are unlikely to be a representative sample of any large population of interest to social scientists. Can they be expected to react to the experimental treatment in the same way as members of the larger population? The generalizability of the treatment and of the setting for the experiment also must be considered (Cook & Campbell, 1979:73–74). The more artificial the experimental arrangements, the greater the problem (Campbell & Stanley, 1966:20–21).

In some limited circumstances, a researcher may be able to sample subjects randomly for participation in an experiment and thus select a generalizable sample—one that is representative of the population from which it is selected. This approach is occasionally possible in **field experiments.** For example, some studies of the effects of income supports on the work behavior of poor persons have randomly sampled persons within particular states before randomly assigning them to experimental and comparison groups. Sherman and Berk's (1984) field experiment about the impact of arrest in actual domestic violence incidents (see Chapter 2) used a slightly different approach. In this study, all eligible cases were treated as subjects in the experiment during the data collection periods. As a result, we can place a good deal of confidence in the generalizability of the results to the population of domestic violence arrest cases in Minneapolis.

Cross-Population Generalizability

Researchers often are interested in determining whether treatment effects identified in an experiment hold true across different populations, times, or settings. When random selection is not feasible, the researchers may be able to increase the cross-population generalizability of their findings by selecting several different experimental sites that offer marked contrasts on key variables (Cook & Campbell, 1979:76–77).

Within a single experiment, researchers also may be concerned with whether the relationship between the treatment and the outcome variable holds true for certain subgroups. This demonstration of "external validity" is important evidence about the conditions that are required for the independent variable(s) to have an effect. Price, Van Ryn, and Vinokur (1992) found that intensive job-search assistance reduced depression among individuals who were at high risk for it because of other psychosocial characteristics; however, the intervention did not influence the rate of depression among individuals at low risk for depression. This is an important limitation on the generalizability of the findings, even if the sample taken by Price et al. was representative of the population of unemployed persons.

Finding that effects are consistent across subgroups does not establish that the relationship also holds true for these subgroups in the larger population, but it does provide supportive evidence. We have already seen examples of how the existence of treatment effects in particular subgroups of experimental subjects can help us predict the cross-population generalizability of the findings. For example, Sherman and Berk's research (see Chapter 2) found that arrest did not deter subsequent domestic violence for unemployed individuals; arrest also failed to deter subsequent violence in communities with high levels of unemployment.

There is always an implicit tradeoff in experimental design between maximizing causal validity and generalizability. The more that assignment to treatments is randomized and all experimental conditions are controlled, the less likely it is that the research subjects and setting will be representative of the larger population. College students are easy to recruit and to assign to artificial but controlled manipulations, but both practical and ethical concerns preclude this approach with many groups and with respect to many treatments. However, although we need to be skeptical about the generalizability of the results of a single experimental test of a hypothesis, the body of findings accumulated from many experimental tests with different people in different settings can provide a very solid basis for generalization (Campbell & Russo, 1999:143).

Exhibit 5.7 Solomon Four-Group Design Testing the Interaction of Pretesting and Treatment				
Experimental group:	R	O_1	X	O_2
Comparison group:	R	O_1		O_2
Experimental group:	R		X	O_2
Comparison group:	R			O_2

Key: R = Random assignment
     O = Observation (pretest or posttest)
     X = Experimental treatment

Interaction of Testing and Treatment

A variant on the problem of external validity occurs when the experimental treatment has an effect only when particular conditions created by the experiment occur. One such problem occurs when the treatment has an effect only if subjects have had the pretest. The pretest sensitizes the subjects to some issue so that when they are exposed to the treatment, they react in a way they would not have reacted if they had not taken the pretest. In other words, testing and treatment interact to produce the outcome. For example, answering questions in a pretest about racial prejudice may sensitize subjects so that when they are exposed to the experimental treatment, seeing a film about prejudice, their attitudes are different from what they would have been. In this situation, the treatment truly had an effect, but it would not have had an effect if it were repeated without the sensitizing pretest. This possibility can be evaluated by using the Solomon Four-Group Design to compare groups with and without a pretest (see Exhibit 5.7). If testing and treatment do interact, the difference in outcome scores between the experimental and comparison groups will be different for subjects who took the pretest compared to those who did not.

As you can see, there is no single procedure that establishes the external validity of experimental results. Ultimately, we must base our evaluation of external validity on the success of replications taking place at different times and places and using different forms of the treatment.

HOW DO EXPERIMENTERS PROTECT THEIR SUBJECTS?

Social science experiments often involve subject deception. Primarily because of this feature, some experiments have prompted contentious debates about research ethics. Experimental evaluations of social programs also pose ethical dilemmas because they require researchers to withhold possibly beneficial treatment from some of the subjects just on the basis of chance. Such research may also yield sensitive information about program compliance, personal habits, and even illegal activity—information that is protected from legal subpoenas only in some research concerning mental illness or criminal activity (Boruch, 1997). In this section, we will give special attention to the problems of deception and the distribution of benefits in experimental research.

Deception

Deception occurs when subjects are misled about research procedures in order to determine how they would react to the treatment if they were not research subjects. Deception is a critical component of many social experiments, in part because of the difficulty of simulating real-world stresses and dilemmas in a laboratory setting. Stanley Milgram's (1965) classic study of obedience to authority provides a good example. Volunteers were recruited for what they were told was a study of the learning process. The experimenter told the volunteers they were to play the role of "teacher" and to administer an electric shock to a "student" in the next room when the student failed a memory test. The shocks were phony (and the students were actors), but the real subjects, the volunteers, didn't know this. They were told to increase the intensity of the shocks, even beyond what they were told was a lethal level. Many subjects continued to obey the authority in the study (the experimenter), even when their obedience involved administering what they thought were potentially lethal shocks to another person.

But did the experimental subjects actually believe that they were harming someone? Observational data suggest they did: "Persons were observed to sweat, tremble, stutter, bite their lips, and groan as they found themselves increasingly implicated in the experimental conflict" (Milgram 1965:66).

Verbatim transcripts of the sessions also indicated that participants were in much agony about administering the "shocks." So it seems that Milgram's deception "worked"; moreover, it seemed "necessary," since Milgram could not have administered real electric shocks to the students, nor would it have made sense for him to order the students to do something that wasn't so troubling, nor could he have explained what he was really interested in before conducting the experiment. The real question: Is this sufficient justification to allow the use of deception?

Aronson and Mills's study (1959) of severity of initiation (at an all-women's college in the 1950s) provides a very different example of the use of deception in experimental research—one that does not pose greater-than-everyday risks to subjects. The students who were randomly assigned to the "severe initiation" experimental condition had to read a list of embarrassing words. Even in the 1950s, reading a list of potentially embarrassing words in a laboratory setting and listening to a taped discussion were unlikely to increase the risks to which students were exposed in their everyday lives. Moreover, the researchers informed subjects that they would be expected to talk about sex and could decline to participate in the experiment if this requirement would bother them. No one dropped out.

To further ensure that no psychological harm was caused, Aronson and Mills (1959) explained the true nature of the experiment to the subjects after the experiment, in what is called **debriefing**. The subjects' reactions were typical:

> None of the Ss expressed any resentment or annoyance at having been misled. In fact, the majority were intrigued by the experiment, and several returned at the end of the academic quarter to ascertain the result. (1959:179)

Although the American Sociological Association's *Code of Ethics* does not discuss experimentation explicitly, one of its principles highlights the ethical dilemma posed by deceptive research:

(a) Sociologists do not use deceptive techniques (1) unless they have determined that their use will not be harmful to research participants; is justified by the study's prospective scientific, educational, or applied value; and that equally effective alternative procedures that do not use deception are not feasible, and (2) unless they have obtained the approval of institutional review boards or, in the absence of such boards, with another authoritative body with expertise on the ethics of research.

(b) Sociologists never deceive research participants about significant aspects of the research that would affect their willingness to participate, such as physical risks, discomfort, or unpleasant emotional experiences. (American Sociological Association, 1997:3)

Selective Distribution of Benefits

Field experiments conducted to evaluate social programs also can involve issues of informed consent (Hunt, 1985:275–276). One ethical issue that is somewhat unique to field experiments is the **distribution of benefits:** How much are subjects harmed by the way treatments are distributed in the experiment? For example, Sherman and Berk's (1974) experiment, and its successors, required police to make arrests in domestic violence cases largely on the basis of a random process. When arrests were not made, did the subjects' abused spouses suffer? Price et al. (1992) randomly assigned unemployed individuals who had volunteered for job-search help to an intensive program. Were the unemployed volunteers who were assigned to the comparison group at a big disadvantage?

Is it ethical to give some potentially advantageous or disadvantageous treatment to people on a random basis? Random distribution of benefits is justified when the researchers do not know whether some treatment actually is beneficial or not—and, of course, it is the goal of the experiment to find out. Chance is as reasonable a basis for distributing the treatment as any other. Also, if insufficient resources are available to fully fund a benefit for every eligible person, distribution of the benefit on the basis of chance to equally needy persons is ethically defensible (Boruch, 1997:66–67).

CONCLUSION

Causation and the means for achieving causally valid conclusions in research is the last of the three legs on which the validity of research rests. In this chapter, you have learned about the five criteria used to evaluate the extent to which particular research designs may achieve causally valid findings. You have been exposed to the problem of spuriousness and the way that randomization deals with it. You also have learned why we must take into account the units of analysis in a research design in order to come to appropriate causal conclusions.

True experiments help greatly to achieve more valid causal conclusions—they are the "gold standard" for testing causal hypotheses. Even when conditions preclude use of a true experimental design, many research designs can be improved by adding some experimental components. However, although it may be possible to test a hypothesis with an experiment, it is not always desirable to do so. Laboratory experiments may be inadvisable when they do not test the real hypothesis of interest but test instead a limited version that is amenable to laboratory manipulation. It also does not make sense to test the impact of social programs that cannot actually be implemented because of financial or political problems (Rossi & Freeman, 1989:304–307). Yet the virtues of experimental designs mean that they should always be considered when explanatory research is planned.

We emphasize that understandings of causal relationships are always partial. Researchers must always wonder whether they have omitted some relevant variables from their controls or whether their experimental results would differ if the experiment were conducted in another setting or at another time in history. But the tentative nature of causal conclusions means that we must give more—not less—attention to evaluating the causal validity of social science research whenever we need to ask the simple question, "What caused variation in this social phenomenon?"

KEY TERMS

Association
Before-and-after design
Causal effect
Ceteris paribus
Compensatory rivalry (John Henry effect)
Contamination
Context
Control group
Debriefing
Differential attrition (mortality)
Distribution of benefits
Double-blind procedure
Endogenous change
Evaluation research
Ex post facto control group design
Expectancies of experimental staff
Experimental group
External event
Field experiment
Hawthorne effect
History effect
Matching

Mechanism
Multiple group before-and-after design
Nonequivalent control group design
Nonspuriousness
Placebo effect
Posttest
Pretest
Process analysis
Quasi-experimental design
Random assignment
Randomization
Regression effects
Repeated cross-sectional design
Repeated measures panel design
Selection bias
Self-fulfilling prophecy
Spurious relationship
Time order
Time series design
Treatment misidentification
True experiment

HIGHLIGHTS

• Three criteria generally are viewed as necessary for identifying a causal relationship: association between the variables, proper time order, and nonspuriousness of the association. In addition, the basis for concluding that a causal relationship exists is strengthened by identification of a causal mechanism and the context.

• Association between two variables by itself is insufficient evidence of a causal relationship. This point is commonly made by the expression "Correlation does not prove causation."

• The independent variable in an experiment is represented by a treatment or other intervention. Some subjects receive one type of treatment; others may receive a different treatment or no treatment. In true experiments, subjects are assigned randomly to comparison groups.

• Experimental research designs have three essential components: use of at least two groups of subjects for comparison, measurement of the change that occurs as a result of the experimental treatment, and use of random assignment. In addition, experiments may include identification of a causal mechanism and control over experimental conditions.

• Random assignment of subjects to experimental and comparison groups eliminates systematic bias in group assignment. The odds of there being a difference between the experimental and comparison groups on the basis of chance can be calculated. They become very small for experiments with at least 30 subjects per group.

• Random assignment and random sampling both rely on a chance selection procedure, but their purposes differ. Random assignment involves placing predesignated subjects into two or more groups on the basis of chance; random sampling involves selecting subjects out of a larger population on the basis of chance. Matching of cases in the experimental and comparison groups is a poor substitute for randomization because identifying in advance all important variables on which to make the match is not possible. However, matching can improve the comparability of groups when it is used to supplement randomization.

• Ethical and practical constraints often preclude the use of experimental designs.

• Quasi-experimental designs can be either a nonequivalent control group design or a before-and-after design. Nonequivalent control groups can be created through either individual matching of subjects or matching of group characteristics. In either case, these designs can allow us to establish the existence of an association and the time order of effects, but they do not ensure that some unidentified extraneous variable did not cause what we think of as the effect of the independent variable. Before-and-after designs can involve one or more pretests and posttests. Although multiple pretests and posttests make it unlikely that another, extraneous influence caused the experimental effect, they do not guarantee it.

• Ex post facto control group designs involve a comparison group that individuals could decide to join precisely because they prefer this experience rather than what the experimental group offers. This creates differences in subject characteristics between the experimental and control groups that might very well result in a difference on the dependent variable. Because of this possibility, this type of design is not considered a quasi-experimental design.

- Invalid conclusions about causality may occur when relationships between variables measured at the group level are assumed to apply at the individual level (the ecological fallacy) and when relationships between variables measured at the level of individuals are assumed to apply at the group level (the reductionist fallacy). Nonetheless, many research questions point to relationships at multiple levels and may profitably be answered by studying different units of analysis.

- Causal conclusions derived from experiments can be invalid because of selection bias, endogenous change, the effects of external events, cross-group contamination, or treatment misidentification. In true experiments, randomization should eliminate selection bias and bias due to endogenous change. External events, cross-group contamination, and treatment misidentification can threaten the validity of causal conclusions in both true experiments and quasi-experiments.

- Process analysis can be used in experiments to identify how the treatment had (or didn't have) an effect—a matter of particular concern in field experiments. Treatment misidentification is less likely when process analysis is used.

- The generalizability of experimental results declines if the study conditions are artificial and the experimental subjects are unique. Field experiments are likely to produce more generalizable results than experiments conducted in the laboratory.

- The external validity of causal conclusions is determined by the extent to which they apply to different types of individuals and settings. When causal conclusions do not apply to all the subgroups in a study, they are not generalizable to corresponding subgroups in the population; consequently, they are not externally valid with respect to those subgroups. Causal conclusions can also be considered externally invalid when they occur only under the experimental conditions.

- Subject deception is common in laboratory experiments and poses unique ethical issues. Researchers must weigh the potential harm to subjects and debrief subjects who have been deceived. In field experiments, a common ethical problem is selective distribution of benefits. Random assignment may be the fairest way of allocating treatment when treatment openings are insufficient for all eligible individuals and when the efficacy of the treatment is unknown.

To assist you in completing the Web Exercises, please access the Study Site at http://www.pineforge.com/mssw2 where you'll find the Web Exercises with accompanying links. You'll find other useful study materials like self-quizzes and e-flashcards for each chapter, along with a group of carefully selected articles from research journals that illustrate the major concepts and techniques presented in the book.

EXERCISES

Discussing Research

1. Review articles in several newspapers, copying down all causal assertions. These might range from assertions that the stock market declined because of uncertainty in the Middle East to explanations about why a murder was committed or why test scores are declining in U.S. schools. Inspect the articles carefully, noting all evidence used to support the causal assertions. Which of the five criteria for establishing causality are met? What other potentially important influences on the reported outcome have been overlooked? Can you spot any potentially spurious relationships?

2. Select several research articles in professional journals that assert, or imply, that they have identified a causal relationship between two or more variables. Are each of the criteria for establishing the existence of a causal relationship met? Find a study in which subjects were assigned randomly to experimental and comparison groups to reduce the risk of spurious influences on the supposedly causal relationship. How convinced are you by the study?

3. The practice CD-ROM contains lessons on units of analysis. Choose the Units of Analysis lesson from the main menu. It describes several research projects and asks you to identify the units of analysis in each.

4. The National Institutes of Health provides a tutorial for learning about current ethical standards in research. Complete this tutorial at http://cme.nci.nih.gov/intro.htm. Be prepared to spend one-half to one hour completing the tutorial. You must register as a college student and provide a bit of other information. Indicate that you do not need a certificate of completion. After you complete the registration fields, begin with the section on History. In this section, you will find a subsection on "The Development of Codes of Research Ethics." When you get to the heading in this subsection on the "Belmont Report," you will find a link to the federal "Common Rule" document. Click on this link and take the time to print the document out and read it. When you are finished with the tutorial and have read the Common Rule, you will be well on your way to becoming an expert on human subjects regulations. Identify the human subjects rules that are most important for research on human subjects.

Finding Research

1. Read an original article describing a social experiment. (Social psychology "readers," collections of such articles for undergraduates, are a good place to find interesting studies.) Critique the article, using as your guide the article review questions presented in Exhibit 10.2. Focus on the extent to which experimental conditions were controlled and the causal mechanism was identified. Did inadequate control over conditions or inadequate identification of the causal mechanism make you feel uncertain about the causal conclusions?

2. Go to the Web site of the Community Policing Consortium at www.communitypolicing .org/about2.html. What causal assertions are made? Pick one of these assertions and propose a research design with which to test this assertion. Be specific.

3. Go to Sociosite at www.pscw.uva.nl/sociosite. Choose "Subject Areas." Choose a sociological subject area you are interested in. Find an example of research that has been

done using experimental methods in this subject. Explain the experiment. Choose at least five of the Key Terms listed at the end of this chapter that are relevant to and incorporated in the research experiment you have located on the Internet. Explain how each of the five Key Terms you have chosen plays a role in the research example you found on the Web.

Critiquing Research

1. From newspapers or magazines, find two recent studies of education (reading, testing, etc.). For each study, list in order what you see as the most likely sources of internal invalidity (e.g., selection, mortality, etc.).

2. Select a true experiment, perhaps from the *Journal of Experimental and Social Psychology,* the *Journal of Personality and Social Psychology*, or sources suggested in class. Diagram the experiment using the exhibits in this chapter as a model. Discuss the extent to which experimental conditions were controlled and the causal mechanism was identified. How confident can you be in the causal conclusions from the study, based on review of the threats to internal validity discussed in this chapter: selection bias, endogenous change, external events, contamination, and treatment misidentification? How generalizable do you think the study's results are to the population from which the cases were selected? To specific subgroups in the study? How thoroughly do the researchers discuss these issues?

3. Repeat the previous exercise with a quasi-experiment.

4. Critique the ethics of one of the experiments presented in this chapter, or some other experiment you have read about. What specific rules do you think should guide researchers' decisions about subject deception and the selective distribution of benefits?

Doing Research

1. Try out the process of randomization. Go to the Web site www.randomizer.org. Now just type numbers into the randomizer for an experiment with two groups and 20 individuals per group. Repeat the process for an experiment with four groups and 10 individuals per group. Plot the numbers corresponding to each individual in each group. Does the distribution of numbers within each group truly seem to be random?

2. Participate in a social psychology experiment on the Internet. Go to www.social psychology.org/expts.htm. Pick an experiment in which to participate and follow the instructions. After you finish, write a description of the experiment and evaluate it using the criteria discussed in the chapter.

3. Volunteer for an experiment. Contact the psychology department and ask about opportunities for participating in laboratory experiments. Discuss the experience with your classmates.

Chapter 6

Survey Research

Some six months after the September 11, 2001, attacks on the World Trade Center and the Pentagon, a small group of students at Hamilton College and their professor, Dennis Gilbert, conducted a nationwide survey of American Muslims. The survey found that nearly 75% of the respondents either knew someone who had, or had themselves, experienced anti-Muslim discrimination since the attacks. "You are demons," "Pig religion," "You guys did it," some were told. Respondents described actions such as "He spit in my face," "He pulled off my daughter's hajib [her head covering]"—the list of abuses went on. In all, 517 American Muslims were contacted, through a careful sampling procedure, and were interviewed via telephone by Gilbert's students and by employees of the Zogby International polling firm. This survey provided a quick snapshot of the views of an important segment of American society.

In this chapter, we will use the "Muslim America" project, a "youth and guns" survey also done by Gilbert, and other surveys to illustrate some key features of survey research. We explain the major steps in questionnaire design and then consider the features of four types of surveys, highlighting the unique problems attending each one and suggesting some possible solutions. (For instance, how do we develop an initial list—a sampling frame—of American Muslims?) We discuss ethics issues in the final section. By the chapter's end, you should be well on your way to becoming an informed consumer of survey reports and a knowledgeable developer of survey designs.

WHY IS SURVEY RESEARCH SO POPULAR?

Survey research collects information from a *sample of individuals* through their responses to *standardized questions*. As you probably have observed, a great many social scientists rely on surveys as their primary method of data collection. In fact, surveys have become so common that we cannot evaluate much of what we read in the newspaper or see on TV without having some understanding of this method of data collection (Converse, 1984).

Survey research owes its popularity to three advantages: versatility, efficiency, and generalizability. The *versatility* of surveys is apparent in the wide range of uses to which they are put, including opinion polls, election campaigns, marketing surveys, community needs assessments, and program evaluations. Surveys are *efficient* because they are a relatively fast means of collecting data on a wide range of issues at relatively little cost—ranging from about $10 to $15 per respondent in mailed surveys of the general population to $30 for a telephone survey, and then as much as $300 for in-person interview surveys (Fowler, 1998; see also Dillman, 1982; Groves & Kahn, 1979). Because they can be widely distributed to representative samples (see Chapter 4), surveys also help in achieving *generalizable* results.

Perhaps the most efficient type of survey is an **omnibus survey**, which includes a range of topics of interest to different social scientists or to other sponsors. The General Social Survey (GSS) of the National Opinion Research Center at the University of Chicago is a prime example of an omnibus survey. It is a 90-minute interview administered biennially to a probability sample of almost 3,000 Americans, with a wide range of questions and topic areas chosen by a board of overseers. The resulting datasets are made available to many universities, instructors, and students (Davis & Smith, 1992; National Opinion Research Center, 1992).

HOW SHOULD WE WRITE SURVEY QUESTIONS?

Questions are the centerpiece of survey research, so selecting good questions is the single most important concern for survey researchers. All hope for achieving measurement validity is lost unless the questions in a survey are clear and convey the intended meaning to respondents.

Question writing for a particular survey might begin with a brainstorming session or a review of previous surveys. The Muslim America survey began with students formulating questions, with help from Muslim students and professors. Most professionally prepared surveys contain previously used questions as well as some new ones, but every question that is considered for inclusion must be reviewed carefully for clarity and for its ability to convey the intended meaning to the respondents.

Adherence to the following basic principles will go a long way toward ensuring clear and meaningful questions.

Be Clear; Avoid Confusing Phrasing

In most cases, a *simple direct approach* to asking a question minimizes confusion ("Overall, do you enjoy living in Ohio?"). Use shorter rather than longer words and sentences: "brave" rather than "courageous"; "job concerns" rather than "work-related employment issues" (Dillman, 2000:52). On the other hand, questions shouldn't be abbreviated so much that the results are ambiguous. The simple statement,

Residential location: _____

is *too* simple. Does it ask for town? Country? Street address? In contrast, asking, "In what city or town do you live?" focuses attention clearly on a specific geographic unit, a specific time, and a specific person.

Avoid *negative phrases or words,* especially **double negatives:** "Do you disagree that there should not be a tax increase?" Respondents have a hard time figuring out which response matches their sentiments. Such errors can easily be avoided with minor wording changes, but even experienced survey researchers can make this mistake.

Avoid **double-barreled questions**; these actually ask two questions but allow only one answer. For example, during the Watergate scandal, the Gallup poll asked "Do you think President Nixon should be impeached and compelled to leave the presidency, or not?" Only about a third of Americans said yes. But when the wording was changed to ask whether President Nixon should be brought to trial before the Senate more than half answered yes. The first version combined impeachment—trial—with conviction, and may have confused people (Kagay & Elder, 1992:E5).

It is also important to identify clearly what kind of information each question is to obtain. Some questions focus on attitudes, or on what people say they want or how they feel. Some questions focus on beliefs, or what people think is true. Some questions focus on behavior, or on what people do. And some questions focus on attributes, or on what people are like or have experienced (Dillman, 1978:79–118; Gordon, 1992). Rarely can a single question effectively address more than one of these dimensions at a time.

Minimize Bias

Specific words in survey questions should not trigger biases, unless that is the researcher's conscious intent. Biased words and phrases tend to produce misleading answers. Some polls ask obviously loaded questions such as "Isn't it time for Americans to stand up for morality and stop the shameless degradation of the air waves?" Especially when describing abstract ideas (e.g., "freedom," "justice," "fairness"), your choice of words can dramatically affect how respondents answer. Take the difference between "welfare" and "assistance for the poor." On average, surveys have found that public support for "more assistance for the poor" is about *39 percentage points higher* than for "welfare" (Smith, 1987). Most people favor helping the poor; most people oppose welfare. The "truly needy" gain our sympathy, but "loafers and bums" do not.

Sometimes responses can be distorted through the lack of good alternative answers. For example, the Detroit Area Study (Turner & Martin, 1984:252) asked the following question: "People feel differently about making changes in the way our country is run. In order to keep America great, which of these statements do you think is best?" When the only two response choices were, "We should be very cautious of making changes" or "We should be free to make changes," only 37% said that we should be free to make changes. However, when a stronger response choice was added suggesting that we should "constantly" make changes, 24% chose that response and another 32% still chose the "free to make changes" response. So instead of 37%, we now had a total of 56% who seemed open to making changes in the way our country is run (Turner & Martin, 1984:252). Including the more extreme positive alternative ("constantly" make changes) made the less extreme positive alternative more attractive.

To minimize biased responses, researchers have to test reactions to the phrasing of a question.

Allow for Disagreement

Some respondents tend to "agree" with a statement just to avoid disagreeing. In a sense, they want to be helpful. You can see the impact of this human tendency in a 1974 Michigan Survey Research Center survey about crime and lawlessness in the United States (Schuman & Presser, 1981). When one question stated that individuals were more to blame for crime than were social conditions, 60% of the respondents agreed. But when the question was rephrased so respondents were asked, "In general, do you believe that individuals or social conditions are more to blame for crime and lawlessness in the United States?" only 46% chose individuals.

As a rule, you should present both sides of attitude scales in the question itself (Dillman, 2000:61–62). The response choices themselves should be phrased to make each one seem as socially approved, as "agreeable," as the others.

Most people, for instance, won't openly admit to having committed a crime or other disreputable activities. In this situation, you should write questions that make agreement seem more acceptable. Rather than ask "Have you ever shoplifted something from a store?" Dillman (2000:75) suggests "Have you ever taken anything from a store without paying for it?" Asking about a range of behaviors or attitudes can also facilitate agreeing with those that are socially unacceptable.

Don't Ask Questions They Can't Answer

Respondents should be *competent* to answer questions. Too many surveys expect accurate answers from people who couldn't reasonably know the answers. One campus survey we've seen asked professors to agree or disagree with statements such as the following:

"Minority students are made to feel they are second-class citizens."

"The Campus Center does a good job of meeting the informal needs of students."

"The Campus Center is where students go to meet one another and socialize informally."

"Alcohol contributes to casual sex among students."

But of course, most professors are in no position to know the answers to these questions about students' lives. To know what students do or feel, one should ask students, not professors. You should also realize that memory isn't a perfect tool—most of us, for instance, cannot accurately report what we ate for lunch on a Tuesday two weeks ago. To get accurate lunch information, ask about today's meal.

Sometimes your survey itself can sort people by competence, so they answer the appropriate questions. For instance, if you include a question about job satisfaction in a survey of the general population, first ask respondents whether they

---

Exhibit 6.1   Filter Questions and Skip Patterns

9. (GUNSHOT) Not including military combat, have you or anyone close to you ever been shot by a gun?

   1. Yes   2. No (**skip to 11**)   3. Not sure (**do not read**)

10. (OPENSHOT) Could you explain the circumstances? _____

11. (GUNLAWS) In general, do you feel that laws covering the sale of firearms should be made more strict, less strict, or kept as they are now?

   1. More strict
   2. Less strict
   3. Kept as are
   4. Not sure (**do not read**)

Source: Filter Questions and Skip Patterns, Youth and Guns Survey, 2000.

have a job. These **filter questions** create **skip patterns**. For example, respondents who answer "no" to one question are directed to skip ahead to another question, but respondents who answer "yes" go on to the **contingent question**. Skip patterns should be indicated clearly, as demonstrated in Exhibit 6.1.

Allow for Uncertainty

Some respondents just don't know—about your topic, about their own feelings, about what they think. Or they like to be neutral and won't take a stand on anything. Or they don't have any information. All of these choices are OK, but you should recognize and allow for them.

Many people, for instance, are **floaters:** respondents who choose a substantive answer even when they really don't know. Asked for their opinion on a law of which they're completely ignorant, a third of the public will give an opinion anyway, if "Don't know" isn't an option. But if it *is* an option, 90% of that group will pick that answer. You should give them the chance to say that they don't know (Schuman & Presser, 1981:113–160).

Because there are so many floaters in the typical survey sample, the decision to include an explicit "Don't know" option for a question is important, especially with surveys of less-educated populations. "Don't know" responses are chosen more often by those with less education (Schuman & Presser, 1981:113–146). Unfortunately, the inclusion of an explicit "Don't know" response choice also allows some people who *do* have a preference to take the easy way out and choose "Don't know."

Fence-sitters, people who see themselves as being neutral, may skew the results if you force them to choose between opposites. In most cases, about 10 to 20% of respondents—those who do not have strong feelings on an issue—will choose an explicit middle, neutral alternative (Schuman & Presser, 1981:161–178). Adding an explicit neutral response option is appropriate when you want to find out who is a fence-sitter.

Fence-sitting and floating can be managed by including an explicit "no opinion" category after all the substantive responses. If neutral sentiment is a possibility, also include a neutral category in the middle of the substantive responses (such as "neither agree nor disagree") (Dillman, 2000:58–60). Finally, adding an open-ended question in which respondents are asked to discuss their opinions (or reasons for having no opinion) can help by shedding some light on why some persons choose "Don't know" in response to a particular question (Smith, 1984).

Make Response Categories Exhaustive and Mutually Exclusive

Questions with fixed response choices must provide one and only one possible response for everyone who is asked the question. First, all of the possibilities should be offered (choices are "exhaustive"). In one survey of employees exiting from a telecommunications company, respondents were given these choices for "Why are you leaving [the company]? (a) poor pay, (b) poor working environment, (c) poor benefits, or (d) poor relations with my boss." Clearly, there may be other reasons (e.g., family or health reasons, geographical preferences, etc.) to leave an employer. The response categories were not exhaustive. Or when asking college students their class (senior, junior, etc.), you should probably consider having an "other" category for nontraditional matriculants who may be on an unusual track.

Second, response choices shouldn't overlap—they should be mutually exclusive, so that picking one rules out picking another. If I say, for instance, that I'm 25 years old, I cannot also be 50 years old; but I may claim to be both "young" and "mature." Those two choices aren't mutually exclusive, so they shouldn't be used as response categories for a question about age.

There are two exceptions to these principles: Filter questions may tell some respondents to skip over a question (the response choices do not have to be exhaustive); and respondents may be asked to "check all that apply" (the response choices are not mutually exclusive). Even these exceptions should be kept to a minimum. Respondents to a self-administered questionnaire should not have to do a lot of "skipping around" or else they may lose interest in completing carefully all the applicable questions. And some survey respondents react to a "check all that apply" request by just checking enough responses so that they feel they have "done enough" for that question and then ignoring the rest of the choices (Dillman, 2000:63).

HOW SHOULD QUESTIONNAIRES BE DESIGNED?

Survey questions are asked as part of a **questionnaire** (or **interview schedule,** in interview-based studies); they are not isolated from other questions. The context created by the questionnaire as a whole has a major impact on how individual questions are interpreted and answered. Therefore, survey researchers must carefully design the questionnaire itself, not just each individual question. Several steps, explained in the following sections, will help you design a good questionnaire.

Questionnaire: The survey instrument containing the questions in a self-administered survey.

Interview schedule: The survey instrument containing the questions asked by the interviewer in an in-person or phone survey.

Build on Existing Instruments

If another researcher has already designed a set of questions to measure a key concept and previous surveys indicate that this measure is reliable and valid, then by all means use that instrument. Resources such as the *Handbook of Research Design and Social Measurement, 6th Edition* (Miller & Salkind, 2002) can give you many ideas about existing questionnaires; your literature review at the start of a research project should be an even better source.

But there is a tradeoff here. Questions used previously may not concern quite the right concept or may not be appropriate in some ways to your population. A good rule of thumb is to use a previously designed instrument if it measures the concept of concern to you and it seems appropriate for your survey population.

Refine and Test Questions

The only good question is a pretested question. Before you rely on a question in your research, you need evidence that your respondents will understand what it means. So try it out on a few people (Dillman, 2000:140–147).

One important form of pretesting is discussing the questionnaire with colleagues. You can also review prior research in which your key questions or indexes have been used. Another increasingly popular form of pretesting comes from guided discussions among potential respondents. Such "focus groups" let you check for consistent understanding of terms and identify the range of events or experiences about which people will be asked to report (Fowler, 1995). (See Chapter 7 for more about this technique.)

Professional survey researchers have also developed a technique for evaluating questions called the **cognitive interview** (Fowler, 1995). Although the specifics vary, the basic approach is to ask people to "think aloud" as they answer questions. The researcher asks a test question and then probes with follow-up questions to learn how the question was understood and whether its meaning varied for different respondents. This method can identify many potential problems.

Conducting a pilot study is the final stage of questionnaire preparation. For the Muslim America study, students placed 550 telephone calls and in the process learned (a) the extent of fear that many respondents felt about such a poll; (b) that females were, for cultural reasons, less likely to respond in surveys of the Muslim population; and (c) that some of their questions were worded ambiguously.

To do a pilot study, draw a small sample of individuals from the population you are studying or one very similar to it (it is best to draw a sample of at least 100 respondents) and carry out the survey procedures with them. You may include in the pretest version of a written questionnaire some space for individuals to add comments on each key question or, with in-person interviews, audiotape the test interviews for later review. Review the distribution of responses to each question and revise any that respondents do not seem to understand.

A survey researcher also can try to understand what respondents mean by their responses after the fact—that is, by including additional questions in the survey itself. Adding such **interpretive questions** after key survey questions is always a good idea, but it is of utmost importance when the questions in a survey have not been thoroughly pretested (Labaw, 1980).

Maintain Consistent Focus

A survey (with the exception of an omnibus survey) should be guided by a clear conception of the research problem under investigation and the population to be sampled. Remember to have measures of all of the independent and dependent variables you plan to use. Of course, not even the best researcher can anticipate the relevance of every question. Researchers tend to try to avoid "missing something" by erring on the side of extraneous questions (Labaw, 1980:40).

At the same time, respondents are dismayed by long lists of redundant or unimportant questions, so respect their time and make sure that each question counts. Surveys too often include too many irrelevant questions.

Order the Questions

The sequence of questions on a survey matters. As a first step, the individual questions should be sorted into broad thematic categories which then become separate sections in the questionnaire. Both the sections and the questions within the sections must then be organized in a logical order that would make sense in a conversation.

The first question deserves special attention, particularly if the questionnaire is to be self-administered. This question signals to the respondent what the survey is about, whether it will be interesting, and how easy it will be to complete. ("Overall, would you say your physical health right now is excellent, good, fair, or poor?") For these reasons, the first question should be connected to the primary purpose of the survey, it should be interesting, it should be easy, and it should apply to everyone in the sample (Dillman, 2000:92–94). Don't try to jump right into sensitive issues ("In general, how well do you think your marriage is working?"); respondents have to warm up to talking before they will be ready for such questions. As a standard practice, for instance, most researchers ask any questions about income or finances near the end of a survey, because many people are cautious about discussing such matters.

Question order can lead to **context effects** when one or more questions influence how subsequent questions are interpreted (Schober, 1999:89–98). The potential for context effects is greatest when two or more questions concern the same issue or closely related issues. For example, if an early question asks respondents to state whom they plan to vote for in an election, they may hesitate in later questions to support views that are clearly not those of that candidate. In general, people try to appear consistent (even if they are not); be sensitive to this and realize that earlier questions may "commit" respondents to answers on later questions.

Make the Questionnaire Attractive

An attractive questionnaire—neat, clear, clean, and spacious—is more likely to be completed and less likely to confuse either the respondent or, in an interview, the interviewer.

An attractive questionnaire does not look cramped; plenty of "white space"—more between questions than within question components—makes the questionnaire appear easy to complete. Response choices are listed vertically and are distinguished clearly and consistently, perhaps by formatting them in all capital letters and keeping them in the middle of the pages. Skip patterns are indicated with arrows or other graphics. Some distinctive type of formatting should be used to identify instructions. Printing a multi-page questionnaire in booklet form usually results in the most attractive and simple-to-use questionnaire (Dillman, 2000:80–86).

Exhibit 6.2 contains portions of a telephone interview questionnaire that illustrates these features, making it easy for the interviewer to use.

Exhibit 6.2   Sample Interview Guide

Hi, my name is _____. I am calling on behalf of (I am a student at) Hamilton College in New York. We are conducting a national opinion poll of high school students.

SCREENER: Is there a sophomore, junior, or senior in high school in your household with whom I may speak?

    1. Yes   2. No/not sure/refuse **(End)**

(If student not on phone, ask:) Could he or she come to the phone?

(When student is on the phone) Hi, my name is _____. I am calling on behalf of (I am a student at) Hamilton College in New York. We are conducting a national opinion poll of high school students about gun control. Your answers will be completely anonymous. Would you be willing to participate in the poll?

    1. Yes   2. No/not sure/refuse **(End)**

1. (SKOLYR) What year are you in school?
    1. Sophomore
    2. Junior
    3. Senior
    4. Not sure/Refuse **(do not read) (End)**

Now some questions about your school:

2. (SKOL) Is it a public, Catholic, or private school?
    1. Public   2. Catholic   3. Private   4. Not sure **(do not read)**

Source: Sample Interview Guide, Youth and Guns Survey, 2000.

WHAT ARE THE ALTERNATIVES FOR ADMINISTERING SURVEYS?

Surveys can be administered in at least five different ways. They can be *mailed, group-administered,* or conducted *by telephone, in person,* or *electronically.* (Exhibit 6.3 summarizes the typical features of each.) Each approach differs from the others in one or more important features:

- *Manner of administration*—Mailed, group, and electronic surveys are completed by the respondents themselves. During phone and in-person interviews, however, the researcher or a staff person asks the questions and records the respondent's answers.
- *Questionnaire structure*—Most mailed, group, phone, and electronic surveys are highly structured, fixing in advance the content and order of questions

Exhibit 6.3 Typical Features of the Five Survey Designs

Design	Manner of Administration	Setting	Questionnaire Structure	Cost
Mailed survey	Self	Individual	Mostly structured	Low
Group survey	Self	Group	Mostly structured	Very low
Phone survey	Professional	Individual	Structured	Moderate
In-person interview	Professional	Individual or unstructured	Structured	High
Electronic survey	Self	Individual	Mostly structured	Very low

Source: Ross, 1990.

and response choices. In-person interviews may be highly structured, but they also may include many questions without fixed response choices.

- *Setting*—Mailed, electronic, and phone interviews are usually intended for only one respondent. The same is usually true of in-person interviews, although sometimes researchers interview several family members at once. On the other hand, some surveys are distributed simultaneously to a group of respondents, who complete the survey while the researcher (or assistant) waits.
- *Cost*—As mentioned earlier, in-person interviews are clearly the most expensive type of survey. Phone interviews are much less expensive, and surveying by mail is cheaper yet. Electronic surveys are now the least expensive method, because there are no interviewer costs, no mailing costs, and, for many designs, almost no costs for data entry. (Of course, extra staff time and expertise are required to prepare an electronic questionnaire.)

Because of their different features, the five administrative options vary in the types of error to which they are most prone and the situations in which they are most appropriate. The rest of this section focuses on each format's unique advantages and disadvantages.

Mailed, Self-Administered Surveys

A **mailed (self-administered) survey** is conducted by mailing a questionnaire to respondents who then take the survey by themselves. The central problem for a mailed survey is maximizing the response rate. Even an attractive questionnaire with clear questions will probably be returned by no more than 30% of a sample unless extra steps are taken. A response rate of 30%, of course, is a disaster, destroying any hope of a representative sample. That's because people who *do* respond are often systematically different from people who *don't* respond—women respond more often, for instance, to most surveys; people with very strong opinions respond more than those who are indifferent; very wealthy and very poor people, for different reasons, are less likely to respond.

Fortunately, the conscientious use of systematic techniques can push the response rate to 70% or higher for most mailed surveys (Dillman, 2000), which is acceptable. Sending follow-up mailings to nonrespondents is the single most important technique for obtaining an adequate response rate. The follow-up mailings explicitly encourage initial nonrespondents to return a completed questionnaire; implicitly, they convey the importance of the effort. Dillman (2000:155–158, 177–188) has demonstrated the effectiveness of a standard procedure for the mailing process: a preliminary introductory letter, a well-packaged survey mailing with a personalized cover letter, a reminder postcard two weeks after the initial mailing, and then new cover letters and replacement questionnaires 2–4 weeks and 6–8 weeks after that mailing.

The **cover letter**, actually, is critical to the success of a mailed survey. This statement to respondents sets the tone for the entire questionnaire. The cover letter or introductory statement must establish the credibility of the research and the researcher, it must be personalized (including a personal salutation and an original signature), it should be interesting to read, and it must explain issues about voluntary participation and maintaining subject confidentiality (Dillman, 1978:165–172). A carefully prepared cover letter should increase the response rate and result in more honest and complete answers to the survey questions; a poorly prepared cover letter can have the reverse effects. Exhibit 6.4 is an example of a cover letter for a questionnaire.

Other steps that help to maximize the response rate include clear and under-standable questions, not many open-ended questions, a credible research sponsor, a token incentive (such as a $1 coupon), and presurvey advertising (Fowler, 1988:99–106; Mangione, 1995:79–82).

Group-Administered Surveys

A **group-administered survey** is completed by individual respondents assembled in a group. The response rate is usually high because most group members will participate. Unfortunately, this method is seldom feasible because it requires a captive audience. With the exception of students, employees, members of the armed forces, and some institutionalized populations, most people cannot be sampled in such a setting.

Whoever is responsible for administering the survey to the group must be careful to minimize comments that might bias answers or that could vary between different groups in the same survey (Dillman, 2000:253–256). A standard intro-ductory statement should be read to the group that expresses appreciation for their participation, describes the steps of the survey, and emphasizes (in classroom

---

Exhibit 6.4   Sample Questionnaire Cover Letter

University of Massachusetts at Boston
Department of Sociology
May 24, 2003

Jane Doe
AIDS Coordinator
Shattuck Shelter

Dear Jane:

AIDS is an increasing concern for homeless people and for homeless shelters. The enclosed survey is about the AIDS problem and related issues confronting shelters. It is sponsored by the Life Lines AIDS Prevention Project for the Homeless—a program of the U.S. Centers for Disease Control and the Massachusetts Department of Public Health.

As an AIDS coordinator/shelter director, you have learned about homeless persons' problems and about implementing programs in response to those problems. The Life Lines Project needs to learn from your experience. Your answers to the questions in the enclosed survey will improve substantially the base of information for improving AIDS prevention programs.

Questions in the survey focus on AIDS prevention activities and on related aspects of shelter operations. It should take about 30 minutes to answer all the questions.

Every shelter AIDS coordinator (or shelter director) in Massachusetts is being asked to complete the survey. And every response is vital to the success of the survey: The survey report must represent the full range of experiences.

You may be assured of complete confidentiality. No one outside of the university will have access to the questionnaire you return. (The ID number on the survey will permit us to check with nonrespondents to see if they need a replacement survey or other information.) All information presented in the report to Life Lines will be in aggregate form, with the exception of a list of the number, gender, and family status of each shelter's guests.

Please mail the survey back to us by Monday, June 4, and feel free to call if you have any questions.

Thank you for your assistance.

Yours sincerely,

Russell K. Schutt

Russell K. Schutt, Ph.D.
Project Director

---

surveys) that the survey is not the same as a test. A cover letter like that used in mailed surveys also should be distributed with the questionnaires. To emphasize confidentiality, respondents should be given an envelope in which to seal their questionnaire after it is completed.

Another issue of special concern with group-administered surveys is the possibility that respondents will feel coerced to participate and therefore will be less likely to answer questions honestly. Also, because administering group surveys requires approval of the authorities—and this sponsorship is made quite obvious, because the survey is conducted on the organization's premises—respondents may infer that the researcher is in league with the sponsor. No complete solution to this problem exists, but it helps to make an introductory statement emphasizing the researcher's independence and giving participants a chance to ask questions about the survey. The sponsor should keep a low profile and allow the researcher both control over the data and autonomy in report writing.

Telephone Surveys

In a **phone survey**, interviewers question respondents over the phone and then record respondents' answers. Phone interviewing has become a very popular method of conducting surveys in the United States because almost all families have phones. But two matters may undermine the validity of a phone survey: not reaching the proper sampling units and not getting enough complete responses to make the results generalizable.

Reaching Sample Units

Most telephone surveys use random digit dialing at some point in the sampling process (Lavrakas, 1987). A machine calls random phone numbers within the designated exchanges, whether or not the numbers are published. You should try to "capture" unlisted numbers this way because their owners are systematically different—often they are wealthier than the general population. When the machine reaches an inappropriate household (such as a business in a survey of individuals), the phone number is simply replaced with another.

When targeting a specific population, other approaches may be used. Because it targeted a relatively small minority population, the Muslim America survey worked from a national database of Muslim names in telephone books. That's a clever idea, but unfortunately, it misses converts (whose family name is not evidently Muslim) and many African-American Muslims. But random dialing, in an attempt to find a fairly small minority populations, would have produced far too many failed calls. However households are contacted, the interviewers should ask a series of questions at the start of the survey to ensure that they are speaking to the appropriate member of the household (the homeowner, oldest child, etc.).

Maximizing Response to Phone Surveys

Several issues require special attention in phone surveys. First, because people often are not home, multiple call-backs will be needed for many sample members. In the last 20 years, with increasing numbers of single-person households, dual-earner families, and out-of-home activities, survey research organizations have had to increase the usual number of phone contact attempts from just 4–8 to 20—a lot of attempts just to reach one person. The growth of telemarketing has created another problem for telephone survey researchers: Individuals nowadays often "just say no" to calls from unknown individuals and organizations or use their answering machines to screen calls (Dillman, 2000:8, 28). In the Muslim America study, many people were afraid to talk with the researchers or were actively hostile; after all, respondents don't really know who is calling and may have good reason to be suspicious.

Phone surveys also must cope with difficulties due to the impersonal and nonvisual nature of phone contact. The instructions shown in Exhibit 6.5 were developed to clarify procedures for asking and coding a series of questions in the phone interviews conducted for the youth and guns survey. In general, careful interviewer training is essential for phone surveys.

Phone surveying is the method of choice for relatively short surveys of the general population. Response rates in phone surveys traditionally have tended to be very high—often above 80%—because few individuals would hang up on a polite caller or refuse to stop answering questions (at least within the first 30 minutes or so).

Exhibit 6.5   Sample Interviewer Instructions

Sample Interview Instructions, Youth and Guns Survey, 2000

22. (CONSTIT) To your knowledge, does the U.S. Constitution guarantee citizens the right to own firearms?
    1. Yes   2. No **(skip to 24)**   3. Not sure **(do not read)**

23. (CONLAW) Do you believe that laws regulating the sale and use of handguns violate the constitutional rights of gun owners?
    1. Yes   2. No   3. Not sure **(do not read)**

24. (PETITION) In some localities, high school students have joined campaigns to change the gun laws, and sometimes they have been successful. Earlier you said that you thought that the current gun control laws were (**if Q11 = 1, insert "not strict enough"; if Q11 = 2, insert "too strict"**). Suppose a friend who thinks like you do about this asked you to sign a petition calling for (**if Q11 = 1, insert "stronger gun control laws"; if Q11 = 2, insert "less restrictive gun control laws"**). On a scale from 1 to 5, with 1 being very unlikely and 5 being very likely, how likely is it that you would sign the petition?
    1. (Very unlikely)
    2.
    3.
    4.
    5. (Very likely)
    6. Not sure **(do not read)**

Source: Sample Interviewer Instructions, Youth and Guns Survey, 2000.

However, as we have noted, the refusal rate in phone interviews is rising with the prevalence of telemarketing and answering machines.

In-Person Interviews

What is unique to the **in-person interview**, compared to the other survey designs, is the face-to-face social interaction between interviewer and respondent. If money is no object, in-person interviewing is often the best survey design.

In-person interviewing has several advantages: Response rates are higher than with any other survey design; questionnaires can be much longer than with mailed or phone surveys; the questionnaire can be complex, with both open-ended and closed-ended questions and frequent branching patterns; the order in which questions are read and answered can be controlled by the interviewer; the physical and social circumstances of the interview can be monitored; and respondents' interpretations of questions can be probed and clarified. The interviewer therefore is well placed to gain a full understanding of what the respondent really wants to say.

However, researchers must be alert to some special hazards due to the presence of an interviewer. Ideally, every respondent should have the same interview experience—that is, each respondent should be asked the same questions in the same way by the same type of person, who reacts similarly to the answers. Suppose one interviewer is smiling and pleasant while another is gruff and rude; the two interviewers will likely elicit very different results in their surveys, if only in the length of responses. Careful training and supervision are essential (Groves, 1989:404–406).

Maximizing Response to Interviews

Several factors affect the response rate in interview studies. Contact rates tend to be lower in central cities, in part because of difficulties in finding people at home and gaining access to high-rise apartments, and, in part, because of interviewer reluctance to visit some areas at night, when people are more likely to be home (Fowler, 1988:45–60). Households with young children or elderly adults tend to be easier to contact, whereas single-person households are more difficult to reach (Groves & Couper, 1998:119–154).

Refusal rates vary with some respondent characteristics. People with less education participate somewhat less in surveys of political issues (perhaps because they are less aware of current political issues). Less education is also associated with higher rates of "don't know" responses (Groves, 1989). On the other hand, wealthy people often refuse to be surveyed about their income or buying habits, perhaps to avoid being plagued by sales calls. Such problems can be lessened with an advance letter introducing the survey project and by multiple contact attempts throughout the day and evening, but they cannot be entirely avoided (Fowler, 1988:52–53; Groves & Couper, 1998).

Electronic Surveys

The widespread use of personal computers and the growth of the Internet have created new possibilities for survey research. **Electronic surveys** can be prepared in two ways (Dillman, 2000:352–354). **E-mail surveys** can be sent as messages to respondent e-mail addresses. Respondents then mark their answers in the message and send them back to the researcher. This approach is easy for researchers to develop and for respondents to use. However, this approach is cumbersome for surveys that are more than four or five pages long. By contrast, **Web surveys** are stored on a server that is controlled by the researcher; respondents are then asked to visit the Web site and respond to the questionnaire by checking answers. This approach requires more programming by the researcher and in many cases requires more skill on the part of the respondent. However, a well-designed Web survey can show only the questions applicable to a given respondent and so seem much shorter and therefore more attractive.

Web surveys are becoming a popular form of electronic survey because they are so flexible (see Exhibit 6.6). Web surveys can be quite long, with questions that are inapplicable to a given respondent hidden from them so that the survey may actually seem much shorter than it is. The questionnaire design can feature many graphic and typographic elements. Respondents can view definitions of words or instructions for answering questions by clicking on linked terms. Lengthy sets of response choices can be presented with pull-down menus. Pictures and audio segments can be added when they are useful. Because answers are recorded directly in the researcher's database, data entry errors are virtually eliminated and results can be reported quickly.

The most important drawback to either electronic survey approach is the large number of households that are not yet connected to the Internet: In October 2003 just under half of American households were connected to the Internet (U.S. Department of Commerce, 2002). But there's another almost opposite problem with Web surveys: Because they are so easy and cheap to set up, you can find hundreds of Web surveys on a wide range of topics and for many different purposes. It may be possible for any Internet user to just go right ahead and participate in many of these Web surveys. But the large numbers of respondents that this uncontrolled method can generate should not cause you to forget the importance of a representative sample, for this method is guaranteed to produce, instead, a very biased sample (Dillman, 2000:355).

Exhibit 6.6 Survey.Net—Year 2000 Presidential Election Survey

Your source for information, opinions & demographics from the Net Community!

SUR☑EY.NET ™

Year 2000 Presidential Election Survey

Take the year 2000 presidential election survey!

1. **What is your age?**
   No Answer ⬍

2. **Your Sex:**
   No Answer ⬍

3. **Your highest level of education completed:**
   No Answer ⬍

4. **Your political affiliation:**
   No Answer ⬍

5. **Who did you vote for in 1996?**
   No Answer ⬍

6. **Even though not all of these candidates are necessarily running, if the presidential election were held today, who would you vote for?**
   No Answer ⬍

7. **Of the following TWO potential presidential candidates, who would you vote for?**
   No Answer ⬍

8. **Of the following presidential candidates, who would you vote for?**
   No Answer ⬍

9. **Do you consider yourself...**
   No Answer ⬍

(Continued)

10. What political concepts do you agree with? *(check all that apply)*

☐ - We need less government regulation in general
☐ - We need more responsible government regulation
☐ - States should have more responsibility than the Federal Gov.

☐ - The government should NOT mandate moral standards
☐ - The government SHOULD mandate moral standards

☐ - Tax breaks are more important than reducing the deficit
☐ - Reducing the deficit is more important than tax breaks

☐ - Unions are destroying American productivity
☐ - Unions protect the worker

☐ - The economy is more important than the environment
☐ - The environment is more important than the economy

11. In your opinion, what is the worst problem with our society?

    | No Answer | ⬍ |

12. Of those items listed, what should be our next President's highest priority?

    | No Answer | ⬍ |

13. Without turning this into a partisan/rhetorical argument, who do you want to see for president in 2000 and why? (*Limit this to one or two sentences*)

    | | ⬍ |

Thanks very much for participating in the survey!

To submit your survey choices, select:

    SUBMIT SURVEY

or Reset survey settings

You can view the latest survey results after you submit your answers.

We hope you will also participate in other surveys online as well. Please note that you shoul only complete each survey <u>once</u>.

Source: Survey.Net courtesy Otterbein College. Reprinted with permission.

When the population to be surveyed has a high rate of Internet use, however, the Web makes possible fast and effective surveys (Dillman 2000:354–355). For example, Titus K. L. Schleyer and Jane L. Forrest (2000:420) achieved a 74% response rate in a survey of dental professionals who were already Internet users. A skilled Web programmer can generate a survey layout with many attractive features that make it more likely that respondents will give their answers—and have a clear understanding of the question (Smyth, Dillman, Christian, & Stern 2004:4–5). To ensure that the appropriate people respond to a Web-based survey, researchers may require that respondents enter a PIN (Personal Identification Number) in order to gain access to the Internet survey (Dillman, 2000:378).

A COMPARISON OF SURVEY DESIGNS

Which survey design should you use for a study? Let's compare the four major survey designs: mailed surveys, phone surveys, in-person surveys, and electronic surveys. (Group-administered surveys are similar in most respects to mailed surveys except that they require the unusual circumstance of having access to the sample in a group setting.) Exhibit 6.7 summarizes these strong and weak points.

The most important difference among these four methods is their varying response rates. Because of the low response rates of *mailed surveys,* they are weakest from a sampling standpoint. However, researchers with limited time, money, and staff may still prefer a mailed survey. Mailed surveys can be useful in asking sensitive questions (e.g., questions about marital difficulties or financial situation), because respondents won't be embarrassed by answering in front of an interviewer.

Contracting with an established survey research organization for a *phone survey* is often the best alternative to a mailed survey. The persistent follow-up attempts that are necessary to secure an adequate response rate are much easier over the phone than in person. A phone survey limits the length and complexity of the questionnaire but offers the possibility of very carefully monitoring interviewers (Dillman, 1978; Fowler, 1988:61–73).

In-person surveys can be long and complex, and the interviewer can easily monitor the conditions (the room, noise and distractions, etc.). Although interviewers may themselves distort results, either by changing the wording of questions or failing to record answers properly, this problem can be lessened by careful training and monitoring of interviewers, and by tape-recording the answers.

The advantages and disadvantages of *electronic surveys* must be weighed in light of the capabilities at the time that the survey is to be conducted. At this time, too many people do not have Internet connections for general use of Internet surveying, and too many people who have computers lack adequate computer capacity for displaying complex Web pages. But when your entire sample has access and ability (e.g., students at some colleges), Web-based surveys can be very effective.

So overall, in-person interviews are the strongest design and are generally preferable when sufficient resources and a trained interview staff are available; telephone surveys have many of the advantages of in-person interviews at much less cost, but response rates are an increasing problem. Any decision about the best survey design for a particular study must take into account the unique features and goals of the study.

ETHICAL ISSUES IN SURVEY RESEARCH

Survey research designs usually pose fewer ethical dilemmas than do experimental or field research designs. Potential respondents to a survey can easily refuse to participate, and a cover letter or introductory statement that identifies the sponsors of and motivations for the survey gives them the information required to make this decision. Little is concealed from the respondents, and the methods of data collection are quite obvious. Only in group-administered survey designs might the respondents (such as students or employees) be, in effect, a captive audience, so they require special attention to ensure that participation is truly voluntary. (Those who do not wish to participate may be told they can just hand in a blank form.)

Sometimes, political or marketing surveys are used unscrupulously, to sway opinion under the guise of asking for it. So-called "push polls" are sometimes employed in political campaigns to distort an opponent's image ("If you knew Congressman Jones was cheating on his wife, would you consider him fit for high office?"). Advertisers can use surveys that pretend to collect opinions or "register" a purchase for warranty purposes, but they are really trying to collate information about where you live, your phone numbers, your buying habits, and the like.

Confidentiality is most often the primary focus of ethical concern in survey research. Many surveys include questions that might prove damaging to the subjects if their answers were disclosed. When a survey of employees asks "Do you think management here, especially your boss, is doing a good job?" or when student course evaluations ask "On a scale of 1 to 5, how fair would you say the professor is?," respondents may well hesitate; if the boss or professor saw the results, workers or students could be hurt.

To prevent any disclosure of such information, it is critical to preserve subject confidentiality. Only research personnel should have access to information that could be used to link respondents to their responses, and even that access should be limited to what is necessary for specific research purposes. Only numbers should be used to identify respondents on their questionnaires, and the researcher

Exhibit 6.7 Advantages and Disadvantages of Four Survey Designs

Characteristics of Design	Mail Survey	Phone Survey	In-person Survey	Electronic Survey
Representative sample				
Opportunity for inclusion is known				
For completely listed populations	High	High	High	Medium
For incompletely listed populations	Medium	Medium	High	Low
Selection within sampling units is controlled	Medium	High	High	Low
(e.g., specific family members must respond)				
Respondents are likely to be located				
If samples are heterogeneous	Medium	High	High	Low
If samples are homogeneous and	High	High	High	High
specialized				
Questionnaire construction and question design				
Allowable length of questionnaire	Medium	Medium	High	Medium
Ability to include				
Complex questions	Medium	Low	High	High
Open questions	Low	High	High	Medium
Screening questions	Low	High	High	High
Tedious, boring questions	Low	High	High	Low
Ability to control question sequence	Low	High	High	High
Ability to ensure questionnaire	Medium	High	High	Low
completion				
Distortion of answers				
Odds of avoiding social desirability bias	High	Medium	Low	High
Odds of avoiding interviewer distortion	High	Medium	Low	High
Odds of avoiding contamination by others	Medium	High	Medium	Medium
Administrative goals				
Odds of meeting personnel requirements	High	High	Low	Medium
Odds of implementing quickly	Low	High	Low	High
Odds of keeping costs low	High	Medium	Low	High

Source: Adapted from Dillman, 1978:74–75. "Mail and Telephone Surveys: The Total Design Method." Copyright © 1978 Don A. Dillman. Reprinted by permission of John Wiley & Sons.

should keep the names that correspond to these numbers in a safe, private location, unavailable to staff and others who might come across them. Follow-up mailings or contact attempts that require linking the ID numbers with names and addresses should be carried out by trustworthy assistants under close supervision. If an electronic survey is used, encryption technology should be used to make information that is provided over the Internet secure from unauthorized people. Usually confidentiality can be protected readily; the key is to be aware of the issue. Don't allow bosses to collect workers' surveys or professors to pick up course evaluations. Be aware of your respondents' concerns and be even a little more careful than you need to be.

Few surveys can provide true **anonymity**, in which no identifying information is ever recorded to link respondents with their responses. The main problem with anonymous surveys is that they preclude follow-up attempts to contact nonrespondents, and they prevent panel designs, which measure change through repeated surveys of the same individuals. In-person surveys rarely can be anonymous because an interviewer must, in almost all cases, know the name and address of the interviewee. However, phone surveys that are meant only to sample opinion at one point in time, as in political polls, can safely be completely anonymous. When no future follow-up is desired, group-administered surveys also can be anonymous. To provide anonymity in a mail survey, the researcher should omit identifying codes from the questionnaire but could include a self-addressed, stamped postcard so the respondent can notify the researcher that the questionnaire has been returned without creating any linkage to the questionnaire itself (Mangione, 1995:69).

CONCLUSION

Survey research is an exceptionally efficient and productive method for investigating a wide array of social research questions. In addition to the potential benefits for social science, considerations of time and expense frequently make a survey the preferred data-collection method. One or more of the five survey designs reviewed in this chapter can be applied to almost any research question. It is no wonder that surveys have become the most popular research method in sociology and that they frequently inform discussion and planning about important social and political questions. As use of the Internet increases, survey research should become even more efficient and popular.

The relative ease of conducting at least some types of survey research leads many people to imagine that no particular training or systematic procedures are required. Nothing could be further from the truth. But as a result of this widespread misconception, you will encounter a great many nearly worthless survey results. You must be prepared to examine carefully the procedures used in any survey before accepting its findings as credible. And if you decide to conduct a survey, you must be prepared to invest the time and effort required by proper procedures.

KEY TERMS

Anonymity
Cognitive interview
Confidentiality
Context effect
Contingent question
Cover letter
Double-barreled question
Double negative
Electronic survey
E-mail survey
Fence-sitter
Filter question

Floater
Group-administered survey
In-person interview
Interpretive question
Interview schedule
Mailed (self-administered) survey
Omnibus survey
Phone survey
Questionnaire
Skip pattern
Survey research
Web survey

HIGHLIGHTS

• Surveys are the most popular form of social research because of their versatility, efficiency, and generalizability. Many survey datasets, like the General Social Survey, are available for social scientists to use in teaching and research.

• Omnibus surveys cover a range of topics of interest and generate data useful to multiple sponsors.

• Questions must be worded carefully to avoid confusing respondents, encouraging less-than-honest responses, or triggering biases. Inclusion of "Don't know" choices and neutral responses may help, but the presence of such options also affects the distribution of answers. Open-ended questions can be used to determine the meaning that respondents attach to their answers. Answers to any survey questions may be affected by the questions that precede them in a questionnaire or interview schedule.

• Questions can be tested and improved through review by experts, focus group discussions, cognitive interviews, and/or pilot testing. Every questionnaire and interview schedule should be pretested on a small sample that is like the sample to be surveyed.

• The cover letter for a mailed questionnaire should be credible, personalized, interesting, and responsible.

• Response rates in mailed surveys are typically well below 70% unless multiple mailings are made to nonrespondents and the questionnaire and cover letter are attractive, interesting, and carefully planned. Response rates for group-administered surveys are usually much higher than for mailed surveys.

• Phone interviews using random digit dialing allow fast turnaround and efficient sampling. Multiple call-backs are often required, and the rate of nonresponse to phone interviews is rising. Phone interviews should be limited in length to about 30 to 45 minutes.

• In-person interviews have several advantages over other types of surveys: They allow longer and more complex interview schedules, monitoring of the conditions when the questions are answered, probing for respondents' understanding of the questions, and high response rates. However, the interviewer must balance the need to establish rapport with the respondent with the need to adhere to a standardized format.

- Electronic surveys may be e-mailed or posted on the Web. Interactive voice-response systems using the telephone are another option. At this time, use of the Internet is not sufficiently widespread to allow e-mail or Web surveys of the general population, but these approaches can be fast and efficient for populations with high rates of computer use.

- The decision to use a particular survey design must take into account the unique features and goals of the study. In general, in-person interviews are the strongest but most expensive survey design.

- Most survey research poses few ethical problems because respondents can decline to participate—an option that should be stated clearly in the cover letter or introductory statement. Special care must be taken when questionnaires are administered in group settings (to "captive audiences"), and when sensitive personal questions are to be asked; subject confidentiality should always be preserved.

> To assist you in completing the Web Exercises, please access the Study Site at http://www.pineforge.com/mssw2 where you'll find the Web Exercises with accompanying links. You'll find other useful study materials like self-quizzes and e-flashcards for each chapter, along with a group of carefully selected articles from research journals that illustrate the major concepts and techniques presented in the book.

EXERCISES

Discussing Research

1. *Down and Out in America*, by Peter Rossi (1989), includes an appendix containing an annotated bibliography of survey-based studies of homeless and extremely poor populations. Critique the survey designs based on Rossi's descriptions. Which designs seemed likely to produce more generalizable results? Comment on sample generalizability and cross-population generalizability. Propose a plan to survey either homeless persons or those who provide services to homeless persons in some city in your state. How would you draw a sample? How would you approach potential respondents? What survey design do you think would have the greatest chance of success?

2. Review the experiment by Richard Price, Michelle Van Ryn, and Amiram Vinokur (1992). Propose a survey design that would test the same hypothesis but with a sample from a larger population. Your survey design can be longitudinal but should remain experimental, not quasi-experimental. Compare your survey design to the original experimental design. What are the advantages and disadvantages of your survey design in terms of causal validity? Generalizability? Measurement validity?

Finding Research

1. Who does survey research and how do they do it? These questions can be answered through careful inspection of organizations listed at www.ukans.edu/cwis/units/coms2/po/index.html.

Spend some time reading about some of the different survey research organizations, and write a brief summary of the types of research they conduct, the projects in which they are involved, and the resources that they offer on their Web site. What are the distinctive features of different survey research organizations?

2. Go to the Research Triangle Institute (RTI) site at www.rti.org and click on "Tools and Methods," "Surveys," and then "Survey Design & Development." Find the links from the words "cognitive pretesting" and "computer-assisted interviewing." Read about RTI's methods for computer-assisted interviewing and their cognitive laboratory methods for refining questions. What does this add to our treatment of these topics in this chapter?

Critiquing Research

1. Read one of the original articles that reported one of the surveys described in this chapter. Critique the article using the questions presented in Exhibit 10.2 as your guide, but focus particular attention on sampling, measurement, and survey design.

2. Each of the following questions was used in a survey that we received at some time in the past. Evaluate each question and its response choices using the guidelines for question writing presented in this chapter. What errors do you find? Try to rewrite each question to avoid such errors and improve question wording.

a. The first question in an *Info World* (computer publication) "product evaluation survey":

```
How interested are you in PostScript Level 2 printers?

_____ Very _____ Somewhat _____ Not at all
```

b. From the Greenpeace National Marine Mammal Survey:

```
Do you support Greenpeace's nonviolent direct action to inter-
cept whaling ships, tuna fleets and other commercial fisher-
men in order to stop their wanton destruction of thousands of
magnificent marine mammals?

_____ Yes _____ No _____ Undecided
```

c. From a U.S. Department of Education survey of college faculty:

```
How satisfied or dissatisfied are you with each of the follow-
ing aspects of your instructional duties at this institution?

                       Very        Somewhat   Somewhat    Very
                  dissatisfied dissatisfied satisfied satisfied
a. The authority
   I have to make
   decisions about
   what courses
   I teach.........     1            2           3          4
```

b. Time available
   for working
   with students as
   advisor, mentor.. 1   2   3   4

d. From a survey about affordable housing in a Massachusetts community:

   Higher than single-family density is acceptable in order
   to make housing affordable.

   Strongly Agree Agree Undecided Disagree Strongly Disagree
         1   2   3   4   5

e. From a survey of faculty experience with ethical problems in research:

   Are you reasonably familiar with the codes of ethics of
   any of the following professional associations?

	Very Familiar	Familiar	Not too Familiar
American Sociological Association	1	2	0
Society for the Study of Social Problems	1	2	0
American Society of Criminology	1	2	0

   If you are familiar with any of the above codes of ethics,
   to what extent do you agree with them?

   Strongly Agree_____ Agree_____ No Opinion_____
   Disagree_____ Disagree Strongly_____

   Some researchers have avoided using a *professional code
   of ethics* as a guide for the following reasons. Which
   responses, if any, best describe your reasons for not using
   all or any of the parts of the codes?

	Yes	No
1. Vagueness	1	0
2. Political pressures	1	0
3. Codes protect only individuals, not groups	1	0

f. From a survey of faculty perceptions:

   Of the students you have observed while teaching college
   courses, please indicate the percentage who significantly
   improved their performance in the following areas:

   Reading ____%

   Organization ____%

   Abstraction ____%

g. From a University of Massachusetts Boston student survey:

```
A person has a responsibility to stop a friend or relative
from driving when drunk.

Strongly Agree _____ Agree _____ Disagree _____
Strongly Disagree _____

Even if I wanted to, I would probably not be able to stop
most people from driving drunk.

Strongly Agree _____ Agree _____ Disagree _____
Strongly Disagree _____
```

3. We received in a university mailbox some years ago a two-page questionnaire that began with the following "cover letter" at the top of the first page:

Faculty Questionnaire

This survey seeks information on faculty perception of the learning process and student performance in their undergraduate careers. Surveys have been distributed in nine universities in the Northeast, through random deposit in mailboxes of selected departments. This survey is being conducted by graduate students affiliated with the School of Education and the Sociology Department. We greatly appreciate your time and effort in helping us with our study.

Critique this cover letter, and then draft a more persuasive one.

4. Go to the Centre for Applied Social Surveys Question Bank at http://qb.soc.surrey .ac.uk/docs/home.htm. Click on the link for one of the listed surveys. Review 10 questions used in the survey and critique them in terms of the principles for question writing that you have learned. Do you find any question features that might be attributed to the use of British English?

Doing Research

1. Write 10 questions for a one-page questionnaire that concerns your proposed research question. Your questions should operationalize at least three of the variables on which you have focused, including at least one independent and one dependent variable. (You may have multiple questions to measure some variables.) Make all but one of your questions closed-ended. If you completed the "research proposal" exercises in Chapter 3, you can select your questions from the ones you developed for those exercises.

2. Conduct a preliminary pretest of the questionnaire by conducting cognitive interviews with two students or other persons like those to whom the survey is directed. Follow up the closed-ended questions with open-ended probes that ask the respondents what they meant by each response or what came to mind when they were asked each question. Take account of the feedback you receive when you revise your questions.

3. Polish up the organization and layout of the questionnaire, following the guidelines in this chapter. Prepare a rationale for the order of questions in your questionnaire. Write a cover letter directed to the appropriate population that contains appropriate statements about research ethics (human subject issues).

Chapter 7

Qualitative Methods
Observing, Participating, Listening

Qualitative research goes straight to where people live—and die:

We see what those poor bastards go through. Seriously, when [a dying medical patient has] been resuscitated nine or ten times and their chest looks like raw meat, they've been fried from being defibrillated, they've had their chest pumped on, they've got a flat chest because their ribs are no more connected to their sternum . . . You know this guy doesn't have a chance in hell. I mean, he's already blown out, squash, herniated his brain, he doesn't have any spontaneous respirations, he's flat EEGs. You take care of him for eight hours, you know that this person is not viable, and you feel for him and you feel for the family . . . When you're resuscitating somebody and they get no response going into the code for an hour, and now has no EKG, no heart tracing, pupils are blown, fixed, no spontaneous respiration, blood gases are out in the ozone . . . you are the one that's going to turn to the resident and say, "don't you think this is about it, don't you think we should call this?"

—Interview, quoted in Chambliss, 1996:164

Throughout this chapter, you will learn that some of our greatest insights into social processes can result from what appear to be very ordinary activities: observing, participating, listening, and talking. But you will also learn that qualitative research is much more than just doing what comes naturally: Qualitative researchers must observe keenly, take notes systematically, question respondents strategically, and prepare to spend more time and invest more of their whole selves than often occurs with experiments or surveys.

We begin with an overview of the major features of qualitative research. The next section discusses participant observation research, which is the most distinctive qualitative method. We then discuss intensive interviewing—a type of interviewing that qualifies as qualitative rather than quantitative research, and focus groups, an increasingly popular qualitative method. The last two sections discuss how to analyze qualitative data and make ethical decisions in qualitative research.

WHAT ARE "QUALITATIVE" METHODS?

Qualitative methods refer to several distinctive research activities: **participant observation, intensive interviewing,** and **focus groups.**

Participant observation: A qualitative method for gathering data that involves developing a sustained relationship with people while they go about their normal activities.

Intensive interviewing: A qualitative method that involves open-ended, relatively unstructured questioning in which the interviewer seeks in-depth information on the interviewee's feelings, experiences, and perceptions (Lofland & Lofland, 1984:12).

Focus groups: A qualitative method that involves unstructured group interviews in which the focus group leader actively encourages discussion among participants on the topics of interest.

Although these three qualitative designs differ in many respects, they share several features, in addition to the collection of qualitative data itself, that distinguish them from experimental and survey research designs (Denzin & Lincoln, 1994; Maxwell, 1996; Wolcott, 1995).

- Qualitative researchers typically begin with *an exploratory research question* about what people think and how they act, and why, in some social setting. Their research approach is primarily inductive.
- A *focus on previously unstudied processes and unanticipated phenomena,* because previously unstudied attitudes and actions can't adequately be understood with a structured set of questions or within a highly controlled experiment.
- *An orientation to social context,* to the interconnections between social phenomena rather than to their discrete features.
- A *focus on human subjectivity,* on the meanings that participants attach to events and that people give to their lives.
- *Sensitivity to the subjective role of the researcher.* The researcher considers himself or herself as necessarily part of the social process being studied and therefore keeps track of his or her own actions in, and reactions to, that social process.

Case Study: Beyond Caring

In preparing to write his 1996 book *Beyond Caring: Hospitals, Nurses, and the Social Organization of Ethics,* Dan Chambliss spent many months, spread over 12 years, studying hospital nurses at work. Observing in several different hospitals, in different regions of the United States, Chambliss watched countless operations and emergency room crises, but also sat up nights chatting with nurses on geriatric floors (specializing in the care of old people), and quietly watched for hours at a time while nurses did postoperative care, bathed patients, helped patients walk down the hall, or just met with each other and with doctors, technicians, and aides to discuss the day's work. He also conducted more than 100 formal interviews, averaging an hour and a half or more each; he attended birthday parties and softball games and saw nurses in social situations as well as at professional conferences. This project exemplifies **field research**, which combines various forms of qualitative research.

The resulting data are nothing like the clean list of responses given to a survey questionnaire. Instead, Chambliss wrote his book from boxes full of notes on his observations, such as these:

[Today I witnessed] the needle injection of local anesthetic into a newborn (3 weeks) baby's skull, so they could remove a shunt. The two residents doing it discussed whether a local anesthetic would be sufficient; a general [anesthetic] would be dangerous. One said, "I can do it if you can." This exchange was carried out a couple of times. A nurse (man) stroked the infant's hand, talked softly to it, and calmed it immediately as they were setting up, putting in the IVs—hard to do, the veins are so small.

The resident injected the local anesthetic. Everyone around was affected by the immediate widening of the baby's eyes as the needle first went in, and then the screaming. The resident doing it, though, was absolutely concentrated on the task. At one point the female resident mentioned her concern, saying something about the whole point of anesthetic is to lessen pain, not to increase it. The baby was put in pain, couldn't have known any reason for it, was helpless to resist. [Field Notes] (Chambliss, 1996:135–136)

So field work involves, at its simplest, spending time with people in their own settings, watching them do what they do. Gary Allen Fine, a prominent field researcher, has studied little league baseball, restaurant kitchens, high school debate teams, and people who hunt for mushrooms, to name a few different settings. Chambliss had complete access to the working (and sometimes personal) lives of the nurses he studied.

Such research obviously requires a huge investment of time. Chambliss moved his residence several times during his research, living in apartments near the medical centers that he studied. He built his entire schedule, for months on end, around the opportunities for seeing often unseen things—emergency resuscitations, hidden malpractice, even the boredom of some nursing work.

But the investment can be worth the cost. Chambliss's early research on nurses primarily relied on tape-recorded interviews:

These [interviews] produced many dramatic stories and often confirmed theories I already held, but as I began to spend more time in hospitals I began to doubt the veracity of interviews. I began to see how the interviews were a reflection of my interests as much as of my subjects' lives. The stories told were more exciting than the ordinary drudgery I saw; the nurses described in stories seemed more committed and courageous than some of those I actually watched. Interviewees told what they noticed and remembered, which I discovered to be a highly selective version of what actually occurred. Much of life, I found, consists precisely in not noticing what one does all the time. "There aren't any ethical problems here I can think of," said a pediatric research nurse mentioned earlier; "You should talk with people on the ethics committee," said nurses gathered outside the room of an AIDS patient. (Chambliss, 1996:194)

Chambliss wanted to learn about nurses, so in a sense he did the obvious: He worked and talked with nurses, many of them, over a long period of time. But he also took care to study a variety of hospitals, and different services within hospitals; he "sampled" different times of the day and night, and different kinds of patients. True, such research is inductive, and the researcher is open to surprises; Chambliss couldn't run controlled experiments or easily isolate independent and dependent variables. But even the most unstructured kind of research still adheres to the basic discipline of scientific method.

HOW DOES PARTICIPANT OBSERVATION BECOME A RESEARCH METHOD?

Dan Chambliss used **participant observation** (or "field work," or "field research") to study nurses because it leaves natural social processes, in their natural setting, relatively undisturbed. It is a means for seeing the social world as the research subjects see it, in its totality, and for understanding subjects' interpretations of that world (Wolcott, 1995:66). Participant observers seek to avoid the artificiality of experimental designs and the unnatural structured questioning of survey research (Koegel, 1987:8). This method encourages consideration of the context in which social interaction occurs, of the complex and interconnected nature of social relations, and of the sequencing of events (Bogdewic, 1999:49). Through it, we can understand the *mechanisms* (one of the criteria for establishing cause) of social life.

In his study of nursing homes, Timothy Diamond (1992) explained how his exploratory research question led him to adopt the method of participant observation:

> How does the work of caretaking become defined and get reproduced day in and day out as a business? . . . the everyday world of Ina and Aileen and their co-workers, and that of the people they tend. . . . I wanted to collect stories and to experience situations like those Ina and Aileen had begun to describe. I decided that . . . I would go inside to experience the work myself. (Diamond, 1992:5)

The term *participant observer* actually represents a continuum of roles (see Exhibit 7.1), ranging from being a complete observer who does not participate in group activities and is publicly defined as a researcher, to being a covert participant who acts just like other group members and does not disclose his or her research role. Many field researchers develop a role between these extremes, publicly acknowledging being a researcher but nonetheless participating in group activities.

Choosing a Role

The first concern of all participant observers is deciding what balance to strike between observing and participating and whether to reveal their roles as researchers. These decisions must take into account the specifics of the social situation being studied, the researcher's own background and personality, the larger sociopolitical context, and ethical concerns. Which balance of participating and observing is most appropriate also changes during most projects—often many times.

Exhibit 7.1   The Observational Continuum

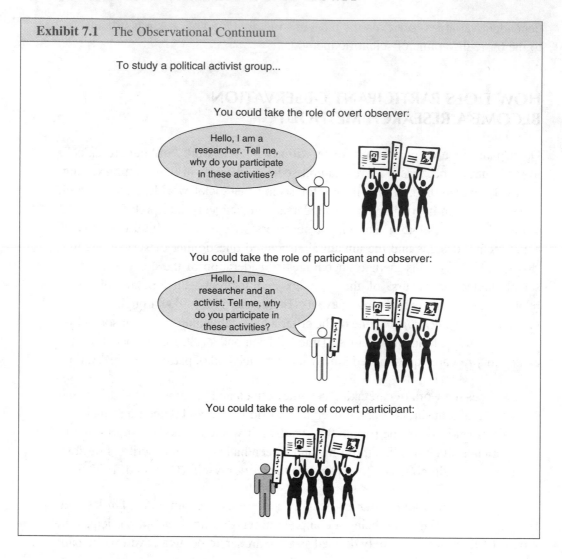

To study a political activist group...

You could take the role of overt observer:

Hello, I am a researcher. Tell me, why do you participate in these activities?

You could take the role of participant and observer:

Hello, I am a researcher and an activist. Tell me, why do you participate in these activities?

You could take the role of covert participant:

Complete Observation

In **complete observation**, researchers try to see things as they happen, without actively participating in these events. Chambliss watched nurses closely, but he never bathed a patient, changed a dressing, started an intravenous line, or told a family that their loved one had died. Once during an emergency surgery for a ruptured ectopic pregnancy—a drastic, immediately life-threatening event—a surgeon ordered him to "put in a Foley" (a urinary catheter) but a nurse quickly said, "He's a researcher, I'll do it." Of course, at the same time that he or she is observing the setting, the researcher must take into account the ways in which his or her presence as an observer itself alters the social situation being observed. Such **reactive effects** occur because it is not "natural" for someone to be present, recording observations for research and publication purposes (Thorne, 1993:20).

Mixed Participation/Observation

Most field researchers adopt a role that involves some active participation in the setting. Usually they inform at least some group members of their research interests, but then they participate in enough group activities to develop rapport with members and to gain a direct sense of what group members experience. This is not an easy balancing act. In his massive, 10-year study of gangs in urban America, Martin Sanchez Jankowski (1991)—

> . . . participated in nearly all the things they did. I ate where they ate, I slept where they slept, I stayed with their families, I traveled where they went, and . . . I fought with them. The only things that I did not participate in were those activities that were illegal . . . (including taking drugs) . . . . (Jankowski, 1991:13)

And Jankowski says that although, for instance, the fights he was in "often left bruises, I was never seriously hurt. Quite remarkably, in the more than 10 years during which I conducted this research, I was only seriously injured twice" (Jankowski, 1991:12).

A strategy of mixed participation and observation has two clear ethical advantages. Because group members know the researcher's real role in the group, they can choose to keep some information or attitudes hidden. By the same token, a researcher such as Jankowski can decline to participate in unethical or dangerous activities. Most field researchers get the feeling that, after they have become known and at least somewhat trusted figures in the group, their presence does not have any palpable effect on members' actions.

One especially interesting example of a "mixed" strategy is Chambliss's work on Olympic-level competitive swimmers. While working as a pure observer with a large number of world-class swimmers and teams, Chambliss himself coached, for six years, a small, local team in New York State—where he tried to apply what he had learned through his years of research about what produces Olympic athletes. If his theories were correct, he reasoned, he should be able to make his *own* team much better. And in fact his swimmers improved dramatically, from being a rather poor local team to producing some state champions and even a few national-class athletes (Chambliss, 1989). His written reports thus include a very unusual mix of observations, theorizing, and practical field experimentation to test the theory.

Complete Participation

Some field researchers adopt a **complete participation** role, in which they operate as a fully functioning member of the setting. Most often, such research is also *covert,* or secret—other members don't know that the researcher is doing research. In one famous covert study, Laud Humphreys (1970) served as a "watch queen" so that he could learn about men engaging in homosexual acts in a public restroom. In another case, Randall Alfred (1976) joined a group of Satanists to investigate group members and their interaction. And Erving Goffman (1961) worked as a state hospital assistant while studying the treatment of psychiatric patients.

Covert participants don't disrupt their settings, but they do face other problems. They must write up notes from memory and must do so when it would be natural for them to be away from group members. Researchers often run to the bathroom to scribble their notes, or jot "reminders" on napkins to expand on later, or whisper into hand-held recorders when they are out of the room. Researchers' spontaneous reactions to every event are unlikely to be consistent with those of the regular participants (Mitchell, 1993), because they are not "really" interested in washroom sex, or Satanists, or psychiatric ward attendants. When Timothy Diamond did covert research as an aide in a nursing home, his economic resources showed:

> "There's one thing I learned when I came to the States," [said a Haitian nursing assistant]. "Here you can't make it on just one job." She tilted her head, looked at me curiously, then asked, "You know, Tim, there's just one thing I don't understand about you. How do you make it on just one job?" (Diamond, 1992:47–48)

Ethical issues have been at the forefront of the debate over the strategy of covert participation. Some covert observers may become so wrapped up in the role they are playing that they adopt not just the mannerisms but also the perspectives and goals of the regular participants—they "go native"—and so may end up "going along to get along" with group activities that are themselves unethical. Kai Erikson (1967) argues that covert participation is therefore by its very nature unethical and should not be allowed except in public settings. If others suspect the researcher's identity or if the researcher contributes to, or impedes, group action, these consequences can be adverse. Covert researchers cannot anticipate the unintended consequences of their actions for research subjects or even for other researchers, because it can increase distrust of social scientists.

Entering the Field

Entering the field, the setting under investigation, is a critical stage in a participant observation project. Chambliss used a very "soft" technique for gaining access to hospitals. Rather than preparing a formal proposal to present to top administrators, he began quite informally:

> . . . I use an informal series of contacts with lower level members of the organization. In the present study, I would try first to meet some staff nurses who worked at the target hospitals, see them socially—for instance, by inviting them to lunch—and tell them I was interested in learning about nursing, hospitals, and ethical problems therein. This gave me a chance, first, to learn a lot about nursing in a comfortable setting. More important, it gave the people I met a chance to see that I was easy to talk to, trustworthy, and a decent human being who was not out to do an exposé.
>
> Typically, such conversations ended with my new acquaintance suggesting that I talk with still another nurse or administrator and providing a phone number. I would immediately follow up on this suggestion. A series of such meetings and introductions typically concluded in my being invited by suitably authorized administrators to visit the hospital, observe various units, and talk with whomever I pleased. At that point, as needed, I would present a formal proposal for research, get necessary permission, and so on. Basically, my assumption is that once potential subjects get to know me, they won't be afraid of my doing research on them. (Chambliss, 1996:190–191)

When participant observing involves public figures who are used to reporters and researchers, a more direct approach may secure entry into the field. Richard Fenno simply wrote a letter to most of the members of Congress whom he sought to study, asking for their permission to observe them at work (Fenno, 1978:257). He received only two refusals and attributed this high rate of subject cooperation to such reasons as interest in a change in the daily routine, commitment to making themselves available, a desire for more publicity, the flattery of scholarly attention, and interest in helping to teach others about politics. Other groups have other motivations, but in every case some consideration of these potential motives in advance should help smooth entry into the field.

In short, field researchers must be very sensitive to the impression they make and the ties they establish when entering the field. This stage lays the groundwork for collecting data from people who have different perspectives and for developing relationships that the researcher can use to surmount the problems in data collection that inevitably arise in the field. The researcher should be ready with a rationale for her participation and some sense of the potential benefits to participants. Discussion about these issues with key participants, or **gatekeepers,** should be honest and should identify what the participants can expect from the research, without necessarily going into detail about the researcher's hypotheses or research questions (Rossman & Rallis, 1998:51–53, 105–108).

Developing and Maintaining Relationships

Researchers must be careful to manage their relationships in the research setting so that they can continue to observe and interview diverse members of the setting throughout the long period typical of participant observation (Maxwell, 1996:66). Interaction early in the research process is particularly sensitive, because participants don't know the researcher and the researcher doesn't know the routines.

In his classic study *Street Corner Society,* William F. Whyte (1955) used what in retrospect was a sophisticated two-part strategy to develop and maintain relationships with poor men whose informal relationships he studied in "Cornerville" (actually a slum neighborhood in Boston). The first part of Whyte's strategy was to maintain good relations with a group leader known as Doc and, through Doc, to stay on good terms with the others. Doc became a **key informant** in the research setting—a knowledgeable insider who knew the group's culture and was willing to share access and insights with the researcher (Gilchrist & Williams, 1999). The less obvious part of Whyte's strategy was a consequence of his decision to move into Cornerville, a move he decided was necessary to really understand and be accepted in the community. The room he rented in a local family's home became his base of operations. In some respects, this family became an important dimension of Whyte's immersion in the community: He tried to learn Italian by speaking with family members, and they conversed late at night as if Whyte were a real family member. But Whyte recognized that he needed a place to unwind after his days of constant alertness in the field, so he made a conscious decision not to include the family as an object of study. Living in this family's home became a means for Whyte to maintain standing as a community insider without becoming totally immersed in the demands of research (Whyte, 1955:294–297).

Experienced participant observers recommend developing a plausible (and honest) explanation for yourself and your study and keeping the support of key individuals in order to maintain relationships in the field. They also suggest being somewhat "laid back," neither showing off your expertise nor being too aggressive in questioning others. Another good bit of advice is not faking social similarity with those you are observing and not offering monetary rewards for participation (Bogdewic, 1999:53–54; Rossman & Rallis, 1998:105–108; Whyte, 1955:300–306; Wolcott, 1995:91–95).

Sampling People and Events

Qualitative researchers intensively study people, places, or other phenomena of interest, and so they tend to limit their focus to just one or a few sites or programs. Still, the sample must be appropriate and adequate for the study, even if it is not representative. The qualitative researcher may select a "critical case" that is unusually rich in information pertaining to the research question, a "typical case" precisely because it is judged to be typical, and/or a "deviant case" that provides a useful contrast (Kuzel, 1999). Within a research site, plans may be made to sample different settings, people, events, and artifacts (see Exhibit 7.2).

Studying more than one case or setting almost always strengthens the causal conclusions and makes the findings more generalizable (King, Keohane, & Verba, 1994). For example, Diamond (1992:5) worked in three different Chicago nursing homes "in widely different neighborhoods" and with different percentages of residents supported by Medicaid. He then "visited many homes across the United States to validate my observations."

Other approaches to sampling in field research are more systematic. Researchers use **theoretical sampling** when they focus their investigation on particular processes that seem to be important and select instances to allow comparisons or checks with which they can test these perceptions (Glaser & Strauss, 1967; Ragin,

Exhibit 7.2   Sampling Plan for a Participant Observation Project in Schools

	Type of Information to Be Obtained				
*Information Source**	*Collegiality*	*Goals & Community*	*Action Expectations*	*Knowledge Orientation*	*Base*
SETTINGS					
Public places (halls, main offices)					
Teacherís lounge	X	X		X	X
Classrooms		X	X	X	X
Meeting rooms	X		X	X	
Gymnasium or locker room		X			
EVENTS					
Faculty meetings	X		X		X
Lunch hour	X				X
Teaching		X	X	X	X
PEOPLE					
Principal		X	X	X	X
Teachers	X	X	X	X	X
Students		X	X	X	
ARTIFACTS					
Newspapers		X	X		X
Decorations		X			

* Selected examples in each category.

Exhibit 7.3   Theoretical Sampling

Original cases interviewed in a study of cocaine users:

Realization: Some cocaine users are businesspeople.
Add businesspeople to sample:

Realization: Sample is low on women.
Add women to sample:

Realization: Some female cocaine users are mothers of young children.
Add mothers to sample:

1994:98–101) (see Exhibit 7.3). Jankowski, again, provides an impressive example of conscientious theoretical sampling in field research:

> It was first essential to investigate *gangs in different cities* in order to control for the different socioeconomic and political environments that they operate in. Second, in order to determine if there were any differences associated with ethnicity, it was critical to *compare gangs composed of different ethnic groups.* Three metropolitan areas were therefore chosen for the study: the greater Los Angeles area, various boroughs of New York City, and the greater Boston area.
>
> Two were eastern cities with certain weather patterns; the other was western with a completely different weather pattern. (Weather has often been thought to have an impact on gang activity, with colder weather restricting activity and warmer weather encouraging it.)

Of the thirty-seven gangs studied, thirteen were in the Los Angeles area, twenty were in the New York City area, and four were in the Boston area. Various ethnic groups are represented in the sample, which includes gangs composed of Irish, African-American, Puerto Rican, Chicano, Dominican, Jamaican, and Central American members. The sample also involves gangs of varying size. The smallest had thirty-four members; the largest had more than one thousand. . . . Within this sample, stratified by ethnicity, I randomly selected ten in each city. It was my intention to study African-American gangs, Latino gangs, Asian gangs, and white gangs, and so gangs representing each of these ethnic groups were chosen. Because I wanted to include gangs of varying membership sizes, I randomly selected gangs from my ethnically stratified list until I obtained a sample representing gangs of different sizes. Since my over-all strategy was to study five gangs in Los Angeles and five in New York for two years, then add more, and finally add several Boston gangs, I selected five of the original ten chosen and began my effort to secure their participation. (Jankowski, 1991:6–7)

Taking Notes

Notes are the primary means of recording participant observation data (Emerson, Fretz, & Shaw, 1995). It is almost always a mistake to try to take comprehensive notes while engaged in the field—the process of writing extensively is just too disruptive. The usual procedure is to jot down brief notes about highlights of the observation period. These brief notes then serve as memory joggers when writing the actual **field notes** at a later session. It will also help to maintain a daily log in which each day's activities are recorded (Bogdewic, 1999:58–67). With the aid of the **jottings** and some practice, researchers usually remember a great deal of what happened—as long as the comprehensive field notes are written immediately afterward, or at least within the next 24 hours, and before they have been discussed with anyone else.

Usually writing up notes takes much longer—at least three times longer—than the observing did. Field notes must be as complete, detailed, and true to what was observed and heard as possible. Direct quotes should be distinguished clearly from paraphrased quotes, and both should be set off from the researcher's observations and reflections. The surrounding context should receive as much attention as possible, and a map of the setting should be included, with indications of where individuals were at different times.

Careful note taking yields a big payoff. On page after page, field notes will suggest new concepts, causal connections, and theoretical propositions. Notes also should include descriptions of the methodology and a record of the researchers' feelings and thoughts while observing. Exhibit 7.4 illustrates these techniques with notes from the Chambliss study.

Exhibit 7.4 Sample Field Notes from the Chambliss Nursing Study

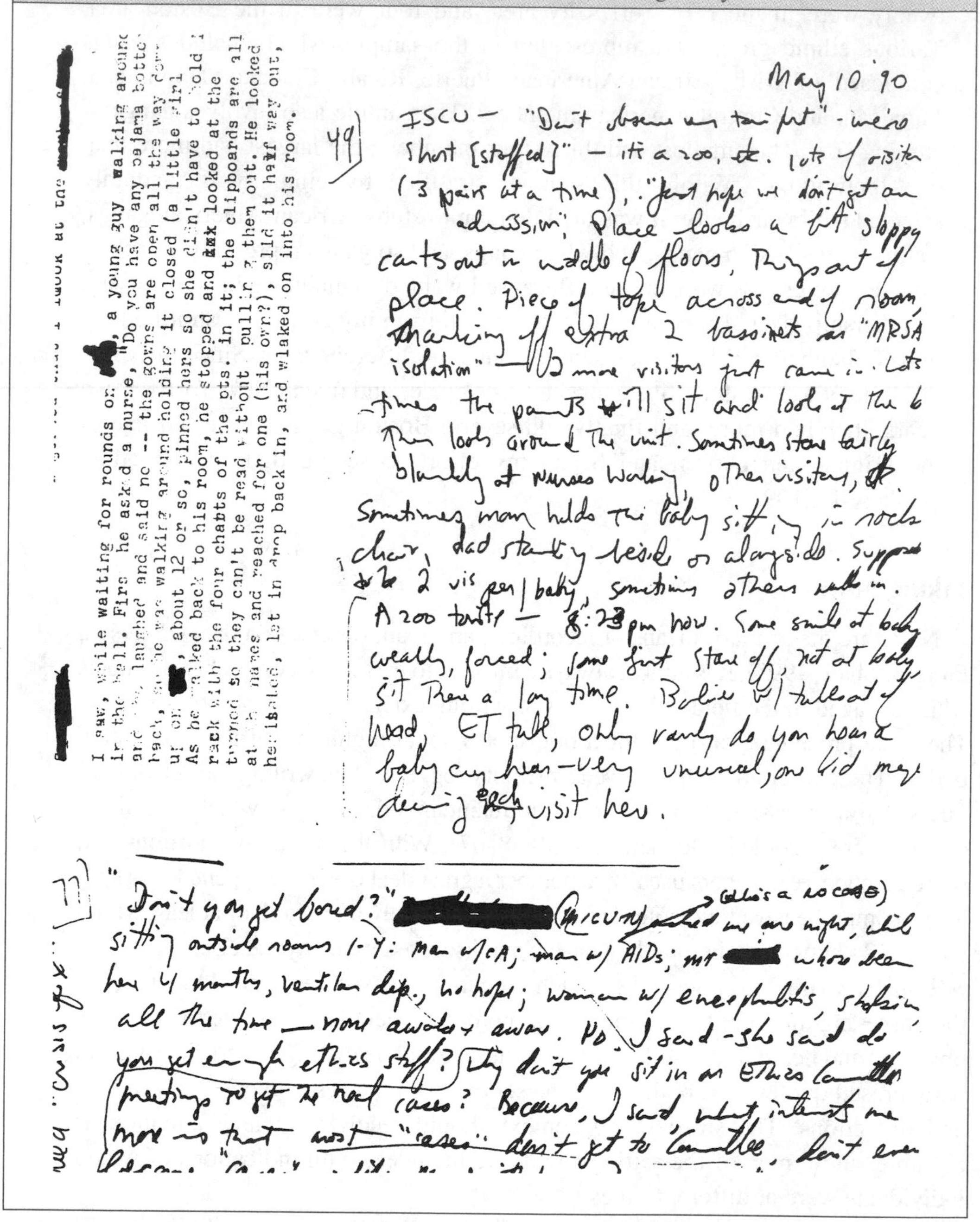

Source: Original field notes, either written on site or typed later that day. Identifying information has been blanked out. "ISCU" stands for "Infant Special Care Unit," where premature infants are cared for. The first sentence reads, "Don't observe us tonight," "we're short [staffed]," a quotation from a nurse in the unit.

Managing the Personal Dimensions

Field researchers cannot help but be affected on a personal, emotional level by social processes in the social situation they are studying. At the same time, those being studied react to researchers not just as researchers but as personal acquaintances—and often as friends. Managing and learning from this personal side of field research is an important part of any project.

> The researcher, like his informants, is a social animal. He has a role to play, and he has his own personality needs that must be met in some degree if he is to function successfully. Where the researcher operates out of a university, just going into the field for a few hours at a time, he can keep his personal social life separate from field activity. His problem of role is not quite so complicated. If, on the other hand, the researcher is living for an extended period in the community he is studying, his personal life is inextricably mixed with his research. (Whyte, 1955:279)

Barrie Thorne, a sociologist known for her research on gender roles among children, wondered whether "my moments of remembering, the times when I felt like a ten-year-old girl, [were] a source of distortion or insight?" She concluded they were both: "Memory, like observing, is a way of knowing and can be a rich resource." But "When my own responses . . . were driven by emotions like envy or aversion, they clearly obscured my ability to grasp the full social situation" (Thorne, 1993:26).

There is no formula for successfully managing the personal dimension of field research. It is much more art than science and flows more from the researcher's own personality and natural approach to other people than from formal training. But novice field researchers often neglect to consider how they will manage personal relationships when they plan and carry out their projects. Attention to a few guidelines based on our personal experience with field research, provided in Exhibit 7.5, should maximize the likelihood of a project's success.

HOW DO YOU CONDUCT INTENSIVE INTERVIEWS?

Participant observation can provide a wonderfully rich view, then, of the social world. But it remains a *view,* seen by the observer. Often we wonder what individuals think or feel, or how they see their world. For this purpose one can use **intensive interviews.**

Unlike the more structured interviewing that may be used in survey research (discussed in Chapter 6), intensive or *depth* interviewing relies on open-ended

Exhibit 7.5   Nine Steps to Successful Field Research

1. *Have a simple, one-sentence explanation of your project.* "I want to learn about the problems nurses face in their work," or "I want to learn what makes a great swimming team." People will ask what you're doing, but no one cares to hear all your theories.

2. *Be yourself.* Don't lie about who you are. First, it's wrong. Second, you'll get caught and ruin the trust you're trying to build. (Yes, there are exceptions, but very few.)

3. *Don't interfere.* They got along just fine before you came along, and they can do it again. Don't be a pest.

4. *Listen, actively.* Be genuinely interested in what they say. Unless you're studying movie stars, politicians, or other celebrities, most people don't listen to them. If you really care to listen, they'll tell you everything.

5. *Show up,* at every opportunity—3:00 in the morning, or if you have to walk five miles. Go to their parties and their funerals. Make a 5-hour trip for a 15-minute interview, and they'll notice—and give you everything you want.

6. *Pay attention to everything,* especially when you're bored. That's when the important stuff is happening, the stuff *no one else* notices.

7. *Protect your sources,* more than is necessary. When word gets around that you can be trusted, you won't believe what people will tell you.

8. *Write everything down, that day.* By tomorrow, you'll forget 90% of the best material, and then it's gone forever.

9. Always remember: *It's not about you, it's about them.* Don't try to be smart, or savvy, or hip; don't try to be the center of attention. Stop thinking about yourself all the time. Pay attention to other people.

Source: Prepared for this volume by Dan Chambliss.

questions to develop a comprehensive picture of the interviewee's background, attitudes, and actions—to "listen to people as they describe how they understand the worlds in which they live and work" (Rubin & Rubin, 1995:3).

For instance:

> We had two or three patients, and they were terminally ill with cancer. We would give the patients, every two or three hours around the clock toward the end, morphine sulphate, intramuscular.
>
> I was really worried about giving them a morphine injection because the morphine depresses the respiration. I thought, well, is this injection going to do them in?
>
> If I don't give the injection, they will linger on longer, but they might also have more pain. If I do give the injection, the end result of death is going to occur faster. Am I playing God?" (Chambliss, 1996:171)

The key to eliciting such a response is *active listening*—which is not the same as just being quiet. Instead, you must actively question, ask for explanations, and show a genuine deep curiosity about the subject's views and feelings. The researcher's own opinions are not important here; you must suspend all judgment of what the respondent is saying, even if you regard her opinions as obnoxious or even immoral. Remember, the goal is to learn what *she* thinks, not to express what *you* think.

Therefore, depth interviews may be highly unstructured. Rather than asking standard questions in a fixed order, a researcher conducting intensive interviews may allow the specific content and order of questions to vary from one interviewee to another. Like participant observation studies, intensive interviewing engages researchers actively with subjects. The researchers must listen to lengthy explanations, ask follow-up questions tailored to the preceding answers, and seek to learn about interrelated belief systems or personal approaches to things, rather than measure a limited set of variables. As a result, intensive interviews are often much longer than standardized interviews, sometimes as long as 15 hours, conducted in several different sessions.

The intensive interview can become more like a conversation between partners than between a researcher and a subject (Kaufman, 1986:22–23). Some call it "a conversation with a purpose" (Rossman & Rallis, 1998:126). Robert Bellah, Richard Madsen, William Sullivan, Ann Swidler, and Steven Tipton (1985) elaborate on this aspect of intensive interviewing in a methodological appendix to their national best-seller about American individualism, *Habits of the Heart:*

> We did not, as in some scientific version of "Candid Camera," seek to capture their beliefs and actions without our subjects being aware of us. Rather, we sought to bring our preconceptions and questions into the conversation and to understand the answers we were receiving not only in terms of the language but also, so far as we could discover, in the lives of those we were talking with. Though we did not seek to impose our ideas on those with whom we talked . . . we did attempt to uncover assumptions, to make explicit what the person we were talking to might rather have left implicit. The interview as we employed it was active, Socratic. (Bellah et al., 1985:304)

Random selection is rarely used to select respondents for intensive interviews, but the selection method still must be considered carefully. Researchers should try to select interviewees who are knowledgeable about the subject of the interview, who are open to talking, and who represent a range of perspectives (Rubin & Rubin, 1995:65–92). Selection of new interviewees should continue, if possible, at least until the **saturation point** is reached, the point when new interviews seem to yield little additional information (see Exhibit 7.6).

Exhibit 7.6   The Saturation Point in Intensive Interviewing

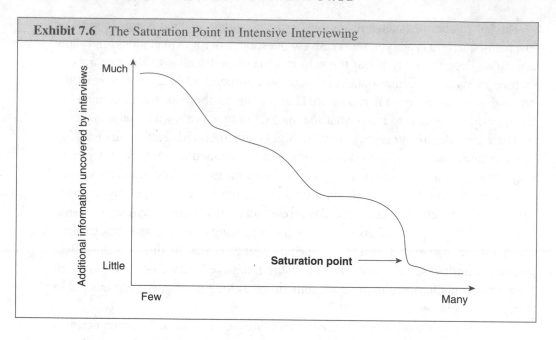

Establishing and Maintaining a Partnership

Because intensive interviewing does not engage researchers as participants in subjects' daily affairs, the problems of entering the field are much reduced. However, the logistics of arranging long periods for personal interviews can still be pretty complicated. It also is important to establish rapport with subjects by considering in advance how they will react to the interview arrangements and by developing an approach that does not violate their standards for social behavior. Interviewees should be treated with respect, as knowledgeable partners whose time is valued (in other words, don't be late for your appointments). A commitment to confidentiality should be stated and honored (Rubin & Rubin, 1995).

Asking Questions and Recording Answers

Intensive interviewers must plan their main questions around an outline of the interview topic. The questions generally should be short and to the point. More details can then be elicited through nondirective probes (such as "Can you tell me more about that?" or "uh-huh," echoing the respondent's comment, or just maintaining a moment of silence). Follow-up questions can then be tailored to answers to the main questions.

Interviewers should strategize throughout an interview about how best to achieve their objectives while taking into account interviewees' answers. *Habits of the Heart* again provides a useful illustration:

[Coinvestigator Steven] Tipton, in interviewing Margaret Oldham [a pseudonym], tried to discover at what point she would take responsibility for another human being:

Q: So what are you responsible for?

A: I'm responsible for my acts and for what I do.

Q: Does that mean you're responsible for others, too?

A: No.

Q: Are you your sister's keeper?

A: No.

Q: Your brother's keeper?

A: No.

Q: Are you responsible for your husband?

A: I'm not. He makes his own decisions. He is his own person. He acts his own acts. I can agree with them, or I can disagree with them. If I ever find them nauseous enough, I have a responsibility to leave and not deal with it any more.

Q: What about children?

A: I . . . I would say I have a legal responsibility for them, but in a sense I think they in turn are responsible for their own acts. (Bellah et al., 1985:304)

Do you see how the interviewer actively encouraged the subject to *explain* what she meant by "responsibility"? This sort of active questioning undoubtedly did a better job of clarifying the interviewee's concept of responsibility than a fixed set of questions would have.

Tape recorders commonly are used for recording intensive interviews and focus group interviews. They do not inhibit most interviewees and, in fact, are routinely ignored. Occasionally a respondent is very concerned with his or her public image and may therefore speak "for the tape recorder," but such individuals are unlikely to speak frankly in any research interview. In any case, constant note-taking during an interview prevents adequate displays of interest and is distracting. Sometimes, though, the very act of visibly turning off the recorder may free a respondent to tell that one great secret she's been keeping—and interviewers often use that very technique.

HOW DO YOU RUN FOCUS GROUPS?

Finally, for quick-and-dirty answers, **focus groups** can be the qualitative researcher's best friend. Long favored by advertisers and political consultants who want to see "what message pushes their buttons," focus groups are groups of unrelated individuals that are formed by a researcher and then led in group discussion of a topic for one to two hours. The researcher asks specific questions and guides the discussion, but the resulting information is qualitative and relatively unstructured. Focus groups do not involve representative samples; instead, a few individuals are recruited for the group who have the time to participate, have some knowledge pertinent to the focus group topic, and share key characteristics with the target population. Throughout the Mellon Project on liberal education at Hamilton College, focus groups—of Dean's List students, or minority students, or study abroad participants—have been used to rapidly assess major problem areas in various programs, and to develop areas for more systematic investigation.

Most focus groups involve 7 to 10 people, a number that facilitates discussion by all in attendance. Homogeneous groups may be more convivial and willing to share feelings, but heterogeneous groups may stimulate more ideas (Brown, 1999:115–117); which kind one uses depends on the goals of the study.

The researcher, or group moderator, uses an interview guide, but the dynamics of group discussion often require changes in the order and manner in which different topics are addressed (Brown, 1999:120). No formal procedure exists for determining the generalizability of focus group answers, but the careful researcher should conduct at least several focus groups on the same topic and check for consistency in the findings. Some focus group experts advise conducting enough focus groups to reach the point of "saturation," when an additional focus group adds little new information to that which already has been generated (Brown, 1999:118).

Richard Krueger provides a good example of a situation in which focus groups were used effectively:

> [A] University recently launched a $100 million fund drive. The key aspect of the drive was a film depicting science and research efforts. The film was shown in over two dozen focus groups of alumni, with surprising results to University officials. Alumni simply did not like the film and instead were more attracted to supporting undergraduate humanistic education. (Krueger, 1988:33–37)

Focus group methods share with other field research techniques an emphasis on discovering unanticipated findings and exploring hidden meanings. Although they do not provide a means for developing reliable, generalizable results (the traditional strong suits of survey research), focus groups can be an indispensable aid for developing hypotheses and survey questions, for investigating the meaning of survey results, and for quickly assessing the range of opinion about an issue.

ANALYZING QUALITATIVE DATA

The data for a qualitative study most often are notes jotted down in the field or during an interview—from which the original comments, observations, and feelings are reconstructed—or text transcribed from audiotapes. What to do with all this material? Chapter 8 is a full discussion of this topic, but a few comments here provide an introduction.

Many field research projects have slowed to a halt because a novice researcher becomes overwhelmed by the quantity of information that has been collected. (A one-hour interview can generate 20 to 25 pages of single-spaced text [Kvale, 1996:169].) Boxes filled with those scribbled notes: old napkins with some words, flyers for events attended, e-mails from informants—all can seem daunting, but a few simple steps can clarify the whole mess rather quickly.

The Phases of Analysis

Basically, there are two approaches to analyzing qualitative data: the *deductive,* or hypothesis-testing, and the *inductive,* or exploratory. Jankowski, in his study of gangs, used a deductive method:

> I began the analysis by establishing topics that would need to be covered in a book about gangs, such as gang recruitment, gang organization, violence, and so on. I then proceeded to read each of my notes (daily notes, daily summaries, weekly summaries) and place them in stacks having to do with each topic I wanted to cover. When notes pertained to more than one topic, I photocopied them and placed each under the additional topics.
>
> My analysis began by taking a topic and reviewing what other researchers had found concerning gangs. Their findings would be written down in hypothesis form and then I would read my notes to determine what my evidence suggested. (Jankowski, 1991:16)

Jankowski created a series of topics and sorted his notes into those categories, which were created in advance. He then used the material in each category to test hypotheses from the literature on gangs.

An *inductive* approach, by contrast, allows themes and topics to emerge from the data themselves. In his nursing study, Chambliss first spent several weeks reading through all of his notes and skimming transcripts, taking notes on the topics covered; then he read through the notes themselves, organizing them into a handful of topics (e.g., routines of work, ethical problems, the role of the nurse) that seemed to arise repeatedly; and finally re-sorted all of his "notes and quotes" into huge piles, one for each of those main topics. (He did this work with notes covering the entire living room floor of his apartment.)

As observation, interviewing, and reflection continue, researchers refine their definitions of problems and concepts and select indicators. They can then check the frequency and distribution of phenomena. How many people made a particular type of comment? How often did social interaction lead to arguments? Hypotheses are modified as researchers gain experience in the setting. For the final analysis, the researchers check their models carefully against their notes and make a concerted attempt to discover negative evidence that might suggest the model is incorrect. Such an approach combines the inductive with the deductive.

ETHICAL ISSUES IN QUALITATIVE RESEARCH

Qualitative research can raise some complex ethical issues. No matter how hard the field researcher strives to study the social world naturally, leaving no traces, the very act of research itself imposes something "unnatural" on the situation. It is up to the researcher to identify and take responsibility for the consequences of her or his involvement. Five main ethical issues arise:

1. *Voluntary participation*—Ensuring that subjects are participating in a study voluntarily is not often a problem with intensive interviewing and focus group research, but it is often a point of contention in participant observation studies. Few researchers or institutional review boards are willing to condone covert participation because it does not offer any way to ensure that participation by the subjects is voluntary. Even when the researcher's role is more open, interpreting the standard of voluntary participation still can be difficult. Should the requirement of voluntary participation apply equally to every member of an organization being observed? What if the manager consents, the workers are ambivalent, and the union says no?

2. *Subject well-being*—Before beginning a project, every field researcher should consider carefully how to avoid harm to subjects. It is not possible to avoid every theoretical possibility of harm or to be sure that a project will cause no adverse consequences whatsoever to any individual, but direct harm to the reputations or feelings of particular individuals should be avoided at all costs. The risk of such harm can be minimized by maintaining the confidentiality of research subjects and by not adversely affecting the course of events while engaged in a

setting. Whyte (1955:335–337) found himself regretting having recommended that a particular politician be allowed to speak to a social club he was observing, because the speech led to serious dissension in the club and strains between Whyte and some club members.

3. *Identity disclosure*—Current ethical standards require informed consent of research subjects and most would argue that this standard cannot be met in any meaningful way if researchers do not disclose fully their identity. But how much disclosure about the study is necessary and how hard should researchers try to make sure that their research purposes are understood? In field research on Codependents Anonymous, Leslie Irvine (1998) found that the emphasis on anonymity and the expectations for group discussion made it difficult for her to disclose her identity. Can a balance be struck between the disclosure of critical facts and a coherent research strategy?

4. *Confidentiality*—Field researchers normally use fictitious names for the characters in their reports, but doing so does not always guarantee confidentiality to their research subjects. In Chambliss's nursing book, reference to "the director of the medical center" might have identified that person, at least to other employees of the center who knew Chambliss did his research there. And anyone studying public figures or national leaders in a social movement must exercise special care, because such people can be privately recognized by their own followers or enemies. Researchers should thus make every effort to expunge any possible identifying material from published information and to alter unimportant aspects of a description when necessary to prevent identity disclosure. In any case, no field research project should begin if some participants clearly will suffer serious harm by being identified in project publications.

5. *Online research*—The large number of discussion groups and bulletin boards on the Internet has stimulated much interest in conducting research like that of Fox and Roberts (1999) who observed physicians' listservs in the United Kingdom. Such research can violate the principles of voluntary participation and identity disclosure when researchers participate in discussions and record and analyze text, but do not identify themselves as researchers (Jesnadum, 2000).

These ethical issues cannot be evaluated independently. The final decision to proceed must be made after weighing the relative benefits and risks to participants. Few qualitative research projects will be barred by consideration of these ethical issues, however, except for those involving covert participation. The more important concern for researchers is to identify the ethically troublesome aspects of their proposed research and resolve them before the project begins and to act on new ethical issues as they come up during the project.

CONCLUSION

Qualitative research has both immediate and lasting attractions. Many of the classic works of social science, from Sigmund Freud's *Interpretation of Dreams* and Margaret Mead's *Coming of Age in Samoa* to Erving Goffman's *Presentation of Self in Everyday Life* and Kristin Luker's *Abortion and the Politics of Motherhood,* rest on qualitative forms of social research. Telling true stories of real people, laying out their feelings and emotions, is qualitative research—interviews, field work, and focus groups cut through the dry numbers and correlations, the abstract variables, and the hypotheses of contemporary quantitative social science. Qualitative research aims to go, as we said at the beginning of this chapter, where real people live. It thereby can become, at its best, a form of literature, beautifully teaching its readers the deeper truths of the human condition. More modestly, many students simply find reading reports of qualitative research to be far more interesting than the statistics used in survey analysis.

But "interesting" is not always the same as accurate, correct, or even representative. The juiciest stories that Dan Chambliss heard from his nurses were not, as it happens, what typically occurred to them. Researchers love a "good quote," but it may not represent the truth of a setting; field workers love finding a key informant whose views may not be those of the average subject. Like journalists, even the best qualitative researchers may be drawn to the odd, the unusual, or the available—and all of those may be poor substitutes for representative sampling, standardized questions, and other more sober approaches to learning about social life. The statistics of survey analysis and the control groups of experiments force us to face reality with self-discipline; they make it harder to fool ourselves about what we see.

In the end, qualitative methods are one—and only one—excellent set of tools, complementary in purpose to the tools of surveys, experiments, and other methods. Each has its strengths and its weaknesses. When surveys find that college students complain about "social life" but also rejoice that they "made my best friends ever here," interviews can explain the (apparent) contradiction. When police statistics and crime surveys can't fathom the logic of gang life, Martin Sanchez Jankowski steps in and tells us the story in all its richness. And remember: no experiment, however carefully designed with an eye to protecting internal validity, could ever have uncovered what Sigmund Freud found by just sitting quietly next to a patient on a couch, and listening.

KEY TERMS

Complete observation	Field research
Complete (covert) participation	Focus group
Field notes	Gatekeeper

Grounded theory

Intensive (depth) interviewing

Jottings

Key informant

Participant observation

Qualitative method

Reactive effect

Saturation point

Tacit knowledge

Theoretical sampling

HIGHLIGHTS

• Qualitative methods are most useful in exploring new issues, in investigating hard-to-study groups, and in determining the meaning people give to their lives and actions. In addition, most social research projects can be improved in some respects by taking advantage of qualitative techniques.

• Qualitative researchers tend to develop ideas inductively; they try to understand the social context and sequential nature of attitudes and actions and explore the subjective meanings that participants attach to events. They rely primarily on participant observation, intensive interviewing, and, in recent years, focus groups.

• Participant observers may adopt one of several roles for a particular research project. Each role represents a different balance between observing and participating. Many field researchers prefer a moderate role, participating as well as observing in a group but acknowledging publicly the researcher role. Such a role avoids the ethical issues posed by covert participation while still allowing the insights into the social world derived from participating directly in it. The role that the participant observer chooses should be based on an evaluation of the problems likely to arise from reactive effects and the ethical dilemmas of covert participation.

• Field researchers must develop strategies for entering the field, developing and maintaining relations in the field, sampling, and recording and analyzing data. Selection of sites or other units to study may reflect an emphasis on typical cases, deviant cases, and/or critical cases that can provide more information than others. Sampling techniques commonly used within sites or in selecting interviewees in field research include theoretical sampling.

• Recording and analyzing notes is a crucial step in field research. Jottings are used as brief reminders about events in the field, whereas daily logs are useful to chronicle the researcher's activities. Detailed field notes should be recorded daily. Periodic analysis of the notes can guide refinement of methods used in the field and of the concepts, indicators, and models developed to explain what has been observed.

• Intensive interviews involve open-ended questions and follow-up probes, with specific question content and order varying from one interview to another.

• Focus groups combine elements of participant observation and intensive interviewing. They can increase the validity of attitude measurement by revealing what people say when presenting their opinions in a group context, instead of the artificial one-on-one interview setting.

• Computer software is used increasingly for the analysis of qualitative, textual, and pictorial data. Users can record their notes, categorize observations, specify links between categories, and count occurrences.

• The four main ethical issues in field research concern voluntary participation, subject well-being, identity disclosure, and confidentiality.

> To assist you in completing the Web Exercises, please access the Study Site at http://www.pineforge.com/mssw2 where you'll find the Web Exercises with accompanying links. You'll find other useful study materials like self-quizzes and e-flashcards for each chapter, along with a group of carefully selected articles from research journals that illustrate the major concepts and techniques presented in the book.

EXERCISES

Discussing Research

1. William Foote Whyte's (1955) classic field study, *Street Corner Society*, raises a number of ethical issues. He lived with a family in the neighborhood he was studying, participated in activities ranging from social gatherings to voting, and portrayed the neighborhood in a way that some residents disagreed with. Which ethical issues do you think are likely to come up in this type of participatory research? What procedures or decisions would you suggest to ensure adequate protection of human subjects? Discuss your opinions with other class members, using Whyte's research for examples.

Finding Research

1. Go to the Annual Review of Sociology's Web site by following the publications link at http://AnnualReviews.org. Search for articles that use qualitative methods as the primary method of gathering data on any one of the following subjects: child development/socialization; gender/sex roles; aging/gerontology. Enter "Qualitative AND Methods" in the subject field to begin this search. Review at least five articles and report on the specific method of field research used in each.

2. Go to the Social Science Information Gateway (SOSIG) at http://sosig.esrc.bris.ac.uk. Choose "Social Science Methodology." Now choose three or four interesting sites and explore them to find out what information they provide regarding field research, what kinds of projects are being done that involve field research, and the purposes that specific field research methods are being used for.

3. You have been asked to do field research on the World Wide Web's impact on the socialization of children in today's world. The first part of the project involves your writing a compare and contrast report on the differences between how you and your generation were socialized as children and the way children today are being socialized. Collect your data by surfing the Web "as if you were a kid." The Web is your field and you are the field researcher.

Using any of the major search engines, explore the Web within the "Kids" or "Children" subject heading, keeping field notes on what you observe.

Write a brief report based on the data you have collected. How has the Web impacted child socialization in comparison to when you were a child?

Critiquing Research

1. Read and summarize one of the qualitative studies discussed in this chapter, or another classic study recommended by your instructor. Review and critique the study using the article review questions presented in Exhibit 10.2. What questions are answered by the study? What questions are raised for further investigation?

2. Write a short critique of the ethics of Ellis's (1986) study (discussed in Chapter 2). Read the book ahead of time to clarify the details, and then focus on each of the ethical guidelines presented in this chapter: voluntary participation, subject well-being, identity disclosure, and confidentiality. Conclude with a statement about the extent to which field researchers should be required to disclose their identities and the circumstances in which they should not be permitted to participate actively in the social life they study.

Doing Research

1. Conduct a brief observational study in a public location on campus where students congregate. A cafeteria, a building lobby, or a lounge would be ideal. You can sit and observe, taking occasional notes unobtrusively and without violating any expectations of privacy. Observe for 30 minutes. Write up field notes, being sure to include a description of the setting and a commentary on your own behavior and your reactions to what you observed.

2. Review the experiments and surveys described in previous chapters. Pick one and propose a field research design that would focus on the same research question but with participant observation techniques in a local setting. Propose the role along the participant observation continuum that you would play in the setting, and explain why you would favor this role. Describe the stages of your field research study, including your plans for entering the field, developing and maintaining relationships, sampling, and recording and analyzing data. Then discuss what you would expect your study to add to the findings resulting from the study described in the book.

3. Develop an interview guide that focuses on a research question addressed in one of the studies in this book. Using this guide, conduct an intensive interview with one person who is involved with the topic in some way. Take only brief notes during the interview; then write up as complete a record of the interview as you can immediately afterward. Turn in an evaluation of your performance as an interviewer and note-taker, together with your notes.

Qualitative Data Analysis

I was at lunch standing in line and he [another male student] came up to my face and started saying stuff and then he pushed me. I said . . . I'm cool with you, I'm your friend and then he push me again and calling me names. I told him to stop pushing me and then he push me hard and said something about my mom. And then he hit me, and I hit him back. After he fell I started kicking him.

—Morrill et al., 2000:521

Unfortunately, this statement was not made by a soap opera actor but by a real student writing an in-class essay about conflicts in which he had participated.

It was written for a team of social scientists who were studying conflicts in high schools, to better understand their origins and to inform prevention policies.

In qualitative data analysis, the raw data to be analyzed are text, rather than numbers. In the high school conflict study by Morrill et al. (2000), there are no variables and hypotheses in this qualitative analysis. The use of text, not numbers, and the (initial) absence of variables are just two of the ways that qualitative analysis differs from quantitative.

In this chapter, we present the features that most qualitative data analyses share and illustrate these features with a wide variety of research. You will quickly see that there is no one way to analyze textual data. To quote Michael Quinn Patton (2002:432),

> Qualitative analysis transforms data into findings. No formula exists for that transformation. Guidance, yes. But no recipe. Direction can and will be offered, but the final destination remains unique for each inquirer, known only when—and if—arrived at.

We will discuss some different types of qualitative data analysis and then describe computer programs for qualitative data analysis. You will see that these increasingly popular programs are blurring the distinctions between quantitative and qualitative approaches to textual analysis.

WHAT IS DISTINCTIVE ABOUT QUALITATIVE DATA ANALYSIS?

The distinctive features of qualitative data collection methods that you studied in Chapter 7 are also reflected in the methods used to analyze that data. The focus on text—on qualitative data rather than on numbers—is the most important feature of qualitative analysis. The "text" that qualitative researchers analyze is most often transcripts of interviews or notes from participant observation sessions, but the term can also refer to pictures or other images that the researcher examines.

What can the qualitative data analyst learn from a "text"? Here qualitative analysts may have two different goals. Some view analysis of a text as a way to understand what participants "really" thought or felt or did in some situation or at some point in time. The text becomes a way to get "behind the numbers" that are recorded in a quantitative analysis to see the richness of real social experience. Other qualitative researchers have adopted a "hermeneutic" perspective on texts—that is, a perspective that views a text as an interpretation that can never be judged true or false. The text is only one possible interpretation among many (Patton, 2002:114).

The meaning of a text, then, is negotiated among a community of interpreters, and to the extent that some agreement is reached about meaning at a particular time and place, that meaning can only be based on consensual community validation.

From a hermeneutic perspective, a researcher is constructing a "reality" with his interpretations of a text provided by the subjects of research; other researchers with different backgrounds could come to markedly different conclusions.

You can see from this discussion about text that qualitative and quantitative data analyses differ in the priority given to the prior views of the researcher and to those of the subjects of the research. Qualitative data analysts seek to describe their textual data in ways that capture the setting or people who produced this text on their own terms, rather than in terms of predefined measures and hypotheses. So qualitative data analysis tends to be inductive—the analyst identifies important categories in the data, as well as patterns and relationships, through a process of discovery. There are often no predefined measures or hypotheses. Anthropologists term this an **emic focus,** which means representing the setting in terms of the participants, rather than an **etic focus,** in which the setting and its participants are represented in terms that the researcher brings to the study.

Emic focus: Representing a setting with the participants' terms.

Etic focus: Representing a setting with the researchers' terms.

Good qualitative data analyses focus on the interrelated aspects of the setting or group, or person, under investigation—the case—rather than breaking the whole up into separate parts. The whole is always understood to be greater than the sum of its parts, and so the social context of events, thoughts, and actions becomes essential for interpretation. Within this framework, it doesn't really make sense to focus on two variables out of an interacting set of influences and test the relationship between just those two.

Qualitative data analysis is an iterative and reflexive process that begins as data are being collected, rather than after data collection has ceased (Stake, 1995). Next to her field notes or interview transcripts, the qualitative analyst jots down ideas about the meaning of the text and how it might relate to other issues. This process of reading through the data and interpreting it continues throughout the project. When it appears that additional concepts need to be investigated, or new relationships explored, the analyst adjusts her data collection. This process is termed **progressive focusing** (Parlett & Hamilton, 1976).

We emphasize placing an interpreter in the field to observe the workings of the case, one who records objectively what is happening but simultaneously examines its meaning and redirects observation to refine or substantiate those meanings. Initial research questions may be modified or even replaced in mid-study by the case researcher. The aim is to thoroughly understand [the case]. If early questions are not working, if new issues become apparent, the design is changed. (Stake, 1995:9)

Progressive focusing: The process by which a qualitative analyst interacts with the data and gradually refines her focus.

Elijah Anderson (2003:38) describes the progressive focusing process in his memoir about his study of Jelly's Bar:

I also wrote conceptual memos to myself to help me sort out my findings. Usually not more than a page long, they represented theoretical insights that emerged from my engagement with the data in my field notes. As I gained tenable hypotheses and propositions, I began to listen and observe selectively, focusing in on those events that I thought might bring me alive to my research interests and concerns. This method of dealing with the information I was receiving amounted to a kind of dialogue with the data, sifting out ideas, weighing new notions against the reality with which I [was] faced there on the streets and back at my desk.

Following a few guidelines will help when a researcher starts analyzing qualitative data (Miller & Crabtree, 1999b:142–143):

- Know yourself, your biases and preconceptions.
- Know your question.
- Seek creative abundance. Consult others and keep looking for alternative interpretations.
- Be flexible.
- Exhaust the data. Try to account for all the data in the texts, then publicly acknowledge the unexplained and remember the next principle.
- Celebrate anomalies. They are the windows to insight.
- Get critical feedback. The solo analyst is a great danger to self and others.
- Be explicit. Share the details with yourself, your team members, and your audiences.

Qualitative Data Analysis as an Art

If you miss the certainty of predefined measures and deductively derived hypotheses, you are beginning to understand the difference between quantitative and qualitative data analyses. Qualitative data analysis is even described by some as involving as much "art" as science—as a "dance," in the words of William Miller and Benjamin Crabtree (1999b:138–139):

> Interpretation is a complex and dynamic craft, with as much creative artistry as technical exactitude, and it requires an abundance of patient plodding, fortitude, and discipline. There are many changing rhythms; multiple steps; moments of jubilation, revelation, and exasperation. . . . The dance of interpretation is a dance for two, but those two are often multiple and frequently changing, and there is always an audience, even if it is not always visible. Two dancers are the interpreters and the texts.

The "dance" of qualitative data analysis is represented in Exhibit 8.1, which captures the alternation between immersion in the text to identify meanings and editing the text to create categories and codes. The process involves three different modes of reading the text:

1. When the researcher reads the text *literally* (L, in Exhibit 8.1), she is focused on its literal content and form, so the text "leads" the dance.

2. When the researcher reads the text *reflexively* (R), she focuses on how her own orientation shapes her interpretations and focus. Now, the researcher leads the dance.

3. When the researcher reads the text *interpretively* (I), she tries to construct her own interpretation of what the text means.

In this artful way, analyzing text involves both inductive and deductive processes: The researcher generates concepts and linkages between them based on reading the text and also checks the text to see whether her concepts and interpretations are reflected in it.

Qualitative Compared to Quantitative Data Analysis

With these points in mind, let's review the differences of the logic behind qualitative vs. quantitative analysis (Denzin & Lincoln, 2000:8–10; Patton, 2002:13–14).

- A focus on meanings rather than on quantifiable phenomena
- Collection of much data on a few cases rather than little data on many cases

Exhibit 8.1   Dance of Qualitative Analysis

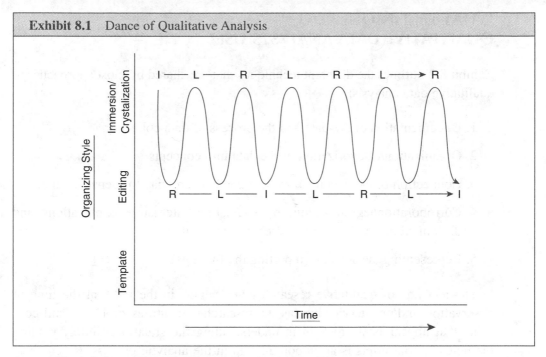

Source: Miller & Crabtree, 1999b:139, Figure 7.1. Based on Addison 1999.

- Study in depth and detail, without predetermined categories or directions, rather than emphasis on analyses and categories determined in advance
- Conception of the researcher as an "instrument," rather than as the designer of objective instruments to measure particular variables.
- Sensitivity to context, rather than seeking universal generalizations
- Attention to the impact of the researcher's and others' values on the course of the analysis, rather than presuming the possibility of value-free inquiry
- A goal of rich descriptions of the world rather than measurement of specific variables

You'll also want to keep in mind features of qualitative data analysis that are shared with those of quantitative data analysis (introduced in Chapter 9 of this book). Both qualitative and quantitative data analysis can involve making distinctions about textual data. Textual data can also be transposed to quantitative data through a process of categorization and counting. Some qualitative analysts also share with quantitative researchers a positivist goal of describing better the world as it "really" is, but others have adopted a postmodern goal of trying to understand how different people see and make sense of the world, without believing that there is any "correct" description.

WHAT TECHNIQUES DO QUALITATIVE DATA ANALYSTS USE?

Exhibit 8.2 outlines the different techniques that are shared by most approaches to qualitative data analysis:

1. Documentation of the data and the process of data collection

2. Organization/categorization of the data into concepts

3. Connection of the data to show how one concept may influence another

4. Corroboration/legitimization, by evaluating alternative explanations and disconfirming evidence and searching for negative cases

5. Representing the account (reporting the findings)

The analysis of qualitative research notes begins in the field, at the time of observation and/or interviewing, as the researcher identifies problems and concepts that appear likely to help in understanding the situation. Simply reading the notes or transcripts is an important step in the analytic process. Researchers should make frequent notes in the margins to identify important statements and to propose ways of coding the data: "husband/wife conflict," perhaps, or "tension reduction strategy."

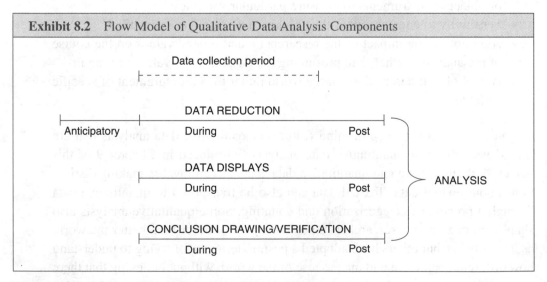

Exhibit 8.2   Flow Model of Qualitative Data Analysis Components

Source: Miles & Huberman, 1994:10, Figure 1.3. Used with permission.

An interim stage may consist of listing the concepts reflected in the notes and diagramming the relationships among concepts (Maxwell, 1996:78–81). In large projects, weekly team meetings are an important part of this process. Susan Miller describes this process in her study of neighborhood police officers. Her research team met both to go over their field notes and to resolve points of confusion, as well as to dialogue with other skilled researchers who helped to identify emerging concepts (as cited in Bachman & Schutt, 2001:309):

> The fieldwork team met weekly to talk about situations that were unclear and to troubleshoot any problems. We also made use of peer-debriefing techniques. Here, multiple colleagues, who were familiar with qualitative data analysis but not involved in our research, participated in preliminary analysis of our findings. (Miller, 1999:233)

This process continues throughout the project and should assist in refining concepts during the report-writing phase, long after data collection has ceased. Let's examine each of the stages of qualitative research in more detail.

Documentation

The data for a qualitative study most often are notes jotted down in the field or during an interview—from which the original comments, observations, and feelings are reconstructed—or text transcribed from audiotapes. "The basic data are these observations and conversations, the actual words of people reproduced to the best of my ability from the field notes" (Diamond, 1992:7). What to do with all this material? Many field research projects have slowed to a halt because a novice researcher becomes overwhelmed by the quantity of information that has been collected. A one-hour interview can generate 20 to 25 pages of single-spaced text (Kvale, 1996:169).

Analysis is less daunting, however, if the researcher maintains a disciplined transcription schedule:

> Usually, I wrote these notes immediately after spending time in the setting or the next day. Through the exercise of writing up my field notes, with attention to "who" the speakers and actors were, I became aware of the nature of certain social relationships and their positional arrangements within the peer group. (Anderson, 2003:38)

You can see the analysis already emerging from this simple process of taking notes.

The first formal analytical step is documentation. The various contacts, interviews, written documents, and notes all need to be saved and listed.

Documentation is critical to qualitative research for several reasons: It is essential for keeping track of what will be a rapidly growing volume of notes, tapes, and documents; it provides a way of developing an outline for the analytic process; and it encourages ongoing conceptualizing and strategizing about the text.

Miles and Huberman (1994:53) provide a good example of a contact summary form that was used to keep track of observational sessions in a qualitative study of a new school curriculum (Exhibit 8.3).

Conceptualization, Coding, and Categorizing

Identifying and refining important concepts is a key part of the iterative process of qualitative research. Sometimes conceptualization begins with a simple observation that is interpreted directly, "pulled apart" and then put back together more meaningfully. Robert Stake provides an example (1995:75):

> When Adam ran a pushbroom into the feet of the children nearby, I jumped to conclusions about his interactions with other children: aggressive, teasing, arresting. Of course, just a few minutes earlier I had seen him block the children climbing the steps in a similar moment of smiling bombast. So I was aggregating, and testing my unrealized hypotheses about what kind of kid he was, not postponing my interpreting. . . . My disposition was to keep my eyes on him. (Stake, 1995:74)

The focus in this conceptualization "on the fly" is to provide a detailed description of what was observed and a sense of why that was important.

More often, analytic insights are tested against new observations, the initial statement of problems and concepts is refined, the researcher then collects more data, interacts with it again, and the process continues. Elijah Anderson (2003) recounts how his conceptualization of social stratification at Jelly's Bar developed over a long period of time:

> I could see the social pyramid, how certain guys would group themselves and say in effect, "I'm here and you're there." I made sense of these crowds [initially] as the "respectables," the "non-respectables," and the "near-respectables." . . . Inside, such non-respectables might sit on the crates, but if a respectable came along and wanted to sit there, the lower status person would have to move. (Anderson, 2003:18, 19)

But this initial conceptualization changed with experience as Anderson realized that the participants themselves used other terms to differentiate social

Exhibit 8.3	Example of a Contact Summary Form

Contact type: Site: Tindale
Visit   X   Contact date: 11/28-29/79
Phone   _____   Today's date: 12/28/79
               (with whom)   Written by: BLT

1. What were the main issues or themes that struck you in this contact?

   Interplay between highly prescriptive, "teacher-proof" curriculum that is top-down imposed and the actual writing of the curriculum by the teachers themselves.

   Split between the "watchdogs" (administrators) and the "house masters" (dept. chairs & teachers) vis a vis job foci.

   District curric, coord'r as decision maker re school's acceptance of research relationship.

2. Summarize the information you got (or failed to get) on each of the target questions you had for this contact.

Question	Information
History of dev. of innov'n	Conceptualized by Curric., Coord'r, English Chairman & Assoc. Chairman; written by teachers in summer; revised by teachers following summer with field testing data
School's org'l structure	Principal & admin'rs responsible for discipline; dept chairs are educ'l leaders
Demographics	Racial conflicts in late 60's; 60% black stud. pop.; heavy emphasis on discipline & on keeping out non-district students slipping in from Chicago
Teachers' response to innov'n	Rigid, structured, etc. at first; now, they say they like it/NEEDS EXPLORATION
Research access	Very good; only restriction: teachers not required to cooperate

3. Anything else that struck you as salient, interesting, illuminating or important in this contact?
   Thoroughness of the innov'n's development and training.

   Its embeddedness in the district's curriculum, as planned and executed by the district curriculum coordinator.

   The initial resistance to its high prescriptiveness (as reported by users) as contrasted with their current acceptance and approval of it (again, as reported by users).

4. What new (or remaining) target questions do you have in considering the next contact with this site?

   How do users really perceive the innov'n? If they do indeed embrace it, what accounts for the change from early resistance?

   Nature and amount of networking among users of innov'n.

   Information on "stubborn" math teachers whose ideas weren't heard initially – who are they? Situation particulars? Resolution?

   Follow-up on English teacher Reilly's "fall from the chairmanship."

   Follow a team through a day of rotation, planning, etc.

   CONCERN: The consequences of eating school cafeteria food two days per week for the next four or five months . . .

                                                                                    Stop

Source: Miles & Huberman, 1994:53, Figure 4.1.

status: "winehead," "hoodlum," and "regular" (Anderson, 2003:28). What did they mean by these terms? "The 'regulars' basically valued 'decency.' They associated decency with conventionality but also with 'working for a living,' or having a 'visible means of support'" (Anderson, 2003:29). In this way, Anderson progressively refined his concept as he gained experience in the setting.

Howard S. Becker (1958:658) provides another excellent illustration of this iterative process of conceptualization in his study of medical students:

> When we first heard medical students apply the term "crock" to patients, we made an effort to learn precisely what they meant by it. We found, through interviewing students about cases both they and the observer had seen, that the term referred in a derogatory way to patients with many subjective symptoms but no discernible physical pathology. Subsequent observations indicated that this usage was a regular feature of student behavior and thus that we should attempt to incorporate this fact into our model of student-patient behavior. The derogatory character of the term suggested in particular that we investigate the reasons students disliked these patients. We found that this dislike was related to what we discovered to be the students' perspective on medical school: the view that they were in school to get experience in recognizing and treating those common diseases most likely to be encountered in general practice. "Crocks," presumably having no disease, could furnish no such experience. We were thus led to specify connections between the student-patient relationship and the student's view of the purpose of his professional education. Questions concerning the genesis of this perspective led to discoveries about the organization of the student body and communication among students, phenomena which we had been assigning to another [segment of the larger theoretical model being developed]. Since "crocks" were also disliked because they gave the student no opportunity to assume medical responsibility, we were able to connect this aspect of the student-patient relationship with still another tentative model of the value system and hierarchical organization of the school, in which medical responsibility plays an important role. (Becker, 1958:658)

In this excerpt, the researcher was first alerted to a concept by observations in the field, then refined his understanding of this concept by investigating its meaning. By observing the concept's frequency of use, he came to realize its importance. Finally, he incorporated the concept into an explanatory model of student-patient relationships.

A well-designed chart, or **matrix,** can facilitate the coding and categorization process. Exhibit 8.4 shows an example of a coding form designed by Miles and Huberman (1994:93–95) to represent the extent to which teachers and teachers'

Exhibit 8.4	Example of Checklist Matrix

Presence of Supporting Conditions

Condition	*For Users*	*For Administrators*
Commitment	*Strong*—"wanted to make it work."	*Weak* at building level. Prime movers in central office committed; others not.
Understanding	*"Basic"* ("felt I could do it, but I just wasn't sure how.") for teacher. *Absent* for aide ("didn't understand how we were going to get all this.")	*Absent* at building level and among staff. *Basic* for 2 prime movers ("got all the help we needed from developer.") *Absent* for other central office staff.
Materials	*Inadequate*: ordered late, puzzling ("different from anything I ever used"), discarded.	N.A.
Front-end training	*"Sketchy"* for teacher ("it all happened so quickly"); no demo class. *None* for aide: ("totally unprepared. I had to learn along with the children.")	Prime movers in central office had training at developer site; none for others.
Skills	*Weak-adequate* for teacher. *"None"* for aide.	One prime mover (Robeson) skilled in substance; others unskilled.
Ongoing inservice	*None*, except for monthly committee meeting; no substitute funds.	*None*
Planning, coordination time	*None*: both users on other tasks during day; lab tightly scheduled, no free time.	*None*
Provisions for debugging	*None* systematized; spontaneous work done by users during summer.	*None*
School admin. support	*Adequate*	N.A.
Central admin. support	*Very Strong* on part of prime movers.	Building admin. only acting on basis of central office commitment.
Relevant prior experience	*Strong* and useful in both cases: had done individualized instruction, worked with low achievers. But aide no diagnostic experience.	*Present* and useful in central office, esp. Robeson (specialist).

Source: Miles & Huberman, 1994:95, Table 5.2. Used with permission.

aides ("users") and administrators at a school gave evidence of various supporting conditions that indicated preparedness for a new reading program. The matrix condenses data into simple categories, reflects further analysis of the data to identify "degree" of support, and provides a multidimensional summary that will facilitate subsequent, more intensive analysis. Direct quotes still impart some of the flavor of the original text.

Examining Relationships and Displaying Data

Examining relationships is the centerpiece of the analytic process because it allows the researcher to move from simple description of the people and settings to explanations of why things happened as they did with those people in that setting. A matrix can show how different concepts are related, or perhaps what causes are linked with what effects.

In Exhibit 8.5, a matrix relates stakeholders' stake in a new program with the researcher's estimate of their attitude toward the program. Each cell of the matrix was to be filled in with a summary of an illustrative case study. In other matrix analyses, quotes might be included in the cells to represent the opinions of these different stakeholders, or the number of cases of each type might appear in the cells. The possibilities are almost endless. Keeping this approach in mind will generate many fruitful ideas for structuring a qualitative data analysis.

The simple relationships that are identified with a matrix like that shown in Exhibit 8.5 can be examined and then extended to create a more complex causal model. Such a model can represent the multiple relationships among the important explanatory constructs. A great deal of analysis must precede the construction of

---

Exhibit 8.5   Coding Form for Relationships: Stakeholders' Stakes

	Estimate of Various Stakeholders' Inclination Toward the Program		
How high are the stakes for various primary stakeholders?	Favorable	Neutral or Unknown	Antagonistic
High			
Moderate			
Low			

Source: Patton, 2002:472.

Note: Construct illustrative case studies for each cell based on fieldwork.

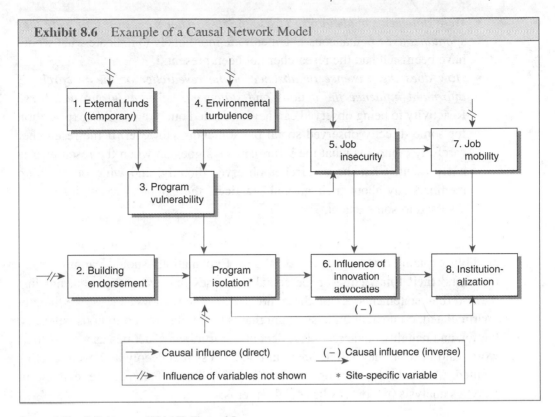

Exhibit 8.6 Example of a Causal Network Model

Source: Miles & Huberman, 1994:159, Figure 6.5.

such a model, with careful attention to identification of important variables and the evidence that suggests connections between them. Exhibit 8.6 provides an example, from a study of the implementation of a school program.

Authenticating Conclusions

No set standards exist for evaluating the validity or "authenticity" of conclusions in a qualitative study, but the need to consider carefully the evidence and methods on which conclusions are based is just as great as with other types of research. Individual items of information can be assessed in terms of at least three criteria (Becker, 1958):

- *How credible was the informant?* Were statements made by someone with whom the researcher had a relationship of trust, or by someone the researcher had just met? Did the informant have reason to lie? If the statements do not seem to be trustworthy as indicators of actual events, can they at least be used to help understand the informant's perspective?

- *Were statements made in response to the researcher's questions, or were they spontaneous?* Spontaneous statements are more likely to indicate what would have been said had the researcher not been present.
- *How does the presence or absence of the researcher or the researcher's informant influence the actions and statements of other group members?* Reactivity to being observed can never be ruled out as a possible explanation for some directly observed social phenomenon. However, if the researcher carefully compares what the informant says goes on when the researcher is not present, what the researcher observes directly, and what other group members say about their normal practices, the extent of reactivity can be assessed to some extent.

A qualitative researcher's conclusions should also be judged by their ability to credibly explain some aspect of social life. Explanations should capture group members' **tacit knowledge** of the social processes that were observed, not just their verbal statements about these processes. Tacit knowledge—"the largely unarticulated, contextual understanding that is often manifested in nods, silences, humor, and naughty nuances"—is reflected in participants' actions as well as their words and in what they fail to state but nonetheless feel deeply and even take for granted (Altheide & Johnson, 1994:492–493). These features are evident in Whyte's analysis of Cornerville social patterns:

> The corner-gang structure arises out of the habitual association of the members over a long period of time. The nuclei of most gangs can be traced back to early boyhood. . . . Home plays a very small role in the group activities of the corner boy. . . .
> . . . The life of the corner boy proceeds along regular and narrowly circum-scribed channels. . . . Out of [social interaction within the group] arises a system of mutual obligations which is fundamental to group cohesion. . . . The code of the corner boy requires him to help his friends when he can and to refrain from doing anything to harm them. When life in the group runs smoothly, the obliga-tions binding members to one another are not explicitly recognized. (Whyte, 1955:255–257)

Comparing conclusions from a qualitative research project to those obtained by other researchers conducting similar projects can also increase confidence in their authenticity. Miller's (1999) study of neighborhood police officers (NPOs) found striking parallels in the ways they defined their masculinity to processes reported in research about males in nursing and other traditionally female jobs (Bachman & Schutt 2001:315):

In part, male NPOs construct an exaggerated masculinity so that they are not seen as feminine as they carry out the social-work functions of policing. Related to this is the almost defiant expression of heterosexuality, so that the men's sexual orientation can never truly be doubted even if their gender roles are contested. Male patrol officers' language—such as their use of terms like "pansy police" to connote neighborhood police officers—served to affirm their own heterosexuality. . . . In addition, the male officers, but not the women, deliberately wove their heterosexual status into conversations, explicitly mentioning their female domestic partner or spouse and their children. This finding is consistent with research conducted in the occupational field. The studies reveal that men in female-dominated occupations, such as teachers, librarians, and pediatricians, over-reference their heterosexual status to ensure that others will not think they are gay. (Miller, 1999:222)

Reflexivity

Confidence in the conclusions from a field research study is also strengthened by an honest and informative account about how the researcher interacted with subjects in the field, what problems he or she encountered, and how these problems were or were not resolved. Such a "natural history" of the development of the evidence enables others to evaluate the findings. Such an account is important first and foremost because of the evolving and variable nature of field research: To an important extent, the researcher "makes up" the method in the context of a particular investigation rather than applying standard procedures that are specified before the investigation begins.

Barrie Thorne provides a good example of this final element of the analysis:

Many of my observations concern the workings of gender categories in social life. For example, I trace the evocation of gender in the organization of every-day interactions, and the shift from boys and girls as loose aggregations to "the boys" and "the girls" as self-aware, gender-based groups. In writing about these processes, I discovered that different angles of vision lurk within seemingly simple choices of language. How, for example, should one describe a group of children? A phrase like "six girls and three boys were chasing by the tires" already assumes the relevance of gender. An alternative description of the same event—"nine fourth-graders were chasing by the tires"—emphasizes age and downplays gender. Although I found no tidy solutions, I have tried to be thoughtful about such choices. . . . After several months of observing at Oceanside, I realized that my field notes were peppered with the words "child" and "children," but that the children themselves rarely used the term. "What do they call themselves?" I badgered in an entry in my field notes. The answer it turned out, is that children use the same practices as adults. They refer to one another by using given names ("Sally," "Jack") or language specific to a given context ("that guy on first base"). They rarely have occasion to use age-generic terms. But when pressed to locate themselves in an age-based way, my informants used "kids" rather than "children." (Thorne, 1993:8–9)

Qualitative data analysts, more often than quantitative researchers, display real sensitivity to how a social situation or process is interpreted from a particular background and set of values and not simply based on the situation itself (Altheide & Johnson, 1994). Researchers are only human, after all, and must rely on their own senses and process all information through their own minds. By reporting how and why they think they did what they did, they can help others determine whether, or how, the researchers' perspectives influenced their conclusions. "There should be clear 'tracks' indicating the attempt [to show the hand of the ethnographer] has been made" (Altheide & Johnson, 1994:493).

Elijah Anderson's (2003) memoir about the Jelly's Bar research illustrates the type of "tracks" that an ethnographer makes as well as how he can describe those tracks. He acknowledges that his tracks began as a child (Anderson, 2003:1–2):

While growing up in the segregated black community of South Bend, from an early age, I was curious about the goings on in the neighborhood, but particularly streets, and more particularly, the corner taverns that my uncles and my dad would go to hang out and drink in. . . . Hence, my selection of Jelly's as a field setting was a matter of my background, intuition, reason, and with a little bit of luck.

After starting to observe at Jelly's, Anderson's (2003:4) "tracks" led to Herman:

After spending a couple of weeks at Jelly's, I met Herman and I felt that our meeting marked a big achievement. We would come to know each other well. . . . something of an informal leader at Jelly's. . . . We were becoming friends. . . . he seemed to genuinely like me, and he was one person I could feel comfortable with.

Anderson's observations were shaped in part by Herman's perspective, but we also learn here that Anderson maintained some engagement with fellow students. This contact outside the bar helped to shape his analysis: "By relating my experiences to my fellow students, I began to develop a coherent perspective or a 'story' of the place which complemented the accounts that I had detailed in my accumulating field notes" (Anderson, 2003:6).

So Anderson's analysis came in part from the way in which he "played his role" as a researcher and participant, not just from the setting itself.

WHAT ARE SOME ALTERNATIVES IN QUALITATIVE DATA ANALYSIS?

The qualitative data analyst can choose from many interesting alternative approaches. Of course, the research question should determine the approach, but a researcher's preferences will also inevitably matter. The alternative approaches we present here (ethnography, ethnomethodology, qualitative comparative analysis, narrative analysis, conversation analysis, case-oriented understanding, and grounded theory) give you a good sense of the different possibilities (Patton, 2002).

Ethnography

Ethnography is the study of a culture or cultures that some group of people share (Van Maanen, 1995:4). As a method, it usually refers to participant observation by a single investigator who immerses himself or herself in the group for a long period of time (often one or more years). Ethnographic research can also be termed "naturalistic," because it seeks to describe and understand the natural social world as it really is, in all its richness and detail. As you learned in Chapter 7, anthropological field research has traditionally been ethnographic, and much sociological fieldwork shares these same characteristics. But there are no particular methodological techniques associated with ethnography other than just "being there." The analytic process relies on the thoroughness and insight of the researcher to "tell us like it is" in the setting, as he or she experienced it.

Code of the Street, Elijah Anderson's (1999:10–11) award-winning study of Philadelphia's inner city, captures the flavor of this approach:

> My primary aim in this work is to render ethnographically the social and cultural dynamics of the interpersonal violence that is currently undermining the quality of life of too many urban neighborhoods. . . . How do the people of the setting perceive their situation? What assumptions do they bring to their decision making?

Anderson's methods are described in the book's preface: participant observation, including direct observation and in-depth interviews; impressionistic materials drawn from various social settings around the city; and interviews with a wide variety of people. Like most traditional ethnographers, Anderson (1999:11) describes his concern with being "as objective as possible" and using his training as other ethnographers do, "to look for and to recognize underlying assumptions, their own and those of their subjects, and to try to override the former and uncover the latter."

From analysis of the data obtained in these ways, a rich description emerges of life in the inner city. Although we often do not "hear" the residents speak, we feel the community's pain in Anderson's (1999:138) description of "the aftermath of death":

> When a young life is cut down, almost everyone goes into mourning. The first thing that happens is that a crowd gathers about the site of the shooting or the incident. The police then arrive, drawing more of a crowd. Since such a death often occurs close to the victim's house, his mother or his close relatives and friends may be on the scene of the killing. When they arrive, the women and girls often wail and moan, crying out their grief for all to hear, while the young men simply look on, in studied silence. . . . Soon the ambulance arrives.

Elijah Anderson uses these descriptions as a foundation on which he develops the key concepts in his analysis, such as "code of the street":

> The "code of the street" is not the goal or product of any individual's actions but is the fabric of everyday life, a vivid and pressing milieu within which all local residents must shape their personal routines, income strategies, and orientations to schooling, as well as their mating, parenting, and neighbor relations. (Anderson, 1999:326)

Anderson's report on his Jelly's Bar study illustrates how an ethnographic analysis deepened as he became more socially integrated into the Jelly's Bar group. He thus became more successful at "blending the local knowledge one has learned with what we already know sociologically about such settings" (Anderson, 2003:39):

> I engaged the denizens of the corner and wrote detailed field notes about my experiences, and from time to time looked for patterns and relationships in my notes. In this way, an understanding of the setting came to me in time, especially as I participated more fully in the life of the corner and wrote my field notes about my experiences; as my notes accumulated, and as I reviewed them occasionally and supplemented them with conceptual memos to myself, their meanings became more clear, while even more questions emerged. (Anderson 2003:15)

This rich ethnographic tradition is being abandoned by some qualitative data analysts, however. Many doubt that social scientists can perceive the social world objectively or receive impressions from people that are unaffected by their being studied (Van Maanen, 2002). As a result, alternative techniques and approaches to qualitative data analysis have proliferated. The next sections introduce several of these alternative approaches.

Ethnomethodology

Ethnomethodology studies the way that participants construct the social world in which they live—how they "create reality"—rather than trying to describe the social world objectively. In fact, ethnomethodologists do not necessarily believe that we can find an objective reality; instead, how participants come to create and sustain a sense of "reality" is the focus of study. In the words of Jaber F. Gubrium and James A. Holstein (1997:41), in ethnomethodology, as compared to the naturalistic orientation of ethnography,

> The focus shifts from the scenic features of everyday life onto the ways through which the world comes to be experienced as real, concrete, factual, and "out there." An interest in members' methods of constituting their worlds supersedes the naturalistic project of describing members' worlds as they know them.

Unlike the ethnographic analyst, who seeks to describe the social world as the participants see it, the ethnomethodological analyst seeks to maintain some distance from that world. The ethnomethodologist views a "code" of conduct like that described by Elijah Anderson (2003) not as a description of a real normative force that constrains social action but as the way that people in the setting create a sense of order and social structure (Gubrium and Holstein, 1997:44–45). The ethnomethodologist focuses on how reality is constructed, not on what it *is*.

Qualitative Comparative Analysis (QCA)

In their study of homeless social movement organizations (SMOs), Daniel Cress and David Snow (2000) asked a series of very specific questions about social movement outcomes. They collected qualitative data about 15 SMOs in eight cities. A content analysis of newspaper articles indicated that these cities represented a range of outcomes, and the SMOs within them were also relatively accessible to Cress and Snow. In each city, Cress and Snow used a snowball sampling strategy to identify the SMOs and the various supporters, antagonists, and significant organizational bystanders with whom they interacted. They then gathered information from representatives of these organizations, including churches, other activist organizations, police departments, mayors' offices, service providers, federal agencies, and of course the SMOs themselves.

To answer their questions, Cress and Snow operationalized each of the various conditions that they believed might affect movement outcomes, using coding procedures that were much more systematic than those often employed in qualitative research. For example, Cress and Snow (2000:1078) defined "sympathetic allies" operationally as

> . . . the presence of one or more city council members who were supportive of local homeless mobilization. This was demonstrated by attending homeless SMO meetings and rallies and by taking initiatives to city agencies on behalf of the SMO. (Seven of the 15 SMOs had such allies.)

Cress and Snow chose a structured method of analysis, **qualitative comparative analysis (QCA)**, to assess how the various conditions influenced SMO outcomes. This procedure identifies the combination of factors that had to be present across multiple cases to produce a particular outcome (Ragin, 1987). Cress and Snow (2000:1079) explain why QCA was appropriate for their analysis:

> QCA . . . is conjunctural in its logic, examining the various ways in which specified factors interact and combine with one another to yield particular outcomes. This increases the prospect of discerning diversity and identifying different pathways that lead to an outcome of interest and thus makes this mode of analysis especially applicable to situations with complex patterns of interaction among the specified conditions.

Exhibit 8.7 summarizes the results of much of Cress and Snow's (2000:1097) analysis. It shows that homeless SMOs that were coded as organizationally viable used disruptive tactics, had sympathetic political allies, and presented a coherent diagnosis and program in response to the problems they were protesting were very likely to achieve all four valued outcomes: representation, resources, protection of basic rights, and some form of tangible relief. Some other combinations of the conditions were associated with increased likelihood of achieving some valued outcomes, but most of these alternatives less frequently had positive effects.

The qualitative textual data on which the codes were based indicate how particular combinations of conditions exerted their influence. For example, one set of conditions that increased the likelihood of achieving increased protection of basic rights for homeless persons included avoiding disruptive tactics in cities that were more responsive to the SMOs. Cress and Snow (2000:1089) use a quote from a local SMO leader to explain this process:

Exhibit 8.7   Multiple Pathways to Outcomes and Level of Impact

Pathways	Outcomes	Impact
1. VIABLE * DISRUPT * ALLIES * DIAG * PROG ………...	Representation, Resources, Rights, and Relief	Very strong
2. VIABLE * disrupt * CITY * DIAG * PROG ……..............	Representation and Rights	Strong
3. VIABLE * ALLIES * CITY * DIAG * PROG ………..........	Resources and Relief	Moderate
4. viable * DISRUPT * allies * diag * PROG ……................	Relief	Weak
5. viable * allies * city * diag * PROG ………..........................	Relief	Weak
6. viable * disrupt * ALLIES * CITY * diag * prog ………..........	Resources	Weak

Source: Cress & Snow, 2000:1097, Table 6. Reprinted with permission from the University of Chicago Press.

Note:—Uppercase letters indicate presence of condition and lowercase letters indicate the absence of a condition. Conditions not in the equation are considered irrelevant. Multiplication signs (*) are read as "and."

We were going to set up a picket, but then we got calls from two people who were the co-chairs of the Board of Directors. They have like 200 restaurants. And they said, "Hey, we're not bad guys, can we sit down and talk?" We had been set on picketing . . . Then we got to thinking, wouldn't it be better . . . if they co-drafted those things [rights guidelines] with us? So that's what we asked them to do. We had a work meeting, and we hammered out the guidelines.

Narrative Analysis

Narrative "displays the goals and intentions of human actors; it makes individuals, cultures, societies, and historical epochs comprehensible as wholes" (Richardson, 1995:200). **Narrative analysis** focuses on "the story itself" and seeks to preserve the integrity of personal biographies or a series of events that cannot adequately be understood in terms of their discrete elements (Riessman, 2002:218). The coding for a narrative analysis is typically of the narratives as a whole, rather than of the different elements within them. The coding strategy revolves around reading the stories and classifying them into general patterns.

For example, Calvin Morrill and his colleagues (2000:534) read through 254 conflict narratives written by the ninth graders (mentioned at the beginning of this chapter) they studied and found four different types of stories:

1. *Action tales,* in which the author represents him- or herself and others as acting within the parameters of taken-for-granted assumptions about what is expected for particular roles among peers

2. *Expressive tales,* in which the author focuses on strong, negative emotional responses to someone who has wronged him or her

3. *Moral tales,* in which the author recounts explicit norms that shaped his or her behavior in the story and influenced the behavior of others

4. *Rational tales,* in which the author represents him- or herself as a rational decision maker navigating through the events of the story

In addition to these dominant distinctions, Morrill et al. (2000:534–535) also distinguished the stories in terms of four stylistic dimensions: plot structure (such as whether the story unfolds sequentially), dramatic tension (how the central conflict is represented), dramatic resolution (how the central conflict is resolved), and predominant outcomes (how the story ends). Coding reliability was checked through a discussion by the two primary coders, who found that their classifications agreed for a large percentage of the stories.

The excerpt that begins this chapter exemplifies what Morrill et al. (2000:536) termed an "action tale." Such tales

> . . . unfold in matter-of-fact tones kindled by dramatic tensions that begin with a disruption of the quotidian order of everyday routines. A shove, a bump, a look . . . triggers a response. . . . Authors of action tales typically organize their plots as linear streams of events as they move briskly through the story's scenes. . . . this story's dramatic tension finally resolves through physical fighting, but . . . only after an attempted conciliation.

You can contrast that "action tale" with the following narrative, which Morrill et al. (2000:545–546) classify as a "moral tale," in which the student authors "explicitly tell about their moral reasoning, often referring to how normative commitments shape their decision making":

> I . . . got into a fight because I wasn't allowed into the basketball game. I was being harassed by the captains that wouldn't pick me and also many of the players. The same type of things had happened almost every day where they called me bad words so I decided to teach the ring leader a lesson. I've never been in a fight before but I realized that sometimes you have to make a stand

against the people that constantly hurt you, especially emotionally. I hit him in the face a couple of times and I got respect I finally deserved.

Morrill et al. (2000:553) summarize their classification of the youth narratives in a simple table that highlights the frequency of each type of narrative and the characteristics associated with each of them (Exhibit 8.8). How does such an analysis contribute to our understanding of youth violence? Morrill et al. (2000:551) first emphasize that their narratives "suggest that consciousness of conflict among youths—like that among adults—is not a singular entity but comprises a rich and diverse range of perspectives."

Theorizing inductively, Morrill et al. (2000:553–554) then attempt to explain why action tales were much more common than the more adult-oriented normative, rational, or emotionally expressive tales. They relate that one possibility is to be found in Gilligan's theory of moral development, which suggests that younger students are likely to limit themselves to the simpler action tales that "concentrate on taken-for-granted assumptions of their peer and wider cultures, rather than on more self-consciously reflective interpretation and evaluation." More generally, Morrill et al. (2000:556) argue, "we can begin to think of the building blocks of cultures as different narrative styles in which various aspects of reality are accentuated, constituted, or challenged, just as others are deemphasized or silenced."

Exhibit 8.8 Summary Comparison of Youth Narratives*

Representation of	*Action Tales (N = 144)*	*Moral Tales (N = 51)*	*Expressive Tales (N = 35)*	*Rational Tales (N = 24)*
Bases of everyday conflict	disruption of everyday routines & expectations	normative violation	emotional provocation	goal obstruction
Decisionmaking	intuitive	principled stand	sensual	calculative choice
Conflict handling	confrontational	ritualistic	cathartic	deliberative
Physical violence†	in 44% (N = 67)	in 27% (N = 16)	in 49% (N = 20)	in 29% (N = 7)
Adults in youth conflict control	invisible or background	sources of rules	agents of repression	institutions of social control

Source: Morrill et al., 2000:551, Table 1. Copyright 2000. Reprinted with permission of Blackwell Publishing Ltd.

*Total *N* = 254.

†Percentages based on the number of stories in each category.

In this way, Morrill et al.'s narrative analysis allowed an understanding of youth conflict to emerge from the youths' own stories while also informing our understanding of broader social theories and processes.

Conversation Analysis

Conversation analysis is a specific qualitative method for analyzing ordinary conversation. Unlike narrative analysis, it focuses on the sequence and details of conversational interaction, rather than on the "stories" that people are telling. Like ethnomethodology, from which it developed, conversation analysis focuses on how reality is constructed, rather than on what it "is." Three premises guide conversation analysis (Gubrium and Holstein, 2000:492):

1. Interaction is sequentially organized and talk can be analyzed in terms of the process of social interaction rather than in terms of motives or social status;
2. Talk, as a process of social interaction, is contextually oriented—it is both shaped by interaction and creates the social context of that interaction;
3. These processes are involved in all social interaction, so no interactive details are irrelevant to understanding it.

Consider these premises as you read the following dialogue between British research Ann Phoenix (2003:235) and a boy she called "Thomas" in her study of notions of masculinity, bullying, and academic performance among 11- to 14-year-old boys in 12 London schools.

Thomas: It's your attitude, but some people are bullied for no reason whatsoever just because other people are jealous of them. . . .

Q: How do they get bullied?

Thomas: There's a boy in our year called James, and he's really clever and he's basically got no friends, and that's really sad because . . . he gets top marks in every test and everyone hates him. I mean, I like him. . . .

Ann Phoenix (2003:235) notes that here,

Thomas dealt with the dilemma that arose from attempting to present himself as both a boy and sympathetic to school achievement. He . . . distanced himself from . . . being one of those who bullies a boy just because they are jealous of his academic attainments . . . constructed for himself the position of being kind and morally responsible.

Do you see how Thomas's presentation of himself reflected his interchange with the researcher, as she probed his orientation? Do you imagine that his talk would have been quite different if his conversation had been with other boys?

An example of the detailed data recorded in a formal conversation analysis appears in Exhibit 8.9. It is from David R. Gibson's (2005:1566) study of the effects of superior-subordinate and friendship interaction on the transitions that occur in the course of conversation—in this case, in meetings of managers. Every

---

Exhibit 8.9 Inventory of P-Shifts With Examples

Type of Information to Be Obtained

Information Source*	*Collegiality*	*Goals & Community*	*Action Expectations*	*Knowledge Orientation*	*Base*
SETTINGS					
Public places (halls, main offices)	X	X	X	X	X
Teacherís lounge	X	X		X	X
Classrooms		X	X	X	X
Meeting rooms	X		X	X	
Gymnasium or locker room		X			
EVENTS					
Faculty meetings	X		X		X
Lunch hour	X				X
Teaching		X	X	X	X
PEOPLE					
Principal		X	X	X	X
Teachers	X	X	X	X	X
Students		X	X	X	
ARTIFACTS					
Newspapers		X	X		X
Decorations		X			

Source: Gibson, 2005:1566.

Note: The initial speaker is denoted A and the initial target B, unless the group is addressed (or the target was ambiguous), in which case the target is 0. Then, the P-shift is summarized in the form (speaker$_1$)(target$_1$)-(speaker$_2$)(target$_2$), with A or B appearing after the hyphen only if the initial speaker or target serves in one of these two positions in the second turn. When the speaker in the second turn is someone other than A or B, X is used, and when the target in the second turn is someone other than A, B, or the group 0, Y is used.

type of "participation-shift" is recorded and distinguished from every other type. Some shifts involve "turn claiming," in which one person (X) begins to talk after the first person (A) has addressed the group as a whole (0), without being prompted by the first speaker. Some shifts involve "turn receiving," in which the first person (A) addresses the second (B), who then responds. In "turn usurping," by contrast, the second person (X) speaks after the first person (A) has addressed a comment to a third person (B), who is thus prevented from responding. Examining this type of data can help us to see how authority is maintained or challenged in social groups.

Case-Oriented Understanding

A **case-oriented understanding** attempts to understand a phenomenon from the standpoint of the participants. It is not geared to identifying causes. For example, Constance Fischer and Fredrick Wertz (2002) constructed such an explanation of the effect of being criminally victimized. They first recounted crime victims' stories, and then identified common themes in these stories.

Their explanation began with a description of what they termed the process of "living routinely" before the crime: "he/she . . . feels that the defended against crime could never happen to him/her. I said, 'nah, you've got to be kidding.'"

In a second stage, "Being Disrupted," the victim copes with the discovered crime and fears worse outcomes: "You imagine the worst when it's happening. . . . I just kept thinking my baby's upstairs." In a later stage, "Reintegrating," the victim begins to assimilate the violation by taking some protective action: "but I clean out my purse now since then and I leave very little of that kind of stuff in there."

Finally, when the victim is "Going On," he/she reflects on the changes the crime produced: "I don't think it made me stronger. It made me smarter."

You can see how Fischer and Wertz (2002:288–290) constructed an explanation of the effect of crime on its victims through this analysis of the process of responding to the experience. This effort to "understand" what happened in these cases gives us a much better sense of *why* things happened as they did.

Grounded Theory

Theory development occurs continually in qualitative data analysis (Coffey & Atkinson, 1996:23). The goal of many qualitative researchers is to create **grounded theory**—that is, to build up inductively a systematic theory that is "grounded" in, or based on, the observations. The observations are summarized into conceptual categories that are tested directly in the research setting with more observations. Over time, as the conceptual categories are refined and linked, a theory evolves (Glaser & Strauss, 1967; Huberman & Miles, 1994:436). Exhibit 8.10 diagrams this process. Notice that it corresponds to the inductive portion of the research circle, which was introduced in Chapter 2 (see Exhibit 2.2).

Exhibit 8.10   The Development of Grounded Theory

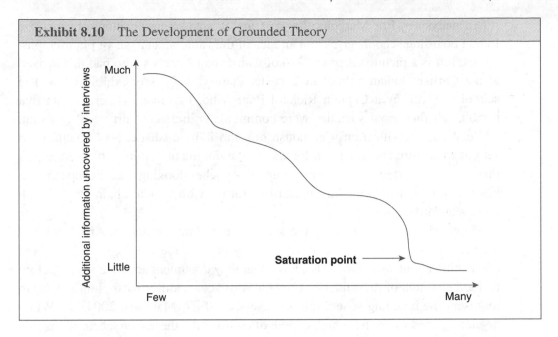

As observation, interviewing, and reflection continue, researchers refine their definitions of problems and concepts and select indicators. They can then check the frequency and distribution of phenomena: How many people made a particular type of comment? How often did social interaction lead to arguments? Social system models may then be developed, which specify the relationships among different phenomena. These models are modified as researchers gain experience in the setting. For the final analysis, the researchers check their models carefully against their notes and make a concerted attempt to discover negative evidence that might suggest the model is incorrect.

VISUAL SOCIOLOGY

The analysis of the "text" of social life, then, can be conducted in a variety of ways. But words are not the only form of qualitative data. For about 150 years, people have been recording the social world with photography. This creates the possibility of "observing" the social world through photographs and films and of interpreting the resulting images as a "text." Visual sociology is a method both to learn how others "see" the social world and to create images of it for further study. As with written text, however, the visual sociologist must be sensitive to the way in which a photograph or film "constructs" the reality that it depicts.

An analysis by Eric Margolis (2004) of photographic representations of American Indian boarding schools gives you an idea of the value of analysis of photographs. On the left is a picture taken in 1886 of Chiricahua Apaches who had just arrived at the Carlisle Indian School in Carlisle, Pennsylvania (see Exhibit 8.11). The school was run by a Captain Richard Pratt, who, like many Americans in that period, felt that tribal societies were communistic, indolent, dirty, and ignorant, while Western civilization was industrious and individualistic. So Captain. Pratt set out to acculturate American Indians to the dominant culture. The second picture shows the result: the same group of Apaches looking like European, not Native, Americans: dressed in standard uniforms, with standard haircuts and with more standard posture.

Many other pictures display the same type of transformation. Are these pictures each "worth a thousand words"? They capture the ideology of the school management, but we can be less certain that they document accurately the "before and after" status of the students. Captain Pratt "consciously used photography to represent the boarding school mission as successful" (Margolis, 2004:79). While he clearly tried to ensure a high degree of conformity, there were accusations that the contrasting images were exaggerated to overemphasize the change (Margolis, 2004:78). Reality was being constructed in these photographs, not just depicted.

Visual sociology will certainly become an increasingly important aspect of qualitative analyses of social settings and the people in them. The result will be richer descriptions of the social world, but whether you examine or also produce pictures for such analyses, remember Darren Newbury's (2005:1) reminder to

---

Exhibit 8.11   Pictures of Chiricahua Apache Children Before and After Starting Carlisle Indian School, Carlisle, Pennsylvania, 1886

Chiricahua Apache Children Upon Arrival at Carlisle School.

Chiricahua Apache Children After Four Months at Carlisle School.

Source: Margolis, 2004:78.

readers of his journal, *Visual Studies*, "that images cannot be simply taken of the world, but have to be made within it."

Pictures, like other "text," are in part a social construction.

HOW CAN COMPUTERS ASSIST QUALITATIVE DATA ANALYSIS?

The analysis process can be enhanced in various ways by using a computer. Programs designed for qualitative data can speed up the analysis process, make it easier for researchers to experiment with different codes, test different hypotheses about relationships, and facilitate diagrams of emerging theories and preparation of research reports (Coffey & Atkinson, 1996; Richards & Richards, 1994). The steps involved in **computer-assisted qualitative data analysis** parallel those used traditionally to analyze such text as notes, documents, or interview transcripts: preparation, coding, analysis, and reporting. We use two of the most popular programs to illustrate these steps: HyperRESEARCH and QSR NVivo. (See Appendix C for an extended introduction to HyperRESEARCH. Check out the software itself and the HyperRESEARCH tutorials on the CD-ROM that accompanies this text.)

Text preparation begins with typing or scanning text in a word processor or, with NVivo, directly into the program's rich text editor. NVivo will create or import a rich text file. HyperRESEARCH requires that your text be saved as a text file (as "ASCII" in most word processors) before you transfer it into the analysis program. HyperRESEARCH expects your text data to be stored in separate files corresponding to each unique case, such as an interview with one subject.

Coding the text involves categorizing particular text segments. This is the foundation of much qualitative analysis. Either program allows you to assign a code to any segment of text (in NVivo, you drag through the characters to select them; in HyperRESEARCH, you click on the first and last words to select text). You can either make up codes as you go through a document or assign codes that you have already developed to text segments. Exhibit 8.12 shows the screens that appear in the two programs at the coding stage, when a particular text segment is being labeled. You can also have the programs "autocode" text by identifying a word or phrase that should always receive the same code, or, in NVivo, by coding each section identified by the style of the rich text document—for example, each question or speaker (of course, you should check carefully the results of autocoding). Both programs also let you examine the coded text "in context"—embedded in its place in the original document.

In qualitative data analysis, coding is not a one-time-only or one-code-only procedure. Both HyperRESEARCH and NVivo allow you to be inductive and holistic in your coding: You can revise codes as you go along, assign multiple

Exhibit 8.12a   HyperRESEARCH Coding Stage

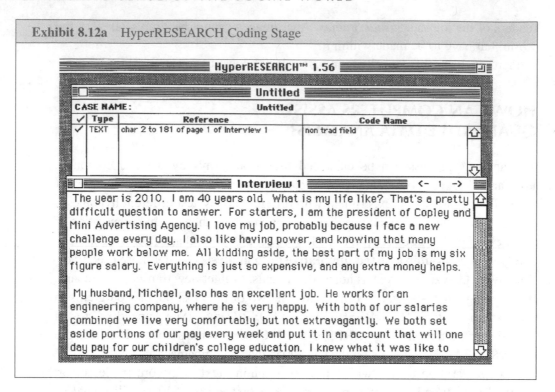

Exhibit 8.12b   NVivo Coding Stage

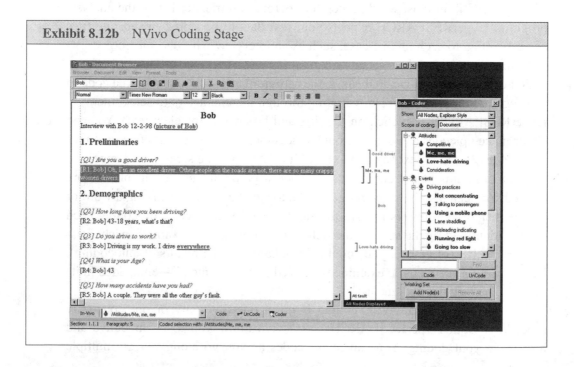

codes to text segments, and link your own comments ("memos") to text segments. In NVivo you can work "live" with the coded text to alter coding or create new, more subtle categories. You can also place hyperlinks to other documents in the project or any multimedia files outside it.

Analysis focuses on reviewing cases or text segments with similar codes and examining relationships among different codes. You may decide to combine codes into larger concepts. You may specify additional codes to capture more fully the variation among cases. You can test hypotheses about relationships among codes. NVivo allows development of an indexing system to facilitate thinking about the relationships among concepts and the overarching structure of these relationships. It will also allow you to draw more free-form models (see Exhibit 8.13). In HyperRESEARCH, you can specify combinations of codes that identify cases that you want to examine.

Reports from both programs can include text to illustrate the cases, codes, and relationships that you specify. You can also generate counts of code frequencies and then import these counts into a statistical program for quantitative analysis. However, the many types of analyses and reports that can be developed with qualitative analysis software do not lessen the need for a careful evaluation of the quality of the data on which conclusions are based.

In reality, using a qualitative data analysis computer program is not always as straightforward as it appears (Bachman & Schutt 2001:314). Scott Decker and

Exhibit 8.13   A Free-Form Model in NVivo

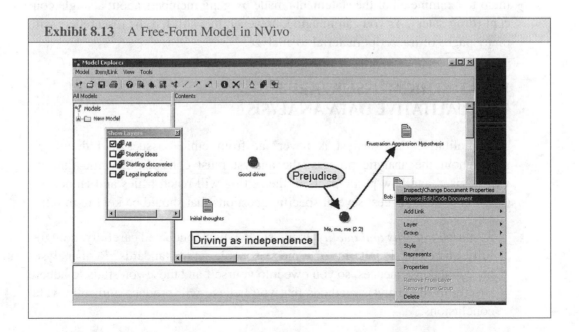

Barrik Van Winkle (1996:53–54) describe the difficulty they faced in using a computer program to identify instances of the concept of "drug sales":

> The software we used is essentially a text retrieval package. . . . One of the dilemmas faced in the use of such software is whether to employ a coding scheme within the interviews or simply to leave them as unmarked text. We chose the first alternative, embedding conceptual tags at the appropriate points in the text. An example illustrates this process. One of the activities we were concerned with was drug sales. Our first chore (after a thorough reading of all the transcripts) was to use the software to "isolate" all of the transcript sections dealing with drug sales. One way to do this would be to search the transcripts for every instance in which the word "drugs" was used. However, such a strategy would have the disadvantages of providing information of too general a character while often missing important statements about drugs. Searching on the word "drugs" would have produced a file including every time the word was used, whether it was in reference to drug sales, drug use, or drug availability, clearly more information than we were interested [in]. However, such a search would have failed to find all of the slang used to refer to drugs ("boy" for heroin, "Casper" for crack cocaine) as well as the more common descriptions of drugs, especially rock or crack cocaine.

Decker and Van Winkle solved this problem by parenthetically inserting conceptual tags in the text whenever talk of drug sales was found. This process allowed them to examine all of the statements made by gang members about a single concept (drug sales). As you can imagine, however, this still left the researchers with many pages of transcript material to analyze.

WHAT ETHICAL ISSUES ARISE IN QUALITATIVE DATA ANALYSIS?

The qualitative data analyst is never far from ethical issues and dilemmas. Throughout the analytic process, the analyst must consider how the findings will be used and how participants in the setting will react. Miles and Huberman (1994:204–205) suggest several specific questions that should be kept in mind:

> *Research integrity and quality.* Is my study being conducted carefully, thoughtfully, and correctly in terms of some reasonable set of standards? Real analyses have real consequences, so you owe it to yourself and those you study to adhere strictly to the analysis methods that you believe will produce authentic, valid conclusions.

Ownership of data and conclusions. Who owns my field notes and analyses: I, my organization, my funders? And once my reports are written, who controls their diffusion? Of course these concerns arise in any social research project, but the intimate involvement of the qualitative researcher with participants in the setting studied makes conflicts of interest between different stakeholders much more difficult to resolve. Working through the issues as they arise is essential.

Use and misuse of results. Do I have an obligation to help my findings be used appropriately? What if they are used harmfully or wrongly? It is prudent to develop understandings early in the project with all major stakeholders that specify what actions will be taken in order to encourage appropriate use of project results and to respond to what is considered misuse of these results.

CONCLUSIONS

The variety of approaches to qualitative data analysis makes it difficult to provide a consistent set of criteria for interpreting their quality. Norman Denzin's (2002:362–363) "interpretive criteria" are a good place to start. Denzin suggests that at the conclusion of their analyses, qualitative data analysts ask the following questions about the materials they have produced. Reviewing several of them will serve as a fitting summary for your understanding of the qualitative analysis process.

- *Do they illuminate the phenomenon as lived experience?* In other words, do the materials bring the setting alive in terms of the people in that setting?
- *Are they based on thickly contextualized materials?* We should expect **thick descriptions** that encompass the social setting studied.
- *Are they historically and relationally grounded?* There must be a sense of the passage of time between events and the presence of relationships between social actors.
- *Are they processual and interactional?* The researcher must have described the research process and his or her interactions within the setting.
- *Do they engulf what is known about the phenomenon?* This includes situating the analysis in the context of prior research and also acknowledging the researcher's own orientation upon first starting the investigation.

When an analysis of qualitative data is judged as successful in terms of these criteria, we can conclude that the goal of "authenticity" has been achieved.

As a research methodologist, you must be ready to use both types of techniques, evaluate research findings in terms of both sets of criteria, and mix and match the methods as required by the research problem to be investigated and the setting in which it is to be studied.

KEY TERMS

Case-oriented understanding
Computer-assisted qualitative data
  analysis
Emic focus
Ethnography
Ethnomethodology
Etic focus

Grounded theory
Matrix
Narrative analysis
Progressive focusing
Qualitative comparative analysis (QCA)
Tacit knowledge
Thick description

HIGHLIGHTS

• Qualitative data analysts are guided by an emic focus of representing persons in the setting on their own terms, rather than by an etic focus on the researcher's terms.

• Case studies use thick description and other qualitative techniques to provide a holistic picture of a setting or group.

• Ethnographers attempt to understand the culture of a group.

• Narrative analysis attempts to understand a life or a series of events as they unfolded, in a meaningful progression.

• Grounded theory connotes a general explanation that develops in interaction with the data and is continually tested and refined as data collection continues.

• Special computer software can be used for the analysis of qualitative, textual, and pictorial data. Users can record their notes, categorize observations, specify links between categories, and count occurrences.

To assist you in completing the Web Exercises, please access the Study Site at http://www.pineforge.com/mssw2 where you'll find the Web Exercises with accompanying links. You'll find other useful study materials like self-quizzes and e-flashcards for each chapter, along with a group of carefully selected articles from research journals that illustrate the major concepts and techniques presented in the book.

EXERCISES

Discussing Research

1. List the primary components of qualitative data analysis strategies. Compare and contrast each of these components with those relevant to quantitative data analysis. What are the similarities and differences? What difference do these make?

2. Does qualitative data analysis result in trustworthy results? Why would anyone question its use? What would you reply to the doubters?

3. Which analytic alternative do you prefer? Why?

Finding Research

1. The Qualitative Report is an online journal about qualitative research. Inspect the table of contents for a recent issue at http://www.nova.edu/ssss/QR/index.html. Read one of the articles and write a brief article review.

2. Be a qualitative explorer! Go to the list of qualitative research Web sites and see what you can find that enriches your understanding of qualitative research (http://www.qualitative research.uga.edu/QualPage/). Be careful to avoid textual data overload.

Critiquing Research

1. Read the complete text of one of the qualitative studies presented in this chapter and evaluate its analysis and conclusions for authenticity, using the criteria in this chapter.

Doing Research

1. Attend a sports game as an ethnographer. Write up your analysis and circulate it for criticism.

2. Write a narrative in class about your first date, car, college course, or something else that you and your classmates agree on. Then collect all the narratives and analyze them in a "committee of the whole." Follow the general procedures discussed in the example of narrative analysis in this chapter.

3. Eight essays written by college-aged women in Hesse-Biber's (1989) "Cinderella Study" are saved on the CD-ROM. The essays touch on how young women feel about combining work and family roles. Using HyperRESEARCH, the qualitative software program on the CD-ROM, open the Cinderella Study. Look over the preliminary code categories that have already been applied to each essay. Do you agree with the code categories/themes already selected? Do they capture the meaning for each of these cases (essays)? What new code categories would you add and why? Which would you delete? Why? What are some of the common themes/codes you see that cut across all 8 cases concerning how young women think about what their life will be like 20 years from now?

4. Work through the HyperRESEARCH tutorials on the CD-ROM. How does it seem that qualitative analysis software facilitates the analysis process? Does it seem to you that it might hinder the analysis process in some ways? Explain your answers.

Elementary Quantitative Data Analysis

"**S**how me the data," says your boss. Presented with a research conclusion, most people—not just bosses—want evidence to support it; presented with piles of data, you the researcher need to uncover what it all means. To handle the data gathered by your research, you need to use straightforward methods of data analysis.

In this chapter we will introduce several common statistics used in social research and explain how they can be used to make sense of "raw" data gathered in your research. Such quantitative analysis, using numbers to discover and describe patterns in your data, is the most elementary use of social statistics.

WHY DO STATISTICS?

A **statistic,** in ordinary language usage, is a numerical description of a population, usually based on a sample of that population. (In the technical language of mathematics, a *parameter* describes a population, and a *statistic* specifically describes a sample.) Some statistics are useful for describing the results of measuring single variables or for constructing and evaluating multi-item scales. These statistics include frequency distributions, graphs, measures of central tendency and variation, and reliability tests. Other statistics are used primarily to describe the association among variables and to control for other variables, and so to enhance the causal validity of our conclusions. Crosstabulation, for example, is one simple technique for measuring association and controlling other variables; it is introduced in this chapter. All of these statistics are termed **descriptive statistics** because they describe the distribution of and relationship among variables. Statisticians also use **inferential statistics** to estimate the degree of confidence that can be placed in generalizations from a sample to the population from which the sample was selected.

Case Study: The Likelihood of Voting

In this chapter, we use for examples some data from the General Social Survey (GSS) on voting and other forms of political participation. What influences the likelihood of voting? Prior research on voting in both national and local settings provides a great deal of support for one hypothesis: The likelihood of voting increases with social status (Milbrath & Goel, 1977:92–95; Salisbury, 1975:326; Verba & Nie, 1972:126). We will find out whether this hypothesis was supported in the 2004 General Social Survey and examine some related issues.

The variables we will use from the 2004 GSS are listed in Exhibit 9.1. We will use these variables to illustrate particular statistics throughout this chapter.

HOW TO PREPARE DATA FOR ANALYSIS

Our analysis of voting in this chapter is an example of what is called **secondary data analysis.** It is secondary because we received the data secondhand. A great many high-quality datasets are available for re-analysis from the Inter-University Consortium for Political and Social Research at the University of Michigan, and many others can be obtained from the government, individual researchers, and other research organizations. (See Appendix C.)

Exhibit 9.1	List of GSS Variables for Analysis of Voting	
Variable	**SPSS Variable Name**	**Description**
Social Status		
Family income	INCOM98R	Family income (in 1998 categories)
Education	EDUCR3	Years of education completed (categories)
Age	AGER	Years old (categories)
Gender	SEX	Sex
Marital status	MARITAL	Married, never married, widowed, divorced
Race	RACE	White, black, other
Politics		
Voting	VOTE00D	Voted in 2000 presidential election (yes/no)
Political views	POLVIEWS	Liberal to conservative rating
Interpersonal trust	TRUST	Believe other people can be trusted

Source: General Social Survey, National Opinion Research Center, 2004.

Note: Weighted to adjust for nonresponse and the number of adults in the eligible households (WT2004NR in the original file).

If you have conducted your own survey or experiment, your quantitative data must be prepared in a format suitable for computer entry. Questionnaires or other data entry forms can be designed to facilitate this process (see Exhibit 9.2). Data from such a form can be entered online, directly into a database, or first on a paper form and then typed or even scanned into a computer database. Whatever data entry method is used, the data must be checked carefully for errors—a process called **data cleaning.** Most survey research organizations now use a database management program to monitor data entry so that invalid codes can be corrected immediately. After data are entered, a computer program must be written to "define the data." A data definition program identifies the variables that are coded in each column or range of columns, attaches meaningful labels to the codes, and distinguishes values representing missing data. The procedures vary depending on the specific statistical package used.

WHAT ARE THE OPTIONS FOR DISPLAYING DISTRIBUTIONS?

The first step in data analysis is usually to discover the variation in each variable of interest. How many people in the sample are married? What is their typical income? Did most of them complete high school? Graphs and frequency distributions are the

Exhibit 9.2   Data Entry Procedures

OMB Control No: 6691-0001
Expiration Date: 04/30/07

Bureau of Economic Analysis
Customer Satisfaction Survey

1. Which data products do you use?

	Frequently (every week)	Often (every month)	Infrequently	Rarely	Never	Don't know or not applicable
GENERAL DATA PRODUCTS (On a scale of 1-5, please circle the appropriate answer.)						
Survey of Current Business	5	4	3	2	1	N/A
CD-ROMs	5	4	3	2	1	N/A
BEA Web site (www.bea.gov)	5	4	3	2	1	N/A
STAT-USA Web site (www.stat-usa.gov)	5	4	3	2	1	N/A
Telephone access to staff	5	4	3	2	1	N/A
E-Mail access to staff	5	4	3	2	1	N/A
INDUSTRY DATA PRODUCTS						
Gross Product by Industry	5	4	3	2	1	N/A
Input-Output Tables	5	4	3	2	1	N/A
Satellite Accounts	5	4	3	2	1	N/A
INTERNATIONAL DATA PRODUCTS						
U.S. International Transactions (Balance of Payments)	5	4	3	2	1	N/A
U.S. Exports and Imports of Private Services	5	4	3	2	1	N/A
U.S. Direct Investment Abroad	5	4	3	2	1	N/A
Foreign Direct Investment in the United States	5	4	3	2	1	N/A
U.S. International Investment Position	5	4	3	2	1	N/A
NATIONAL DATA PRODUCTS						
National Income and Product Accounts (GDP)	5	4	3	2	1	N/A
NIPA Underlying Detail Data	5	4	3	2	1	N/A
Capital Stock (Wealth) and Investment by Industry	5	4	3	2	1	N/A
REGIONAL DATA PRODUCTS						
State Personal Income	5	4	3	2	1	N/A
Local Area Personal Income	5	4	3	2	1	N/A
Gross State Product by Industry	5	4	3	2	1	N/A
RIMS II Regional Multipliers	5	4	3	2	1	N/A

Source: U. S. Bureau of Economic Analysis, 2004:14.

two most popular display formats. Whatever format is used, the primary concern of the analyst is to display accurately the distribution's shape; that is, to show how cases are distributed across the values of the variable.

Three features are important in describing the shape of the distribution: **central tendency, variability,** and **skewness** (lack of symmetry). All three features can be represented in a graph or in a frequency distribution.

Central tendency: The most common value (for variables measured at the nominal level) or the value around which cases tend to center (for a quantitative variable).

Variability: The extent to which cases are spread out through the distribution or clustered in just one location.

Skewness: The extent to which cases are clustered more at one or the other end of the distribution of a quantitative variable rather than in a symmetric pattern around its center. Skew can be positive (a right skew), with the number of cases tapering off in the positive direction, or negative (a left skew), with the number of cases tapering off in the negative direction.

We will now examine graphs and frequency distributions that illustrate the three features of shape. Several summary statistics used to measure specific aspects of central tendency and variability will be presented in a separate section.

Graphs

There are many types of graphs, but the most common and most useful for the statistician are bar charts, histograms, and frequency polygons. Each has two axes, the vertical axis (the y-axis) and the horizontal axis (the x-axis), and labels to identify the variables and the values, with tick marks showing where each indicated value falls along the axis.

A **bar chart** contains solid bars separated by spaces. It is a good tool for displaying the distribution of variables measured in discrete categories (e.g., nominal variables such as religion or marital status) because such categories don't blend into each other. The bar chart of marital status in Exhibit 9.3 indicates that more than half of adult Americans were married at the time of the survey. Smaller percentages were divorced, separated, widowed, or never married. The most common value in the distribution is "married." There is a moderate amount of variability in the distribution, because the half who are not married are spread across the categories of widowed, divorced, separated, and never married. Because marital status

Exhibit 9.3   Bar Chart of Marital Status

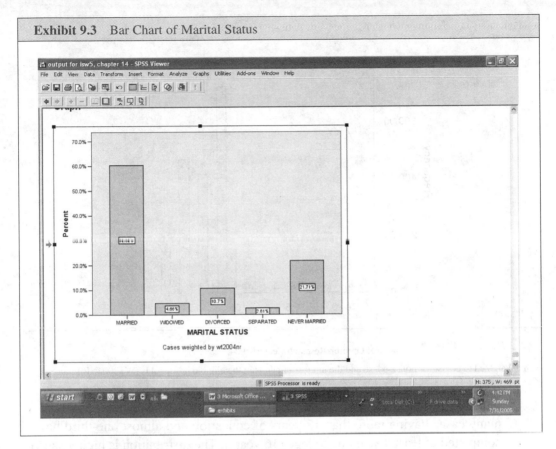

Source: General Social Survey, National Opinion Research Center, 2004.

Note: Weighted to adjust for nonresponse and the number of adults in the eligible households (WT2004NR in the original file).

is not a quantitative variable, the order in which the categories are presented is arbitrary, and there is no need to discuss skewness.

Histograms, in which the bars are adjacent, are used to display the distribution of quantitative variables that vary along a continuum that has no necessary gaps. Exhibit 9.4 shows a histogram of years of education from the 2004 GSS data. The distribution has a clump of cases centered at 12 years. The distribution is skewed because there are more cases just above the central point than below it.

In a **frequency polygon,** a continuous line connects the points representing the number or percentage of cases with each value. It is easy to see in the frequency polygon of years of education in Exhibit 9.5 that the most common value is 12 years (high school completion) and that this value also seems to be the center of the distribution. There is moderate variability in the distribution, with

Exhibit 9.4   Histogram of Years of Education

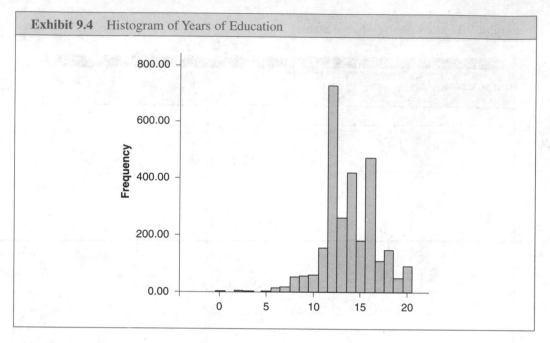

Source: General Social Survey, National Opinion Research Center, 2004.

Note: Weighted to adjust for nonresponse and the number of adults in the eligible households (WT2004NR in the original file).

many cases having more than 12 years of education and almost one-third having completed at least 4 years of college (16 years). The distribution is highly skewed in the negative direction, with few respondents reporting less than 10 years of education.

If graphs are misused, they can distort rather than display the shape of a distribution. Compare, for example, the two graphs in Exhibit 9.6. The first graph shows that high school seniors reported relatively stable rates of lifetime use of cocaine between 1980 and 1985. The second graph, using exactly the same numbers, appeared in a 1986 *Newsweek* article on "the coke plague" (Orcutt & Turner, 1993). To look at this graph, you would think that the rate of cocaine usage among high school seniors had increased dramatically during this period. But, in fact, the difference between the two graphs is due simply to changes in how the graphs were drawn. In the *Newsweek* graph, the percentage scale on the vertical axis begins at 15 rather than at 0, making what was about a 1 percentage point increase look very big indeed. In addition, omission from this graph of the more rapid increase in reported usage between 1975 and 1980 makes it look as if the tiny increase in 1985 were a new, and thus more newsworthy, crisis. Finally, these numbers report "lifetime use," not current or recent use; such numbers can drop only when anyone who has used cocaine dies off. The graph is, in total, grossly misleading.

Exhibit 9.5   Frequency Polygon of Years of Education

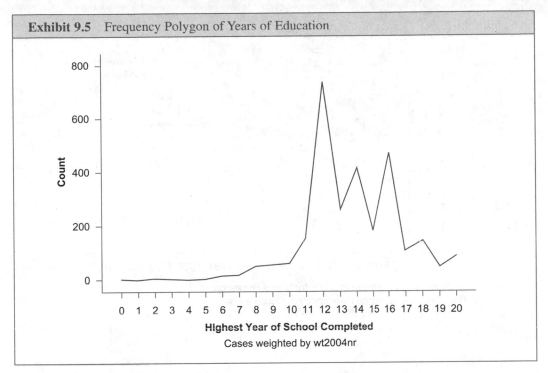

Source: General Social Survey, National Opinion Research Center, 2004.

Note: Weighted to adjust for nonresponse and the number of adults in the eligible households (WT2004NR in the original file).

Adherence to several guidelines (Tufte, 1983; Wallgren et al., 1996) will help you to spot such problems and to avoid them in your own work:

- Begin the graph of a quantitative variable at 0 on both axes. The difference between bars can be misleadingly exaggerated by cutting off the bottom of the vertical axis and displaying less than the full height of the bars. It may at times be reasonable to violate this guideline, as when an age distribution is presented for a sample of adults; but in this case be sure to mark the break clearly on the axis.
- Always use bars of equal width. Bars of unequal width, including pictures instead of bars, can make particular values look as if they carry more weight than their frequency warrants.
- The two axes usually should be of approximately equal length. Either shortening or lengthening the vertical axis will obscure or accentuate the differences in the number of cases between values.
- Avoid "chart junk"—a lot of verbiage or excessive marks, lines, lots of cross-hatching, and the like. It can confuse the reader and obscure the shape of the distribution.

Exhibit 9.6   Two Graphs of Cocaine Usage

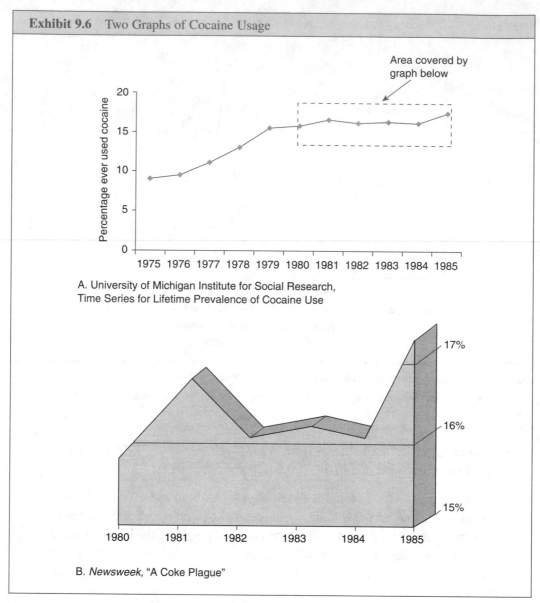

A. University of Michigan Institute for Social Research,
Time Series for Lifetime Prevalence of Cocaine Use

B. *Newsweek*, "A Coke Plague"

Source: Adapted from Orcutt & Turner, 1993. Copyright 1993 by the Society for the Study of Social Problems. Reprinted by permission.

Frequency Distributions

Another good way to present a univariate (one-variable) distribution is with a frequency distribution. A **frequency distribution** displays the number, percentage (the relative frequencies), or both, of cases corresponding to each of a variable's values. A frequency distribution will usually be labeled with a title, a stub (labels for the values), a caption, and perhaps the number of missing cases. If percentages are presented rather than frequencies (sometimes both are included), the total number of cases in the distribution (the **base number** N) should be indicated (see Exhibit 9.7).

Constructing and reading frequency distributions for variables with few values is not difficult. The frequency distribution of voting in Exhibit 9.7, for example, shows that 62.5% of the respondents eligible to vote said they voted, and that 27.8% reported they did not vote. The total number of respondents to this question was 2,791, although 2,813 actually were interviewed. The rest were ineligible to vote, just refused to answer the question, said they did not know whether they had voted or not, or gave no answer.

When the distributions of variables with many values (for instance, age) are to be presented, the values must first be grouped. Exhibit 9.8 shows both an ungrouped and a grouped frequency distribution of age. You can see why it is so important to group the values, but we have to be sure that in doing so we do not distort the distribution. Follow these two rules and you'll avoid problems:

- Categories should be logically defensible and should preserve the shape of the distribution.
- Categories should be mutually exclusive and exhaustive so that every case should be classifiable in one and only one category.

Exhibit 9.7 Frequency Distribution of Voting in the 2000 Presidential Election

Value	Frequency	Valid Percentage
Voted	1,743	69.2%
Did not vote	777	30.8
Not eligible	266	—
Refused to answer	5	—
Don't know	22	—
No answer	7	—
Total	2,813	100.0%
	(2,520)	

Source: General Social Survey, National Opinion Research Center, 2004.

Note: Weighted to adjust for nonresponse and the number of adults in the eligible households (WT2004NR in the original file).

Exhibit 9.8 Ungrouped and Grouped Age Distributions

Ungrouped		Grouped	
Age	Percentage	Age	Percentage
18	1.5%	18–19	3.1%
19	1.6	20–29	18.4
20	1.5	30–39	19.3
21	1.6	40–49	21.9
22	1.5	50–59	18.0
23	2.0	60–69	11.3
24	2.0	70–79	5.2
25	1.9	80–89	42.8
26	2.2		
27	1.6		100.0%
28	2.6		(2,801)
29	1.5		
30	1.9		
31	1.7		
32	1.9		
33	2.0		
34	2.3		
35	2.2		
36	2.1		
37	1.5		
38	1.9		
39	1.7		
40	2.5		
41	2.0		
42	1.9		
43	2.3		
44	2.4		
45	2.2		
46	1.9		

Source: General Social Survey, National Opinion Research Center, 2004.

Note: Weighted to adjust for nonresponse and the number of adults in the eligible households (WT2004NR in the original file).

WHAT ARE THE OPTIONS FOR SUMMARIZING DISTRIBUTIONS?

Summary statistics describe particular features of a distribution and facilitate comparison among distributions. We can, for instance, show that average income is higher in Connecticut than in Mississippi, and higher in New York than in Louisiana.

But if we just use one number to represent a distribution, we lose information about other aspects of the distribution's shape. For example, a measure of central tendency (such as the mean or average) would miss the point entirely for an analysis about differences in income inequality among states. A high average income could as easily be found in a state with little income inequality as in one with much income inequality; the average says nothing about the distribution of incomes. For this reason, analysts who report summary measures of central tendency usually also report a summary measure of variability or just present the distributions themselves to indicate skewness.

Measures of Central Tendency

Central tendency is usually summarized with one of three statistics: the mode, the median, or the mean. For any particular application, one of these statistics may be preferable, but each has a role to play in data analysis. To choose an appropriate measure of central tendency, the analyst must consider a variable's level of measurement, the skewness of a quantitative variable's distribution, and the purpose for which the statistic is used.

Mode

The **mode** is the most frequent value in a distribution. In a distribution of Americans' religious affiliations, Protestant Christian is the most frequently occurring value—the largest single group. In an age distribution of college students, 18- to 22-year-olds are by far the largest group, and therefore the mode. One silly, but easy, way to remember the definition of the mode is to think of apple pie "à la mode," which means pie with a big blob of vanilla ice cream on top. Just remember, the mode is where the big blob is—the largest collection of cases.

The mode is also sometimes termed the *probability average* because, being the most frequent value, it is the most probable. For example, if you were to pick a case at random from the distribution of age (refer back to Exhibit 9.8), the probability of the case being in their 30s would be 0.193 out of 1, or 19.3%—the most probable value in the distribution.

The mode is used much less often than the other two measures of central tendency because it can so easily give a misleading impression of a distribution's central tendency. One problem with the mode occurs when a distribution is **bimodal,** in contrast to being **unimodal.** A bimodal distribution has two categories with a roughly equal number of cases and clearly more cases than the other categories. In this situation, there is no single mode.

Nevertheless, there are occasions when the mode is very appropriate. The mode is the only measure of central tendency that can be used to characterize the central tendency of variables measured at the nominal level. In addition, because it is the most probable value, it can be used to answer questions such as which ethnic group is most common in a given school.

Median

The **median** is the position average, or the point that divides the distribution in half (the 50th percentile). Think of the median of a highway—it divides the road exactly in two parts. To determine the median, we simply array a distribution's values in numerical order and find the value of the case that has an equal number of cases above and below it. If the median point falls between two cases (which happens if the distribution has an even number of cases), the median is defined as the average of the two middle values and is computed by adding the values of the two middle cases and dividing by 2. The median is not appropriate for variables that are measured at the nominal level because their values cannot be put in order and so there is no meaningful middle position.

The median in a frequency distribution is determined by identifying the value corresponding to a cumulative percentage of 50. Starting at the top of the years of education distribution in Exhibit 9.9, for example, and adding up the percentages, we find that we have reached 38.9% in the 12 years category, and then 69.3% in the 13–15 years category. The median is therefore 13–15.

Exhibit 9.9	Years of Education Completed

Years of Education	*Percentage*
Less than 8	1.7%
8–11	11.3
12	25.9
13–15	30.5
16	16.7
17 or more	13.9
	100.0%
	(2,811)

Source: General Social Survey, National Opinion Research Center, 2004.

Note: Weighted to adjust for nonresponse and the number of adults in the eligible households (WT2004NR in the original file).

Mean

The **mean** is just the arithmetic average. (Many people, you'll notice, use the word *average* a bit more generally, to mean everything we've called "central tendency.") In calculating a mean, any higher numbers pull it up, and any lower numbers pull it down. Therefore, it takes into account the values of each case in a distribution—it is a weighted average. (The median, by contrast, only depends on whether the numbers are higher or lower compared to the middle, not *how* high or low.)

The mean is computed by adding up the values of all the cases and dividing the result by the total number of cases, thereby taking into account the value of each case in the distribution:

Mean = Sum of value of cases / Number of cases

In algebraic notation, the equation is: $X = \Sigma X_i / N$. For example, to calculate the mean value of eight cases, we add the values of all the cases (ΣX_i) and divide by the number of cases (N):

$$(28 + 117 + 42 + 10 + 77 + 51 + 64 + 55) / 8 + 444 / 8 + 55.5$$

Computing the mean obviously requires adding up the values of the cases. So it makes sense to compute a mean only if the values of the cases can be treated as actual quantities—that is, if they reflect an interval or ratio level of measurement, or if we assume that an ordinal measure can be treated as an interval (which is a fairly common practice). It makes no sense to calculate the mean of a qualitative (nominal) variable such as religion, for example. Imagine a group of four people in which there were two Protestants, one Catholic, and one Jew. To calculate the mean you would need to solve the equation (Protestant + Protestant + Catholic + Jew) / 4 = ?. Even if you decide that Protestant = 1, Catholic = 2, and Jewish = 3 for data entry purposes, it still doesn't make sense to add these numbers because they don't represent quantities of religion. In general, certain statistics (such as the mean) can apply only if there is a high enough level of measurement.

Median or Mean?

Because the mean is based on adding the value of all the cases, it will be pulled in the direction of exceptionally high (or low) values. In a positively skewed distribution, the value of the mean is larger than the median—more so the more extreme the skew. For instance, in Seattle, the presence of Microsoft owner Bill Gates—the world's richest person—probably pulls the mean wealth number up quite a bit. One extreme case can have a disproportionate effect on the mean.

This differential impact of skewness on the median and mean is illustrated in Exhibit 9.10. On the first balance beam, the cases (bags) are spread out equally, and the median and mean are in the same location. On the second balance beam, the median corresponds to the value of the middle case, but the mean is pulled toward the value of the one case with an extremely low value. For this reason, the mean age (44.7) for the 2,801 cases represented partially in the detailed age distribution in Exhibit 9.8 is higher than the median age (43.0). Although in this instance the difference is small, in some distributions the two measures will have markedly different values, and in such instances usually the median is preferred. (Income is a very common variable that is best measured by the median, for instance.)

Exhibit 9.10   The Mean as a Balance Point

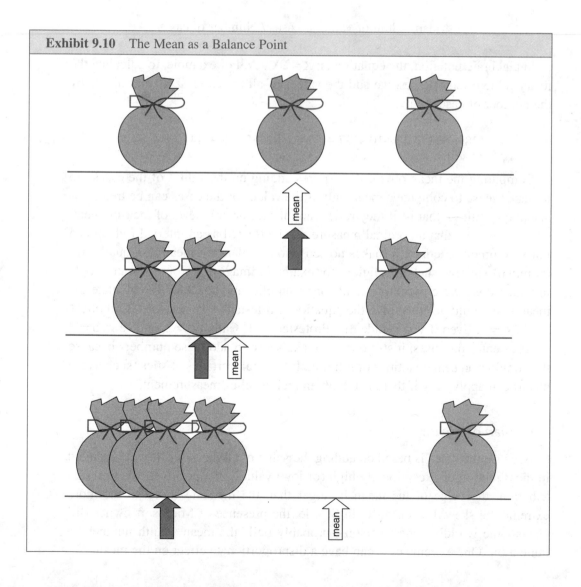

Measures of Variation

Central tendency is only one aspect of the shape of a distribution—the most important aspect for many purposes, but still just a piece of the total picture. The distribution, we have seen, also matters. It is important to know that the median household income in the United States is a bit over $50,000 a year, but if the variation in income isn't known—the fact that incomes range from zero up to hundreds of millions of dollars—we haven't really learned much. Measures of variation capture how widely and densely spread income (for instance) is. Four popular measures of variation for quantitative variables are the range, the interquartile range, the variance, and the standard deviation (which is the single most popular measure of variability). Each conveys a certain kind of information, with strengths and weaknesses. Statistical measures of variation are used infrequently with qualitative variables and are not presented here.

Range

The **range** is the simplest measure of variation, calculated as the highest value in a distribution minus the lowest value, plus 1:

$$\text{Range} = \text{Highest value} - \text{Lowest value} + 1$$

It often is important to report the range of a distribution—to identify the whole range of possible values that might be encountered. However, because the range can be altered drastically by just one exceptionally high or low value (termed an **outlier**), it's not a good summary measure for most purposes.

Interquartile Range

The **interquartile range** avoids the problem created by outliers, by showing the range where most cases lie. **Quartiles** are the points in a distribution that correspond to the first 25% of the cases, the first 50% of the cases, and the first 75% of the cases. You already know how to determine the second quartile, corresponding to the point in the distribution covering half of the cases—it is another name for the median. The interquartile range is the difference between the first quartile and the third quartile (plus 1).

Variance

The **variance,** in its statistical definition, is the average squared deviation of each case from the mean; you take each case's distance from the mean, square that

Exhibit 9.11   Calculation of the Variance

Case #	Score (X_i)	$X_i - \bar{X}$	$(X_i - \bar{X})^2$
1	21	−3.27	10.69
2	30	5.73	32.83
3	15	−9.27	85.93
4	18	−6.27	39.31
5	25	0.73	0.53
6	32	7.73	59.75
7	19	−5.27	27.77
8	21	−3.27	10.69
9	23	−1.27	1.61
10	37	12.73	162.05
11	26	1.73	2.99
	267		434.15

Mean: $\bar{X} = 267/11 = 24.27$
Sum of squared deviations = 434.15
Variance: $\sigma^2 = 434.15/11 = 39.47$

number, and take the average of all such numbers. Thus, variance takes into account the amount by which each case differs from the mean. The variance is mainly useful for computing the standard deviation, which comes next in our list here. An example of how to calculate the variance, using the following formula, appears in Exhibit 9.11:

$$\sigma^2 = \frac{\sum(X_i - \bar{X})^2}{N}$$

Symbol key: X = mean; N = number of cases;
Σ = sum over all cases; X_i = value of case i on variable X.

The variance is used in many other statistics, although it is more conventional to measure variability with the closely related standard deviation than with the variance.

Standard Deviation

Very roughly, the standard deviation is the distance from the mean that covers a clear majority of cases (about two-thirds). More precisely, the **standard**

deviation is simply the square root of the variance. It is the square root of the average squared deviation of each case from the mean:

$$\sigma = \sqrt{\dfrac{\sum (X_i - \bar{X})^2}{N}}$$

Symbol key: X = mean; N = number of cases;
Σ = sum over all cases; X_i = value of case i on variable X; $\sqrt{}$ square root.

The standard deviation has mathematical properties that make it the preferred measure of variability in many cases, particularly when a variable is normally distributed. A graph of a **normal distribution** looks like a bell, with one "hump" in the middle, centered around the population mean, and the number of cases tapering off on both sides of the mean (see Exhibit 9.12). A normal distribution is symmetric: If you were to fold the distribution in half at its center (at the population mean), the two halves would match perfectly. If a variable is normally distributed, 68% of the cases (almost exactly two-thirds) will lie between ±1 standard deviation from the distribution's mean, and 95% of the cases will lie between 1.96 standard deviations above and below the mean.

So the standard deviation, in a single number, tells you quickly about how wide the variation is of any set of cases—or, the range in which most cases will fall. It's very useful.

Exhibit 9.12   The Normal Distribution

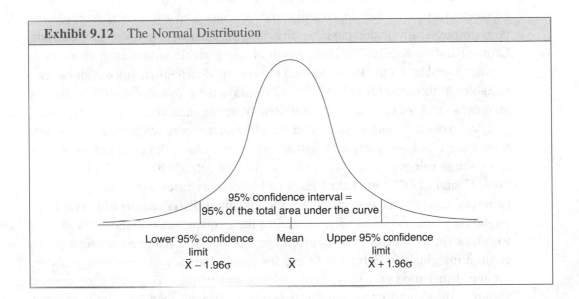

95% confidence interval =
95% of the total area under the curve

Lower 95% confidence limit
$\bar{X} - 1.96\sigma$

Mean
$\bar{X}$

Upper 95% confidence limit
$\bar{X} + 1.96\sigma$

Exhibit 9.13 Crosstabulation of Voting in 2000 by Family Income

	FAMILY INCOME: CELL COUNTS			
Voting	**<$20,000**	**$20,000–$34,999**	**$35,000–$59,999**	**$60,000+**
Voted	178	239	364	761
Did not vote	182	135	168	193
Total (*n*)	(360)	(374)	(532)	(954)

	FAMILY INCOME: PERCENTAGES			
Voting	**<$20,000**	**$20,000–$34,999**	**$35,000–$59,999**	**$60,000+**
Voted	49%	64%	68%	80%
Did not vote	51%	36%	32%	20%
Total	100%	100%	100%	100%

Source: General Social Survey, National Opinion Research Center, 2004.

Note: Weighted to adjust for nonresponse and the number of adults in the eligible households (WT2004NR in the original file).

HOW CAN WE TELL WHETHER TWO VARIABLES ARE RELATED?

Univariate distributions are nice, but they don't say how variables relate to each other—for instance, if religion affects education, or if marital status is related to income. To establish cause, of course, one's first task is to show an association between independent and dependent variables (cause and effect). **Crosstabulation** is a simple, easily understandable first step in such quantitative data analysis. Crosstabulation displays the distribution of one variable within each category of another variable; it can also be termed a *bivariate distribution,* since it shows two variables at the same time. Exhibit 9.13 displays the crosstabulation of voting by income, so that we can see if the likelihood of voting increases as income goes up.

The "crosstab" table is presented first (the upper part) with frequencies, and then again (the lower part) with percentages. The *cells* of the table are where row and column values intersect; for instance, the first cell is where "<$20,000" meets "voted," and "178" is the value. Each cell represents cases with a unique combination of values of the two variables. The **marginal distributions** of the table are on the right and underneath. These are just the frequency distributions for the two variables (in number of cases, percentages, or both), considered separately (the column marginals in Exhibit 9.13 are for family income; the row marginals are for the distribution of voting). The independent variable is usually the column variable, listed across the top; the dependent variable, then, is usually the row variable. This format isn't necessary, but social scientists typically use it.

Reading the Table

The first (upper) table in Exhibit 9.13 shows the raw number of cases with each combination of values of voting and family income. It is hard to look at the table in this form and determine whether there is a relationship between the two variables. What we really want to know is the likelihood, for any level of income, that someone voted. So we need to convert the cell frequencies into percentages. Percentages show the likelihood per 100 ("per cent") that something occurs. The second table, then, presents the data as **percentages** within the categories of the independent variable (the column variable, in this case). In other words, the cell frequencies have been converted into percentages of the column totals (the *n* in each column). For example, in Exhibit 9.13, the number of people earning less than $20,000 who voted is 178 out of 360, or 49%. Because the cell frequencies have been converted to percentages of the column totals, the numbers add up to 100 in each column but not across the rows.

Note carefully: You must *always percentage within levels of the independent variable*—adding numbers down the columns, in our standard format. In this example, we want to know the chance that a poor person (income less than $20,000) voted, so we calculate what percentage of poor people voted. Then we will *compare* that to the chance that people of other income levels voted. Percentaging across the table, by contrast, will not show the effect of the independent variable on voting. To repeat: *Always percentage within levels of the independent variable* (with*in* the *in*dependent variable, to remember).

To read the percentage table, compare the percentage distribution of voting/not voting across the columns. Start with the lowest income category (in the left column). Move slowly from left to right, looking at each distribution down the columns. As income increases, you will see, the percentage who voted also increases, from 49% of those with annual incomes under $20,000 (in the first cell in the first column) up to 80% of those with incomes of $60,000 or more (the last cell in the body of the table in the first row). This result is consistent with the hypothesis: It seems that higher income is moderately associated with a greater likelihood of voting.

Now look at Exhibit 9.14, which relates gender (as the independent variable) to voting (the dependent variable). The independent variable is listed across the top, and the table has been percentaged, correctly, down the columns, with values of the independent variable. Does gender affect voting? As you look down the first column, you see that 67% of men voted; then, in the second column, 71% of women voted. The difference is so small that it's probably negligible. Gender does not, in this table, have an effect on voting.

Some standard practices should be followed in formatting percentage tables (crosstabs): When a table is converted to percentages, usually just the percentages in each cell should be presented, not the number of cases in each cell. Include 100% at the bottom of each column (if the independent variable is the column variable) to indicate that the percentages add up to 100, as well as the **base**

	Gender	
Exhibit 9.14 Voting in 2000 by Gender		
Voting	*Male*	*Female*
Voted	67%	71%
Did not vote	33%	29%
Total	100%	100%
(*n*)	(1,158)	(1,362)

Source: General Social Survey, National Opinion Research Center, 2004.

Note: Weighted to adjust for nonresponse and the number of adults in the eligible households (WT2004NR in the original file).

number (*N*) for each column (in parentheses). If the percentages add up to 99 or 101 due to rounding error, just indicate so in a footnote. As noted already, there is no requirement that the independent variable always be the column variable, although consistency within a report or paper is a must. If the independent variable is the row variable, we calculate percentages in the cells of the table on the row totals (the *n* in each row), and so the percentages add up to 100 across the rows.

Try your hand at the table reading process with the larger table in Exhibit 9.15. This table describes the relationship between education and income. Examine the distribution of income for those with only a grade school education (first column). Almost half (45%) reported an income under $20,000, whereas just 12% reported an income of $60,000 or more. Then examine the distribution of income for the respondents who had finished high school but had gone no further. Here, the distribution of income has shifted upward, with just 21% reporting an income under $20,000 and 28% reporting incomes of $60,000 or more—that's three times the percentage in that category than we saw for those with a grade school education. You can see there are also more respondents in the $35,000–$59,999 category than there were for the grade schoolers. Now examine the column representing those who had completed at least some college. The percentage with incomes under $20,000 has dropped again, to 11%, whereas the percentage in the highest income category has risen to 52%. If you step back and compare the income distributions across the three categories of education, you see that incomes increased markedly and consistently. The relationship is positive (fortunately for all of us in the college crowd).

When you read research reports and journal articles, you will find that social scientists usually judge the strength of association on the basis of more statistics than just a crosstabulation table. A **measure of association** is a descriptive statistic used to summarize the strength of an association. One measure of association in crosstabular analyses with ordinal variables is called **gamma.** The value of gamma ranges from −1 to +1. The closer a gamma value is to −1 or +1, the stronger the

Income by Education			
		Education	
Income	*Grade School*	*High School*	*Some College*
<$20,000	45%	21%	11%
$20,000–$34,999	26%	23%	13%
$35,000–$59,999	16%	28%	24%
$60,000+	12%	28%	52%
Total	99%*	100%	100%
(*n*)	(299)	(610)	(1,548)

Exhibit 9.15   Income by Education

Source: General Social Survey, National Opinion Research Center, 2004.

Note: Weighted to adjust for nonresponse and the number of adults in the eligible households (WT2004NR in the original file).

*Percentages do not add to 100 due to rounding error.

relationship between the two variables; a gamma of zero indicates that there is no relationship between the variables. Inferential statistics go further, addressing whether an association exists in the larger population from which the (random) sample was drawn. Even when the empirical association between two variables supports the researcher's hypothesis, it is possible that the association was just due to the vagaries of random sampling. In a crosstab, estimation of this probability can be based on the inferential statistic, **chi-square.** The probability is customarily reported in a summary form such as "$p < .05$," which can be translated as "The probability that the association was due to chance is less than 5 out of 100 (5%)."

When the analyst feels reasonably confident (at least 95% confident, or $p < .05$) that an association was not due to chance, it is said that the association is **statistically significant.** Statistical significance basically means the relationship is actually there; it's not a chance occurrence. Convention (and the desire to avoid concluding that an association exists in the population when it doesn't) dictates that the criterion be a probability less than 5%. Statistical significance, though, doesn't equal substantive significance. That is, while the relationship is really occurring, not just happening accidentally, it may still not matter very much. It may be a minor part of what's happening.

Controlling for a Third Variable

Crosstabulation also can be used to study the relationship between three or more variables. The single most important reason for introducing a third variable into a bivariate relationship is to see whether that relationship is spurious. A third,

extraneous variable, for instance, may influence both the independent and dependent variables, creating an association between them that disappears when the extraneous variable is controlled. Ruling out possible extraneous variables will help to strengthen considerably the conclusion that the relationship between the independent and dependent variables is causal—that it is nonspurious. In general, adding variables is termed **elaboration analysis:** the process of introducing control or intervening variables into a bivariate relationship in order to better understand the relationship (Davis, 1985; Rosenberg, 1968).

For example, we have seen a positive association between incomes and the likelihood of voting. But perhaps that association only exists because both income and likelihood of voting are influenced by education; maybe when we control for education—that is, when we hold the value of education constant—we will find that there is no longer an association between income and voting. This possibility is represented by the hypothetical three-variable causal model in Exhibit 9.16, in which the arrows show that education influences both income and voting, thereby creating a relationship between the two. To test whether there is such an effect of education, we create the trivariate table in Exhibit 9.17, showing the bivariate crosstabs for various levels of education separately. This allows us to see if the income/voting relationship still exists after we hold education constant.

The trivariate crosstabulation in Exhibit 9.17 shows that the relationship between voting and income is *not* spurious due to the effect of education. The association between voting and income occurs in both subtables. So our original hypothesis—that income as a social status indicator has an effect on voting—is not weakened.

Our goal in introducing you to crosstabulation has been to help you think about the association among variables and to give you a relatively easy tool for describing association. In order to read most statistical reports and to conduct more sophisticated analyses of social data, you will have to extend your statistical knowledge, at

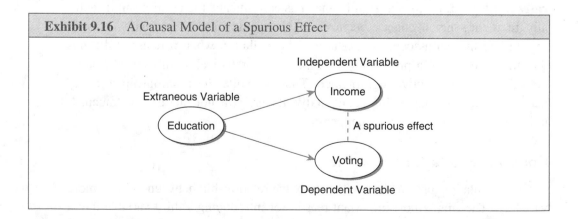

Exhibit 9.16   A Causal Model of a Spurious Effect

Exhibit 9.17   Voting in 2000 by Income and Education

Education = Grade School

	Family Income			
Voting	*<$20,000*	*$20,000–$34,999*	*$35,000–$59,999*	*$60,000+*
Voted	39%	47%	19%	62%
Did not vote	61%	53%	81%	38%
Total	100%	100%	100%	100%
(*n*)	(114)	(72)	(37)	(29)

Education = High School

	Family Income			
Voting	*<$20,000*	*$20,000–$34,999*	*$35,000–$59,999*	*$60,000+*
Voted	54%	63%	68%	68%
Did not vote	46%	37%	32%	32%
Total	100%	100%	100%	100%
(*n*)	(114)	(132)	(159)	(158)

Education = Some College

	Family Income			
Voting	*<$20,000*	*$20,000–$34,999*	*$35,000–$59,999*	*$60,000+*
Voted	54%	72%	74%	83%
Did not vote	46%	28%	26%	17%
Total	100%	100%	100%	100%
(*n*)	(132)	(169)	(336)	(767)

Source: General Social Survey, National Opinion Research Center, 2004.

Note: Weighted to adjust for nonresponse and the number of adults in the eligible households (WT2004NR in the original file).

least to include the technique of *regression* or *correlation analysis*. These statistics have many advantages over crosstabulation—as well as some disadvantages. You will need to take a course in social statistics in order to become proficient in the use of statistics based on regression and correlation.

ANALYZING DATA ETHICALLY: HOW NOT TO LIE WITH STATISTICS

Using statistics ethically means first and foremost being honest and open. Findings should be reported honestly, and the researcher should be open about the thinking that guided her decision to use particular statistics. Although this section has a mildly humorous title (after Darrell Huff's [1954] little classic, *How to Lie with Statistics*), make no mistake about the intent. It is possible to distort social reality with statistics, and it is unethical to do so knowingly, even when the error is due more to carelessness than deceptive intent.

There are a few basic rules to keep in mind:

- Inspect the shape of any distribution for which you report summary statistics, to ensure that the statistic does not mislead us (or anyone else) because of an unusual degree of skewness.
- When you create graphs, be sure to consider how the axes you choose may change the distribution's apparent shape; don't deceive your readers. You have already seen that it is possible to distort the shape of a distribution by manipulating the scale of axes, clustering categories inappropriately, and the like.
- Whenever you need to group data in a frequency distribution or graph, inspect the ungrouped distributions and then use a grouping procedure that does not distort the distribution's basic shape.
- Hypotheses formulated in advance of data collection must be tested as they were originally stated. When evaluating associations between variables, it becomes very tempting to search around in the data until something interesting emerges. Social scientists sometimes call this a "fishing expedition." Although it's not wrong to examine data for unanticipated relationships, inevitably some relationships between variables will appear just on the basis of chance association alone. Exploratory analyses must be labeled in research reports as such.
- Be honest about the limitations of using survey data to test causal hypotheses. Finding that a hypothesized relationship is not altered by controlling for some other variables does not establish that the relationship is causal. There is always a possibility that some other variable that we did not think to control, or that was not even measured in the survey, has produced a spurious relationship between the independent and dependent variables in our hypothesis (Lieberson, 1985). We have to think about the possibilities and be cautious in our causal conclusions.

CONCLUSION

With some simple statistics (means, standard deviations, and the like) a researcher can describe social phenomena, identify relationships among them, explore the reasons for these relationships (especially through elaboration), and test hypotheses about them. Statistics—carefully constructed numbers that describe an entire population of data—are amazingly helpful in giving a simple summation of complex situations.

Statistics provide a remarkably useful tool for developing our understanding of the social world, a tool that we can use both to test our ideas and to generate new ones.

Unfortunately, to the uninitiated, the use of statistics can seem to end debate right there—one can't argue with the numbers. But you now know better. Numbers are worthless if the methods used to generate the data are not valid, and numbers can be misleading if they are not used appropriately, taking into account the type of data to which they are applied. In a very poor town with one wealthy family, the mean income may be fairly high—but grossly misleading. And even assuming valid methods and proper use of statistics, there's one more critical step, because the numbers do not speak for themselves. Ultimately, it is how we interpret and report statistics that determines their usefulness.

KEY TERMS

Bar chart	Mean
Base number (*N*)	Measure of association
Bimodal	Median
Central tendency	Mode (probability average)
Chi-square	Normal distribution
Crosstabulation (crosstab)	Outlier
Data cleaning	Percentage
Descriptive statistics	Quartile
Elaboration analysis	Range
Extraneous variable	Secondary data analysis
Frequency distribution	Skewness
Frequency polygon	Standard deviation
Gamma	Statistic
Histogram	Statistical significance
Inferential statistics	Unimodal
Interquartile range	Variability
Marginal distribution	Variance

HIGHLIGHTS

• Data entry options include direct collection of data through a computer, use of scannable data entry forms, and use of data entry software. All data should be cleaned during the data entry process.

• Use of secondary data can save considerable time and resources, but may limit data analysis possibilities.

• Bar charts, histograms, and frequency polygons are useful for describing the shape of distributions. Care must be taken with graphic displays to avoid distorting a distribution's apparent shape.

• Frequency distributions display variation in a form that can be easily inspected and described. Values should be grouped in frequency distributions in a way that does not alter the shape of the distribution. Following several guidelines can reduce the risk of problems.

- Summary statistics are often used to describe the central tendency and variability of distributions. The appropriateness of the mode, mean, and median vary with a variable's level of measurement, the distribution's shape, and the purpose of the summary.

- The variance and standard deviation summarize variability around the mean. The interquartile range is usually preferable to the range to indicate the interval spanned by cases, due to the effect of outliers on the range. The degree of skewness of a distribution is usually described in words rather than with a summary statistic.

- Cell frequencies in crosstabulation should normally be converted to percentages within the categories of the independent variable. A crosstabulation can be used to determine the existence, strength, direction, and pattern of an association.

- Elaboration analysis can be used in crosstabular analysis to test for spurious relationships.

- Inferential statistics are used with sample-based data to estimate the confidence that can be placed in a statistical estimate of a population parameter. Estimates of the probability that an association between variables may have occurred on the basis of chance are also based on inferential statistics.

- Honesty and openness are the key ethical principles that should guide data summaries.

To assist you in completing the Web Exercises, please access the Study Site at http://www.pineforge.com/mssw2 where you'll find the Web Exercises with accompanying links. You'll find other useful study materials like self-quizzes and e-flashcards for each chapter, along with a group of carefully selected articles from research journals that illustrate the major concepts and techniques presented in the book.

EXERCISES

Discussing Research

1. Review the statistical analysis of voting in this chapter. Referring to this analysis, discuss some ways you think that statistics do and don't describe social reality. What are the strong and weak points of statistical analysis for social scientists? What are the advantages of using numbers?

2. Do you see how it is possible to "lie with statistics"? Identify three ways to distort social reality with statistics, even when the "numbers" are accurate. (Hint: You should review the chapter carefully to identify guidelines about statistics that might be violated in order to "change the picture.")

Finding Research

1. Do a Web search for information on a social science subject you are interested in. How much of the information you find relies on statistics as a tool for understanding the subject? How do statistics allow researchers to test their ideas about the subject and generate new ideas? Write your findings in a brief report, referring to the Web sites that you relied on.

2. The U.S. Bureau of the Census provides many graphs and numeric tables about current economic conditions. Review some of these presentations at http://www.census .gov/

cgi-bin/briefroom/BriefRm. Which displays are most effective in conveying information? Summarize what you can learn from this site about economic conditions in just one of the "briefing rooms."

Critiquing Research

1. Become a media critic. For the next week, scan a newspaper or some magazines for statistics. How many articles can you find that use frequency distributions, graphs, and the summary statistics introduced in this chapter? Are these statistics used appropriately and interpreted correctly? Would any other statistics have been preferable or useful in addition to those presented?

Doing Research

1. Create frequency distributions from lists in U.S. Bureau of the Census reports on the characteristics of cities or counties, or any similar listing of data for at least 100 cases. You will have to decide on a grouping scheme for the distribution of variables such as average age and population size, how to deal with outliers in the frequency distribution, and how to categorize qualitative variables such as the predominant occupation. Decide what summary statistics to use for each variable. How well were the features of each distribution represented by the summary statistics? Describe the shape of each distribution. Propose a hypothesis involving two of these variables, and develop a crosstab to evaluate the support for this hypothesis. Describe each relationship in terms of the four aspects of an association, after converting cell frequencies to percentages in each table within the categories of the independent variable. Does the hypothesis appear to have been supported?

2. Exhibit 9.18 is a three-variable table created with survey data from 355 employees hired during the previous year at a large telecommunications company. Employees were asked if the presence of on-site child care at the company's offices was important in their decision to join the company.

Reading the table:

(a) Does gender affect attitudes?

(b) Does marital status affect attitudes?

(c) Which of the preceding two matters more?

(d) Does being married affect men's attitudes more than women's?

3. If you have access to the SPSS statistical program, you can analyze data contained in the 2004 General Social Survey (GSS) file contained on the CD-ROM that comes with this text. See Appendix E for instructions on using SPSS.

Call up the GSS 2004 mini file from the CD-ROM and use it to describe basic social and demographic characteristics of the U.S. population in 2004.

a. From the menu, select

Graphs → Bar

From the Bar Graph window, select

Simple Define [Marital—Category Axis]

Exhibit 9.18	Is Child Care Important? By Gender and Marital Status			
	MEN		WOMEN	
	Single	Married	Single	Married
Not Important	54%	48%	33%	12%
Somewhat Important	24%	30%	45%	31%
Very Important	22%	22%	22%	57%
	100%	100%	100%	100%
N =	(125)	(218)	(51)	(161)

Bars represent % of cases. Select Options (do not display groups defined by missing values). Repeat this process with the variable SEX.

Describe the distribution of both variables.

b. Select

Histogram [EDUC,CHILDS,AGE]

Describe the distributions.

c. Generate frequency distributions and descriptive statistics for these variables. From the menu, select

Analyze → Descriptive Statistics → Frequencies From the Frequencies window, set

MARITAL,EDUC,INCOME98, ATTEND

Statistics [mean, median, range, std deviation]

d. Which statistics are appropriate to summarize the central tendency and variation of each variable? Do the values of any of these statistics surprise you?

4. Does support for capital punishment vary with political party affiliation? Generate a crosstabulation of CAPPUN by PARTYID in order to answer this question.

a. From the menu, select

Analyze → Descriptive Statistics → Crosstabs.

From the Crosstabs box, click CAPPUN into Rows and click

PARTYID into Columns.

Click on CELLS and select Column Percentages.

b. Describe how the percentage that supports capital punishment varies by party identification.

Chapter 10

Reviewing, Proposing, and Reporting Research

In a sense, we end this book where we began. As you begin writing up your findings, you can see the gaps in the research. While reviewing the literature—and finding where your own work fits in—you may discover more interesting possibilities or more exciting studies to be started. In the process of concluding each study, we almost naturally begin the next.

The primary goals of this chapter are to guide you in evaluating the research of other scholars, developing research proposals, and writing worthwhile reports of your own. We discuss how to evaluate prior research—a necessary step before writing a research report or proposal. We then focus on writing research proposals and reports.

COMPARING RESEARCH DESIGNS

From different methods, we learn different things. Even when used to study the same social processes, the central features of experiments, surveys, qualitative methods, and evaluation research provide distinct perspectives. Comparing subjects randomly assigned to a treatment group and to a comparison group, asking standard questions of the members of a random sample, observing while participating in a natural social setting, or studying program impact involve markedly different decisions about measurement, causality, and generalizability. As you can see in Exhibit 10.1, not one of these methods can reasonably be graded as superior to the others in all respects, and each varies in its suitability to different research questions and goals. Choosing among them for a particular investigation requires consideration of the research problem, opportunities and resources, prior research, philosophical commitments, and research goals.

Experimental designs are strongest for testing nomothetic causal hypotheses (law-like explanations that identify a common influence on a number of cases or events). These designs are most appropriate for studies of treatment effects (see Chapter 5). Research questions that are believed to involve basic social psychological processes are most appealing for laboratory studies, because the problem of generalizability is reduced. Random assignment reduces the possibility of preexisting differences between treatment and comparison groups to small, specifiable, chance levels, so many of the variables that might create a spurious association are controlled. Laboratory experiments permit unsurpassed control over conditions, and are excellent for establishing internal validity (causality).

But experimental designs have weaknesses. For most laboratory experiments, people volunteer as subjects, and volunteers aren't like other people, so generalizability is not good. Ethical and practical constraints limit your treatments (for

Exhibit 10.1   Comparison of Research Methods

Design	Measurement Validity	Generalizability	Causal Validity
Experiments	+	−	+
Surveys	+	+	−/+[a]
Participant Observation	−/+[b]	−	−

a. Surveys are a weaker design for identifying causal effects than true experiments, but use of statistical controls can strengthen causal arguments.

b. Reliability is low compared to surveys, and systematic evaluation of measurement validity is often not possible. However, direct observations may lead to great confidence in the validity of measures.

instance, you can't randomly assign race or social class). Although some processes may be the same for all people, so that generalizing from volunteer subjects will work, it's difficult to know in advance which processes are really invariant. Field experiments, unlike apparently more generalizable studies, allow for less control than lab experiments; hence, treatments may not be delivered as intended, or other influences may intrude (see Chapter 8). And field experiments typically require unusual access (e.g., permission to revise a school curriculum or change police department policy) and can be very expensive.

Surveys, because of their probability sampling and standardized questions, are excellent for generalizable descriptive studies of large populations (see Chapter 6). They can include a large number of variables, unlike experiments, so that potential spuriousness can be statistically controlled; therefore, surveys can be used readily to test hypothesized causal relationships. And because many closed-ended questions are available that have been used in previous studies, it's easy to find reliable measures of commonly used variables.

But surveys, too, have weaknesses. Survey questionnaires can measure only what respondents are willing to say; they may not uncover behavior or attitudes that are socially unacceptable. Survey questions, being standardized, may miss the nuances of a respondent's feelings or the complexities of an attitude; they lump together what may be interestingly different responses. They rely on the truthfulness of respondents and on their accuracy in reporting (for instance, by asking students how many hours a week they study—do they know? Is it constant?).

Qualitative methods allow intensive measurement of new or developing concepts, subjective meanings, and causal mechanisms (see Chapter 7). In field research, a "grounded theory" approach helps you create and refine concepts and theories based on direct observation or in depth interviewing. Interviewing reveals what people really mean by their ideas, and allows you to explore their feelings at great length. How, exactly, social processes unfold over time can be explored using interviews and fieldwork. Qualitative methods can identify the multiple successive events that might have led to some outcome, thus identifying idiographic causal processes; they are excellent for studying new or poorly understood settings, or populations that seek to remain hidden. When exploratory questions are posed or new groups studied, qualitative methods are preferred.

But such intensive study is time-consuming, so fewer cases can be examined. Single or a few cases or unique settings are interesting but don't produce generalizable results. Also, most researchers can't spend six months away from home doing a project. Open-ended interviews take time—not just the one or two hours of the interview itself, but the time in scheduling, in missed appointments, in travel to reach your subjects, and so on.

When qualitative methods can find real differences in an independent variable—for example, several different management styles in a manufacturing company—you can test nomothetic causal hypotheses. But the impossibility of controlling numerous possible extraneous influences makes qualitative methods a weak approach to hypothesis testing.

REVIEWING RESEARCH

A good literature review is the foundation for a research proposal, both in identifying gaps in current knowledge and in considering how to design a research project. It is also important to review the literature prior to writing an article about the research findings—the latest findings on your topic should be checked, and prior research on new issues should be consulted. This section helps you learn how to review the research that you locate. First, we focus on the process of reviewing single articles; then, we explain how to combine reviews of single articles into an overall literature review.

Exhibit 10.2 lists the questions you should ask when critiquing a social research study, and the following paragraphs provide an example. This particular critique

---

Exhibit 10.2   Questions to Ask About a Research Article

In reading a research article you want to know (a) What is the author's conclusion? and (b) Does the research presented adequately support that conclusion? The questions below will help you determine the answers.

I. *Overall assessment of the article*
1. What is the basic question being posed?
2. Is the theoretical approach appropriate?
3. Is the literature review adequate?
4. Does the research design suit the question?
5. Is the study scientific in its fundamentals?
6. Are the ethical issues adequately addressed?
7. What are the key findings?

II. *Detailed assessment*
1. What are the key concepts? Are they clearly defined?
2. What are the main hypotheses?
3. What are the main independent and dependent variables?
4. Are the measurements valid?
5. What are the units of analysis? Are they appropriate?
6. Are any causal relationships successfully established?
7. Is the effective sample (sampling plus response rate) representative?
8. Does context matter to the causal relationship?

does not answer all of the review questions, nor does it provide complete answers to all these questions, but it gives you the basic idea. In any case, remember that your goal is to evaluate research projects as integrated wholes. In addition to considering how valid the measures were and whether the causal conclusions were justified, you must consider how the *measurement approach* might have affected the causal validity of the researcher's conclusions and how the *sampling strategy* might have altered the quality of measures. In other words, all the parts of a study affect each other. Our goal here is just to illustrate the process of critically thinking about a piece of research.

Case Study: "Night as Frontier"

A minor classic in sociological literature, Murray Melbin's 1978 article "Night as Frontier," compares 20th-century extension of human activity into nighttime hours with 19th-century geographic expansion into the American West. Melbin argues that just as there was a "frontier lifestyle" in the old West of cowboys, a similar style of behavior, particularly toward strangers, prevails among late-night inhabitants of contemporary American cities. In developing this comparison of spatial frontiers with temporal frontiers, Melbin accomplished an insightful reconceptualization of how human beings live on a sparsely populated "frontier" of a different kind (Melbin, 1978).

Suppose that you are a student of urban life and curious as to whether city dwellers, such as New Yorkers, are really as unfriendly and brusque as stereotypes portray them. Melbin's article describes a number of field experiments, conducted entirely in Boston, to discover whether people were more or less helpful to others at nighttime than during the day. Perhaps you could use his findings. But was his research properly conducted?

The Research Design

Melbin and his assistants conducted four different experiments, all designed to measure if time of day affected people's willingness to be "helpful or friendly" to strangers. He drew in part on a sizable literature in this area conducted by social psychologists, but his studies were simpler in design than most psychology experiments; in most cases he had one independent variable—time of day— and one dependent variable—how likely people were to be helpful or friendly. Melbin's assistants, using a detailed sampling procedure (sampling both times of the day and subjects) approached random people on (also sampled) streets in Boston. In one study the researchers asked for directions; in another, they requested that subjects answer several interview questions. In a third study, they observed customers' interactions with cashiers at grocery stores. Finally, they left keys, tagged with "Please return" and an address, in various locations. In each case, the independent variable was time of day (for instance, when subjects were approached or the key was dropped on the street); the dependent variable was whether people were cooperative (directions, interviews), helpful (returning key), or friendly (smiling, conversational). A clear, simple coding scheme was used for all of these measures.

Analysis of the Design

Melbin's study was exploratory, designed to propose a new idea of how to understand nighttime in contemporary America. His experiments, therefore, were more in the manner of demonstrations—a first test of a new idea—than of continuing an established line of scientific research. Indeed, Melbin himself claimed to be advancing "the hypothesis that night is a frontier"; yet his experiments only test the idea that people at night are more "helpful and friendly" to strangers, which he argues is one of about a dozen characteristics of frontier communities.

But we can narrow our view to his specific question about helpfulness. His measures certainly have face validity, and in fact in three of his four studies people were indeed more friendly at night. And he didn't simply ask people if they would be helpful; he tested them in real situations in which they didn't know that it was an experiment. He also was open to surprises: In the "lost key" study, people were in fact *less* likely to return the key at night. Melbin realized that he had unintentionally slipped in another variable—whether the act of helpfulness was anonymous (the key study) or not (all the others). Only the community of face-to-face contact, he suggests, exists at night; help is not just generally extended to those not part of the nighttime community. So the different trials also lend plausibility to his argument. He only studied city residents, and only in Boston; it may be that the "nighttime community" exists only in urban settings, but an urban setting was a constant, not a variable, here.

There are at least two important problems in Melbin's design, despite its conscientious use of sampling, reliable coding procedures, and multiple measures. First, the studies don't really show that nighttime makes particular people more helpful and friendly; they show that people who are up at night—a self-selected group—are more helpful and friendly. Perhaps the kind of people who prefer night life, and not nighttime itself, is the true causal agent. And second, again, the studies were all conducted in a Northeastern city. Rural or suburban settings—a different context—could very well reveal different patterns.

An Overall Assessment

"Night as Frontier" certainly makes a persuasive argument, with far more historical and theoretical detail than we've mentioned here. It tends to be research of the "exploratory" type, so its experiments were somewhat crude; neither the measures nor the studies themselves have been widely replicated. Ethically, the work is benign. Its main value may lie in the persuasiveness of the argument that nighttime is different than daytime, and that the difference is much like the difference between densely settled areas and the old frontier West. For its conceptual insights, "Night as Frontier" deserves a respected place in the social science literature. In a detailed study of urban life and community it may be helpful, but perhaps it is not fundamental.

Case Study: When Does Arrest Matter?

The goal of the literature review process is to integrate the results of your separate article reviews and develop an overall assessment of the implications of prior research. The integrated literature review should accomplish three goals (Hart 1998:186–187):

- Summarize prior research
- Critique prior research
- Present pertinent conclusions

I'll discuss each of these goals in turn.

Summarize Prior Research

Your summary of prior research must focus on the particular research questions that you will address, but you may need also to provide some more general background. Carolyn Hoyle and Andrew Sanders (2000:14) begin their *British Journal of Criminology* research article about mandatory arrest policies in domestic violence cases with what they term a "provocative" question: What is the point of making it a crime for men to assault their female partners and ex-partners? They then review the different theories and supporting research that has justified different police policies: the "victim choice" position, the "pro-arrest" position, and the "victim empowerment" position. Finally, they review the research on the "controlling behaviors" of men that frames the specific research question on which they focus: how victims view the value of criminal justice interventions in their own cases (Hoyle and Sanders 2000:15).

Ask yourself three questions about your summary of the literature (Pyrczak 2005:51–59):

1. *Have you been selective?* If there have been more than a few prior investigations of your research question, you will need to narrow your focus to the most relevant and highest quality studies. Don't cite a large number of prior articles "just because they are there."

2. *Is the research up-to-date?* Be sure to include the latest research, not just the "classic" studies.

3. *Have you used direct quotes sparingly?* In order to focus your literature review, you need to express the key points from prior research in your own words. Use direct quotes only when they are essential for making an important point.

Critique Prior Research

Evaluate the strengths and weaknesses of the prior research. In addition to all the points you develop as you answer the "article review questions" in Appendix B, you should also select articles for review that reflect the work of credible authors in peer-reviewed journals who have been funded by reputable sources. Consider the following questions as you decide how much weight to give each article (Locke, Silverman, & Spirduso 1998:37–44):

1. *How was the report reviewed prior to its publication or release?* Articles published in academic journals go through a very rigorous review process, usually involving careful criticism and revision. Top "refereed" journals may accept only 10% of submitted articles, so they can be very selective. Dissertations go through a lengthy process of criticism and revision by a few members of the dissertation writer's home institution. A report released directly by a research organization is likely to have had only a limited review, although some research organizations maintain a rigorous internal review process. Papers presented at professional meetings may have had little prior review. Needless to say, more confidence can be placed in research results that have been subject to a more rigorous review.

2. *What is the author's reputation?* Reports by an author or team of authors who have published other work on the research question should be given somewhat greater credibility at the outset.

3. *Who funded and sponsored the research?* Major federal funding agencies and private foundations fund only research proposals that have been evaluated

carefully and ranked highly by a panel of experts. They also often monitor closely the progress of the research. This does not guarantee that every such project report is good, but it goes a long way toward ensuring some worthwhile products. On the other hand, research that is funded by organizations that have a preference for a particular outcome should be given particularly close scrutiny.

Present Pertinent Conclusions

Don't leave the reader guessing about the implications of the prior research for your own investigation. Present the conclusions you draw from the research you have reviewed. As you do so, follow several simple guidelines (Pyrczak, 2005:53–56):

- Distinguish clearly your own opinion of prior research from conclusions of the authors of the articles you have reviewed.
- Make it clear when your own approach is based on the theoretical framework you are using rather than on the results of prior research.
- Acknowledge the potential limitations of any empirical research project. Don't emphasize problems in prior research that you can't avoid either.

Explain how the unanswered questions raised by prior research or the limitations of methods used in prior research make it important for you to conduct your own investigation (Fink, 2005:190–192).

A good example of how to conclude an integrated literature review is provided by an article based on the replication in Milwaukee of the Minneapolis Domestic Violence Experiment. For this article, Ray Paternoster, Robert Brame, Ronet Bachman, and Lawrence Sherman (1997) sought to determine whether police officers' use of fair procedures when arresting assault suspects would lessen the rate of subsequent domestic violence. Paternoster et al. (1997:164) conclude that there has been a major gap in the prior literature:

> Even at the end of some seven experiments and millions of dollars, then, there is a great deal of ambiguity surrounding the question of how arrest impacts future spouse assault.

Specifically, they note that each of the seven experiments focused on the effect of arrest itself, but ignored the possibility that "particular kinds of police *procedure* might inhibit the recurrence of spouse assault" (Paternoster et al. 1997:165).

So Paternoster and his colleagues ground their new analysis in additional literature on procedural justice and conclude that their new analysis will be:

. . . the first study to examine the effect of fairness judgments regarding a punitive criminal sanction (arrest) on serious criminal behavior (assaulting one's partner). (Paternoster et al. 1997:172)

PROPOSING NEW RESEARCH

Be grateful for people who require you to write a formal research proposal—and even more for those who give you constructive feedback. Whether your proposal is written for a professor, a thesis committee, an organization seeking practical advice, or a government agency that funds basic research, the proposal will force you to set out a problem statement and a research plan. Too many research projects begin without a clear problem statement or with only the barest of notions about which variables must be measured or what the analysis should look like. Such projects often wander along, lurching from side to side, and then collapse entirely or just peter out with a report that is ignored—and should be. Even in circumstances when a proposal is not required, you should prepare one and present it to others for feedback. Just writing your ideas down will help you to see how they can be improved, and feedback in almost any form will help you to refine your plans.

A well-designed proposal can go a long way toward shaping the final research report and will make it easier to progress at later research stages (Locke, Spirduso, & Silverman, 2000). Every research proposal should have at least six sections:

- *An introductory statement of the research problem,* in which you clarify what it is that you are interested in studying
- *A literature review,* in which you explain how your problem and plans build on what has already been reported in the literature on this topic
- *A methodological plan,* detailing just how you will respond to the particular mix of opportunities and constraints you face
- *A budget,* presenting a careful listing of the anticipated costs
- *An ethics statement,* identifying human subjects issues in the research and how you will respond to them in an ethical fashion
- *A statement of limitations,* reviewing weaknesses of the proposed research and presenting plans for minimizing their consequences

A research proposal also can be strengthened considerably by presenting a result of a pilot study of the research question. This might involve administering the proposed questionnaire to a small sample, conducting a preliminary version of the proposed experiment with a group of available subjects, or making observations over a limited period of time in a setting like that proposed for a qualitative study. Careful presentation of the methods used in the pilot study and the problems that were encountered will impress anyone who reviews the proposal.

If your research proposal will be reviewed competitively, it must present a compelling rationale for funding. The research problem that you propose to study is crucial; its importance cannot be overstated (see Chapter 2). If you propose to test a hypothesis, be sure that it is one for which there are plausible alternatives, so your study isn't just a boring report of the obvious (Dawes, 1995:93).

Case Study: Treating Substance Abuse

Particular academic departments, grant committees, and funding agencies will have specific proposal requirements. As an example, Exhibit 10.3 lists the primary required sections of the "Research Plan" for proposals to the National Institutes of Health (NIH), together with excerpts from a proposal Russell Schutt submitted in this format to the National Institute of Mental Health (NIMH) with colleagues from the University of Massachusetts Medical School. The research plan is limited by NIH guidelines to 25 pages. It must be preceded by an abstract (which is excerpted), a proposed budget, biographical sketches of project personnel, and a discussion of the available resources for the project. Appendixes may include research instruments, prior publications by the authors, and findings from related work.

As you can see from the excerpts, the proposal was to study the efficacy of a particular treatment approach for homeless mentally ill persons who abuse substances. The proposal included a procedure for recruiting subjects in two cities, randomly assigning half of the subjects to a recently developed treatment program, and measuring a range of outcomes. The NIMH review committee (composed of social scientists who were experts in these issues) approved the project for funding but did not rate it highly enough so that it actually was awarded funds. (It often takes several resubmissions before even a worthwhile proposal is funded.) The committee members recognized the proposal's strengths but also identified several problems that they believed had to be overcome before the proposal could be funded. The problems were primarily

Exhibit 10.3 A Grant Proposal to the National Institute of Mental Health

Relapse Prevention for Homeless Dually Diagnosed

Abstract

This project will test the efficacy of shelter-based treatment that integrates Psychosocial Rehabilitation with Relapse Prevention techniques adapted for homeless mentally ill persons who abuse substances. Two hundred and fifty homeless persons, meeting . . . criteria for substance abuse and severe and persistent mental disorder, will be recruited from two shelters and then randomly assigned to either an experimental treatment condition . . . or to a control condition.

For one year, at the rate of three two-hour sessions per week, the treatment group ($n = 125$) will participate for the first six months in "enhanced" Psychosocial Rehabilitation . . . , followed by six months of Relapse Prevention training. . . . The control group will participate in a Standard Treatment condition (currently comprised of a twelve-step peer-help program along with counseling offered at all shelters). . . .

Outcome measures include substance abuse, housing placement and residential stability, social support, service utilization, level of distress. . . . The integrity of the experimental design will be monitored through a process analysis. Tests for the hypothesized treatment effects . . . will be supplemented with analyses to evaluate the direct and indirect effects of subject characteristics and to identify interactions between subject characteristics and treatment condition. . . .

Research Plan

1. Specific Aims

The research demonstration project will determine whether an integrated clinical shelter-based treatment intervention can improve health and well-being among homeless persons who abuse alcohol and/or drugs and who are seriously and persistently ill—the so-called "dually diagnosed." . . . We aim to identify the specific attitudes and behaviors that are most affected by the integrated psychosocial rehabilitation/relapse prevention treatment, and thus to help guide future service interventions.

2. Background and Significance

Relapse is the most common outcome in treating the chronically mentally ill, including the homeless. . . . Reviews of the clinical and empirical literature published to date indicate that treatment interventions based on social learning experiences are associated with more favorable outcomes than treatment interventions based on more traditional forms of psychotherapy and/or chemotherapy. . . . However, few tests of the efficacy of such interventions have been reported for homeless samples.

3. Progress Report/Preliminary Studies

Four areas of Dr. Schutt's research help to lay the foundation for the research demonstration project here proposed. . . . The 1990 survey in Boston shelters measured substance abuse with selected ASI [Addiction Severity Index] questions. . . . About half of the respondents evidenced a substance abuse problem. Just over one-quarter of respondents had ever been treated for a mental health problem. . . . At least three-quarters were interested in help with each of the problems mentioned other than substance abuse. Since help with benefits, housing, and AIDS prevention will each be provided to all study participants in the proposed research demonstration project, we project that this should increase the rate of participation and retention in the study. . . . Results [from co-investigator Dr. Walter Penk's research] . . . indicate that trainers were more successful in engaging the dually diagnosed in Relapse Prevention techniques. . . .

(Continued)

4. Research Design and Methods

Study Sample.
Recruitment. The study will recruit 350 clients beginning in month 4 of the study and running through month 28 for study entry. The span of treatment is 12 months and is followed by 12 months of follow-up. . . .

Study Criteria.
Those volunteering to participate will be screened and declared eligible for the study based upon the following characteristics:
1. Determination that subject is homeless using criteria operationally defined by one of the accepted definitions summarized by . . .

Attrition.
Subject enrollment, treatment engagement, and subject retention each represent potentially significant challenges to study integrity and have been given special attention in all phases of the project. Techniques have been developed to address engagement and retention and are described in detail below. . . .

Research Procedures.
All clients referred to the participating shelters will be screened for basic study criteria. . . . Once assessment is completed, subjects who volunteer are then randomly assigned to one of two treatment conditions—RPST or Standard Treatment. . . .

Research Variables and Measures.
Measures for this study . . . are of three kinds: subject selection measures, process measures, and outcome measures. . . .

5. Human Subjects

Potential risks to subjects are minor. . . . Acute problems identified . . . can be quickly referred to appropriate interventions. Participation in the project is voluntary, and all subjects retain the option to withdraw . . . at any time, without any impact on their access to shelter care or services regularly offered by the shelters. Confidentiality of subjects is guaranteed. . . . [They have] . . . an opportunity to learn new ways of dealing with symptoms of substance abuse and mental illness.

methodological, stemming from the difficulties associated with providing services to and conducting research on this particular segment of the homeless population.

The proposal has many strengths, including the specially tailored intervention derived from psychiatric rehabilitation technology developed by Liberman and his associates and relapse prevention methods adapted from Marlatt.

[T]his fully documented treatment . . . greatly facilitates the generalizability and transportability of study findings. . . . The investigative team is excellent . . . also attuned to the difficulties entailed in studying this target group. . . . While these strengths recommend the proposal . . . eligibility criteria for inclusion of subjects in the study are somewhat ambiguous. . . . .This volunteer procedure could substantially underrepresent important components of the shelter population. . . . The projected time frame for recruiting subjects . . . also seems unrealistic for a three-year effort. . . . Several factors in the research design seem to mitigate against maximum participation and retention. . . .

If you get the impression that researchers cannot afford to leave any stone unturned in working through procedures in an NIMH proposal, you are right. It is very difficult to convince a government agency that a research project is worth spending a lot of money on (we requested about $2 million). And that is as it should be: Your tax dollars should be used only for research that has a high likelihood of yielding findings that are valid and useful. But even when you are proposing a smaller project to a more generous funding source—or even presenting a proposal to your professor—you should scrutinize the proposal carefully before submission and ask others to comment on it. Other people will often think of issues you neglected to consider, and you should allow yourself time to think about these issues and to reread and redraft the proposal. Besides, you will get no credit for having thrown together a proposal as best you could in the face of an impossible submission deadline.

When you develop a research proposal, it will help to work through each of the issues in Exhibit 10.4 (also see Herek, 1995). It is too easy to omit important details and to avoid being self-critical while rushing to put a proposal together. However, it is painful to have a proposal rejected (or to receive a low grade). Better to make sure the proposal covers what it should and confronts the tough issues that reviewers (or your professor) will be sure to spot.

The points in Exhibit 10.4 can serve as a map to preceding chapters in this book and as a checklist of decisions that must be made throughout any research project. The points are organized in five sections, each concluding with a *checkpoint* at which you should consider whether to proceed with the research as planned, modify the plans, or stop the project altogether. The sequential ordering of these questions obscures a bit the way in which they should be answered: not as single questions, one at a time, but as a unit—first as five separate stages, and then as a whole. Feel free to change your answers to earlier questions on the basis of your answers to later questions.

A brief review of how the questions in Exhibit 10.4 might be answered with respect to Schutt's NIMH relapse prevention proposal (with Walter E. Penk and others) should help you to review your own work. The research question concerned the effectiveness of a particular type of substance abuse treatment in a shelter for homeless persons; an evaluation research question (Question 1). This problem certainly was suitable for social research, and it was one that could have

Exhibit 10.4   Decisions in Research Design

PROBLEM FORMULATION (Chapters 1–2)
  1. Developing a research question
  2. Assessing researchability of the problem
  3. Consulting prior research
  4. Relating to social theory
  5. Choosing an approach: Deductive? Inductive? Descriptive?
  6. Reviewing research guidelines

> CHECKPOINT 1
> Alternatives: • Continue as planned.
>   • Modify the plan.
>   • STOP. Abandon the plan.

RESEARCH VALIDITY (Chapters 3–5)
  7. Establishing measurement validity
  8. Establishing generalizability
  9. Establishing causality
  10. Data required: Longitudinal or cross-sectional?
  11. Units of analysis: Individuals or groups?
  12. What are major possible sources of causal invalidity?

> CHECKPOINT 2
> Alternatives: • Continue as planned.
>   • Modify the plan.
>   • STOP. Abandon the plan.

RESEARCH DESIGN (Chapters 6–8)
  13. Choosing a research design, such as survey or participant observation
  14. Specifying the research plan: Types of experiments, surveys, observations, etc.
  15. Assessing ethical concerns

> CHECKPOINT 3
> Alternatives: • Continue as planned.
>   • Modify the plan.
>   • STOP. Abandon the plan.

DATA ANALYSIS (Chapter 9)
  16. Choosing statistics, such as frequencies, crosstabulation, etc.

> CHECKPOINT 4
> Alternatives: • Continue as planned.
>   • Modify the plan.
>   • STOP. Abandon the plan.

REVIEWING, PROPOSING, AND REPORTING RESEARCH (Chapter 10)
  17. Organizing the text
  18. Reviewing ethical and practical constraints

> CHECKPOINT 5
> Alternatives: • Continue as planned.
>   • Modify the plan.
>   • STOP. Abandon the plan.

been handled for the money we requested (Question 2). Prior research demonstrated clearly that our proposed treatment had potential and also that it had not previously been tried with homeless persons (3). The treatment approach was connected to psychosocial rehabilitation theory (4) and, given prior work in this area, a deductive, hypothesis-testing stance was called for (5). Our review of research guidelines continued up to the point of submission, and we felt that our proposal took each into account (6). So it seemed reasonable to continue to develop the proposal (Checkpoint 1).

Measures would include direct questions, observations by field researchers, and laboratory tests (of substance abuse) (7). The proposal's primary weakness was in the area of generalizability (8). We proposed to sample persons in only two homeless shelters in two cities, and we could offer only weak incentives to encourage potential participants to start the study and stay in it. The review committee believed that these procedures might result in an unrepresentative group of initial volunteers beginning the treatment and perhaps an even less representative group continuing through the entire program. The problem was well suited to a randomized, experimental design (9) and was best addressed with longitudinal data (10) involving individuals (11). Our randomized design controlled for selection bias and endogenous change, but external events, treatment contamination, and treatment misidentification were potential sources of causal invalidity (12). Clearly we should have modified the proposal with some additional recruitment and retention strategies—although it may be that the research could not actually be carried out without some major modification of the research question (Checkpoint 2).

A randomized experimental design was preferable because this was to be a treatment-outcome study, but we did include a field research component so that we could evaluate treatment implementation (13, 14). Because the effectiveness of our proposed treatment strategy had not been studied before among homeless persons, we could not propose doing a secondary data analysis or meta-analysis (15). We sought only to investigate causation from a nomothetic perspective, without attempting to show how the particular experiences of each participant may have led to their outcome (16). Because participation in the study was to be voluntary and everyone received *something* for participation, the research design seemed ethical (and it was approved by the University of Massachusetts Medical School's Institutional Review Board and by the state mental health agency's human subjects committee) (17). We planned several statistical tests, but here the review committee remarked that we should have been more specific (18). Our goal was to use our research as the basis for several academic articles, and we expected that the funding agency would also require us to prepare a report for general distribution

(19, 20). We had reviewed the research literature carefully (21), but as is typical in most research proposals, we did not develop our research reporting plans any further (22, 23).

REPORTING RESEARCH

The goal of research is not just to discover something but to communicate that discovery to a larger audience: other social scientists, government officials, your teachers, the general public—perhaps several of these audiences. Whatever the study's particular outcome, if the research report enables the intended audience to comprehend the results and learn from them, the research can be judged a success. If the intended audience is not able to learn about the study's results, the research should be judged a failure—no matter how expensive the research, how sophisticated its design, or how much of yourself you invested in it.

You began writing your research report when you worked on the research proposal, and you will find that the final report is much easier to write, and more adequate, if you write more material for it as you work out issues during the project. It is very disappointing to discover that something important was left out when it is too late to do anything about it. And we don't need to point out that students (and professional researchers) often leave final papers (and reports) until the last possible minute (often for understandable reasons, including other course work and job or family responsibilities). But be forewarned: *The last-minute approach does not work for research reports.*

Writing and Organizing

A successful report must be well organized and clearly written. Getting to such a product is a difficult but not impossible goal. Consider the following principles formulated by experienced writers (Booth, Colomb, & Williams, 1995:150–151):

- Respect the complexity of the task and don't expect to write a polished draft in a linear fashion. Your thinking will develop as you write, causing you to reorganize and rewrite.
- Leave enough time for dead ends, restarts, revisions, and so on, and accept the fact that you will discard much of what you write.
- Write as fast as you comfortably can. Don't worry about spelling, grammar, and so on until you are polishing things up.

- Ask anyone you trust for their reactions to what you have written.
- Write as you go along, so you have notes and report segments drafted even before you focus on writing the report.

It is important to outline a report before writing it, but neither the organization of the report nor the first written draft should be considered fixed. As you write, you will get new ideas about how to organize the report. Try them out. As you review the first draft, you will see many ways to improve your writing. Focus particularly on how to shorten and clarify your statements. Make sure that each paragraph concerns only one topic. Remember the golden rule of good writing: Writing is revising!

You can ease the burden of writing in several ways:

- Draw on the research proposal and on project notes. You aren't starting from scratch; you have all the material you've written during the course of the project.
- Refine your word processing skills on the computer so that you can use the most efficient techniques when reorganizing and editing.
- Seek criticism from friends, teachers, or other research consumers before you turn in the final product. They will alert you to problems in the research or the writing.

We often find it helpful to use *reverse outlining.* After you have written a first draft, read through the draft, noting down the key ideas as they come up. Do those notes reflect your original outline or did you go astray? Are the paragraphs clean? How could your organization be improved?

Most important, leave yourself enough time so that you *can* revise, several times if possible, before turning in the final draft.

You can find more detailed reviews of writing techniques in Becker (1986), Booth et al. (1995), Mullins (1977), Strunk and White (1979), and Turabian (1967).

Your report should be clearly organized into sections, probably following a standard format that readers will immediately understand. Any research report should include an *introductory statement of the research problem,* a *literature review,* and a *methodology section.* These are the same three sections that should begin a research proposal. In addition, a research report must include a *findings section* with pertinent data displays. A *discussion section* may be used to interpret the findings and review the support for the study's hypotheses. A *conclusions section* should summarize the findings and draw implications for the theoretical framework used. Any weaknesses in the research design and ways to improve future research should be identified in this section. Compelling foci for additional research on the research question also should be noted. Most journals require a short abstract at the beginning that summarizes the research question and findings. A *bibliography* is also necessary. Depending on how the report is being published, *appendixes* containing the instruments used and specific information on the measures also may be included.

Exhibit 10.5 presents an outline of the sections in an academic journal article, with some illustrative quotes. The article's introduction highlights the importance of the problem selected—the relation between marital disruption (divorce) and depression. The introduction also states clearly the gap in the research literature that the article is meant to fill—the untested possibility that depression might cause marital disruption rather than, or in addition to, marital disruption causing depression. The findings section (labeled "Results") begins by presenting the basic

---

Exhibit 10.5   Sections in a Journal Article

INTRODUCTION
Despite 20 years of empirical research, the extent to which marital disruption causes poor mental health remains uncertain. The reason for this uncertainty is that previous research has consistently overlooked the potentially important problems of selection into and out of marriage on the basis of prior mental health. (p. 237)

SAMPLE AND MEASURES
Sample
Measures

RESULTS
The Basic Association Between Marital Disruption and Depression
Sex Differences
The Impact of Prior Marital Quality
The Mediating Effects of Secondary Changes
The Modifying Effects of Transitions to Secondary Roles

DISCUSSION [includes conclusions]

. . . According to the results, marital disruption does in fact cause a significant increase in depression compared to pre-divorce levels within a period of three years after the divorce. (p. 245)

Source: Robert H. Aseltine, Jr. and Ronald C. Kessler, 1993. "Marital Disruption and Depression in a Community Sample." *Journal of Health and Social Behavior, 34* (September):237–251.

association between marital disruption and depression. Then, it elaborates on this association by examining sex differences, the impact of prior marital quality, and various mediating and modifying effects. As indicated in the combined discussion and conclusions section, the analysis shows that marital disruption does indeed increase depression and specifies the time frame (three years) during which this effect occurs.

These basic report sections present research results well, but many research reports include subsections tailored to the issues and stages in the specific study being reported. Lengthy applied reports on elaborate research projects may, in fact, be organized around the research project's different stages or foci.

What can be termed the *front matter* and the *back matter* of an applied report also are important. Applied reports usually begin with an executive summary: a summary list of the study's main findings, often with bullet points. Appendixes, the "back matter," may present tables containing supporting data that were not discussed in the body of the report. Applied research reports also often append a copy of the research instrument(s).

For instance, Exhibit 10.6 outlines the sections in an applied research report. This particular report was mandated by the California State Legislature in order to review a state-funded program for the homeless mentally disabled. The goals of the report are described as both description and evaluation. The body of the report presents findings on the number and characteristics of homeless persons and on the operations of the state-funded program in each of 17 counties. The discussion section highlights service needs that are not being met. Nine appendixes then provide details on the study methodology and the counties studied.

An important principle for the researcher writing for a nonacademic audience is to make the findings and conclusions engaging and clear. You can see how Schutt did this in a report from a class research project designed with his graduate methods students (and in collaboration with several faculty knowledgeable about substance abuse) (Exhibit 10.7). These report excerpts indicate how he summarized key findings in an executive summary (Schutt et al., 1996:iv), emphasized the importance of the research in the introduction (Schutt et al., 1996:1), used formatting and graphing to draw attention to particular findings in the body of the text (Schutt et al., 1996:5), and tailored recommendations to his own university context (Schutt et al., 1996:26).

A well-written research report requires (to be just a bit melodramatic) blood, sweat, and tears—and more time than you may at first anticipate. But writing one report will help you write the next report. And the issues you consider, if you approach your writing critically, will be sure to improve your subsequent research projects and sharpen your evaluations of other investigators' research projects.

Exhibit 10.6 Sections in an Applied Report

SUMMARY

In 1986, the California State Legislature mandated an independent review of the HMD programs that the counties had established with the state funds. The review was to determine the accountability of funds; describe the demographic and mental disorder characteristics of persons served; and assess the effectiveness of the program. This report describes the results of that review. (p. v)

INTRODUCTION
  Background
  California's Mental Health Services Act of 1985 . . . allocated $20 million annually to the state's 58 counties to support a wide range of services, from basic needs to rehabilitation. (pp. 1–2)
  Study Objectives
  Organization of the Report

HMD PROGRAM DESCRIPTION AND STUDY METHODOLOGY
  The HMD Program
  Study Design and Methods
  Study Limitations

COUNTING AND CHARACTERIZING THE HOMELESS
  Estimating the Number of Homeless People
  Characteristics of the Homeless Population

THE HMD PROGRAM IN 17 COUNTIES
  Service Priorities
  Delivery of Services
  Implementation Progress
  Selected Outcomes
  Effects on the Community and on County Service Agencies
  Service Gaps

DISCUSSION
  Underserved Groups of HMD
  Gaps in Continuity of Care
  A particularly large gap in the continuum of care is the lack of specialized housing alternatives for the mentally disabled. The nature of chronic mental illness limits the ability of these individuals to live completely independently. But their housing needs may change, and board-and-care facilities that are acceptable during some periods of their lives may become unacceptable at other times. (p. 57)
  Improved Service Delivery
  Issues for Further Research

Appendixes
A. SELECTION OF 17 SAMPLED COUNTIES
B. QUESTIONNAIRE FOR SURVEY OF THE HOMELESS
C. GUIDELINES FOR CASE STUDIES
D. INTERVIEW INSTRUMENTS FOR TELEPHONE SURVEY
E. HOMELESS STUDY SAMPLING DESIGN, ENUMERATION, AND SURVEY WEIGHTS
F. HOMELESS SURVEY FIELD PROCEDURES
G. SHORT SCREENER FOR MENTAL AND SUBSTANCE USE DISORDERS
H. CHARACTERISTICS OF THE COUNTIES AND THEIR HMD-FUNDED PROGRAMS
I. CASE STUDIES FOR FOUR COUNTIES' HMD PROGRAMS

Source: Georges M. Vernez, Audrey Burnam, Elizabeth A. McGlynn, Sally Trude, and Brian S. Mirttman, 1988. *Review of California's Program for the Homeless Mentally Disabled.* Santa Monica, CA: RAND, R-3631-CDMH.

Exhibit 10.7   Student Substance Abuse, Report Excerpts

Executive Summary

- Rates of substance abuse were somewhat lower at UMass–Boston than among nationally selected samples of college students.
- Two-thirds of the respondents reported at least one close family member whose drinking or drug use had ever been of concern to them—one-third reported a high level of concern.
- Most students perceived substantial risk of harm due to illicit drug use, but just one-quarter thought alcohol use posed a great risk of harm.

Introduction

Binge drinking, other forms of alcohol abuse, and illicit drug use create numerous problems on college campuses. Deaths from binge drinking are too common and substance abuse is a factor in as many as two-thirds of on-campus sexual assaults (Finn, 1997; National Institute of Alcohol Abuse and Alcoholism, 1995). College presidents now rate alcohol abuse as the number one campus problem (Wechsler, Davenport, Dowdall, Moeykens, & Castillo, 1994) and many schools have been devising new substance abuse prevention policies and programs. However, in spite of increasing recognition of and knowledge about substance abuse problems at colleges as a whole, little attention has been focused on substance abuse at commuter schools.

Findings

The composite index identifies 27% of respondents as at risk of substance abuse (an index score of 2 or higher).[1] One-quarter reported having smoked or used smokeless tobacco in the past two weeks.

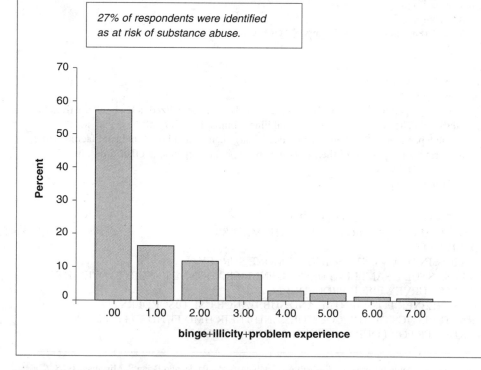

27% of respondents were identified as at risk of substance abuse.

Recommendations

1. Enforce campus rules and regulations about substance use. When possible and where appropriate, communications from campus officials to students should heighten awareness of the UMass–Boston commitment to an alcohol- and drug-free environment.

2. Encourage those students involved in campus alcohol or drug-related problems or crises to connect with the PRIDE program.

3. Take advantage of widespread student interest in prevention by forming a university-wide council to monitor and stimulate interest in prevention activities.

Source: Schutt et al., 1996.

CONCLUSION

Good critical skills are essential in evaluating research reports, whether your own or those produced by others. And it is really not just a question of sharpening your knives and going for the jugular. There are *always* weak points in any research, even published research. Being aware of the weaknesses, both in others' studies and in your own, is a major strength in itself. You need to be able to weigh the results of any particular research, and to evaluate a study in terms of its contribution to understanding the social world—not in terms of whether it gives a definitive answer for all time, or is perfectly controlled, or answers all questions.

This is not to say, however, that "anything goes." Much research lacks one or more of the three legs of validity—measurement validity, causal validity, or generalizability—and contributes more confusion than understanding about the social world. It's true that top scholarly journals maintain very high standards, partly because they have good critics in the review process and distinguished editors who make the final acceptance decisions. But some daily newspapers do a poor job of screening, and research reporting standards in many popular magazines, TV shows, and books are often abysmally poor. Keep your standards high when you read research reports, but not so high or so critical that you dismiss studies that make tangible contributions to understanding the social world. And don't be so intimidated by high standards that you shrink from conducting research yourself.

The growth of social science methods from infancy to adolescence, perhaps to young adulthood, ranks as a key intellectual accomplishment of the 20th century. Opinions about the causes and consequences of homelessness no longer need to depend on the scattered impressions of individuals; criminal justice policies can be shaped by systematic evidence of their effectiveness; and changes in the distribution of poverty and wealth in populations can be identified and charted. Employee productivity, neighborhood cohesion, and societal conflict can each be linked to individual psychological processes and to international economic strains. Systematic researchers looking at truly representative data can make connections and see patterns that no casual observer would ever discern.

Of course, social research methods are only helpful when the researchers are committed and honest. Research methods, like all knowledge, can be used poorly or well, for good purposes or bad, when appropriate or not. A claim that "we're basing this on research!" or "Our statistics prove it!" in itself provides no extra credibility. As you have learned throughout this book, we must first learn which methods were used, how they were applied, and whether final interpretations square with the evidence. But having done all that in good faith, we do emerge from confusion into clarity, in our continuing effort to make sense of the social world.

HIGHLIGHTS

• Research reports should be evaluated systematically, using the review guide in Exhibit 10.2 and also taking account of the interrelations among the design elements.

• Proposal writing should be a time for clarifying the research problem, reviewing the literature, and thinking ahead about the report that will be required. Tradeoffs between different design elements should be considered and the potential for mixing methods evaluated.

• Different types of reports typically pose different problems. Authors of student papers must be guided in part by the expectations of their professor. Thesis writers have to meet the requirements of different committee members, but can benefit greatly from the areas of expertise represented on a typical thesis committee. Applied researchers are constrained by the expectations of the research sponsor; an advisory committee from the applied setting can help to avoid problems. Journal articles must pass a peer review by other social scientists and often are much improved in the process.

• Research reports should include an introductory statement of the research problem, a literature review, a methodology section, a findings section with pertinent data displays, and a conclusions section that identifies any weaknesses in the research design and points out implications for future research and theorizing. This basic report format should be modified according to the needs of a particular audience.

• All reports should be revised several times and critiqued by others before being presented in final form.

To assist you in completing the Web Exercises, please access the Study Site at http://www.pineforge.com/mssw2 where you'll find the Web Exercises with accompanying links. You'll find other useful study materials like self-quizzes and e-flashcards for each chapter, along with a group of carefully selected articles from research journals that illustrate the major concepts and techniques presented in the book.

EXERCISES

Discussing Research

1. How firm a foundation do social research methods provide for understanding the social world? Stage an in-class debate, with the pro and con arguments focusing on the variability of social research findings across different social contexts and the difficulty of understanding human subjectivity.

Finding Research

1. Go to the National Science Foundation's Sociology Program Web site at http://www.nsf.gov/funding/pgm_summ.jsp?pims_id=5369&org=SES&from=home. What are the components that the National Science Foundation's Sociology Program looks for in a proposed piece of research? Outline a research proposal to study a subject of your choice to be submitted to the National Science Foundation for funding.

2. The National Academy of Sciences wrote a lengthy report on ethics issues in scientific research. Visit the site and read the report at www.nap.edu/readingroom/books/obas. Summarize the information and guidelines in the report.

3. Search a social science journal to find five different examples of social science research projects. Briefly describe each. How does each differ in its approach to reporting the research results? To whom do you think the author(s) of each is "reporting" (i.e., who is the "audience"?), How do you think the predicted audience has helped to shape the author's approach to reporting the results? Be sure to note the source in which you located your five examples.

Critiquing Research

1. A good place to start developing your critical skills would be with Murray Melbin's article that is reviewed in this chapter. Try reading it, and fill in the answers to the article review questions that we did not cover (Exhibit 10.2). Do you agree with our answers to the other questions? Could you add some points to our critique, or to the lessons about research designs that we drew from these critiques?

2. Read the journal article "Marital Disruption and Depression in a Community Sample," by Aseltine and Kessler in the September 1993 issue of *Journal of Health and Social Behavior*. How effective is the article in conveying the design and findings

of the research? Could the article's organization be improved at all? Are there bases for disagreement about the interpretation of the findings?

3. Rate four journal articles for overall quality of the research and for effectiveness of the writing and data displays. Discuss how each could have been improved.

Doing Research

1. Call a local social or health service administrator or a criminal justice official and arrange for an interview. Ask the official about his or her experience with applied research reports and conclusions about the value of social research and the best techniques for reporting to practitioners.

2. Interview a student who has written an independent paper or thesis based on collecting original data. Ask her or him to describe her or his experiences while writing the thesis. Review the decisions she or he made in designing the research, and ask about the stages of research design, data collection and analysis, and report writing that proved to be difficult.

3. Design a research proposal, following the outline and guidelines presented in this chapter. Focus on a research question that you could study on campus or in your local community.

Appendix A

Finding Information

ELIZABETH SCHNEIDER, M.L.S.

RUSSELL K. SCHUTT, PH.D.

All research is conducted in order to "find information" in some sense, but the focus of this section is more specifically about finding information to inform a central research project. This has often been termed "searching the literature," but the popularity of the World Wide Web for finding information requires that we broaden our focus beyond the traditional search of the published literature. It may sound trite, but we do indeed live in an "information age," with an unprecedented amount of information of many types available to us with relatively little effort. Learning how to locate and use that information efficiently has become a prerequisite for social science.

SEARCHING THE LITERATURE

It is most important to search the literature before we begin a research study. A good literature review may reveal that the research problem already has been adequately investigated; it may highlight particular aspects of the research problem most in need of further investigation; or it may suggest that the planned research design is not appropriate for the problem chosen. It can highlight the strong and weak points of related theories. When we review previous research about our research question, we may learn about weaknesses in our measures, complexities in our research problem, and possible difficulties in data collection. The more of these problems that can be taken into account before, rather than after, data are collected, the better the final research product will be. Even when the rush to "find out" what people think or are doing creates pressure to just go out and ask or observe, it is important to take the time to search the literature and try to reap the benefit of prior investigations.

But the social science literature is not just a source for guidance at the start of an investigation. During a study, questions will arise that can be answered by careful reading of earlier research. After data collection has ceased, reviewing the literature can help to develop new insights into patterns in the data. Research articles published since a project began may suggest new hypotheses or questions to explore.

The best way of searching the literature will be determined in part by what library and bibliographic resources are available to you, but a brief review of some basic procedures and alternative strategies will help you get started on a productive search.

Preparing the Search

You should formulate a research question before you begin the search, although the question may change after you begin. Identify the question's parts and subparts and any related issues that you think might play an important role in the research. List the authors of relevant studies you are aware of, possible keywords that might specify the subject for your search, and perhaps the most important journals that you are concerned with checking. For example, if your research question is, "What is the effect of informal social control on crime?" you might consider searching the literature electronically for studies that mentioned "informal social control" and "crime" or "crime rate" or "violence" and "arrest." If you are concerned with more specific aspects of this question, you should also include the relevant words in your list, such as "family" or "community policing" or even "Northeast."

Conducting the Search

Now you are ready to begin searching the literature. You should check for relevant books in your library and perhaps in the other college libraries in your area. This usually means conducting a search of an online catalog using a list of subject terms. But most scientific research is published in journal articles so that research results can quickly be disseminated to other scientists. The primary focus of your search must therefore be the journal literature. Fortunately, much of the journal literature can be identified online, without leaving your desktop computer, and an increasing number of published journal articles can be downloaded directly to your own computer (depending on your particular access privileges). But just because there's a lot available online doesn't mean that you need to find it all. Keep in mind that your goal is to find reports of prior research investigations; this means that you should focus on scholarly journals that choose articles for publication after they have been reviewed by other social scientists—"refereed journals." Newspaper and magazine articles just won't do, although you may find some that raise important issues or even that summarize social science research investigations.

The social science literature should be consulted at both the beginning and the end of an investigation. Even while an investigation is in progress, consultations with the literature may help to resolve methodological problems or facilitate supplementary explorations. As with any part of the research process, the method you use will affect the quality of your results. You should try to ensure that your search method includes each of the following steps:

Specify your research question. Your research question should not be so broad that hundreds of articles are judged relevant, or so narrow that you miss important literature. "Is informal social control effective?" is probably too broad. "Does informal social control reduce rates of burglary in large cities?" is probably too narrow. "Is informal social control more effective in reducing crime rates than policing?" provides about the right level of specificity.

Identify appropriate bibliographic databases to search. Sociological Abstracts (Sociofile) may meet many of your needs, but if you are studying a question about social factors in illness you should also search in Medline, the database for searching the medical literature. If your focus is on mental health, you'll also want to include a search in psychological abstracts (Psyc*INFO*). In order to find articles across the social sciences that have referred to a previous publication, like Sherman and Berk's study of the police response to domestic violence, the Social Science Citation Index (SSCI) will be helpful. SSCI has a unique "citation searching" feature that allows you to look up articles or books and see who else has cited them in their work. This is an excellent and efficient way to assemble a number of references that are highly relevant to your research and to find out which articles and books have had the biggest impact in a field. Unfortunately, some college libraries do not subscribe to SSCI, either in its print, CD-ROM, or online version, due to its expense, but if you have access to SSCI, you should consider using it whenever you want to make sure that you develop the strongest possible literature review for your topic. In addition, the search engine Google now offers anyone with Web access "Google Scholar" (which indexes and searches the full text of selected journals) and "Google Print" (which digitizes and searches the full text of the books that are owned by selected research libraries). (When this book went to press the Google Print project was on hold due to copyright concerns raised by some publishers, while the search engine and directory Yahoo was starting a similar venture that focused only on older books that are no longer covered by copyright law.) (Hafner, 2005:C1).

Choose a search technology. For most purposes, an online bibliographic database that references the published journal literature will be all you need to find the relevant social science research literature. However, searches for more obscure topics or very recent literature may require that you also search Web sites or bibliographies of relevant books. You will also need to search Web sites when you need to learn about current debate about particular social issues or you are investigating current social programs.

Create a tentative list of search terms. List the parts and subparts of your research question and any related issues that you think are important: "informal social control," "policing," "influences on crime rates," and perhaps "community cohesion and crime." List the authors of relevant studies. Specify the most important journals that deal with your topic.

Narrow your search. The sheer number of references you find can be a problem. For example, searching for "social capital" resulted in 2,293 citations in *Sociological Abstracts.* Depending on the database you are working with and the purposes of your search, you may want to limit your search to English language publications, to journal articles rather than conference papers or dissertations (both of which are more difficult to acquire), and to materials published in recent years. You should give most attention to articles published in the leading journals in the field. Your professor can help you identify them.

Refine your search. Learn as you go. If your search yields too many citations, try specifying the search terms more precisely. If you have not found much literature, try using more general terms. Whatever terms you search on first, don't consider your search complete until you have tried several different approaches and have seen how many articles you find. A search for "domestic violence" in *Sociological Abstracts* on September 11, 2005, yielded 1,569 hits; by adding "effects" OR "influences" as required search terms the number of hits dropped to 370. A good rule is to cast a net with your search terms that is wide enough to catch most of the relevant articles but not so wide that it identifies many useless citations. In any case, if you are searching a popular topic, you will need to spend a fair amount of time whittling down the list of citations.

Use Boolean search logic. It's often a good idea to narrow your search by requiring that abstracts contain combinations of words or phrases that include more of the specifics of your research question. Using the Boolean connector AND allows you to do this, while using the connector OR allows you to find abstracts containing different words that mean the same thing. Exhibit A.1 provides an example.

Use appropriate subject descriptors. Once you have found an article that you consider to be appropriate, take a look at the "descriptors" field in the citation (see Exhibit A.2). You can then redo your search after requiring that the articles be classified with some or all of these descriptor terms.

Check the results. Read the titles and abstracts you have found and identify the articles that appear to be most relevant. If possible, click on these article titles and generate a list of their references. See if you find more articles that are relevant to your research question but that you have missed so far. You will be surprised (I always am) at how many important articles your initial online search missed.

Read the articles. Now it is time to find the full text of the articles of interest. If you're lucky, many of the articles you need will be available to patrons of your library in online versions, and you'll be able to link to the full text just by clicking on a "full text" link. But many journals and/or specific issues of some journals will only be available in print, so you'll have to find them in your library (or order a

Exhibit A.1   Use of Boolean Connectors in a Literature Search

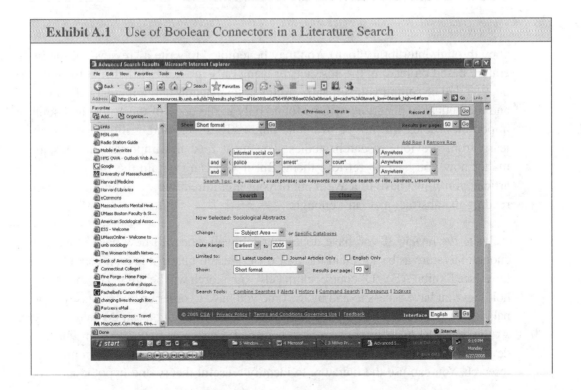

Exhibit A.2   Checking Standard Subject Matter Descriptors

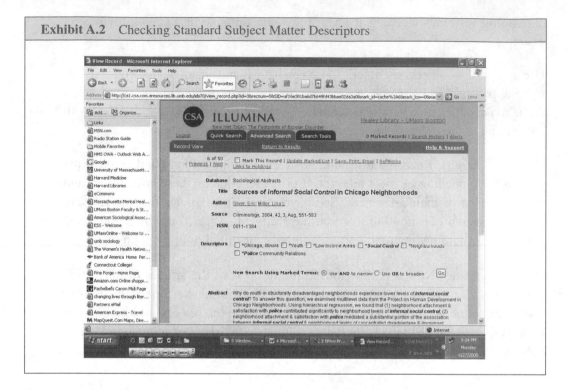

copy through interlibrary loan). You may be tempted to write a "review" of the literature based on reading the abstracts or using only those articles available online, but you will be selling yourself short. Many crucial details about methods, findings, and theoretical implications will be found only in the body of the article and some important articles will not be available online. To understand, critique, and really learn from previous research studies, you must read the important articles, no matter how you have to retrieve them. But if you can't obtain the full text of an article, you'll just have to leave it out of your literature review and bibliography—reading the abstract just isn't enough.

Write the review. If you have done your job well, you will now have more than enough literature as background for your own research unless it is on a very obscure topic (see Exhibit A.3). (Of course, ultimately your search will be limited by the library holdings you have access to and by the time you have to order or find copies of journal articles, conference papers, and perhaps dissertations that you can't obtain online.) At this point, your main concern is to construct a coherent framework in which to develop your research question, drawing as many lessons as you can from previous research. You can use the literature to identify a useful theory and hypotheses to be

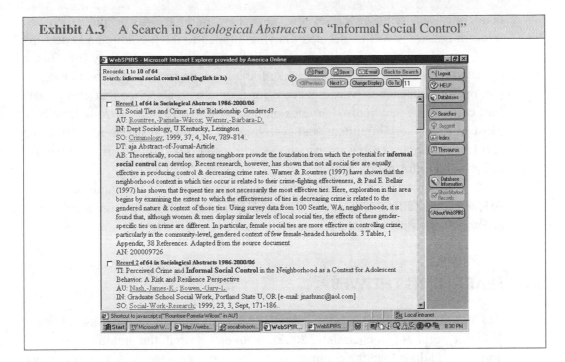

Exhibit A.3   A Search in *Sociological Abstracts* on "Informal Social Control"

reexamined, to find inadequately studied specific research questions, to explicate the disputes about your research question, to summarize the major findings of prior research, and to suggest appropriate methods of investigation.

Be sure to take notes on each article you read, organizing your notes into standard sections: theory, methods, findings, conclusions. In any case, write the literature review so that it contributes to your study in some concrete way; don't feel compelled to discuss an article just because you have read it. Be judicious. You are conducting only one study of one issue; it will only obscure the value of your study if you try to relate it to every tangential point in related research.

Continue to search. Don't think of searching the literature as a one-time-only venture—something that you leave behind as you move on to your *real* research. You may encounter new questions or unanticipated problems as you conduct your research or as you burrow deeper into the literature. Searching the literature again to determine what others have found in response to these questions or what steps they have taken to resolve these problems can yield substantial improvements in your own research. There is so much literature on so many topics that it often is not possible to figure out in advance every subject you should search the literature for or what type of search will be most beneficial.

Another reason to make searching the literature an ongoing project is that the literature is always growing. During the course of one research study, whether it takes only one semester or several years, new findings will be published and relevant questions will be debated. Staying attuned to the literature and checking it at least when you are writing up your findings may save your study from being outdated. Of course, this does not make life any easier for researchers. For example, one of your authors was registered for a time with a service that every week sent citations of new journal articles on homelessness to his electronic mailbox. Most were not very important, and even looking over the abstracts for between 5 and 15 new articles each week is quite a chore—that's part of the price we pay for living in the information age!

Refer to a good book for even more specific guidance about literature searching. Arlene Fink's (2005) *Conducting Research Literature Reviews: From the Internet to Paper,* Sage Publications, is an excellent guide.

SEARCHING THE WEB

The World Wide Web provides access to vast amounts of information of many different sorts (O'Dochartaigh, 2002). You can search the holdings of other libraries and download the complete text of government reports, some conference papers, and newspaper articles. You can find policies of local governments, descriptions of individual social scientists and particular research projects, and postings of advocacy groups. It's also hard to avoid finding a lot of information in which you have no interest, such as commercial advertisements, third-grade homework assignments, or college course syllabi. In 1999, there were already about 800 million publicly available pages of information on the Web (Davis 1999). Today there may be as many as 15 billion pages on the Web (Novak 2003).

After you are connected to the Web with a browser like Microsoft Internet Explorer or Netscape Navigator, you can use three basic strategies for finding information: direct addressing—typing in the address, or URL, of a specific site; browsing—reviewing online lists of Web sites; and searching—the most common approach. "Google" is currently the most popular search engine for searching the Web. For some purposes, you will need to use only one strategy; for other purposes, you will want to use all three. End-of-chapter Web exercises and the Pine Forge Press Study Site for this text both provide many URLs relevant to social science research.

Exhibit A.4 illustrates the first problem that you may encounter when searching the Web: the sheer quantity of resources that are available. It is a much bigger problem than when searching bibliographic databases. On the Web, less is usually more. Limit your inspection of Web sites to the first few pages that turn

Exhibit A.4   Google Search Results for "Informal Social Control"

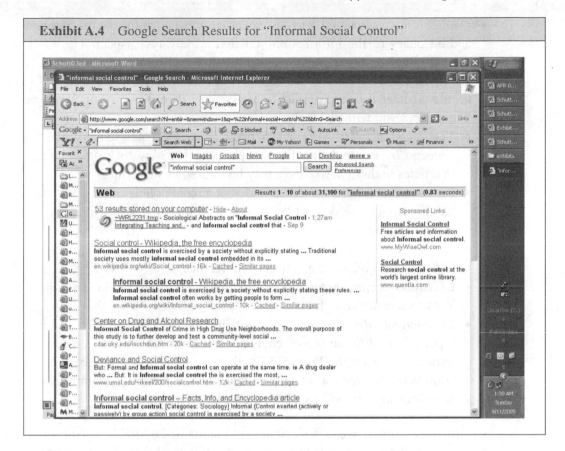

up in your list (they're ranked by relevance). See what those first pages contain and then try to narrow your search by including some additional terms. Putting quotation marks around a phrase that you want to search will also help to limit your search—searching for "informal social control" on Google (on September 11, 2005) produced 31,100 sites, compared to the 15,500,000 sites retrieved when I omitted the quotes, so Google searched "informal" *and* "social" *and* "control."

Remember the following warnings when you conduct searches on the Web:

- *Clarify your goals.* Before you begin the search, jot down the terms that you think you need to search for as well as a statement of what you want to accomplish with your search. This will help to ensure that you have a sense of what to look for and what to ignore.

- *Quality is not guaranteed.* Anyone can post almost anything, so the accuracy and adequacy of the information you find are always suspect. There's no journal editor or librarian to evaluate quality and relevance. You need to anticipate the different sources of information available on the Web and to decide whether it is appropriate to use each of them for specific purposes. The sources you will find include:
  - *Newspaper articles*—These can range from local newspapers like the *Chicago Tribune* to national newspapers like The *New York Times*. Access to articles in these newspapers may be limited to subscribers
  - *Government policies*—You can find government policies and publications ranging from those done at the city or town level to those written by foreign governments.
  - *Presented papers*—You may find the complete text of a formal presentation that was given at a meeting or conference.
  - *Classroom lecture notes and outlines; listings from college catalogs*—These are pretty straightforward.
  - *Commercial advertisements*—Advertising abounds on the Web and it is especially prolific on search engine pages. Your search engine will even retrieve ads from the Web and list them as results of your search! The boundaries between academic, nonprofit, and commercial information have become very porous, so you can't let your guard down.

- *Anticipate change.* Web sites that are not maintained by stable organizations can come and go very quickly. Any search will result in attempts to link to some URLs that no longer exist.
- *One size does not fit all.* Different search engines use different procedures for indexing Web sites. Some attempt to be all-inclusive whereas others aim to be selective. As a result, you can get different results from different search engines (such as Google or Yahoo) even though you are searching for exactly the same terms.
- *Be concerned about generalizability.* You might be tempted to characterize police department policies by summarizing the documents you find at police department Web sites. But how many police departments are there? How many have posted their policies on the Web? Are these policies representative of all police departments? In order to answer all these questions, you would have to conduct a research project just on the Web sites themselves.
- *Evaluate the sites.* There's a lot of stuff out there; so how do you know what's good? Some Web sites contain excellent advice and pointers on how to differentiate the good from the bad. You can find one example at: http://www.library.cornell.edu/olinuris/ref/research/webeval.html.

- *Avoid Web addiction.* Another danger of the extraordinary quantity of information available on the Web is that one search will lead to another and to another and. . . . There are always more possibilities to explore and one more interesting source to check. Establish boundaries of time and effort to avoid the risk of losing all sense of proportion.
- *Cite your sources.* Using text or images from Web sources without attribution is plagiarism. It is the same as copying someone else's work from a book or article and pretending that it is your own. Record the Web address (URL), the name of the information provider, and the date on which you obtain material from the site. Include this information in a footnote to the material that you use in a paper.

Appendix B

Secondary Data Sources

Many quantitative studies and some qualitative investigations use data available from previous research or government agencies. In the United States, the U.S. Bureau of the Census and many other government agencies make data available for general use. Data are also available for research purposes from many other countries as well as from world bodies like the United Nations and the World Bank. Academic researchers and students can draw on a very large data archive at the Inter-university Consortium for Political and Social Research (ICPSR). Qualitative researchers can also use information in published histories or other secondary sources, such as documents found in archival collections. This appendix identifies important sources of such "secondary data."

U.S. Bureau of the Census

The U.S. government has conducted a census of the population every 10 years since 1790; since 1940, this census also has included a census of housing (see also Chapter 4). This decennial Census of Population and Housing is a rich source of social science data (Lavin, 1994). The Census Bureau's monthly *Current Population Survey (CPS)* provides basic data on labor force activity that is then used in Bureau of Labor Statistics reports. The Census Bureau also collects data on agriculture, manufacturers, construction and other business, foreign countries, and foreign trade.

The U.S. Census of Population and Housing aims to survey an adult in every household in the United States. The basic "complete-count" census contains questions about household composition as well as ethnicity and income. More questions are asked in a longer form of the census that is administered to a sample of the households. A separate census of housing characteristics is conducted at the same time (Rives & Serow, 1988:15). Participation in the census is required by law, and confidentiality of the information obtained is mandated by law for 72 years after collection. Census data are reported for geographic units, including states, metropolitan areas, counties, census tracts (small, relatively permanent areas within counties), and even blocks (see Exhibit B.1). These different units allow units of analysis to be tailored to research questions.

Census data are used to apportion seats in the U.S. House of Representatives and to determine federal and state legislative district boundaries, as well as to inform other decisions by government agencies. An interactive data retrieval system, *American FactFinder,* is the primary means for distributing results from the 2000 Census: You can review it at http://factfinder.census.gov/home/saff/main.html?_ lang=en.

Those without direct Internet access can use 1,800 state data centers and 1,400 federal depository libraries, universities, and private organizations (U.S. Bureau of the Census 1999:12). The U.S. Census Web site (http:// www.census.gov) provides much information about the nearly 100 surveys and censuses that the Census directs each year, including direct access to many statistics for particular geographic units. The catalog of the Inter-university Consortium for Political and Social Research (http://www.icpsr.umich.edu) also lists many Census reports. Some detailed information is available only after paying a subscription fee of $40 per quarter for individuals (as of 1997). Summary tapes and CD-ROMs also can be purchased that contain census data in various geographic levels, including counties, cities, census tracts, and even blocks (for an example, check the following U.S. Census Web site: http://www.census.gov/apsd/www/TestDrive/usaprof.htm).

Exhibit B.1 Census Small-Area Geography

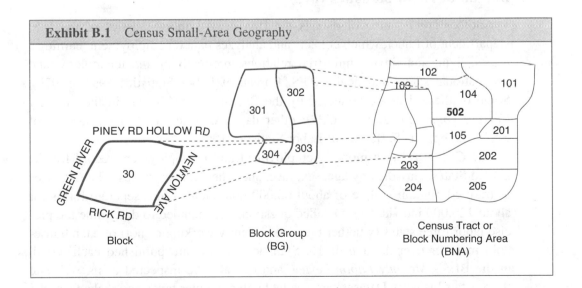

States also maintain census bureaus and may have additional resources. Some contain the original census data collected in the state 100 or more years ago. The ambitious historical researcher can use these returns to conduct detailed comparative studies at the county or state level (Lathrop, 1968:79).

Integrated Public Use Microdata Series

Individual-level samples from U.S. Census data for the years 1850 to 1990, as well as historical census files from several other countries, are available through the Integrated Public Use Microdata Series (IPUMS) at the University of Minnesota's Minnesota Population Center (MPC). These data are prepared in an easy-to-use format that provides consistent codes and names for all the different samples.

This exceptional resource offers 25 samples of the American population selected from 13 federal censuses, with at least 100,000 persons in each sample; in recent years the samples contained more than 1 million persons. Each sample is independently selected, so that individuals are not linked between samples. In addition to basic demographic measures, variables in the U.S. samples include educational, occupational, and work indicators; respondent income; disability status; immigration status; veteran status; and various household characteristics, including family composition and dwelling characteristics. The international samples include detailed characteristics from hundreds of thousands of individuals in countries ranging from France and Mexico to Kenya and Vietnam. You can view these resources at www.ipums.umn.edu.

Many other government agencies provide data for social scientists.

Bureau of Labor Statistics (BLS)

Another good source of data is the Bureau of Labor Statistics of the U.S. Department of Labor, which collects and analyzes data on employment, earnings, prices, living conditions, industrial relations, productivity and technology, and occupational safety and health (U.S. Bureau of Labor Statistics 1991, 1997b). Some of these data are collected by the Bureau of the Census in the monthly *Current Population Survey (CPS);* other data are collected through surveys of establishments (U.S. Bureau of Labor Statistics 1997a).

The *CPS* provides a monthly employment and unemployment record for the United States, classified by age, sex, race, and other characteristics. The *CPS* uses a stratified random sample of about 60,000 households (with separate forms for about 120,000 individuals). Detailed questions are included to determine the precise labor force status (whether they are currently working or not) of each household member over the age of 16. Statistical reports are published each month in the BLS's *Monthly Labor Review* and can also be inspected at its Web site (http://stats.bls.gov). Datasets are available on computer tapes and disks from the

BLS and services like the Inter-university Consortium for Political and Social Research (ICPSR).

Other U.S. Government Sources

Many more datasets useful for historical and comparative research have been collected by federal agencies and other organizations. The National Technical Information Service (NTIS) of the U.S. Department of Commerce maintains a Federal Computer Products Center that collects and catalogs many of these datasets and related software.

By 1993, more than 1,850 datasets from 50 agencies were described in the NTIS *Directory*. The *Directory* is the essential source of information about the datasets and can be purchased from the U.S. Department of Commerce (National Technical Information Service, 1993). Dataset summaries can be searched in the *Directory* by either subject or agency. Government research reports cataloged by NTIS can be searched online at the NTIS Web site (http://www. fedworld.gov) and in a CD-ROM catalog available in some libraries.

International Data Sources

Comparative researchers can find datasets on population characteristics, economic and political features, and political events in many nations. Some of these are available from U.S. government agencies. For example, the Social Security Administration reports on the characteristics of social security throughout the world (Wheeler, 1995). This comprehensive report classifies nations in terms of their type of social security program and provides detailed summaries of the characteristics of each nation's programs. The 1999 volume is available on the Internet at http://www.ssa.gov/policy/docs/progdesc/ssptw/1999/index.html#toc. More recent data are organized by region. A broader range of data is available in the *World Handbook of Political and Social Indicators,* with political events and political, economic, and social data coded from 1948 to 1982 (http://www.icpsr.umich. edu, study no. 7761) (Taylor & Jodice, 1986).

The European Commission administers the Eurobarometer Survey Series at least twice yearly across all the member states of the European Union. The survey monitors social and political attitudes and reports are published regularly online: http://www.gesis.org/en/data_service/eurobarometer/index.htm.

Case level Eurobarometer survey data are stored at the ICPSR.

ICPSR

The University of Michigan's Inter-university Consortium for Political and Social Research (ICPSR) is the premier source of secondary data useful to social science researchers. ICPSR was founded in 1962 and now includes more than 325 colleges and universities in North America and hundreds of institutions on other continents. ICPSR archives the most extensive collection of social science datasets in the United States outside of the federal government: More than 6,000 studies are represented in 450,000 files from 130 countries and from sources that range from U.S. government agencies such as the Census Bureau to international organizations like the United Nations, social research organizations like the National Opinion Research Organization, and individual social scientists who have completed funded research projects.

The datasets archived by ICPSR are available for downloading directly from the ICPSR Web site, http://www.icpsr.umich.edu. ICPSR makes datasets obtained from government sources available directly to the general public, but many other datasets are available only to individuals at the more than 500 colleges and universities around the world that have paid the fees required to join ICPSR. The availability of some datasets is restricted due to confidentiality issues; in order to use them, researchers must sign a contract and agree to certain conditions. http://www.icpsr.umich.edu/help/newuser.html, 7/15/2005.

Survey datasets obtained in the United States and in many other countries that are stored at the ICPSR provide data on topics ranging from elite attitudes to consumer expectations. For example, data collected in the British Social Attitudes Survey in 1998, designed by the University of Chicago's National Opinion Research Center, are available through the ICPSR (go to the ICPSR Web site, http://www.icpsr.umich.edu, and search for study no. 3101). Data collected in a monthly survey of Spaniards' attitudes, by the Center for Research on Social Reality [Spain] Survey, are also available (study no. 17). Survey data from Russia, Germany, and other countries can also be found in the ICPSR collection.

Do you have an interest in events and interactions between nations, such as threats of military force? A dataset collected by Charles McClelland includes characteristics of 91,240 such events (study no. 5211). The history of military interventions in nations around the world between 1946 and 1988 is coded in a dataset developed by Frederic Pearson and Robert Baumann (study no. 6035). This dataset identifies the intervener and target countries, the starting and ending dates of military intervention, and a range of potential motives (such as foreign policies, related domestic disputes, and pursuit of rebels across borders).

Census data from other nations are also available through the ICPSR, as well as directly through the Internet. In the ICPSR archives, you can find a dataset from the Statistical Office of the United Nations on the 1966–1974 population of 220 nations throughout the world (study no. 7623). More current international population data are provided by the Center for International Research and the U.S. Census Bureau (study no. 8490). See also the preceding description of the Eurobarometer Survey Series.

Obtaining Data From ICPSR

You begin a search for data in the ICPSR archives at http://www.icpsr.umich.edu/access/index.html.

Exhibit B.2 shows the search screen as I began a search for data from studies involving the subject, domestic violence. You can also see in this screen that you can search the data archives for specific studies, identified by study number or title, as well as for studies by specific investigators (this would be a quick way to find the dataset contributed by Lawrence Sherman from his research, discussed in Chapter 2, on the police response to domestic violence).

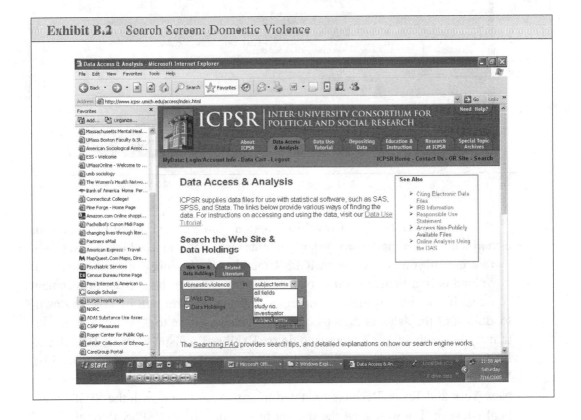

Exhibit B.2 Search Screen: Domestic Violence

Exhibit B.3 displays the results of my search: a list of 63 datasets that involved research on domestic violence and that are available through ICPSR. For most datasets, you can obtain a description, the files that are available for downloading, and a list of "related literature"—that is, reports and articles that use the listed dataset. Some datasets are made available in collections on a CD-ROM; the CD-ROM's contents are described in detail on the ICPSR site, but you have to place an order to receive the CD-ROM itself.

Exhibit B.3   Search Screen: Domestic Violence Results

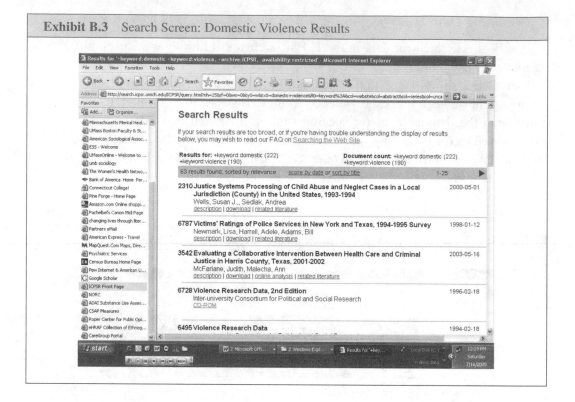

When you click on the "Download" option, you are first asked to enter your e-mail address and password. What you enter will determine which datasets you can access; if you are not at an ICPSR member institution, you will be able to download only a limited portion of the datasets—mostly those from government sources. If you are a student at a member institution, you will be able to download most of the datasets directly, although you may have to be using a computer that is physically on your campus to do so. Exhibit B.4 displays the ICPSR download screen after I selected files I wanted to download from the study by Lisa Newmark, Adele Harrell, and Bill Adams of victim ratings of police response in New York and Texas. Because I wanted to analyze the data with the SPSS statistical package, I downloaded the dataset in the form of an "SPSS Portable File." The files downloaded in a "zip" file, so I had to use the WinZip© program to unzip them. After unzipping the SPSS portable file, I was able to start my data analysis with the SPSS program. If you'd like to learn how to analyze data with the SPSS statistical program, review Appendix D.

If you prepare your own paper based on an analysis of ICPSR data, be sure to include a proper citation. Here's an example from the ICPSR itself (http://www.icpsr.umich.edu/org/citation.html):

Exhibit B.4   ICPSR Download Screen

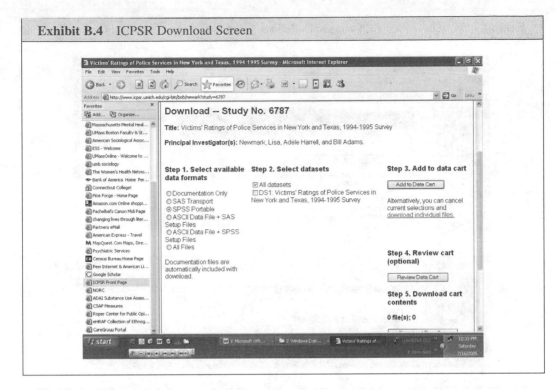

Reif, Karlheinz, and Anna Melich. *Euro-Barometer 39.0: European Community Policies and Family Life, March-April 1993* [Computer file]. Conducted by INRA (Europe), Brussels. ICPSR06195 v4. Ann Arbor, MI: Inter-university Consortium for Political and Social Research [producer], 1995. Koeln, Germany: Zentralarchiv fuer Empirische Sozialforschung/Ann Arbor, MI: Inter-university Consortium for Political and Social Research [distributors], 1997.

Some of the datasets are also offered with the option of "online analysis." If you have this option, you can immediately inspect the distributions of responses to each question in a survey and examine the relation between variables, without having any special statistical programs of your own. At the bottom of Exhibit B.5, you'll find the wording reported in the study "codebook" for a question used in the study of a collaborative health care and criminal justice intervention in Texas, as well as, in the top portion, the available statistical options. After choosing one or more variables from the codebook, you can request the analysis.

My analysis began with a chart of the distribution of victims' responses to a question about their current relationship with the abuser. As you can see in Exhibit B.6, about half had left the relationship, but half were still married or living as married with the abuser. This approach to analysis with secondary data can get you jumpstarted in your work. An online analysis option is also starting to appear at other Web sites that offer secondary data.

Exhibit B.5 ICPSR Online Analysis: Codebook Information and Statistical Options

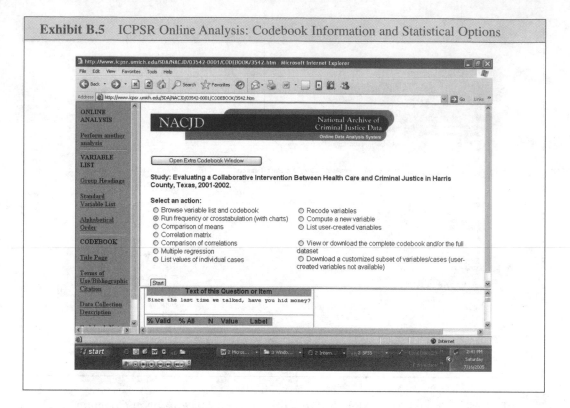

ICPSR also catalogs reports and publications containing analyses that have used ICPSR datasets since 1962—more than 34,000 citations were in this archive in July 2005. This superb resource provides an excellent starting point for the literature search that should precede a secondary data analysis. In most cases, you can learn from detailed study reports a great deal about the study methodology, including the rate of response in a sample survey and the reliability of any indexes constructed. Published articles provide examples of how others have described the study methodology, let you know what research questions have already been studied with the dataset, and outline what issues remain to be resolved. You can search this literature at the ICPSR site simply by entering the same search terms that you used to find datasets, or else by entering the specific study number of the dataset on which you have focused (see Exhibit B.7). Don't start a secondary analysis without reviewing such reports and publications.

Qualitative Data Sources

Far fewer qualitative datasets are available for secondary analysis. By far the richest source, if you are interested in cross-cultural research, is the Human Relations Area Files at Yale University. The HRAF has made anthropological field data available for international cross-cultural research since 1949 and currently

Exhibit B.6   ICPSR Online Analysis Bar Chart

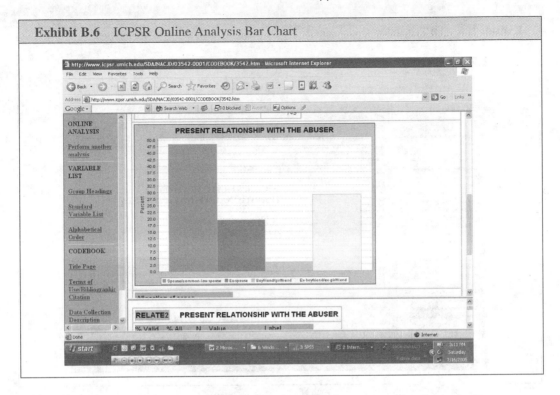

Exhibit B.7   ICPSR Search of "Related Literature" on Domestic Violence

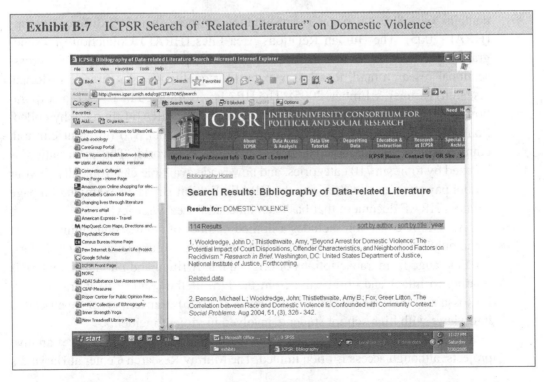

Exhibit B.8 HRAF Indexed Document

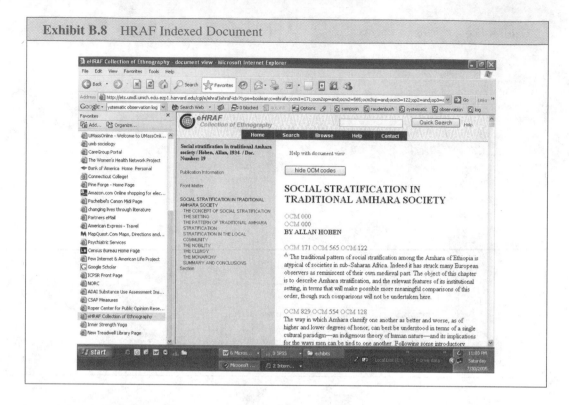

contains over 800,000 pages of information on more than 365 different groups (HRAF 2005). The Human Relations Area Files (HRAF) Collection of Ethnography provides an extraordinary resource for qualitative comparative cross-sectional research (and, to a lesser extent, for qualitative comparative historical research) (Ember & Ember, 2005). The HRAF was founded in 1949 as a corporation designed to facilitate cross-cultural research. The HRAF Ethnography collection now contains over 800,000 pages of material about 370 different cultural, ethnic, religious, and national groups all over the world. The information is indexed by topic, in 710 categories, and now made available electronically (if your school pays to maintain access to the HRAF). Exhibit B.8 is an example of a page from an HRAF document that has been indexed for easy retrieval.

The ICPSR collection includes a limited number of studies containing at least some qualitative data (19 as of July 2005), but these include some very rich data. Studies range from transcriptions of original handwritten and published materials relating to infant and child care, from the turn of the century to World War II. LaRossa's (1995) and Daniel Lockwood's (1996) transcripts of open-ended interviews with high school students involved in violent incidents.

Several other university-based centers have developed qualitative archive projects, although access is often limited. The Murray Research Center at Harvard's

Radcliffe Institute for Advanced Study (http://murraydata.hmdc.harvard.edu/VDC/) focuses on studies of lives over time, with special interest in issues of concern to women. Although the Murray Center's collection of about 300 studies contains both quantitative and qualitative datasets, it has had a special interest in qualitative data, including videotape and audiotape collections, case study data, and transcripts from intensive interview studies and data from surveys that included many open-ended questions. The Murray Research Center has now been merged with the larger Harvard-MIT Data Center, which makes available a much larger set of datasets from quantitative studies, although only to members of Harvard-Radcliffe. Access to archived datasets requires submission of an online application.

Holdings of the Economic and Social Data Service of the Universities of Sussex and Manchester in England (www.esds.ac.uk/qualitdata/online/), ESDS Qualidata, include interview transcripts and other materials from several qualitative studies, including Paul Thompson's "100 Families: Families, Social Mobility and Aging, an Intergenerational Approach." Subsets of the interviews can be browsed or searched directly online, but access is restricted to those at member institutions. Although a great many universities in Britain and throughout the world have joined the ESDS, they include very few colleges and universities in the United States.

The University of Southern Maine's Center for the Study of Lives (www.usm.maine.edu/cehd/csl) collects interview transcripts that record the life stories of people of diverse ages and backgrounds. As of July 2005, their collection included transcripts from almost 400 life stories, representing 36 different ethnic groups, telling of experiences of historical events ranging from the Great Depression to the Vietnam War, and including reports on dealing with health problems like HIV/AIDS. These qualitative data are available directly online without any registration or fee.

References

Adler, Patricia. 1993. *Wheeling and Dealing: An Ethnography of an Upper-Level Drug Dealing and Smuggling Community*, 2nd ed. New York: Columbia University Press.

Adler, Patricia A. and Peter Adler. 2000. "Intense Loyalty in Organizations: A Case Study of College Athletics." Pp. 31–50 in *Qualitative Studies of Organizations,* edited by John Van Maanen. Thousand Oaks, CA: Sage.

Adorno, Theodor W., Nevitt Sanford, Else Frenkel-Brunswik, and Daniel Levinson. 1950. *The Authoritarian Personality.* New York: Harper.

Alfred, Randall. 1976. "The Church of Satan." Pp. 180–202 in *The New Religious Consciousness,* edited by Charles Glock and Robert Bellah. Berkeley: University of California Press.

Altheide, David L. and John M. Johnson. 1994. "Criteria for Assessing Interpretive Validity in Qualitative Research." Pp. 485–499 in *Handbook of Qualitative Research,* edited by Norman K. Denzin and Yvonna S. Lincoln. Thousand Oaks, CA: Sage.

American Psychiatric Association. 1994. *Diagnostic and Statistical Manual of Mental Disorders,* 4th ed. Washington, DC: American Psychiatric Association.

American Sociological Association. 1997. *Code of Ethics.* Washington, DC: American Sociological Association.

Aronson, Elliot and Judson Mills. 1959. "The Effect of Severity of Initiation on Liking for a Group." *Journal of Abnormal and Social Psychology,* 59 (September): 177–181.

Aseltine, Robert H., Jr., and Ronald C. Kessler. 1993. "Marital Disruption and Depression in a Community Sample." *Journal of Health and Social Behavior,* 34 (September): 237–251.

Becker, Howard S. 1958. "Problems of Inference and Proof in Participant Observation." *American Sociological Review,* 23: 652–660.

Becker, Howard S. 1963. *Outsiders: Studies in the Sociology of Deviance.* New York: Free Press.

Becker, Howard S. 1986. *Writing for Social Scientists.* Chicago: University of Chicago Press. [This can be ordered directly from the American Sociological Association, 1722 N Street, NW, Washington, DC 20036, 202–833–3410.]

Bellah, Robert N., Richard Madsen, William M. Sullivan, Ann Swidler, and Steven M. Tipton. 1985. *Habits of the Heart: Individualism and Commitment in American Life.* New York: Harper & Row.

Bogdewic, Stephan P. 1999. "Participant Observation." Pp. 33–45 in *Doing Qualitative Research,* 2nd ed., edited by Benjamin F. Crabtree and William L. Miller. Thousand Oaks, CA: Sage.

Booth, Wayne C., Gregory G. Colomb, and Joseph M. Williams. 1995. *The Craft of Research.* Chicago: University of Chicago Press.

Boruch, Robert F. 1997. *Randomized Experiments for Planning and Evaluation: A Practical Guide.* Thousand Oaks, CA: Sage.

Bramel, Dana and Ronal Friend. 1981. "Hawthorne, the Myth of the Docile Worker, and Class Bias in Psychology." *American Psychologist,* 38 (September): 867–878.

Brewer, John and Albert Hunter. 1989. *Multimethod Research: A Synthesis of Styles.* Newbury Park, CA: Sage.

Brown, Judith Belle. 1999. "The Use of Focus Groups in Clinical Research." Pp. 109–124 in *Doing Qualitative Research,* 2nd ed., edited by Benjamin F. Crabtree and William L. Miller. Thousand Oaks, CA: Sage.

Brown v. Board of Education (Brown I), 347 U.S. 483 (1954).

Bureau of the Census. 2004–2005. *Statistical Abstract of the United States.* Washington, DC: U.S. Department of Commerce, Bureau of the Census. Online edition, http://www.censusgov/prod/www/statistical-abstract-04.html, retrieved 8/8/2005.

Butterfield, Fox. 1996a. "After 10 Years, Juvenile Crime Begins to Drop." *The New York Times,* August 9, pp. A1, A25.

Butterfield, Fox. 1996b. "Gun Violence May Be Subsiding, Studies Find." *The New York Times,* October 14, p. A10.

Butterfield, Fox. 2000. "As Murder Rates Edge Up, Concern, but Few Answers." *The New York Times,* June 18, p. A12.

Buzawa, Eve S. and Carl G. Buzawa (Eds.). 1996. *Do Arrests and Restraining Orders Work?* Thousand Oaks, CA: Sage.

Campbell, Donald T. and Julian C. Stanley. 1966. *Experimental and Quasi-Experimental Designs for Research.* Chicago: Rand McNally.

Campbell, Donald T. and M. Jean Russo. 1999. *Social Experimentation.* Thousand Oaks, CA: Sage.

Campbell, Richard T. 1992. "Longitudinal Research." Pp. 1146–1158 in *Encyclopedia of Sociology,* edited by Edgar F. Borgatta and Marie L. Borgatta. New York: Macmillan.

Campbell, Wilson. 2001. "A Statement from The Governmental Accounting Standards Board and Performance Measurement Staff." Online Forum on Performance Measurement, Government and Sustainability. Washington, DC: Center for Accountability and Performance. Retrieved November 3, 2002, from www.aspanet.org/cap/forum_statement.html.

Center for Survey Research, University of Massachusetts at Boston. 1987. "Methodology: Designing Good Survey Questions." Newsletter, April, p. 3.

Chambliss, Daniel F. 1988. *Champions: The Making of Olympic Swimmers.* New York: Morrow.

Chambliss, Daniel F. 1989."The Mundanity of Excellence: An Ethnographic Report on Stratification and Olympic Swimmers," *Sociological Theory,* 7(1): 70–86.

Chambliss, Daniel F. 1996. *Beyond Caring: Hospitals, Nurses, and the Social Organization of Ethics.* Chicago: University of Chicago Press.

Chen, Huey-Tsyh. 1990. *Theory-Driven Evaluations.* Newbury Park, CA: Sage.

Chen, Huey-Tsyh and Peter H. Rossi. 1987. "The Theory-Driven Approach to Validity." *Evaluation and Program Planning,* 10: 95–103.

Coffey, Amanda and Paul Atkinson. 1996. *Making Sense of Qualitative Data: Complementary Research Strategies.* Thousand Oaks, CA: Sage.

Cohen, Gary E. and Barbara A. Kerr. 1998. "Computer-Mediated Counseling: An Empirical Study of a New Mental Health Treatment." *Computers in Human Services,* 15: 13–26.

Cohen, Susan G. and Gerald E. Ledford, Jr. 1994. "The Effectiveness of Self-Managing Teams: A Quasi-Experiment." *Human Relations,* 47: 13–43.

Coleman, James S. and Thomas Hoffer. 1987. *Public and Private High Schools: The Impact of Communities.* New York: Basic Books.

Coleman, James S., Thomas Hoffer, and Sally Kilgore. 1982. *High School Achievement: Public, Catholic, and Private Schools Compared.* New York: Basic Books.

Collins, Randall. 1975. *Conflict Sociology: Toward an Explanatory Science.* New York: Academic Press.

Converse, Jean M. 1984. "Attitude Measurement in Psychology and Sociology: The Early Years." Pp. 3–40 in *Surveying Subjective Phenomena,* vol. 2, edited by Charles F. Turner and Elizabeth Martin. New York: Russell Sage Foundation.

Cook, Thomas D. and Donald T. Campbell. 1979. *Quasi-Experimentation: Design and Analysis Issues for Field Settings.* Chicago: Rand McNally.

Coontz, Stephanie. 1997. *The Way We Really Are: Coming to Terms with America's Changing Families.* New York: Basic Books.

Core Institute. 1994. *Core Alcohol and Drug Survey: Long Form.* Carbondale, IL: Fund for the Improvement of Postsecondary Education (FIPSE) Core Analysis Grantee Group, Core Institute, Student Health Programs, Southern Illinois University.

Costner, Herbert L. 1989. "The Validity of Conclusions in Evaluation Research: A Further Development of Chen and Rossi's Theory-Driven Approach." *Evaluation and Program Planning,* 12: 345–353.

Davies, Philip, Anthony Petrosino, and Iain Chalmers. 1999. *Report and Papers from the Exploratory Meeting for The Campbell Collaboration.* London: School of Public Policy, University College.

Davis, James A. 1985. *The Logic of Causal Order.* Sage University Paper Series on Quantitative Applications in the Social Sciences, series no. 07–055. Beverly Hills, CA: Sage.

Davis, James A. and Tom W. Smith. 1992. *The NORC General Social Survey: A User's Guide.* Newbury Park, CA: Sage.

Davis, Ryan. 1999. "Study: Search Engines Can't Keep Up with Expanding Net." *The Boston Globe,* July 8, pp. C1, C3.

Dawes, Robyn. 1995. "How Do You Formulate a Testable Exciting Hypothesis?" Pp. 93–96 in *How to Write a Successful Research Grant Application: A Guide for Social and Behavioral Scientists,* edited by Willo Pequegnat and Ellen Stover. New York: Plenum Press.

Dentler, Robert A. 2002. *Practicing Sociology: Selected Fields.* Westport, CT: Praeger.

Denzin, Norman K. and Yvonna S. Lincoln. 1994. "Introduction: Entering the Field of Qualitative Research." Pp. 1–17 in *Handbook of Qualitative Research,* edited by Norman K. Denzin and Yvonna S. Lincoln. Thousand Oaks, CA: Sage.

DeParle, Jason. 1999. "Project to Rescue Needy Stumbles Against the Persistence of Poverty." *The New York Times,* May 15, pp. A1, A10.

Derber, Charles. 2000. *The Pursuit of Attention: Power and Ego in Everyday Life,* 2nd ed. New York: Oxford University Press.

Diamond, Timothy. 1992. *Making Gray Gold: Narratives of Nursing Home Care.* Chicago: University of Chicago Press.

Dillman, Don A. 1978. *Mail and Telephone Surveys: The Total Design Method.* New York: Wiley.

Dillman, Don A. 1982. "Mail and Other Self-Administered Questionnaires." Chapter 12 in *Handbook of Survey Research,* edited by Peter Rossi, James Wright, and Andy Anderson. New York: Academic Press. As reprinted on pp. 637–638 in Delbert C. Miller, 1991. *Handbook of Research Design and Social Measurement,* 5th ed. Newbury Park, CA: Sage.

Dillman, Don A. 2000. *Mail and Internet Surveys: The Tailored Design Method,* 2nd ed. New York: John Wiley & Sons.

Donath, Judith S. 1999. "Identity and Deception in the Virtual Community." Pp. 29–59 in *Communities in Cyberspace,* edited by Peter Kollock and Marc A. Smith. New York: Routledge.

Drake, Robert E., Gregory J. McHugo, Deborah R. Becker, William A. Anthony, and Robin E. Clark. 1996. "The New Hampshire Study of Supported Employment for People with Severe Mental Illness." *Journal of Consulting and Clinical Psychology,* 64: 391–399.

Durkheim, Emile. 1951. *Suicide.* New York: Free Press.

Durkheim, Emile. 1956 [1906]. "The Evolution and the Role of Secondary Education in France." Pp. 135–154 in *Education and Sociology,* translated by Sherwood D. Fox. New York: Free Press.

Ellis, Carolyn. 1986. *Fisher Folk: Two Communities on Chesapeake Bay.* Lexington: University Press of Kentucky.

Emerson, Robert M., ed. 1983. *Contemporary Field Research.* Prospect Heights, IL: Waveland Press.

Emerson, Robert M., Rachel I. Fretz, and Linda L. Shaw. 1995. *Writing Ethnographic Fieldnotes.* Chicago: University of Chicago Press.

Erikson, Kai T. 1967. "A Comment on Disguised Observation in Sociology." *Social Problems,* 12: 366–373.

Erikson, Kai T. 1976. *Everything in Its Path: Destruction of Community in the Buffalo Creek Flood.* New York: Simon and Schuster.

Fenno, Richard F., Jr. 1978. *Home Style: House Members in Their Districts.* Boston: Little, Brown.

Fielding, Nigel G. and Raymond M. Lee. 1998. *Computer Analysis and Qualitative Research.* London: Sage.

Fink, Arlene. 2005. *Conducting Research Literature Reviews: From the Internet to Paper,* 2nd ed. Thousand Oaks, CA: Sage.

Fowler, Floyd J. 1988. *Survey Research Methods,* revised ed. Newbury Park, CA: Sage.

Fowler, Floyd J. 1995. *Improving Survey Questions: Design and Evaluation.* Thousand Oaks, CA: Sage.

Fowler, Floyd J. 1998. Personal communication, January 7. Center for Survey Research, University of Massachusetts, Boston.

Fox, Nick and Chris Roberts. 1999. "GPs in Cyberspace: The Sociology of a 'Virtual Community.'" *The Sociological Review,* 47: 643–669.

Gilbert, Dennis. May 2002. *Hamilton College Muslim America Poll.* In collaboration with Zogby International. Unpublished research report.

Gilchrist, Valerie J. and Robert L. Williams. 1999. "Key Informant Interviews." Pp. 71–88 in *Doing Qualitative Research,* 2nd ed., edited by Benjamin F. Crabtree and William L. Miller. Thousand Oaks, CA: Sage.

Glaser, Barney G. and Anselm L. Strauss. 1967. *The Discovery of Grounded Theory: Strategies for Qualitative Research.* London: Weidenfeld and Nicholson.

Glueck, Sheldon and Eleanor Glueck. 1950. *Unraveling Juvenile Delinquency.* New York: Commonwealth Fund.

Goffman, Erving. 1961. *Asylums: Essays on the Social Situation of Mental Patients and Other Inmates.* Garden City, NY: Doubleday.

Goldfinger, Stephen M. and Russell K. Schutt. 1996. "Comparisons of Clinicians' Housing Recommendations of Homeless Mentally Ill Persons." *Psychiatric Services,* 47(4): 413–415.

Goldfinger, Stephen M., Russell K. Schutt, George S. Tolomiczenko, Winston M. Turner, Norma Ware, Walter E. Penk, et al. 1997. "Housing Persons Who Are Homeless and Mentally Ill: Independent Living or Evolving Consumer Households?" Pp. 29–49 in *Mentally Ill and Homeless: Special Programs for Special Needs,* edited by William R. Breakey and James W. Thompson. Amsterdam, The Netherlands: Harwood Academic Publishers.

Goleman, Daniel. 1993. "Placebo Effect Is Shown to Be Twice as Powerful as Expected." *The New York Times,* August 17, p. C3.

Goode, Erich. 2002. "Sexual Involvement and Social Research in a Fat Civil Rights Organization," *Qualitative Sociology,* 25(4): 501–504.

Gordon, Raymond. 1992. *Basic Interviewing Skills.* Itasca, IL: Peacock.

Government Performance Results Act of 1993. (n.d.). Retrieved July 13, 2002, from www.whitehouse.gov/omb/mgmt-gpra/gplaw2m.html.

Gray, Mark M. 2004. "Sixty-three Percent of Catholics Voted in the 2004 Presidential Election." Washington, DC: Center for Applied Research in the Apostolate, Georgetown University. Retrieved August 8, 2005, from http://cara.georgetown.edu/Press112204.pdf.

Groves, Robert M. 1989. *Survey Errors and Survey Costs.* New York: Wiley.

Groves, Robert M. and Mick P. Couper. 1998. *Nonresponse in Household Interview Surveys.* New York: Wiley.

Groves, Robert M. and Robert L. Kahn. 1979. *Surveys by Telephone: A National Comparison with Personal Interviews.* New York: Academic Press. As adapted in Delbert C. Miller, 1991. *Handbook of Research Design and Social Measurement,* 5th ed. Newbury Park, CA: Sage.

Guba, Egon G. and Yvonna S. Lincoln. 1989. *Fourth Generation Evaluation.* Newbury Park, CA: Sage.

Hadaway, C. Kirk, Penny Long Marler, and Mark Chaves. 1993. "What the Polls Don't Show: A Closer Look at U.S. Church Attendance." *American Sociological Review,* 58 (December): 741–752.

Hafner, Katie. 2005. "In Challenge To Google, Yahoo Will Scan Books." *The New York Times*, October 3, pp. C1, C4.

Hagan, John. 1994. *Crime and Disrepute*. Thousand Oaks, CA: Pine Forge Press.

Hage, Jerald and Barbara Foley Meeker. 1988. *Social Causality*. Boston: Unwin Hyman.

Haney, C., C. Banks, and Philip G. Zimbardo. 1973. "Interpersonal Dynamics in a Simulated Prison." *International Journal of Criminology and Penology,* 1: 69–97.

Hart, Chris. 1998. *Doing a Literature Review: Releasing the Social Science Research Imagination*. London: Sage.

Herek, Gregory. 1995. "Developing a Theoretical Framework and Rationale for a Research Proposal." Pp. 85–91 in *How to Write a Successful Research Grant Application: A Guide for Social and Behavioral Scientists,* edited by Willo Pequegnat and Ellen Stover. New York: Plenum.

Hesse-Biber, Sharlene J. 1989. "Eating Patterns and Disorders in a College Population: Are College Women's Eating Problems a New Phenomenon?" *Sex Roles,* 20: 71–89.

Hesse-Biber, Sharlene and Gregg Lee Carter. 2001. "Family Socialization and Eating Disorders in College-Age Women." Pp. 136–145 in *Empirical Approaches to Sociology,* 3rd ed., edited by Gregg Lee Carter. Boston: Allyn & Bacon.

Hite, Shere. 1987. *Women and Love: A Cultural Revolution in Progress*. New York: Alfred A. Knopf.

Holmes, Steven A. 1994. "Census Officials Plan Big Changes in Gathering Data." *The New York Times,* May 16, pp. A1, A13.

Hoyle, Carolyn and Andrew Sanders. 2000. "Police Response to Domestic Violence: From Victim Choice to Victim Empowerment." *British Journal of Criminology* 40: 14–26.

Huberman, A. Michael and Matthew B. Miles. 1994. "Data Management and Analysis Methods." Pp. 428–444 in *Handbook of Qualitative Research,* edited by Norman K. Denzin and Yvonna S. Lincoln. Thousand Oaks, CA: Sage.

Huff, Darrell. 1954. *How to Lie with Statistics*. New York: W. W. Norton.

Humphrey, Nicholas. 1992. *A History of the Mind: Evolution and the Birth of Consciousness*. New York: Simon & Schuster.

Humphreys, Laud. 1970. *Tearoom Trade: Impersonal Sex in Public Places*. Chicago: Aldine.

Hunt, Morton. 1985. *Profiles of Social Research: The Scientific Study of Human Interactions*. New York: Russell Sage Foundation.

Inter-University Consortium for Political and Social Research. 1996. *Guide to Resources and Services 1995–1996*. Ann Arbor, MI: ICPSR.

Irvine, Leslie. 1998. "Organizational Ethics and Fieldwork Realities: Negotiating Ethical Boundaries in Codependents Anonymous." Pp. 167–183 in *Doing Ethnographic Research: Fieldwork Settings*. Thousand Oaks, CA: Sage.

Jankowski, Martin Sanchez. 1991. *Islands in the Street: Gangs and American Urban Society*. Berkeley: University of California Press.

Jesnadum, Anick. 2000. "Researchers Fear Privacy Breaches with Online Research." Accessed on September 15, 2000, from www.digitalmass.com/news/daily/09/15/researchers.html.

Jones, James H. 1993. *Bad Blood: The Tuskegee Syphilis Experiment,* new and expanded ed. New York: Free Press.

Kagay, Michael R. with Janet Elder. 1992. "Numbers Are No Problem for Pollsters. Words Are." *The New York Times,* October 9, p. E5.

Kaufman, Sharon R. 1986. *The Ageless Self: Sources of Meaning in Late Life*. Madison: University of Wisconsin Press.

Kenney, Charles. 1987. "They've Got Your Number." *The Boston Globe Magazine,* August 30, pp. 12, 46–56, 60.

Kershaw, David and Jerilyn Fair. 1976. *The New Jersey Income-Maintenance Experiment*. Vol. 1. New York: Academic Press.

King, Gary, Robert O. Keohane, and Sidney Verba. 1994. *Scientific Inference in Qualitative Research*. Princeton, NJ: Princeton University Press.

Kinsey, Alfred C., Wardell B. Pomeroy, and Clyde E. Martin. 1948. *Sexual Behavior in the Human Male.* Philadelphia: W. B. Saunders.

Kinsey, Alfred, C., et al. 1953. *Sexual Behavior in the Human Female,* by the Staff of the Institute for Sex Research, Indiana University. Philadelphia: W. B. Saunders.

Koegel, Paul. 1987. *Ethnographic Perspectives on Homeless and Homeless Mentally Ill Women.* Washington, DC: Alcohol, Drug Abuse, and Mental Health Administration, Public Health Service, U.S. Department of Health and Human Services.

Krauss, Clifford. 1996. "New York Crime Rate Plummets to Levels Not Seen in 30 Years." *The New York Times,* December 20, pp. A1, B4.

Krueger, Richard A. 1988. *Focus Groups: A Practical Guide for Applied Research.* Newbury Park, CA: Sage.

Kuzel, Anton J. 1999. "Sampling in Qualitative Inquiry." Pp. 33–45 in *Doing Qualitative Research,* 2nd ed., edited by Benjamin F. Crabtree and William L. Miller. Thousand Oaks, CA: Sage.

Kvale, Steinar. 1996. *Interviews: An Introduction to Qualitative Research Interviewing.* Thousand Oaks, CA: Sage.

Labaw, Patricia J. 1980. *Advanced Questionnaire Design.* Cambridge, MA: ABT Books.

Larson, Calvin J. 1993. *Pure and Applied Sociological Theory: Problems and Issues.* New York: Harcourt Brace Jovanovich.

Latour, Francie. 2002. "Marching Orders: After 10 Years, State Closes Prison Boot Camp." *Boston Sunday Globe,* June 16, pp. B1, B7.

Lavin, Michael R. 1994. *Understanding the 1990 Census: A Guide for Marketers, Planners, Grant Writers and Other Data Users.* Kenmore, NY: Epoch Books.

Lavrakas, Paul J. 1987. *Telephone Survey Methods: Sampling, Selection, and Supervision.* Newbury Park, CA: Sage.

Lelieveldt, Herman. 2003. "Increasing Social Capital Through Direct Democracy? A Case Study of the 'It's Our Neighbourhood's Turn' Project." *Paper for ECPR-Joint Sessions Edinburgh, March 28–April 2, 2003.* Enschede, The Netherlands: University of Twente.

Lelieveldt, Herman. 2004. "Helping Citizens Help Themselves: Neighborhood Improvement Programs and the Impact of Social Networks, Trust, and Norms on Neighborhood-Oriented Forms of Participation." *Urban Affairs Review* 39: 531–551.

Lempert, Richard and Joseph Sanders. 1986. *An Invitation to Law and Social Science: Desert, Disputes, and Distribution.* New York: Longman.

Levy, Paul S. and Stanley Lemeshow. 1999. *Sampling of Populations: Methods and Applications,* 3rd ed. New York: Wiley.

Lewin, Tamar. 2001a. "Surprising Result in Welfare-to-Work Studies." *The New York Times,* July 31, p. A16.

Lewin, Tamar. 2001b. "Income Education Is Found to Lower Risk of New Arrest." *The New York Times,* November 16, p. A18.

Lieberson, Stanley. 1985. *Making It Count: The Improvement of Social Research and Theory.* Berkeley: University of California Press.

Litwin, Mark S. 1995. *How to Measure Survey Reliability and Validity.* Thousand Oaks, CA: Sage.

Locke, Lawrence F., Waneen Wyrick Spirduso, and Stephen J. Silverman. 2000. *Proposals That Work: A Guide for Planning Dissertations and Grant Proposals,* 4th ed. Thousand Oaks, CA: Sage.

Lofland, John and Lyn H. Lofland. 1984. *Analyzing Social Settings: A Guide to Qualitative Observation and Analysis,* 2nd ed. Belmont, CA: Wadsworth.

Mangione, Thomas W. 1995. *Mail Surveys: Improving the Quality.* Thousand Oaks, CA: Sage.

Marini, Margaret Mooney and Burton Singer. 1988. "Causality in the Social Sciences." Pp. 347–409 in *Sociological Methodology,* vol. 18, edited by Clifford C. Clogg. Washington, DC: American Sociological Association.

Marshall, Catherine and Gretchen B. Rossman. 1999. *Designing Qualitative Research,* 3rd ed. Thousand Oaks, CA: Sage.

Marshall, S. L. A. 1978. *Men Against Fire.* Gloucester, MA: Peter Smith [reprinted from original 1947 edition].

Martin, Lawrence L. and Peter M. Kettner. 1996. *Measuring the Performance of Human Service Programs.* Thousand Oaks, CA: Sage.

Maxwell, Joseph A. 1996. *Qualitative Research Design: An Interactive Approach.* Thousand Oaks, CA: Sage.

Melbin, Murray. 1978. "Night as Frontier." *American Sociological Review,* 43(1): 3–22.

Milbrath, Lester and M. L. Goel. 1977. *Political Participation,* 2nd ed. Chicago: Rand McNally.

Milgram, Stanley. 1965. "Some Conditions of Obedience and Disobedience to Authority." *Human Relations* 18: 57–75.

Miller, Delbert C. 1991. *Handbook of Research Design and Social Measurement,* 5th ed. Newbury Park, CA: Sage.

Miller, Delbert C., and Nell J. Salkind. 2002. *Handbook of Research Design and Social Measurement,* 6th ed. Newbury Park, CA: Sage.

Mitchell, Richard G., Jr. 1993. *Secrecy and Fieldwork.* Newbury Park, CA: Sage.

Mohr, Lawrence B. 1992. *Impact Analysis for Program Evaluation.* Newbury Park, CA: Sage.

Mooney, Christopher Z. and Mei Hsien Lee. 1995. "Legislating Morality in the American States: The Case of Abortion Regulation Reform." *American Journal of Political Science,* 39: 599–627.

Mullins, Carolyn J. 1977. *A Guide to Writing and Publishing in the Social and Behavioral Sciences.* New York: Wiley.

Myrdal, Gunnar. 1964. *An American Dilemma.* New York: McGraw-Hill [original work published in 1944].

National Geographic Society. 2000. *Survey 2000.* Retrieved from http://survey2000.national-geographic.com.

National Opinion Research Center (NORC). 1992. *National Data Program for the Social Sciences. The NORC General Social Survey: Questions and Answers.* Chicago: Mimeographed.

National Opinion Research Center (NORC). 1996. *General Social Survey.* Chicago: National Opinion Research Center, University of Chicago.

National Technical Information Service, U.S. Department of Commerce. 1993. *Directory of U.S. Government Datafiles for Mainframes and Microcomputers.* Washington, DC: Federal Computer Products Center, National Technical Information Service, U.S. Department of Commerce.

Newport, Frank. 2000. "Popular Vote in Presidential Race Too Close to Call." www.gallup.com/poll/releases/pr001107.asp. Accessed on December 13, 2000. Princeton: The Gallup Organization.

Ó Dochartaigh, Niall. 2002. *The Internet Research Handbook: A Practical Guide for Students and Researchers in the Social Sciences.* Thousand Oaks, CA: Sage.

Orcutt, James D. and J. Blake Turner. 1993. "Shocking Numbers and Graphic Accounts: Quantified Images of Drug Problems in the Print Media." *Social Problems,* 49 (May): 190–206.

Papineau, David. 1978. *For Science in the Social Sciences.* London: Macmillan.

Parks, Malcolm and Kory Floyd. 1996. "Making Friends in Cyberspace." *Journal of Computer-Mediated Communication,* 1: 1–16. Retrieved from www.ascusc.org/jcmc/vol1/issue4/parks.html.

Parsons, Talcott, ed. 1947. *Max Weber: The Theory of Social and Economic Organization,* translated by A. M. Henderson and Talcott Parsons. New York: The Free Press.

Patton, Michael Quinn. 2002. *Qualitative Research & Evaluation Methods,* 3rd ed. Thousand Oaks, CA: Sage.

Phillips, David P. 1982. "The Impact of Fictional Television Stories on U.S. Adult Fatalities: New Evidence on the Effect of the Mass Media on Violence." *American Journal of Sociology,* 87 (May): 1340–1359.

Pipher, Mary. 1994. *Reviving Ophelia: Saving the Selves of Adolescent Girls.* New York: Ballantine Books.

Posavac, Emil J. and Raymond G. Carey. 1997. *Program Evaluation: Methods and Case Studies,* 5th ed. Upper Saddle River, NJ: Prentice Hall.

Presley, Cheryl A., Philip W. Meilman, and Rob Lyerla. 1994. "Development of the Core Alcohol and Drug Survey: Initial Findings and Future Directions." *Journal of American College Health,* 42: 248–255.

Price, Richard H., Michelle Van Ryn, and Amiram D. Vinokur. 1992. "Impact of a Preventive Job Search Intervention on the Likelihood of Depression Among the Unemployed." *Journal of Health and Social Behavior,* 33 (June): 158–167.

Putnam, Robert D. 2000. *Bowling Alone: The Collapse and Revival of American Community.* New York: Touchstone.

Pyrczak, Fred. 2005. *Evaluating Research in Academic Journals: A Practical Guide to Realistic Evaluation,* 3rd ed. Glendale, CA: Pyrczak Publishing.

Radin, Charles A. 1997. "Partnerships, Awareness Behind Boston's Success." *The Boston Globe,* February 19, pp. A2, B7.

Radloff, Lenore. 1977. "The CES-D Scale: A Self-Report Depression Scale for Research in the General Population." *Applied Psychological Measurement,* 1: 385–401.

Ragin, Charles C. 1994. *Constructing Social Research.* Thousand Oaks, CA: Pine Forge Press.

Ramirez, Anthony. 2002. "One More Reason You're Less Likely to Be Murdered." *The New York Times,* August 25, p. WK3.

Rankin, Bruce H. and James M. Quane. 2002. "Social Contexts and Urban Adolescent Outcomes: The Interrelated Effects of Neighborhoods, Families, and Peers on African-American Youth." *Social Problems,* 49: 79–100.

Reisman, David. 1969 [1950]. *The Lonely Crowd: A Study of the Changing American Character.* New Haven: Yale University Press.

Reiss, Albert J., Jr. 1971. *The Police and the Public.* New Haven, CT: Yale University Press.

Reynolds, Paul Davidson. 1979. *Ethical Dilemmas and Social Science Research.* San Francisco: Jossey-Bass.

Richards, Thomas J. and Lyn Richards. 1994. "Using Computers in Qualitative Research." Pp. 445–462 in *Handbook of Qualitative Research,* edited by Norman K. Denzin and Yvonna S. Lincoln. Thousand Oaks, CA: Sage.

Ringwalt, Christopher L., Jody M. Greene, Susan T. Ennett, Ronaldo Iachan, Richard R. Clayton, and Carl G. Leukefeld. 1994. *Past and Future Directions of the D.A.R.E. Program: An Evaluation Review.* Research Triangle Park, NC: Research Triangle Institute.

Rosenberg, Morris. 1968. *The Logic of Survey Analysis.* New York: Basic Books.

Rossi, Peter H. 1989. *Down and Out in America: The Origins of Homelessness.* Chicago: University of Chicago Press.

Rossi, Peter H. and Howard E. Freeman. 1989. *Evaluation: A Systematic Approach,* 4th ed. Newbury Park, CA: Sage.

Rossman, Gretchen B. and Sharon F. Rallis. 1998. *Learning in the Field: An Introduction to Qualitative Research.* Thousand Oaks, CA: Sage.

Rubin, Herbert J. and Irene S. Rubin. 1995. *Qualitative Interviewing: The Art of Hearing Data.* Thousand Oaks, CA: Sage.

Sacks, Stanley, Karen McKendrick, George DeLeon, Michael T. French, and Kathryn E. McCollister. 2002. "Benefit-Cost Analysis of a Modified Therapeutic Community for Mentally Ill Chemical Abusers." *Evaluation & Program Planning,* 25: 137–148.

Salisbury, Robert H. 1975. "Research on Political Participation." *American Journal of Political Science,* 19 (May): 323–341.

Sampson, Robert J. and Janet L. Lauritsen. 1994. "Violent Victimization and Offending: Individual-, Situational-, and Community-Level Risk Factors." Pp. 1–114 in *Understanding and Preventing Violence.* vol. 3, edited by Albert J. Reiss, Jr., and Jeffrey A. Roth. Washington, DC: National Academy Press.

Sampson, Robert J. and John H. Laub. 1994. "Urban Poverty and the Family Context of Delinquency: A New Look at Structure and Process in a Classic Study." *Child Development,* 65: 523–540.

Schalock, Robert and John Butterworth. 2000. *A Benefit-Cost Analysis Model for Social Service Agencies.* Boston: Institute for Community Inclusion.

Schober, Michael F. 1999. "Making Sense of Survey Questions." Pp. 77–94 in *Cognition and Survey Research*, edited by Monroe G. Sirken, Douglas J. Herrmann, Susan Schechter, Norbert Schwartz, Judith M. Tanur, and Roger Tourangeau. New York: Wiley.

Schorr, Lisbeth B. and Daniel Yankelovich. 2000. "In Search of a Gold Standard for Social Programs." *The Boston Globe,* February 18, p. A19.

Schuman, Howard and Stanley Presser. 1981. *Questions and Answers in Attitude Surveys: Experiments on Question Form, Wording, and Context.* New York: Academic Press.

Schutt, Russell K. and M. L. Fennell. 1992. "Shelter Staff Satisfaction with Services, the Service Network and Their Jobs." *Current Research on Occupations and Professions,* 7: 177–200.

Schutt, Russell K. and Stephen M. Goldfinger. 1996. "Housing Preferences and Perceptions of Health and Functioning Among Mentally Ill Persons." *Psychiatric Services,* 47(4): 381–386.

Scriven, Michael. 1972. "Prose and Cons About Goal-Free Evaluation." *Evaluation Comment,* 3: 1–7.

Sherman, Lawrence. 1997. "Do Fair Procedures Matter? The Effect of Procedural Justice on Spouse Assault." *Law & Society Review* 31(1): 163–204.

Sherman, Lawrence W. and Richard A. Berk. 1984. "The Specific Deterrent Effects of Arrest for Domestic Assault." *American Sociological Review,* 49: 261–272.

Sieber, Joan E. 1992. *Planning Ethically Responsible Research: A Guide for Students and Internal Review Boards.* Thousand Oaks, CA: Sage.

Sjoberg, Gideon, ed. 1967. *Ethics, Politics, and Social Research.* Cambridge, MA: Schenkman.

Smith, Beverly A. and Sharlene Hesse-Biber. 1996. "Users' Experiences with Qualitative Data Analysis Software." *Social Science Computer Review,* 14: 423–432.

Smith, Tom W. 1984. "Nonattitudes: A Review and Evaluation." Pp. 215–255 in *Surveying Subjective Phenomena,* vol. 2, edited by Charles F. Turner and Elizabeth Martin. New York: Russell Sage Foundation.

Smith, Tom. 1987. "That Which We Call Welfare by Any Other Name Would Smell Sweeter: An Analysis of the Impact of Question Wording on Response Patterns." *Public Opinion Quarterly,* 51(1): 75–83.

Stake, Robert E., ed. 1975. *Evaluating the Arts in Education: A Responsible Approach.* Columbus, OH: Merrill.

Stake, Robert E. 1995. *The Art of Case Study Research.* Thousand Oaks, CA: Sage.

Stille, Alexander. 2000. "A Happiness Index with a Long Reach: Beyond G.N.P. to Subtler Measures." *The New York Times,* May 20, pp. A17, A19.

Straus, Murray and Richard Gelles. 1988. *Intimate Violence.* New York: Simon and Schuster.

Strunk, William, Jr., and E. B. White. 1979. *The Elements of Style,* 3rd ed. New York: Macmillan.

Sudman, Seymour. 1976. *Applied Sampling.* New York: Academic Press.

Taylor, Jerry. 1999. "DARE Gets Updated in Some Area Schools, Others Drop Program." *The Boston Sunday Globe,* May 16, pp. 1, 11.

The Gallup Organization. August 20, 2002. *Poll Analyses, July 29, 2002. Bush Job Approval Update.* www.gallup.com/poll/releases/pr020729.asp.

Thorne, Barrie. 1993. *Gender Play: Girls and Boys in School.* New Brunswick, NJ: Rutgers University Press.

Tufte, Edward R. 1983. *The Visual Display of Quantitative Information.* Cheshire, CT: Graphics Press.

Turabian, Kate L. 1967. *A Manual for Writers of Term Papers, Theses, and Dissertations,* 3rd ed., rev. Chicago: University of Chicago Press.

Turner, Charles F. and Elizabeth Martin, eds. 1984. *Surveying Subjective Phenomena,* vols. I and II. New York: Russell Sage Foundation.

U.S. Bureau of the Census. 1996. *Census Catalog and Guide, 1996.* Washington, DC: Department of Commerce, U.S. Bureau of the Census.

U.S. Bureau of the Census. 1999. *United States Census 2000, Updated Summary: Census 2000 Operational Plan.* Washington, DC: U.S. Department of Commerce, Bureau of the Census, February.

U.S. Bureau of Labor Statistics, Department of Labor. 1991. *Major Programs of the Bureau of Labor Statistics*. Washington, DC: U.S. Bureau of Labor Statistics, Department of Labor.

U.S. Bureau of Labor Statistics, Department of Labor. 1997a. *Employment and Earnings*. Washington, DC: U.S. Bureau of Labor Statistics, Department of Labor.

U.S. Bureau of Labor Statistics, Department of Labor. 1997b. *Handbook of Methods*. Washington, DC: U.S. Bureau of Labor Statistics, Department of Labor.

U.S. Department of Health, Education, and Welfare. 1979. *The Belmont Report: Ethical Principles and Guidelines for the Protection of Human Subjects of Research*. Washington, DC: The National Commission for the Protection of Human Subjects of Biomedical and Behavioral Research, Office of the Secretary, Department of Health, Education, and Welfare. Retrieved June 20, 2005, from http://www.hss.gov/ohrp/humansubjects/guidance/belmont.htm.

U.S. Government Accounting Office. June 2001. *Health and Human Services: Status of Achieving Key Outcomes and Addressing Major Management Challenges*. Retrieved November 3, 2002, from www.gao.gov/new.items/d01748.pdf.

Van Maanen, John. 1982. "Fieldwork on the Beat." Pp. 103–151 in *Varieties of Qualitative Research*, edited by John Van Maanen, James M. Dabbs, Jr., and Robert R. Faulkner. Beverly Hills, CA: Sage.

Verba, Sidney and Norman Nie. 1972. *Political Participation: Political Democracy and Social Equality*. New York: Harper & Row.

Verba, Sidney, Norman Nie, and Jae-On Kim. 1978. *Participation and Political Equality: A Seven-Nation Comparison*. New York: Cambridge University Press.

Vernez, Georges M., Audrey Burnam, Elizabeth A. McGlynn, Sally Trude, and Brian S. Mirttman. 1988. *Review of California's Program for the Homeless Mentally Disabled*. Santa Monica, CA: RAND, R-3631-CDMH.

Wageman, Ruth. 1995. "Interdependence and Group Effectiveness." *Administrative Science Quarterly*, 40: 145–180.

Wallgren, Anders, Britt Wallgren, Rolf Persson, Ulf Jorner, and Jan-Aage Haaland. 1996. *Graphing Statistics and Data: Creating Better Charts*. Thousand Oaks, CA: Sage.

Ware, Norma C. 1991. Unpublished ethnographic notes. Department of Psychiatry, Harvard Medical School, Boston, MA.

Webb, Eugene J., Donald T. Campbell, Richard D. Schwartz, and Lee Sechrest. 2000. *Unobtrusive Measures*, rev. ed. Thousand Oaks, CA: Sage.

Weber, Max. 1992. *The Protestant Ethic and the Spirit of Capitalism*, trans. Talcott Parsons. London: Routledge; originally published in English in 1930.

Weber, Robert Philip. 1985. *Basic Content Analysis*. Thousand Oaks, CA: Sage.

Weitzman, Eben and M. B. Miles. 1994. *Computer Programs for Qualitative Data Analysis*. Thousand Oaks, CA: Sage.

Wellman, Barry and Keith Hampton. 1999. "Living Networked in a Wired World." *Comparative Sociology*, 28: 1–12.

Wheeler, Peter M. 1995. *Social Security Programs Throughout the World—1995*. Research Report #64, SSA Publication No. 13–11805. Washington, DC: Office of Research and Statistics, Social Security Administration.

Wholey, J. S. 1979. *Evaluation: Promise and Performance*. Washington, DC: Urban Institute.

Wholey, J. S. 1987. "Evaluability Assessment: Developing Program Theory." Pp. 77–92 in *Using Program Theory in Evaluation: New Directions for Program Evaluation (no. 33)*, edited by Leonard Bickman. San Francisco: Jossey-Bass.

Whyte, William Foote. 1955. *Street Corner Society*. Chicago: University of Chicago Press.

Wilson, William Julius. 1987. *The Truly Disadvantaged: The Inner City, the Underclass, and Public Policy*. Chicago: University of Chicago Press.

Witkin, Belle Ruth and James W. Altschuld. 1995. *Planning and Conducting Needs Assessments: A Practical Guide*. Thousand Oaks, CA: Sage.

Wolcott, Harry F. 1995. *The Art of Fieldwork*. Walnut Creek, CA: AltaMira Press.

Glossary/Index

Note: Page numbers followed by *e* refer to exhibits.

the process used to make sense of related observations, 52-55, 200-202

Concurrent validity   The type of validity that exists when scores on a measure are closely related to scores on a criterion measured at the same time, 73

Confidentiality   Provided by research in which identifying information that could be used to link respondents to their responses is available only to designated research personnel for specific research needs, 45, 157-159, 186-187

Conflict theory, 23-24

Consistency, internal. *See* **Interitem reliability**

Constant   A number that has a fixed value in a given situation; a characteristic or value that does not change, 55

Construct validity   The type of validity that is established by showing that a measure is related to other measures as specified in a theory, 73-74

Contact summary forms, 200, 201*e*

Contamination   A source of causal invalidity that occurs when either the experimental and/or the comparison group is aware of the other group and is influenced in the posttest as a result, 124

Content analysis   A research method for systematically analyzing and making inferences from text, 64

Content validity   The type of validity that exists when the full range of a concept's meaning is covered by the measure, 72

Context   A focus of idiographic causal explanation; a particular outcome is understood as part of a larger set of interrelated circumstances, 110-111

Context effects   Relationships among variables that vary among geographic units or other contexts, 145

Contingent question   A question that is asked of only a subset of survey respondents, 141

Control group   A comparison group that receives no treatment, 111
  comparability, 121
  contamination, 124
  ex post facto, 115, 119
  matching, 113, 115-116
  mortality, 121-122
  nonequivalent, 115-117, 116*e*
  random assignment to, 113
  selection bias, 121, 122

Conversation analysis, 216-218, 217*e*

Converse, Jean M., 137

Cook, Thomas D., 109, 115, 126

Coontz, Stephanie, 110

Core Alcohol and Drug Survey, 60, 69-70, 69*e*

Core Institute, Southern Illinois University, 60, 69

Cornerville study, 174, 187, 206

Correlation. *See* **Association**

Correlation analysis, 251-252

Costner, Herbert L., 110

Counseling, computer-mediated, 15, 16*e*

Couper, Mick P., 152, 153

Cover letter   The letter sent with a mailed questionnaire. It explains the survey's purpose and auspices and encourages the respondent to participate, 148, 149*e*

Covert participation. *See* **Complete participation**

Crabtree, Benjamin F., 195, 196

Cress, Daniel M., 211-213

Crime
  broken windows theory, 21-22
  deterrence theory, 24, 28
  homicide rates, 106-107
  statistics, 58-59, 66
  victimization surveys, 66
  See also Domestic violence

Criterion validity   The type of validity that is established by comparing the scores obtained on the measure being validated to those obtained with a more direct or already validated measure of the same phenomenon (the criterion), 72-73

Cross-population generalizability This type of generalizability exists when findings about one group or population or setting hold true for other groups, populations, or settings. Also called external validity, 14, 14*e*, 15, 88
threats to, 126-127
See also **Generalizability**

Cross-sectional research design A study in which data are collected at only one point in time, 31-32
repeated, 33, 34-35, 36

Crosstabulation (crosstab) In the simplest case, a bivariate (two-variable) distribution, showing the distribution of one variable for each category of another variable; can also be elaborated using three or more variables, 246-250
controlling for third variable, 250-251, 251*e*
examples, 246*e*, 248*e*, 249*e*

Data
levels of measurement, 67-71
qualitative, 68
sources, 58-59
See also **Operation**;
Secondary data sources

Data analysis. *See* **Qualitative data analysis**;
Quantitative data analysis

Data cleaning The process of checking data for errors after the data have been entered in a computer file, 230

Data collection. *See* **Participant observation**; **Qualitative method**; **Survey research**

Davis, James A., 137, 250

Davis, Ryan, 290

Dawes, Robyn, 267

Debriefing A researcher's informing subjects after an experiment about the experiment's purposes and methods, and evaluating subjects' personal reactions to the experiment, 44, 129

Deception, 128-130

Decker, Scott H., 223-224

Deductive research The type of research in which a specific expectation is deduced from a general premise and is then tested, 25-28, 26*e*, 185

Denzin, Norman K., 166, 196, 225

Dependent variable A variable that is hypothesized to vary depending on or under the influence of another variable, 27

Depth interviewing. *See* **Intensive (depth) interviewing**

Descriptive research Research in which social phenomena are defined and described, 9, 30-31

Descriptive statistics Statistics used to describe the distribution of and relationship among variables, 229

Deterrence theory, 24, 28

Detroit Area Study, 139

Dewey, Thomas E., 94

Diamond, Timothy, 169, 172, 175, 199

Differential attrition (mortality) A problem that occurs in experiments when comparison groups become different because subjects are more likely to drop out of one of the groups for various reasons, 121-122

Dillman, Don A., 137, 138, 139, 140, 142, 143, 145, 148, 151, 153, 156

Direction of association A pattern in a relationship between two variables—the values of variables tend to change consistently in relation to change on the other variable. The direction of association can be either positive or negative, 27

Direct observation, 63-64

Disasters, responses to, 30

Disproportionate stratified sampling Sampling in which elements are selected from strata in different proportions from those that appear in the population, 97, 98*e*

two members of each pair are assigned to the two groups. For aggregate matching, groups are chosen for comparison that are similar in terms of the distribution of key characteristics, 113, 115-116

Matrix A chart used to condense qualitative data into simple categories and provide a multidimensional summary that will facilitate subsequent, more intensive analysis. *See also* Exhibit 8.4 in the text., 202-204, 203*e*

Maxwell, Joseph A., 166, 174, 199

Mead, Margaret, 188

Mean The arithmetic, or weighted, average, computed by adding up the value of all the cases and dividing by the total number of cases, 241-242, 242*e*

Measurement levels. *See* **Level of measurement**

Measurement validity This type of validity exists when a measure measures what we think it measures, 12, 13, 72-74, 119, 122
See also **Validity**

Measure of association A type of descriptive statistic that summarizes the strength of an association, 249
See also **Association**

Mechanism A discernible process that creates a causal connection between two variables, 109-110

Median The position average, or the point that divides a distribution in half (the 50th percentile), 240, 240*e*, 241-242

Medical students, 202

Meeker, Barbara Foley, 110

Meilman, Philip W., 60

Melbin, Murray, 261-263

Mellon Foundation Assessment Project, Hamilton College, 35, 184

Mental health
depression, 61-62
homeless mentally ill, 267-273, 276
measures, 76

Michigan Survey Research Center, 140

Milbrath, Lester, 229

Miles, Matthew B., 200, 202-204, 218, 224-225, 250

Miles, M. B., 64

Milgram, Stanley, 129

Miller, Delbert C., 35, 143

Miller, Susan, 199, 206-207

Miller, William L., 195, 196

Mills, Judson, 129

Minneapolis Domestic Violence Experiment
conclusion, 107, 127
deterrence theory, 24, 28
ethical issues, 130
hypothesis, 28
police actions, 121
replications, 265-266
research circle and, 28, 28*e*
research question, 23
sample, 126
selection bias, 121
theoretical background, 24, 25*e*

Minnesota Population Center, 296

Miringoff, Marc, 52

Mitchell, Richard G., Jr., 172

Mode The most frequent value in a distribution; also termed the probability average, 239-240

Mohr, Lawrence B., 115

Montagnier, Luc, 41

Mooney, Christopher Z., 62

Morrill, Calvin, 192-193, 214-216

Mortality. *See* **Differential attrition**

Mullins, Carolyn J., 274

Multiple group before-and-after design A type of quasi-experimental design in which several before-and-after comparisons are made involving the same independent and dependent variables but different groups, 117, 118*e*

Murray Research Center, 304-305

Muslim America project, 136-137, 138, 144, 150, 151

Mutually exclusive A variable's attributes (or values) are mutually exclusive when